BRIDGING AUSTRALIA AND JAPAN

VOLUME 2

THE WRITINGS OF DAVID SISSONS, HISTORIAN AND POLITICAL SCIENTIST

BRIDGING AUSTRALIA AND JAPAN

VOLUME 2

THE WRITINGS OF DAVID SISSONS, HISTORIAN AND POLITICAL SCIENTIST

EDITED BY KEIKO TAMURA
AND ARTHUR STOCKWIN

PRESS

ASIAN STUDIES SERIES MONOGRAPH 15

Published by ANU Press
The Australian National University
Acton ACT 2601, Australia
Email: anupress@anu.edu.au

Available to download for free at press.anu.edu.au

ISBN (print): 9781760463755
ISBN (online): 9781760463762

WorldCat (print): 962408104
WorldCat (online): 962408205

DOI: 10.22459/BAJ.2020

Cover design and layout by ANU Press

CONTENTS

PREFACE

This is the second volume of *Bridging Australia and Japan: The writings of David Sissons, historian and political scientist*. This volume is the third and final publication in the series of Sissons' writings, which started with *Breaking Japanese Diplomatic Codes: David Sissons and D Special Section during the Second World War*, edited by Desmond Ball and Keiko Tamura in 2013. The first volume of *Bridging Australia and Japan*, with a focus on Sissons' writings on Australia–Japan relations, was released in 2016. For this volume, the editors chose his work on the Pacific War, war crimes trials and investigations, and Japanese politics in the 1950s and 1960s. Sissons' previously unpublished work in this volume was selected from the Papers of DCS Sissons (MS 3092) at the National Library of Australia (NLA) in Canberra.[1]

An idea of a publication project was discussed soon after David Sissons' death in 2006. Right from its outset, its main goal has always been to make his writings available to a wider readership. Sissons dedicated his life to research and writing, and his articles are often cited by succeeding researchers due to their high-quality content backed by meticulous research. In recent years, however, some articles became difficult to access. In addition, Sissons left unpublished research papers in the NLA collection. We selected those articles that we consider seminal in the fields of studies in which Sissons was involved. All three books are now available in digital format through ANU Press, and we hope a wide circle of readers and researchers are able to learn from his writings for years to come.

This volume starts with Georgina Fitzpatrick's chapter on her experience of encountering and engaging with Sissons' manuscript at the NLA while she was carrying out research on Australian war crimes trials. Chapter 2 covers the Japanese intentions towards Australia, particularly on the contentious issue of whether or not Japan had a plan to invade Australia. Sissons' research clearly demonstrates that Japan did not have any plans to invade Australia many years before the issue

1 To review the finding aid for this collection, go to nla.gov.au/nla.obj-337994618/findingaid.

attracted a big controversy.[2] Sissons' thorough research is showcased in Chapter 3 in his detailed account of the Cowra breakout. As a young recruit, he joined a search party at Cowra soon after the breakout. Although his personal experience is not included, his writing is riveting and sheds new light on the incident. Sissons' essay in Chapter 4 on the Australian war crimes trials and investigations is a significant contribution to the field of war crime research. This paper was uploaded on the internet after Sissons' death, but did not have a secure hosting website. We are happy to provide a permanent home for this significant work in this publication.

The following two chapters include Sissons' writing and correspondence on his research on war crime trials. Readers will appreciate the depth and rigour of his questioning in his observations and the extent of his efforts to reach out to informants. Contemporary researchers might carry out a similar level of enquiry, but it would be much more difficult to capture their efforts in the digital era.

The last two chapters cover Sissons' writings in political science at the early stage of his academic career. As Stockwin's introduction indicates, these papers, which were written 50 years ago, still have some relevance in contemporary research.

The last chapter by Keiko Tamura discusses Sissons' legacy and records the project's history. A selected bibliography of Sissons shows the breadth of the field in which Sissons carried out his research and writing.

Many of the writings that were included in these publications were originally produced decades ago. It is obvious that some new research results have appeared, and some of Sissons' writings might require updating and revision. Yet, the essence of his enquiries and the references that he recorded are still relevant to contemporary scholars to learn from and be inspired by. Were that to happen, our efforts in bringing this project to a conclusion are worthwhile.

2 About public controversy on this issue, see Peter Stanley, *Invading Australia: Japan and the battle for Australia, 1942* (Camberwell, Victoria: Viking, 2008), Chapter 11.

ACKNOWLEDGEMENTS

This is the second of two volumes of the works of David Sissons, historian and political scientist. In preparing volume two, the last of the ANU Press series on David's writings, we would like to acknowledge David's widow, Bronwen Sissons, for her invaluable support for the project. In fact, her continuous enthusiasm for this project sustained us over its 13 years duration. David was lucky to have such a partner as Bronwen, who understood his passion for research and supported him intellectually and emotionally throughout his career. After his death, Bronwen provided necessary financial assistance for the project. Through discussion with Bronwen, we learned more about David's attitudes not only to his research topics, but also to his life. That insight was valuable in compiling his writings for the publication. We would also like to express our gratitude to their children for their understanding and support for the project. They are Meredith, Miranda, and Hilary who sadly passed away in December 2017.

We thank many people who played invaluable roles in the production of this volume. First of all, we would like to thank Dr Georgina Fitzpatrick. Georgina contributed the first chapter of this volume, which reveals interesting insights into working on David's papers at the National Library of Australia (NLA) for her research on war crimes trials. In addition, she made a significant contribution towards resurrecting David's lecture that was delivered at the Royal Military College, Duntroon, in 1978. She skilfully transcribed David's handwritten lecture manuscript as well as providing comprehensively updated references. Georgina also prepared the notes associated with Sissons' article in the *Sydney Morning Herald*, which is reproduced in the same chapter. Georgina's enthusiasm as well as her deep academic insights into the field of war crimes trials helped us significantly in our consideration of this important and complex issue and guided us in the process of compiling this volume.

We would like to thank Dr Craig Reynolds, the chair of the Asian Studies Editorial Board of ANU Press and series editor of the Asian Studies Monograph Series, for his continuing support throughout the publication project. We owe greatly to his enthusiasm and measured patience in overseeing this project to its successful completion. We thank Emeritus Professor Tessa Morris-Suzuki and Professor Donna Weeks for their useful comments and encouragement. We thank Professor David Cohen, who gave permission to include David's seminal paper on Australian war crimes trials and investigations as Chapter 4 in this volume. We are grateful to Amy Ng who offered her expertise to assist us in production of the manuscript.

We would like to thank the ANU Publication Subsidy Committee for a grant to assist towards the copyediting of this volume as well as the first volume. The copyediting was ably done by Justine Molony as for volume one of this series. We also would like to thank Emily Tinker and her staff at ANU Press for their skilful assistance.

Above all, we would like to acknowledge David Sissons' legacy. He had the foresight to deposit his papers at the NLA for researchers who would follow in his footsteps. We hope that, in a published form, his writings will be available to a wider readership and further research will be undertaken as a result.

Keiko Tamura and Arthur Stockwin

1

DAVID SISSONS AND THE HISTORY OF AUSTRALIA'S WAR CRIMES TRIALS: A SPECTRAL INTERACTION IN THE ARCHIVES

Georgina Fitzpatrick

I never met David Sissons; he died a few years before I began to work on a history of the 300 Australian-run war crimes trials of Japanese suspects in the aftermath of the Pacific War. However, I believe that I have 'met' Sissons in some spectral netherworld where academics engage with each other over the generations. This essay is a study of our interaction, which began in January 2009 and reached its major outcome in 2016 with the publication and dedication to him of the edited volume of essays, *Australia's War Crimes Trials, 1945–51*.[1]

In the final throes of submitting my doctoral thesis,[2] I was interviewed in October 2008 for one of two research fellowships to work on an ARC Linkage project, entitled 'Australia's Post-World War II Crimes Trials of the Japanese: A systematic and comprehensive law reports series'.[3] I became the historian on the project, working half time and based at the Australian War Memorial (AWM), Canberra. I was to

1 Georgina Fitzpatrick, Tim McCormack & Narrelle Morris, *Australia's War Crimes Trials, 1945–51* (Brill, 2016). This book was one of three books shortlisted for the NSW Premier's Australian History Award in September 2017.

2 Georgina Fitzpatrick, 'Britishers Behind Barbed Wire: Internment in Australia during the Second World War', PhD thesis, The Australian National University, 2009. This is now available online through the ANU Library at openresearch-repository.anu.edu.au/handle/1885/109224.

3 The Linkage project was between the Asia Pacific Centre for Military Law, Melbourne Law School; Defence Legal (the legal arm of the Australian Defence Forces); and the Australian War Memorial (Project LP0882300, 2010–2012 and LP120100204, 2012–2013).

provide the historical context for the main study — a series of law reports on each of the 300 trials. At the first meeting[4] of the international humanitarian law academics and senior historians behind the project, they decided that the law reports were to be organised by the locations of the trials rather than the nature of the crimes being tried. I was asked to prepare essays on the eight locations — Morotai, Wewak, Labuan, Darwin, Rabaul, Singapore, Hong Kong and Manus Island — to serve as an introduction to each set of law reports.[5]

I put aside a small document I had been drawing up about the issues and types of crimes — this more thematic approach later formed the basis for the published volume of essays — and set to work to survey the existing secondary literature. I soon found that my work would be mostly archival. Very little had been published. Among the few items I found, however, were two succinct essays, one on sources[6] and one an overview of the trials,[7] both by someone called David Sissons. What a relief for me. I wasn't alone. And it turned out that he had been an interpreter at some of the Morotai trials in 1946.[8] As he wrote to one of many participants from whom he sought information: 'My interest in this subject dates from December 1945 when I acted as interpreter for Captain Kato and some of the other accused at the Morotai trials.'[9] Thus, he combined personal experience with his academic research and analysis. However, his research did not begin in earnest until the trial transcripts were released by the Labor government under Prime Minister Gough Whitlam in the 1970s.[10]

Unfortunately, Sissons published very little on Australia's war crimes trials, a research interest of his for some 30 years. Only three pieces of extended writing on the trials were deemed by him to have met his high standards sufficiently for public perusal: the article on sources and the overview essay already mentioned[11] and the

4 Held in Melbourne in February 2009.

5 The law reports were assigned to Dr Narrelle Morris, the other research fellow.

6 David Sissons, 'Sources on Australian investigations into Japanese war crimes in the Pacific', *Journal of the Australian War Memorial*, no. 30, April 1997, www.awm.gov.au/articles/journal/j30.

7 DCS Sissons, *The Australian War Crimes Trials and Investigations (1942–51)*, c. 1997. From 2006, this document wandered around online on different parts of a website hosted by the War Crimes Center at University of California, Berkeley.

8 He is listed as one of the interpreters at three trials at Morotai — M32 (5 February 1946), M29 (6–7 February 1946) and M34 (7 February 1946).

9 National Library of Australia (NLA), Papers of David Sissons, MS 3092, Box 28: Death Sentence. Sissons to Noel A Fowler, 27 June 1978. Fowler was a Medical Officer, responsible for certifying the deaths of some of the war criminals executed by firing squad at Morotai.

10 NLA, MS 3092, Box 30: Hook. Sissons to John Hook, 26 January 1977. These were not of course digitised as they are now. Sissons had to consult the typed transcripts.

11 See notes 6 and 7 above.

various iterations of his entry on 'War crimes trials' for successive editions of the *Australian Encyclopedia*.[12] For all those working on any of the Australian-run trials, these publications may be regarded as the foundational studies.

Sissons' legacy to war crimes trials' researchers also lies in his papers deposited in the National Library of Australia (NLA). Of the 60 archival boxes constituting his manuscript collection, 15 boxes in Series 10, plus a box on the Webb inquiries into war crimes, two boxes on Webb's role at the International Military Tribunal for the Far East and a box on Linguists and the Allied Translator and Interpreter Section (ATIS), are stuffed with his notes, photocopies of sources, his observations and the new materials he himself generated, all organised in a very logical sequence of subject files. I do not believe that other researchers into the Australian war crimes trials have realised what a treasure trove is contained in these 19 boxes. Even Michael Carrel, who had the advantage of preparing his doctoral thesis while Sissons was alive and acknowledged his help, only used copies of such items as Sissons passed on to him.[13] Whereas anyone looking at my eight 'location' chapters and my 'thematic' chapters on executed airmen, cannibalism and death sentences in *Australia's War Crimes Trials, 1945–51* need only look at my footnotes to see how often I cited a source I had discovered in 'DCS Sissons papers, NLA MS 3092, Box such-and-such'. But let me take you now on the voyage of discovery as the collection revealed itself to me.

***

From the dates of my notes on his archival boxes, my first foray was within weeks of the start of my appointment.[14] It was decided by Professor Tim McCormack, leader of the project, that the first set of trials to be explored should be those held at Darwin. While Narrelle Morris prepared law reports from the digitised transcripts of the three trials,[15] my chapter on Darwin was to serve as a pilot for my other 'location' essays. Off I went to the NLA to see what Sissons had thought worth pursuing about these three trials.

12 I have not been able to source all the editions but, judging from his 1982 draft for the fourth edition (NLA, MS 3092, Box 3, folder 30A), successive editions grew briefer and briefer, presumably as editors wanted to make space for new entries. I always used the fifth edition, published in 1988, which contained substantially more facts and figures than later versions. The fifth edition included criticisms about the procedures at the trials, which were cut for the next edition published in 1996.

13 Michael Carrel, 'Australia's Prosecution of Japanese War Criminals: Stimuli and constraints', PhD thesis, Faculty of Law, University of Melbourne, 2005. Carrel completed his research before the Sissons papers were open to the public. See my discussion of Carrel's interactions with Sissons below.

14 I began work at the beginning of 2009; my original file of notes using Box 28 dates from 29 January.

15 The transcripts may be found on the website of the National Archives of Australia (NAA). For the three Darwin trials, see NAA, A471, 80708 (Darwin D1), A471, 81630 (Darwin D2) and A471, 80709 (Darwin D3).

Box 1.1. Series 10. Australian War Crimes Trials, 1945–51

The large group of files in this series contain papers relating to Sissons' research into Australian War Crimes Trials. The files are arranged alphabetically, by file title.

- Australian War Crimes Section (Box 20)
- Adachi — Ambon (Box 21)
- Ambon (Box 22)
- Ambon — Bismark Sea (Box 23)
- Borneo (Box 24)
- Burma–Siam Railway (Box 25)
- Bougainville (Box 26)
- 'C' (Box 27)
- 'C' — 'E' (Box 28)
- Finding aids and inventories (Box 29)
- 'G' — Laha (Box 30)
- Manus — Miscellaneous (Box 31)
- Morotai trials — 'P' (Box 32)
- Rabaul trials (Box 33)
- Reconnaissance parties — Wewak trials (Box 34)

Source. Finding aid, Papers of David Sissons, MS 3092, NLA, nla.gov.au/nla.obj-337994618/findingaid

My first task was to work out the right box to order for retrieval. Fortunately, I was to discover that if I thought about what subject heading I would use, I found that Sissons had usually picked the same one. He was so logical in his organisation. That was my first wonderful discovery — that his mind and mine were running along the same lines. He had used a straightforward alphabetical sequence within Series 10. Darwin started with 'D' so I filled in the first of many orders I was to place over the next seven or eight years. I ordered Box 28.

I had been asked to organise my research by posing the question: 'Why were these trials held at X?' I soon found that this was not a question of interest to Sissons. My very own viewpoint! I cannot remember now whether this bonded me to him there and then but I did note two other headings of files in Box 28, 'Cannibalism' and 'Death sentences', as files to be pursued later in my own time. They were just the sorts of themes that interested me; much more than explaining the logistics involved in setting up the trials at the eight locations.[16] However, Sissons did not ignore the location of trials altogether. One of his organising principles for his war crimes files was to use a 'location' heading to gather together information about specific trials that took place at that location and then include lots of cross-referencing to his major files on types of crimes or to places where crimes had been committed or to people who were major suspects. I noted at the time that 'Darwin' was a thin file but Sissons had included notes from what I later discovered was an army investigation

16 When the project publication changed to a book of essays, I returned to these themes. See my 'Cannibalism and the war crimes trials' and 'Death sentences, Japanese war criminals and the Australian military' in Fitzpatrick, McCormack & Morris, 2016, pp. 291–325 and pp. 326–70 respectively.

file.[17] These notes gave me an outline of the subject matter of one of the Darwin trials, useful at a time when I did not yet have a draft law report to consult. If that had been all one found in a typical Sissons' file, then their usefulness would have been limited. However, there was more.

In this file were some other items of the type I learned were the gold nuggets hidden within all the files of his that I consulted: his extensive additions of archival material he had himself created. In Box 28 were letters to Sissons written in 1987 from a friend who was in touch with one of the Australian officers whose torture was part of the matter tried at Darwin.[18] Because this friend felt at ease with Sissons, he passed on personal observations about the surviving victim, expressing frank views that I am certain I would never have been told had I approached the officer in question.[19] It was the first time I found exchanges of correspondence that Sissons conducted with participants (victims, witnesses, legal officers, interpreters and even accused) most of whom were long dead by the time I began my research. Invaluable sets of letters, dating from the 1970s to the 1990s, offered insights and answers to my questions time and time again as I tunnelled through the subject files. Sissons had tracked down and questioned almost every possible person I would have liked to interview but was 30 years too late to do so.

The Darwin file also contained a newspaper clipping illustrated with photos from the Darwin trials, sourced from the AWM.[20] This alerted me to the fact that there were official photographers at these war crimes trials and that photographs would constitute a whole set of contemporary materials to study and cross-reference with written materials.[21] As a consequence of inserting photographs into my draft Darwin chapter,[22] showing, for example, the hut interiors where the trials took place, the Australian personnel in situ and the suspects being escorted to the hearings, we included over 100 photographs in *Australia's War Crimes Trials, 1945–51*. It was quite a novelty to have photographic material included in a legal publication.

In his affectionate contribution to the first volume of Sissons' edited writings, *Bridging Australia and Japan*, John Welfield noted Sissons' advice to him about notes. Rather than buying expensive index cards, Sissons suggested he cut recycled

17 NAA, MP742/1, 336/1/1213. This file from the Department of Army files in Melbourne was not one I subsequently read since the logistics and details of the trials were my focus rather than the investigation into the crimes being prosecuted. It later emerged that the original intention of Peter Londey, then at the Military History Section, AWM, and involved in the original submission with McCormack for ARC funding, was that the investigation files held at the AWM would be a main focus of the historian's task. By the time I was employed, however, this seems to have been set aside. It is an aspect of the Australian war crimes apparatus that still awaits its historian.

18 For the trial transcript of D1, see NAA, A471, 80708.

19 I did, however, have a discussion with the officer's son in 2010. His father was alive at that stage but was not willing to talk to me about the events all those years before.

20 F Harari, 'Crime without punishment', *Weekend Australian*, 22–23 May 1993, p. 21.

21 Sissons may not have been aware of this. He annotated the pictures in the news item as being 'claimed' as photos of the Darwin Court and of a group of the accused.

22 The draft chapter with photos was circulated in May 2009 to the participants involved in the project.

scraps of paper into a standard size.[23] I smiled when I saw this practice in action for the first time in Box 28. I was somewhat reminded of thrifty aspects of myself. Sissons also advised Welfield to file the paper scraps in shoeboxes. Although I use index cards for my basic notes, I have always stored them in shoeboxes.[24] However I have never seen scraps of recycled paper used to such an extent before. He cut up memos to ANU staff, minutes of meetings and other circulars from the days of the gestetner machine. After discounting the material on the back of his notes as irrelevant, occasionally, I began to roughly date his notes from what appeared there. In Box 28 ('Darwin'), in the first file I consulted, I decided that he must have been working on these particular trials in 1981 because on the back was a dated notice of the closure of a National Archives of Australia (NAA) office. I not only connected to him in terms of admiring the frugality of practice, but also with him over closed NAA offices and over the years separating our time of research. He explored the Darwin trials in 1981. I had returned to them in 2009. I felt we had begun a parallel study.

Another early parcel of research on war crimes trials that I undertook were the two Wewak trials so I ordered Box 34 for 'Wewak trials' consisting mostly of his notes on the trial transcripts and his notes on the personnel of the court. I noted in an email: 'As always I have started with Sissons — this time a very small file but full of goodies. Apart from extensive notes on the letters from Ottaway … giving me a good idea of the pressure brought on Sturdee to commute the sentence … . Sissons' notes gave me some missing names.'[25] Providing first names and enlistment numbers of court members was often something Sissons did for us as we tried to complete the full details of Australian personnel involved in each trial but it is minor compared with so many other contributions his research made to the underpinning of my chapters for *Australia's War Crimes Trials, 1945–51*.

***

In the next part of this chapter, I would like to demonstrate the many ways Sissons helped me get my thoughts in order, offered me shortcuts along trails on which he had hacked through the thickets of the thousands of relevant files in the NAA, confirmed some of my tentative hypotheses and, above all, provided me with new sources of evidence he had generated himself. This is the aspect I will first address.

---

23 John Welfield, 'David Sissons, his methods of supervision and the adventures of one of his students', in Arthur Stockwin & Keiko Tamura (eds), *Bridging Australia and Japan: The writings of David Sissons, historian and political scientist, Volume 1* (ANU Press, 2016), pp. 35–36.

24 I began this practice for my MA research at the Public Record Office in Chancery Lane. The shoeboxes are clearly labelled and proved excellent for stacking in tea chests and removal boxes as I moved from one side of the world to another at least four times between 1971 and 1999. However, the shoeboxes have needed replacing with newer ones.

25 G Fitzpatrick to NE Morris, email, 'Wewak MW1 trial', 21 December 2010.

Archival items generated by Sissons

Apart from getting summaries of the content of thousands of NAA files, a wonderful shortcut for someone given a full-time task but only a half-time job, and cross-referencing to connected files, I also found an extensive collection of interview notes and correspondence with Australian participants (now long dead) such as Herbert Dick,[26] Roland Beard,[27] Noel Fowler[28] and John Williams.[29] The first three people in particular gave insights I was able to use in my chapter on death sentences.[30] Sissons asked the questions I would like to have asked and, because he could present himself as a fellow participant at the trials, he surely got franker and fuller answers than I would ever have achieved. Even if I interviewed a participant, Sissons had preceded me and often elicited more nuanced observations of the trials and specific aspects. It was so with his correspondence with John Wright whom I interviewed in 2009; too early in my research to ask the right questions.[31] It was also true of his 1977 correspondence with John Hook, whom I interviewed in old age in 2010.[32] Sissons' technique with Hook was to provide a lot of information from the accounts by Lieutenant Katayama Hideo and General Imamura Hitoshi[33] and even translated passages, in particular, where Katayama mentions his contacts with Hook. The effect, of course, was to jog Hook's memory but maybe also to shape it. When I interviewed Hook, he spoke of the contacts with Katayama but as something he had not remembered until Sissons brought it up.

26 Major Herbert Francis Dick was a former prisoner of war, captured at Singapore who, after his liberation, was taken on as a Legal Officer at the Directorate of Prisoners of War and Internees (DPW&I) in Melbourne and 1 Australian War Crimes Section (1AWCS) in Singapore. He later appeared as Defending Officer or Prosecuting Officer at trials held in Rabaul and Hong Kong. His frank correspondence (when a country solicitor) with Sissons in the 1970s gave me many details about the British approach to death sentences (see NLA, MS 3092, Box 22: Ambon: Major Dick).

27 Dr Roland Beard was the Medical Officer (MO) who certified the death of Katayama at Rabaul. See his 1970s correspondence with Sissons: NLA, MS 3092, Box 28: Dr Beard.

28 Noel Fowler was MO at Morotai. One of his responsibilities was to certify that an executed Japanese man was indeed dead. Fowler was the MO at the first firing squad in March 1946. See his 1970s correspondence with Sissons: NLA, MS 3092, Box 28: Death sentence.

29 John Williams was the Prosecuting Officer at Morotai M45. He and Sissons began a correspondence in 1990 about the trial and the related film, *Blood Oath*, which also incorporated some detail from the trial of Katayama (M43), copies of Williams' correspondence with other participants and Williams' MA coursework on the trial (see NLA, MS 3092, Box 21: Ambon).

30 Georgina Fitzpatrick, 'Death sentences, Japanese war criminals and the Australian military', in Fitzpatrick, McCormack & Morris, 2016, pp. 326–70.

31 NLA, MS 3092, Box 32: Morotai: Morotai trials general (excluding Ambon): John Wright. Wright was another interpreter at Morotai with Sissons and they trained together in Melbourne. This correspondence throughout the 1970s contained many frank stories about the death sentences; a subject not touched upon in our interview. Wright died a few months later, before I could return better informed about him and his role.

32 NLA, MS 3092, Box 30 and my interview with John Hook, 11 March 2010.

33 Hideo Katayama, *Ai to shi to eien to: aru senpansha no nikki* (Tokyo, 1958) and Hitoshi Imamura, *Shiki ichi gunjin rokujū-nen no aikan* (Tokyo, 1970). Both books (in Japanese) are held in the NLA.

Another category of participant with whom Sissons corresponded and interviewed was surviving Japanese tried in the Australian courts. In his long search for leads to anyone who had known Katayama,[34] he sought an interview with Dr Mukohata Sadami who was a Medical Officer with the 20th Special Sea Service Company and was prosecuted in four trials at Rabaul.[35] In January 1979, Sissons, on one of his trips to Japan, interviewed Mukohata about Katayama but also about Australian personnel at the Rabaul and Manus compounds and the conditions there.[36] Five days later, he interviewed Takebayashi Tsuruichi and Furuye Eisuke, tried together at Rabaul for the murder of 24 Chinese prisoners of war held captive at Rabaul.[37] They served their sentences first at Rabaul (where they overlapped with Katayama) and then the Manus Island War Criminals Compound until repatriated.[38] Providing extended eyewitness accounts of life in the two compounds from the other side of the barbed wire to researchers long after the deaths of all concerned is yet another contribution made by Sissons.

Another wonderful discovery for me — a researcher without Japanese language skills[39] — was finding his translations from relevant Japanese sources. Apart from many sections of the Katayama diary mentioned already, a major example was his extended translation of an account by Captain Kokaze Ichitano, the Japanese Defending Officer at many of the Rabaul trials.[40] Although Kokaze's specifics were not quite accurate as he was remembering his experience some years later, it was a fascinating insight into his thoughts about the trials and the procedures and the Australian personnel. One observation by Kokaze confirmed my suspicion that it was probably better for a Japanese defendant to have an Australian Defending Officer, knowledgeable in the procedures and in Australian military law. To have access to a Japanese eyewitness account validated my interpretation on this point

---

34 Sub Lt Katayama Hideo, tried at Morotai (NAA, A471, 80918) for his role in the execution of a captured airman, was sentenced to death by firing squad on 28 February 1946, but not executed until 23 October 1947 at Rabaul. Sissons' time as an interpreter at Morotai finished two weeks before Katayama arrived there (23 February 1946) (Hank Nelson, '*Blood Oath*: A reel history', *Australian Historical Studies*, vol. 24, no. 97 (October 1991), p. 436). Sissons left Morotai for Japan on 11 February, so he did not witness the Katayama trial nor meet him then or during his earlier investigation employment in the region. For Sissons' service file, see NAA, B883, VX128886.

35 Found not guilty in R157, NAA 471, 81228, Mukohata was sentenced to 15 years in R158 (NAA, A471, 81221), five years in R168 (NAA, 471, 81219) and 25 years in R164 (NAA, 471, 81236). His sentences were served first at Rabaul (where Katayama spent his last months) and then on Manus until remaining war criminals were repatriated and eventually parolled in the 1950s.

36 NLA, MS 3092, Box 31: Manus: Compounds Manus: Correspondence with Dr Sadami Mukohata [sic], Notes of Sissons' interview with Dr Mukohata, 15 January 1979.

37 NLA, MS 3092, Box 31: Manus: Compounds Manus: Notes of Sissons' interview with Takebayashi Tsuruichi and Furuye Eisuke, 20 January 1979, tried together at Rabaul (R55), NAA, A471, 80915.

38 For a study of the repatriation process, see Dean Aszkielowicz, 'Changing direction: repatriation of Japanese war criminals in Australian custody' in Fitzpatrick, McCormack & Morris, 2016, pp. 732–54.

39 This was not required in my part of the project, I was only expected to work through the Australian files.

40 The title was *Shusen zengo to sempan bengo no kaiso* (Tokyo, 1980). See Sissons' translation of pp. 160–82 in NLA, MS 3092, Box 32: Rabaul & NG.

and would have been a closed door to me without the translation.[41] Of necessity, I had to reduce my discussion about the Kokaze account but that translation lies there in Sissons' boxes for other scholars without linguistic skills. What a legacy! Sissons' translations of Japanese publications constitute a major element of the debt I owe him.

Providing me with hard-to-locate sources

Sissons' files contained primary source materials that I would have been unlikely to locate. For example, he had a 1987 newspaper cutting from the *Sun-Herald* (Sydney), a year not digitised in Trove, the online library database hosted by the National Library of Australia, describing how photographs were surreptitiously taken of the execution by firing squad on Changi Beach of Lt Gen. Shimpei Fukuya, Commanding Officer of all prisoner-of-war camps in Malaya (and reproducing the sequence of photographs as well). I noted this item in Sissons' Box 28 but, as the execution was the outcome of a British-run trial, I set it aside. Later, when I was writing my chapter on the trials in Singapore, I realised that this would be relevant in a section concerning the British approach to death sentences there. As was often the case, I went back to his collection, took fuller details about the photos and included a summary in a footnote.[42]

In his archival boxes, I was always finding a cutting or notes from a newspaper or magazine not yet digitised. How many hours did David Sissons save me from fruitless checking of hard-to-read microfilms to see if a publication contained anything relevant? For example, I would never have found an article from *People* relating the offer from a blind ex-serviceman, who had been a prisoner of war, to act as hangman.[43] Another time, finds in another box reduced research time interstate on limited means consulting the papers of Williams.[44] Sissons had already collected Williams' MA coursework essay and his 'Impromptu address to the cast of *Blood Oath*'. It meant that, before I travelled to Sydney, I had time to digest these interesting items written by one of the prosecuting officers at Ambon and Morotai as he contemplated his role in later years.[45]

41 See my use of this account in Georgina Fitzpatrick, 'The trials in Rabaul' in Fitzpatrick, McCormack & Morris, 2016, pp. 546–47.

42 Georgina Fitzpatrick, 'The trials in Singapore', in Fitzpatrick, McCormack & Morris, 2016, p. 600, note 131, in which I cite my source as NLA, MS 3092, Box 28: Death sentence: Picture of hanging [sic] — a Sissons' title, although the photographs were of an execution by firing squad.

43 NLA, MS 3092, Box 28: Death sentence: People. Having the date and page reference to the article sent me straight to the publication and on a quest for other examples of men volunteering for this task.

44 Williams' papers are held at the Mitchell Library, Sydney, MLMSS 5426.

45 NLA, MS 3092, Box 21: Ambon: Impromptu address to cast of *Blood Oath*, Warner Studios Qld, 12 August 1989; and JM Williams, 'Australian War Crimes Trials 1945–1951: National sentiment, Australian ethos, their historical genesis, and impact on trials', MA Coursework, University of Sydney, November 1988.

Giving me confidence as a novice researcher in this field

At times I felt quite isolated as the historian on this large Linkage project. Although the two existing doctoral theses (by Caroline Pappas and Carrel)[46] often backed up facts and figures, I was less certain about the way the trials were conducted. Sissons, from beyond the grave, so often seemed to give me a reassuring nod. When I was working on the Singapore trials, I found existing published research confusing. When some assertions about the Singapore trials by Utsumi Aiko and Gavan McCormack[47] did not match up with what I was finding, I realised that they must have treated the trials by both British and Australians as one set. Whereas my co-researcher, Morris, and I had decided that British trials were those conducted under the Royal Warrant and Australian trials were those conducted under the *War Crimes Act 1945* (Cth).[48] So no wonder our names, facts and figures were different. Sorting out the two sets of Singapore trials became a major feature of my work for the Singapore chapter and was the subject of a conference paper I delivered in Singapore in 2012.[49] It was such a relief to have Sissons confirm that there was 'a division of labour between the British and the Australian war crimes courts in Singapore'. 'As a result,' Sissons continued, 'there were a large number of British trials where the charge included atrocities perpetuated against Australians.'[50] He identified some of these trials (S1, S15 and others) as *British* trials, just as we had decided, with trial records held by the British in the WO series in the UK National Archives and not in the A471 series in the NAA.

Mentoring from the grave

Several of those who published on the Australian-run war crimes trials leant very heavily on an account by Athol Moffitt of the three trials he prosecuted at Labuan.[51] My instinctive distrust of this approach was confirmed when I read what Sissons had to say about Moffitt's book, *Project Kingfisher*,[52] which he had been asked to review for the *Canberra Times*. Sissons made it very clear that it was most unwise to base

46 Caroline Pappas, 'Law and Politics: Australia's war crimes trials in the Pacific, 1943–1961', PhD thesis, University of NSW, 1998; and Carrel, 2005.

47 Utsumi Aiko, 'Prisoners of war in the Pacific War' (Gavan McCormack trans.) and Gavan McCormack, 'Apportioning the blame: Australian trials for railway crimes', in Gavan McCormack & Hank Nelson (eds), *Burma/Thailand Railway: memory and history* (Sydney: Allen & Unwin), 1993, pp. 68–84 and pp. 85–115 respectively.

48 Exchange of emails between us, 24 August 2011, in possession of this author.

49 Georgina Fitzpatrick, 'Cutting the apron strings? Australian and British war crimes trials at Singapore', conference paper, *Legal Histories of the British Empire*, National University of Singapore, July 2012.

50 Sissons to Michael Pigott, AWM, 22 August 1983 in NLA, MS 3092, Box 25: Singapore: British trials.

51 Capt. Athol Moffitt was the Prosecuting Officer at three trials — ML28 (8–20 January 1946), ML36 (23–28 January 1946) and ML35 (30 January 1946). The middle one had to be retried.

52 Athol Moffit, *Project Kingfisher* (North Ryde, NSW: Angus & Robertson), 1989.

one's view of the trials through the lens of one man at one place with experience only of three trials. His draft review exposes time after time Moffitt's airy generalisations and errors of fact. Unfazed by the lofty position of Moffitt as a judge in the NSW Supreme Court (1962) and then in the Court of Appeal (1970), Sissons gave his judgement that 'it was sloppily written nonsense delivered with an air of supreme authority'. So much fault did he find with it that he explained to Robert Hefner, literary editor at the *Canberra Times*, that he could not deliver the review as he had found the book 'an awful shock to me'.[53]

He also gave warning in relation to another book, Ian Ward's *Snaring the Other Tiger*, concerning the last set of trials at Manus Island and, in particular, the trial of Lieutenant General Nishimura Takuma (LN2).[54] I would not have had the patience he had in analysing the evidence upon which Ward relied — supposedly the investigation reports of Captain James Godwin (some of which were reproduced in the book). Sissons summed up his findings in an unpublished paper, dated 30 January 1997, 'Weekly investigation reports by Godwin reproduced in *Snaring the Other Tiger* — forgeries?'[55] Sissons compared the files Godwin sent from 2 Australian War Crimes Section (2AWCS) to the DPW&I in Melbourne[56] with the reproductions in the Ward book. He compared abbreviations (different). He compared typeface (different) and the typewriter codes used on the originals (absent on the reproduced ones). I do not know why he bothered with the question mark in his title. As established by two later researchers, Gregory Hadley and James Oglethorpe, the forgeries were not the fault of Godwin but the concoction of the late James Mackay.[57] Ward had assumed the 'Godwin' weekly reports, supposedly collected in a 'File 125M' and discussed by Mackay in his book[58] were the genuine ones. When I was given a copy of Ward's book at the AWM, it came with a verbal warning about the forged bits of evidence. Hadley and Oglethorpe acknowledged their debt too to Sissons ('respected Australian historian') in an endnote. He had sent them his unpublished paper[59] and it seems to have inspired their work on the typewriters and formatting used and other details.

53 NLA, MS 3092, Box 23: Borneo: *Canberra Times*, Sissons to Mr Heffner, 5 March 1991. The draft review is in this box too. For a list of errors made by Moffitt, especially in his Chapter 8, see 'Moffitt errors' in same box. In correspondence with Williams (Prosecuting Officer for M45 at Ambon and Morotai), Sissons was explicit that his reason for not producing the review for publication was that he could only see its faults (NLA, MS 3092, Box 21: Ambon, Sissons to Williams, 15 August 1991).

54 Ian Ward, *Snaring the Other Tiger* (Singapore, 1996).

55 NLA, MS 3092, Box 31: Manus.

56 NAA, MP742/1, 336/1/1965 PART 1.

57 Gregory Hadley & James Oglethorpe, 'Mackay's betrayal: Solving the mystery of the "Sado Island prisoner-of-war massacre"', *Journal of Military History*, vol. 71, no. 2 (April 2007), pp. 441–64.

58 James Mackay, *Betrayal in High Places* (Stockport, UK, 1996).

59 'First revealed by respected Australian historian David Sissons … unpublished manuscript [PDF] in D.C.S. possession, 1997' (Hadley & Oglethorpe, 2007, n. 32). This was, of course, before Sissons deposited his archives in the NLA. I have since seen correspondence between Sissons and Oglethorpe enclosing his unpublished paper in a file of materials that Sissons passed on to Carrel.

Sissons in the last years of his life was also mentoring Carrel, as I discovered from Carrel's research files. While I was at the AWM working on my chapters for *Australia's War Crimes Trials, 1945–51*, Carrel, on the eve of moving to Britain, passed on to me his files accumulated from his doctoral thesis (filling one four-drawer cabinet).[60] Among them was a manila folder of Sissons' writings and some correspondence between them. It was another pathway for me, via Carrel, to the thoughts and unpublished writings of Sissons. Even more importantly, Sissons had provided Carrel and, subsequently, me with a database of records organised alphabetically by the Japanese surnames of defendants. Carrel entered all this information from a typescript that Sissons gave him into an Excel database, which was much easier for me to search, but it had started with Sissons.[61]

The designated legatee or the ventriloquist's dummy

As I progressed with my use of Sissons' archival boxes, I began to feel that he had organised his materials specifically for me.[62] This emerged in his cross-referencing. In his box on Japanese language and linguists in Australia, for example, I read this command from him (concerning the recruitment of four ethnic Chinese skilled in the Japanese language) on one of his cut-down notes: 'Suggest that A71 may lead to them under EVACUATION or NON-EURO & RESTRICTED: WARTIME ARRIVAL. DCSS 6/10/87'. There he was, in 1987, realising that he might not be able to follow every thread and that I, his inheritor in this area of his research, should be guided posthumously from the grave to the right file.[63]

On another occasion, when I began research on the trials held at Singapore, many of them concerning the treatment of prisoners of war along the Burma–Thai railway, I came across another suggestion. Sissons had annotated photocopies of chapters by Utsumi Aiko and Gavin McCormack[64] with the following: 'It would be interesting to look at the investigation files and see why more officers and railways personnel were not charged. See how many railway officers were proscribed in the Aust

60 See n. 13. Carrel's files were mostly printouts or photocopies and transcripts of NAA files, organised by file number and not by subject. If it was obvious from his thesis that a file would be relevant for a particular aspect, I would check his file before heading off to the archives to fill in any gaps. Carrel, as well as Sissons, by his generous sharing of his files with me ensured that I could trawl through hundreds of thousands of NAA files in the time allocated to me.

61 Michael Carrel, 'Defendants', Excel database, in my possession. Carrel also passed on to me his file entitled 'Sissons documents', including an appendix to the draft guide for the NAA, which Sissons had decided not to proceed with. The appendix was entitled 'War criminals tried by Australian courts: Index to court transcripts & Dept of Army records by name of accused'. This is also now in my possession.

62 I was told by one of the librarians that he had been working on the arrangement in the manuscript room even in his last weeks of life.

63 NLA, MS 3092, Box 39, File: T.S. Lim (and ex-Malayan Special Branch evacuees).

64 See n. 47.

questionnaires and how many were placed on Aust wanted lists.'[65] I considered this suggestion for a moment and then typed my response: 'I feel he is speaking to me from the grave but for me to explore at that depth would be fatal. I too would not complete my task.'[66] One thing I had learnt from Sissons (as a negative example) was to know when to stop: when to limit oneself within boundaries and leave an aspect of the immense war crimes trials research for another day or for another researcher.

Identifying with Sissons the researcher

At times, I identified with Sissons in certain of his obsessions. For example, some people thought there was something distasteful in my wanting to explore the mechanics of how the Australian military organised the hangings and firing squads required for death sentences. All that I needed to do to set aside any concerns that I was somehow twisted, however, was to remember Sissons' own pursuit of the smallest details on the same subject. He collected NAA material as well as items from obscure or non-digitised publications.[67] One 1987 interview with Harry Morris, the senior official in charge of the Department of Works and Housing on Manus Island during the period of the war crimes trials there, prompted Sissons to draft a few pages of rebuttal.[68] It was clear that Sissons was also intrigued by the question of who acted as hangman on Manus and at Rabaul. In his transcriptions of instructions to those who had to carry out the firing squads or organise the hangings, he alerted me to material I might not have judged significant.[69]

Apart from discovering that I shared many methods and practices in archival research with Sissons, I also wryly grimaced in sympathy at times. When he was delving deeply into death sentences and attempting to pin down which military tradition — British, American or Canadian — had been the source for Australia's procedure, he wrote to the old Public Record Office (PRO) in London, forerunner of the UK National Archives in Kew. In a letter of 1975, at a time when I was spending months commuting from Cambridge to Chancery Lane to work on my MA research, he

65 His emphasis. NLA, MS 3092, Box 24: Burma–Siam: Korean WCs.

66 Unfortunately I have not dated this transcript of mine on the paper version as usual but it would have been in late 2011 when I was working on the Singapore trials. Interestingly, at a meeting in May 2009, I discovered from Peter Londey that the initial intention of AWM staff involved in mapping out the Linkage proposal was to extend the existing research work by Pappas and Carrel in their respective theses (see n. 46) to the investigation files held in the AWM. This was not the path chosen but it is still a good idea for future research.

67 These included a report from someone who had witnessed the Manus hangings the day before and who had identified the hangman (*South Pacific Post*, 15 June 1951).

68 NLA, MS 3092, Box 31: Manus: H. Morris's recollections of the Tol Massacre and the Manus trials'. Morris was on the interviewing committee on Manus when the hangman was chosen from several volunteers. For the original item, see 'War veteran pleads for end to Nazi hunt' (*Age*, 13 March 1987), in the same box. On the Manus hangings, see Fitzpatrick, 'Death sentences', 2016, pp. 360–69.

69 His transcription of a 'Memo upon execution of prisoners by hanging with the long drop' included the information that the Melbourne file had diagrams in the instructions (NLA, MS 3092, Box 28: Death sentence).

asked for information about British policy and requested a copy of standing orders. In a typically curt reply, someone told him to get a professional researcher. That was the PRO as I remembered it! The staff at Chancery Lane was notorious in the 1970s for rudeness and general obstructiveness. Those on the desk got quite cranky and truculent when you approached them with your orders for files. After a gap of many years, I returned to the new premises at Kew and I could not get over the contrast. I think staff had been sent to charm school or, at least, recognised that they were the front face of a public service and that researchers had legitimate requests.[70]

Glimpses of his viewpoint

Sissons' file headings were usually placenames, events, people's names or statements of fact, but occasionally the headings expressed his concerns. One example, occurring in his box of Ambon materials, was headed: 'Subordinates should not be tried until after Seniors'.[71] Another folder was labelled: 'Katayama beaten up at Rabaul'. It became obvious that he was very troubled by the Katayama case as he followed up every trail to anyone who had known Katayama on Morotai and the Rabaul War Criminals Compound. In a letter to Herbert Dick, he wrote:

> At the time I was quite sure that the trials were a necessity and that as a result of them prisoners and civilians were more likely in future wars to be treated with humanity. I thought, however, that some of the Morotai courts were unduly severe in imposing the death penalty on very junior officers and other ranks who had carried out death sentences as a result of specific orders from superior officers and had not aggravated the offence by additional barbarities or indignities.[72]

His concerns seemed to widen out from the Katayama case to the whole process. The clearest statement I found came in his letter applying to present a paper to the 1975 Australian and New Zealand Association for the Advancement of Science (ANZAAS) conference. He set out his doubts about the trials, including the speed of the trials and the short time the defending counsel had with their clients. He also pointed out that the legal officers had inadequate legal reference books. It worried him that the delegation to confirm sentences fell to a single military officer rather than the Governor-General.[73] He also found fault with the failure to ensure conformity in sentencing. As had happened to Katayama, subalterns tried in January

70 The exchange of letters may be found in NLA, MS 3092, Box 28: Death sentence: British Army. Sissons to PRO, 18 September 1975 and the reply.

71 NLA, MS 3092, Box 22: Ambon.

72 NLA, MS 3092, Box 22: Ambon: Major Dick. Sissons to Dick, 5 August 1976. This is a typescript letter of six pages.

73 Initially this was the Commander-in-Chief of the Australian Army, Lt Gen. Vernon Sturdee. In 1947, confirming power was transferred to the Adjutant-General Maj. Gen. WM Anderson (Pappas, 1998, p. 71).

and February 1946 got tougher sentences than their commanding officers tried later on. He also pointed to the failure of the Australian authorities in investigating cases of ill-treatment of Japanese prisoners of war.[74]

These were good points that he made and I looked out for evidence in relation to them, making sure I included sections in my chapters at the relevant points. However, I do wish that he had expressed his opinions more fully towards the end of his life, when, for example, he wrote the overview essay.[75] Or better still, I wish that I had been able to discus my overview essay with him in which I finally concluded that, in the context of the time, the trials made a determined effort to be fair.[76]

Why did he publish so little on the Australian war crimes trials?

Early in my research, when I was exploring Sissons' Morotai files, I came across an envelope marked 'Duntroon lecture'. Inside were notes and the draft of a lecture to be given at the Royal Military College, Duntroon. The few typescript pages of the lecture gave me an inkling of his perfectionism and filled me with a sympathetic horror. Almost every word was crossed out (including 'the' and 'and') in black pen with alternative words supplied. In turn, some of the alternatives were scored through.[77] If his writing was always as hard-wrung from him as this example showed, then his publishing record in this area has an explanation.

His research on the war crimes trials also lasted over decades — from the 1970s to the 2000s. There must come a point at which one is sick of it. Certainly, his focus changed over the years, judging from hints he gave in correspondence. In an early letter in the archive, he described himself as writing a biography of Sub Lieutenant Katayama Hideo.[78] By 1982, he was describing his work on Katayama as an article.[79] However, the amount of detail collected by Sissons by that stage may have overwhelmed him. There seemed no avenue he failed to explore.

74 NLA, MS 3092, Box 32: Morotai trials: ANZAAS. Sissons letter, 19 June 1975. I do not know whether he presented such a paper. I have not found a draft.

75 See n. 7.

76 Georgina Fitzpatrick, 'War crimes trials, "victor's justice" and Australian military justice in the aftermath of the Second World War', in Kevin Jon Heller & Gerry Simpson (eds), *The Hidden Histories of War Crimes Trials*, Oxford University Press, 2013, pp. 327–47.

77 NLA, MS 3092, Box 32: Morotai trials: Duntroon lecture. In my notes from this box which I worked through in October 2009, I wrote: 'I should read this first for an overview. But it is hard to use as it doesn't have footnotes and it has lots crossed out.' In the end, I did not return to it until transcribing it recently for this volume.

78 NLA, MS 3092, Box 28: Death sentence: British Army. Sissons to CM McDougall, 7 April 1975; CM McDougall to Sissons, 7 April 1975.

79 NLA, MS 3092, Box 31: Manus; Correspondence with Dr Sadami Mukohata 1979-82. Sissons to Mukohata, 23 December 1982. For information about Dr Mukohata, see above n. 35.

Katayama received the death sentence; the aspect of his case that Sissons was investigating in 1975. As I found in 2009, when I began to look for material on this aspect of the war crimes trials, there was very little in the public domain about the mechanics of conducting executions. Sissons came across a novel by Colin McDougall[80] containing a description of a firing squad that he believed was based on the British Army standing orders. McDougall was a lieutenant colonel in the Canadian infantry during the Second World War. Sissons tracked him down to the University Secretariat at McGill University and wrote to him for information. McDougall replied that he did not know if the procedure described in his novel followed British Army standing orders. So of course, Sissons wrote another letter, the one to the PRO discussed above, mentioning McDougall and his novel and requesting the British standing orders.[81] In this episode, I observed the extent to which he would follow a trail.

He collected so much material that at some stage he must have realised that he had the makings of a general book on the trials. The focus was still Katayama's case but it snowballed to address many other aspects. As time went on and the folders and envelopes of notes accumulated, he may have been overwhelmed by the scale and complexity of what he had gathered. And the same problem may have applied to the 'Research guide to war crimes trials' that he was preparing for the NAA.[82]

Conclusion

Although Sissons published very little about the war crimes trials in which he pulled together all the source material he had collected and set out his opinions and findings, combining his academic training with his personal experience as a participant in some of the trials — and that is a terrible pity — he still left behind a treasure trove in his boxes of archival material. It helped to live in Canberra, as I did, and could set aside days and weeks to work through his boxes, but perseverance will repay the excavation.

I acknowledged my debt to Sissons in the dedication of the co-authored book *Australia's War Crimes Trials, 1945–51* in the following words: 'Dedicated to the memory of David Sissons upon whose shoulders all who research Australia's war crimes trials stand.' However, writing this chapter and going through my notes and thought processes again has made me realise that his legacy was not just our private two-way spectral conversation. If this chapter makes more historians realise the buried treasure lying in his archival boxes, then perhaps my debt will have been paid.

80 Colin McDougall, *Execution*, Macmillan, 1958.

81 See n. 69.

82 NLA, MS 3092, Box 2: File 25: Australian Archives Guide 9.

DAVID SISSONS' WARTIME SERVICE

Note by Georgina Fitzpatrick

David Sissons combined his later academic interest in Australia's war crimes trials, 1945–51, with personal experience as an interpreter at three of the Morotai trials in early 1946 before his transfer to Japan as a member of the British Commonwealth Occupation Force (BCOF).

He was a student at the University of Melbourne studying the Classics when he was called up six months after his 18th birthday and 'taken on strength' at Royal Park near the university campus on 26 June 1944.[1] A few days later, he went (or 'marched out') to a training course in New South Wales. In the army parlance of the time, the course was noted as 'Jap class'. It must have been during this period that, according to family information, he was present at Cowra on 5 August 1944 during the mass breakout of Japanese prisoners in which 231 Japanese died. This, however, is not mentioned in his service file. The official transfer to the AIF and the allocation of his VX number occurred in September. For the next two-and-a-half years, he belonged to them, setting aside his university education.

During 1944–45, he was one of the students at the intensive course offered at the Military Intelligence and Censorship School in the Olderfleet Building, Collins Street, Melbourne.[2] His first posting was to No. 4 Internment Compound at Tatura in northern Victoria between 28 March and 14 April 1945. This was the Japanese Compound. Unfortunately, his dossier does not detail his task at the camp, but this compound held Japanese civilian internees including Australian-born people with some Japanese descent and the odd Australian of Anglo-Celtic ethnicity who was

1 See his completed Attestation form in his Service File, NAA, B883, VX128886.

2 He is listed in Colin Funch, *Linguists in Uniform: The Japanese Experience* (Clayton, Vic.: Japanese Studies Centre, 2003), p. 284.

suspected of pro-Japanese sympathies.[3] He was then sent to the Cowra prisoner-of-war camp in New South Wales. Once more there is no detail on his role there or even how long his deployment lasted.[4]

As soon as the war ended, thousands of Japanese surrendered to the Australian forces on islands to the north of Australia.[5] As a member of the Allied Translator and Interpreter Section (ATIS), Sissons was attached to the headquarters of 9th Division AIF at Morotai, arriving by plane on 17 September. He was promoted to corporal a week later. Soon after, he was sent to Labuan, an island off the coast of British North Borneo. His two months there must have been confronting. Although his service file does not specify his work, investigators such as Captain Davern Wright (with whom he corresponded in later years) were interrogating war criminal suspects about the Sandakan–Ranau death marches across Borneo, the conditions at the Sandakan and Kuching prisoner-of-war camps and the treatment of Allied prisoners used as forced labour on the island. It is quite likely he was employed translating captured documents or statements taken from suspects. His kindness to a Japanese suspect, 'Nakase', during this time on Labuan was remembered later in a letter Nakase sent to a fellow interpreter, Allan Clifton.[6] Although Sissons was not an interpreter at the subsequent set of 16 Australian-run trials on the island he may well have attended the first three trials held between 3–8 December 1945.[7] He did not leave Labuan until 13 December (on the AS *Merriman*).

Soon after his return to Morotai, he was promoted to sergeant. Although his service file consistently lacks detail about what he did at Morotai, the war crimes trial transcripts reveal that he interpreted at three of the trials held in early February 1946.[8] All three cases concerned the mistreatment or killing of captured Australian airmen and, in all three cases, he interpreted for the defence. Unfortunately, apart

3 See my accounts of Veronica Connelly and Harry Woodfield interned in Tatura 4, in Georgina Fitzpatrick, 'Britishers Behind Barbed Wire: Internment in Australia during the Second World War', PhD thesis, The Australian National University, 2009. This is now available online through the ANU Library at openresearch-repository.anu.edu.au/handle/1885/109224.

4 For the dates and places of his postings to Tatura and Cowra (and his subsequent movements), see his Service and Casualty form, NAA, B883, VX128886.

5 For an account of the role of linguists during this period, see Georgina Fitzpatrick, 'Interpreters at Australia's war crimes trials, 1945–51: From "ready-mades" to "happenchancers"', in Amanda Laugesen & Richard Gehrmann (eds), *Communication, Interpreting and Language in Wartime: Historical and Contemporary Aspects* (Basingstoke: Palgrave Macmillan), 2019, pp. 153–70.

6 'Nakase' wrote that he had looked for familiar faces among the Australian troops with BCOF on his return to Japan, including 'Sergeant Sissons, who had been so kind to me on Labuan'. See the letter, transcribed in Allan S Clifton, *Time of Fallen Blossoms* (Sydney: Cassell, 1960), p. 56.

7 ML2, ML3 and ML4. For an account of the Labuan trials, see Georgina Fitzpatrick, 'The trials on Labuan', in Fitzpatrick, McCormack & Morris, 2016, pp. 429–70.

8 He is listed as one of the two interpreters at three trials at Morotai — M32 (5 February 1946), M29 (6–7 February 1946) and M34 (7 February 1946). He also mentioned interpreting for Captain Katō Kihachirō in a letter to Noel Fowler, 27 June 1978, NLA, Papers of David Sissons, MS 3092, Box 28: Death sentence. This could be either during the investigation period or Katō's trial (M23) held on 14 January 1946. Unfortunately, no interpreter is named in the listing of court personnel for M23, NAA, A471, 80774, p. 10.

from the occasional placing of himself at a specific trial in his archive,[9] Sissons, to my knowledge, did not leave a firsthand account of his experiences. However, at the trials of Captain Murakami Hiroshi (M34) and Sergeant Morimoto Kiyomitsu (M32), Sissons, as interpreter for the defence, would have interpreted any cross-examinations of Japanese witnesses conducted by the Australian Defending Officer and the latter's examination of the accused.[10] In the trial of Corporal Baba Hidetoshi (M29), there is even a glimpse of Sissons, when the Defending Officer, Captain Philip Allen, asked the Court's permission 'to explain through my Interpreter the Accused's rights'. The transcript then noted that the accused and the accused's interpreter retired 'temporarily', and that '[l]ater they return[ed] to Court.'[11] Alas, no official photographer captured that consultation, as happened in the very earliest of the Morotai trials when the novelty of the events prompted a visual record to be made.

Some of the men with whom he later corresponded about the trials were there at Morotai at the same time, appearing in various roles at either the mass trial about conditions at the Tan Toey prisoner-of-war camp (M45) or a related trial (M44). These trials overlapped with those he worked on. Among them was the Prosecuting Officer, Captain John Williams (M45); and from M44, Captain Leo Travers, a member of the Court, and Staff Sergeant John Wright (the interpreter).[12]

On 11 February 1946, he embarked by plane for Japan where he spent the next year with BCOF. He returned to Australia on the *Manoora*, embarking at Kure on 15 February 1947. In his service file, a typed slip of paper, signed by Captain FL Gower, Acting Officer Commanding CSDIC, BCOF, vouched for him as an 'Excellent Translator/Interpreter. Often left to work on his own and produced good results. Conduct excellent. Would make a good Linguist Officer'. However, Sissons did not apply to be an officer. He was discharged from military service to resume his university studies in Melbourne. In his service file, it is noted that he had spent 532 days overseas and only 450 in Australia.[13] These wartime years set his path towards his lifetime research interest into all matters involving Australian–Japanese relations.

9 For example, he noted his role as defence interpreter at M34 in his materials on that trial (NLA, Papers of David Sissons, MS 3092, Box 32: N. Celebes and Halmaheras).

10 For the trial transcript of M34, see NAA, A471, 80788 and for M32, see NAA, A471, 80722.

11 Trial transcript of M29, NAA. A471, 81059, p. 17.

12 For his correspondence with Williams, see NLA, Papers of David Sissons, MS 3092, Box 21: Ambon; for John Wright, see NLA, Papers of David Sissons, MS 3092, Box 32: Morotai trials: John Wright; and for Leo Travers, see NLA, Papers of David Sissons, MS 3092, Box 21.

13 See Proceedings for Discharge, NAA, B883, VX128886.

2

JAPANESE INTENTIONS TOWARD AUSTRALIA (1939–42)

DCS Sissons

Editors' note

The Australian War Memorial (AWM) commissioned David Sissons to write this 1997 essay as a part of the development project for a new Second World War gallery, which opened in 1999. Peter Stanley was the head of the AWM's Military History Section and the project's concept leader. Stanley asked Sissons to produce a scholarly assessment of Japanese intentions towards Australia during the Second World War and his resulting historical interpretation of the issue was included on one of the gallery's interpretive boards.

In this essay, Sissons explains how the Japanese military proposed and rejected the idea of invading Australia in mid-1942, and argues that Japan did not subsequently plan to invade and occupy the mainland. Yet, the Australian publics' belief in Japan's plan to invade Australia remained prevalent for many decades. The myth was finally debunked during fierce public debates in the early 2000s, and Stanley published *Invading Australia: Japan and the battle for Australia* in 2008. Stanley credits Sissons with inspiring him to pursue the topic. This essay again demonstrates Sissons' thorough research and comprehensive review of Japanese source materials.

Fortunately, enough is available from Japanese sources to demonstrate what Japan's objectives were in the Second World War and what part the Japanese planners saw for Australia in the achievement of those objectives.

Japan's objectives were clarified in mid-1940 in the weeks following Hitler's conquest of the Low Countries and France and the evacuation of the British Expeditionary Force at Dunkirk. Japan took this opportunity to conclude the Tripartite Alliance with Germany and Italy on September 27th. The purpose of this was to deter the United States from interfering while Japan: (i) achieved victory in her war with China; (ii) secured the oil, rubber and other resources of the Netherlands East Indies; (iii) organised Asia and the South Seas into a Japanese sphere of interest. In pursuit of the first objective she then proceeded to cut off China's sources of arms and materials by placing an occupation force in French Indo-China and by requiring Britain to close the Burma Road. In pursuit of the second she despatched a negotiating mission to Batavia demanding exclusive prospecting concessions and contracts that would enable her to purchase there three-fifths of her overall oil requirements. The importance of this was that Japan was dependent for oil on her potential enemies and, without oil for her armed services, lacked both the capacity to wage war and the diplomatic power that this conferred.

The breadth of Japan's ambitions are revealed in the brief for negotiating the Alliance adopted at the Four Ministers' (Prime Minister, Army, Navy and Foreign Affairs) conference of September 4th. In this Japan's sphere of interest was described as extending to 'the islands of the Pacific held by Germany in 1914, French Indo-China and France's Pacific islands, Thailand, Malaya, British Borneo, the Netherlands East Indies, Burma, Australia, New Zealand, India, etc.'.[1] It is clear, therefore, that Japan hoped to include Australia within her 'Greater East Asia Co-prosperity Sphere'. It is also clear, however, that the plans in accordance with which Japan went to war in December 1941 did not include the capture of Australia, New Zealand or India.

The strategic policy for the conduct of the war adopted by Cabinet, General Staff Headquarters and Naval Staff Headquarters at the Liaison Conference of November 15th (1941) commences with the statement:

> Our policy is: by quickly destroying American, British and Dutch bases in the Far East to establish self-reliant defence; by the adoption of more vigorous measures against the Chiang Kai-shek regime to hasten its fall: in co-operation with Germany and Italy, to defeat Britain first and destroy America's will to continue the struggle.

1 International Military Tribunal for the Far East, Exhibit 541, Item 3, 'Decisions made by the Conference of the Prime-Minister and the ministers of War, Navy and Foreign Affairs on 4 September 1940 …', Cited in H Feis, *The Road to Pearl Harbor* (Princeton, 1950), p. 114.

The very minor place occupied by Australia and India in this strategy is made apparent in the portion of this document in which the means of first defeating Britain are spelt out:

> Japan, Germany and Italy will act together to defeat Britain first. To this end Japan will: (i) by political tactics and the destruction of commerce sever the connection between the United Kingdom and India and Australia and cause them to revolt; (ii) hasten the independence of Burma and thereby stimulate India to Independence.[2]

The limits of Phase 1 Operations

The orders, 'Outline of overall operational plan', issued by General Staff Headquarters to Commander-in-Chief Southern Expeditionary Force at this time indicate clearly the limits of the operations to be undertaken.

> *Aim* — The object of operations in the Southern Region is to destroy the principal American, British and Dutch bases in East Asia and to occupy and secure the key areas of the region. The area we plan to occupy in these operations consists of the Philippines, Guam, Hong Kong, Malaya, Burma, Sumatra, Borneo, the Celebes, the Bismarck Archipelago, Dutch Timor, etc.
>
> *Method* — With close co-operation between the Army and the Navy operations will commence simultaneously in the Philippines and Malaya to complete the mission in the shortest possible time [3]

It was pursuant to the above plan that an invasion force of brigade group strength ('South Seas Force') supported by 7th Fleet landed at Rabaul on January 23rd (1942).

The operations in the Pacific and South-East Asia progressed so smoothly that Naval Staff Headquarters sought the approval of General Staff Headquarters to enlarge the scope of the plan to include the occupation of points in Papua/New Guinea and the Solomons. Their reasoning was as follows:

> In order to make secure the occupation of the Bismarck Archipelago region, we should make Rabaul the main base for air, sea and land forces and occupy as advanced bases Port Moresby in the south and Tulagi in the east to forestall the enemy's sea-borne counter-attack. Accordingly, the major portion of the

2 Resolutions of 69th Liaison Conference, 15 November 1941, reproduced in S Takagi, *Taiheiyō Kaisenshi* (Tokyo: Iwanami, 1959), pp. 186–89. For translations of the proceedings of these conferences see N Ike, *Japan's Decision for War: Records of the 1941 Policy conferences* (Stanford: University Press, 1967).

3 Reproduced in T Hattori, *Daitōa Sensō* (Tokyo: Masu Shobō, 1953), vol. 1, pp. 299–307. An English translation of this work, T Hattori, *The Complete History of the Greater East Asia War* (Tokyo: US 500th Military Intelligence Group, 1953) is available on microfilm at the Australian War Memorial.

> Navy's air strength allotted to operations in the Southern theatre should be transferred to this area and to the Marshalls in readiness to destroy the American counter-offensive.[4]

Accordingly on February 2nd agreement was reached that, in order to sever communications with the Australian mainland and to secure command of the sea to the north-east of Australia, the Army and Navy should together promptly capture Lae and Salamaua, and thereafter Port Moresby if possible, and that the Navy, either alone or with the Army, should seize any opportunity to establish an air base at Tulagi.[5] Lae and Salamaua were duly occupied on March 7th, Tulagi on May 3rd. The force to occupy Port Moresby set out from Rabaul on May 4th but as a result of the Battle of the Coral Sea was forced to return there.

The Naval Staff's Australian proposals

The Phase 1 operations were substantially completed with the surrender of the Netherlands East Indies on March 9th (1942). Naturally, planning for Phase 2 had been under way throughout Phase 1.

In the 1960s the authors of the official history of the Japanese Navy in the Pacific War interviewed the two officers principally concerned in the Navy's contribution to the planning of the Phase 1 and Phase 2 operations, R/Adm. Fukudome (Director, Operations Division, Naval Staff Headquarters 10/4/41 – 15/6/43) and Capt. Tomioka, who headed Fukudome's Operations Section 7/10/40 – 20/1/43. Both were critical of their own and the Army's thinking in the period preceding the outbreak of hostilities. Engrossed in the task of planning the complicated and large-scale initial operations, they had given inadequate attention to the problem, how to make success in the Phase 1 operations contribute positively to bringing the war to an end. They had, accordingly, to address their minds to this after operations had actually begun. They went to war undecided about how far they intended to advance.[6]

In November (1941), when the plans for Phase 1 had been sent to Combined Fleet for their comments, the latter had enquired how the Naval Staff proposed to make secure the gains acquired in Phase 1. According to Tomioka, the Naval Staff's response had been that, although they had not given the matter careful thought, they desired to destroy, if they could, the enemy's strategic points in: (i) East New Guinea,

4 *Senshi Sōsho* (Tokyo: Asagumo, 1970), vol. 35 [Official War History: Army Division of Imperial Headquarters — Part 3 (to April 1942)], p. 353 citing recollections of Cdr Miyo (Senior SO Air, Operations Division, Naval Staff Headquarters, 1940–42).

5 Imperial Headquarters, Army: Shi [Direction] no. 1915 of 2 Feb. 42 reproduced in *Senshi Sōsho*, 1970. pp. 334–35.

6 *Senshi Sōsho* (Tokyo: Asagumo, 1975), vol. 80 [Official War History: Naval Division of Imperial Headquarters/ Combined Fleet – Part 2 (to June 1942)], p. 296.

New Britain, Fiji, Samoa, etc.; (ii) the Aleutians and Midway; (iii) the Andamans; (iv) the Australian area. When Combined Fleet replied that not just destruction, but occupation, was necessary, the Naval Staff had agreed on the formula 'destruction or occupation'.[7] In retrospect, Fukudome and Tomioka felt that, to the extent that the Naval Staff had before the outbreak of hostilities considered subsequent strategy, their favourite concept for Phase 2 operations had been the capture of some strategic points in northern Australia and on the lines of communication between Australia and the United States.[8] Their argument was that Australia would become a base for air and submarine attacks threatening the areas gained in Phase 1 and for the enemy's counter-offensive. Because of northern Australia's isolation it would be difficult for the enemy to reinforce it. They could therefore capture strategic points there relatively cheaply, move in their planes, and from there strike at the bases from which the enemy's counter-offensive would be launched.[9]

It was in the weeks immediately following the outbreak of hostilities that the Naval Staff developed their thinking with greater precision. They considered that America's losses in capital ships at Pearl Harbor dramatically increased her need of Australia as the base for the counter-offensive. They also now, belatedly, gave thought to the fundamental strategic problem: the capture and occupation of South-East Asia provided Japan with the resources with which to fight but it did not threaten the capacity of Britain and America to fight or enlarge their fighting power. Time was on the side of the Allies and what Japan needed was a means to bring the war to an end. The Naval Staff now reinforced their preference for action against Australia with the argument that to force Australia to surrender would be a very direct contribution to the accepted strategy of defeating Britain first. They therefore proposed that, in addition to points in northern Australia, points in north-east Australia should also be captured. This together with operations against Australia's lines of communication with America and the destruction of the enemy's naval forces in the Australian region would cause Australia to sue for a separate peace.[10] The loss of Australia could, they argued, bring about the surrender of Great Britain.

By about December 20th (1941) Tomioka had conveyed these views to his opposite number in the Army's Directorate of Military Operations at General Staff Headquarters and learnt that the Army was opposed to them.[11] Nevertheless the Naval Staff persisted and on January 4th explained to General Staff Headquarters this approach together with others being considered by Combined Fleet such as the capture of Ceylon or the capture of Hawaii.[12] Of these the Naval Staff continued to prefer the Australian operation. They argued that the Phase 2 operations should

7 *Senshi Sōsho*, 1975, p. 299.
8 *Senshi Sōsho*, 1975, p. 296.
9 *Senshi Sōsho*, 1975, p. 307.
10 *Senshi Sōsho*, 1975, p. 308.
11 *Senshi Sōsho*, 1975, p. 312.
12 *Senshi Sōsho*, 1975, p. 314.

commence with it and that it was the only plan available that would contribute to bringing the war to a speedy conclusion. They argued that, if the areas of Australia to be occupied were limited to northern Australia and the northern part of the east coast and that if this was co-ordinated with an attack by the Navy on strategic points on the east coast and on the Australian fleet, then only three divisions would be required to capture and hold the areas concerned.[13] This the Army would not accept. According to its calculations, operations in Australia would require at least 10 divisions and 200,000 tons of merchant shipping and were therefore, in the situation then prevailing, completely out of the question. The Army, however, acknowledged that in order to defend vital areas of the newly acquired possessions it was necessary to control northern Australia. In an entry in the War Diary of the Director of Military Operations (DMO) dated December 6th (two days before the commencement of hostilities) Darwin is included among the places where, after the completion of Phase 1, forces should be deployed for the purpose of defence. Another diary entry also shows that on January 23rd a temporary lodgement at Darwin to destroy installations there was under consideration.[14]

On January 26th at the planners' level the Army agreed to the Navy's proposal that Samoa, Fiji, and New Caledonia, key points on the lines of communication between America and Australia, be captured. The Naval Staff, however, continued to press for operations on the Australian mainland. The debate increased in intensity when on February 4th the Prime Minister directed urgent discussions to be undertaken to enable a Liaison Conference promptly to agree on 'Future strategic guidance' for Phase 2 operations.

From the records of various participants it is evident that the Naval Staff, in the discussions with the Army, continued to press its Australian proposal as the preferred option.

The War Diary of the Army division of Imperial Headquarters contains the following entries for conferences between the two Services:

> *February 8th*. Conference at 1000 hrs in the General and Flag Officers Conference Room at which representatives of Army, Navy and Foreign Affairs discuss the proposed list of topics for 'Future Strategic Guidance'.
>
> The Navy, who are aiming at Australia are not happy …
>
> *February 14th*. On the subject whether or not the existing plan for operations was sufficient we expended much effort restraining Navy's simplistic view that it was insufficient — in other words, in restraining their dash to Australia.

---

13 *Senshi Sōsho*, 1975, p. 312.

14 *Senshi Sōsho*, 1975, p. 314.

> *February 22nd.* Difficulty of reconciling our overriding principle of 'resilience of national defence capacity' [i.e. sufficient reserve capacity for flexible response to any likely enemy move in any theatre?] and Navy's proposed advance to Australia, which would extend our deployment and prevent us making any move in Manchuria …
>
> *February 25th.* … No agreement yet reached on whether to include the India and Australia issues in our plans. Each side merely reiterated its existing position.[15]

The reasons for the Army's opposition

An invasion of Australia would have been quite inconsistent with the basic principle of the Army's strategy for future operations. These are set out in a brief for the DMO by his Operations Section dated January 20th (1942).

> 1. We should establish an impregnable position in this war by bringing to a successful conclusion our plan for Southern operations, securing the area in which operations have been conducted and establishing self-sufficiency.
> 2. In order to bring the war to a speedy end our political and military strategy towards enemy countries should be: (a) to pick off the Allies one by one; (b) to defeat Great Britain and destroy America's will to fight; (c) to cause China to make a separate peace; (d) to make our best efforts to avoid war with Russia while at the same time making preparations for such an eventuality.
> 3. By conserving and expanding the defence potential of the nation we should build up the capacity both to endure a long war and break up the enemy's counter-offensive.[16]

The Army's reluctance to extend the offensive in the Pacific and its preference for operations in the Indian Ocean are spelt out in the following brief for the Chief of the General Staff (CGS) or discussions that he had with the Chief of the Naval Staff (CNS) on January 30th.

> Although at the end of the Southern operations it is desirable to apply effort to conducting operations to hasten the war's end, we must nevertheless give particular emphasis to establishing quickly self-sufficiency and to increasing the resilience of the nation's defence potential. We should bear this in mind when considering the occupation of further territory and place limits on this lest we become bogged down in a profitless war of attrition. Furthermore, in Southern operations after the end of Phase 1 it is absolutely essential always to have in mind the situation on the Manchurian border. In so far as our aims

15 *Senshi Sōsho*, 1970, pp. 471–73, 477.

16 *Senshi Sōsho*, 1970, p. 339.

> lay weight on the defeat of Great Britain, operations in the Indian Ocean are important. Britain and America are building up their strength. It is greatly to be hoped that our Navy will concentrate its strength in that area.[17]

In addition to these questions of principle, the Army advanced specific objections against conducting operations in Australia.

In a communication to the CNS dated February 12th the CGS contested the Navy's claim that it was possible to conduct limited operations in Australia without fear of their escalating into full-scale operations throughout the continent:

> Australia can be regarded as a very large base from which Britain and America can mount their counter-offensive against us and it is essential that we preempt this. But, if we were to conduct operations in part of Australia without a plan to deal with Australia as a whole, this could involve us in a war of attrition on that front which could progressively escalate in a piecemeal fashion into a profitless full-scale war. Accordingly we must eschew operations for the capture of part of the country that do not form part of a plan to deal with the whole continent.
>
> To preempt the counter-offensive it is essential that we prevent troops and materiel being brought into Australia. It is considered that the best way of doing this would be to occupy places in the Pacific such as Fiji, Samoa and New Caledonia.[18]

The most detailed statement of the Army's objections is given in the notes taken by Cdr Sanagi of the views expressed by the Army's spokesman at a conference between the Army and the Navy's Operations sections on February 27th:

> The capture of Australia is not an absolute requirement for the prosecution of the war. It would be useful; but it would not be a death blow to America and England. Nor would it contribute much to our self-sufficiency.
>
> To capture it would require at least 10 divisions and it would be impossible for us to find these. We put Australia's military strength at 300,000 Caucasian troops at present and at 600,000 on full mobilisation. In our operations to date the strength of our forces relative to that of the enemy has been: in Malaya 130,000:70,000, in the Philippines 75,000:100,000, in the Netherlands East Indies 50,000:70,000. We have not sufficient troops to put against 600,000 in Australia. If we put sufficient troops into Australia, we should be in danger in the North [i.e. on the Manchurian frontier]. The operation would require 2 million tons of merchant shipping — perhaps more because of the long distances involved.

17 *Senshi Sōsho*, 1970, p. 344.

18 *Senshi Sōsho*, 1970, p. 470.

> In short, the Army regards the Java operations as the end point of our advance. If we extend further we shall lose our flexibility of response. Beyond there, we are able to do no more than inflict temporary damage.
>
> We have reached the limit in our mobilisation of resources and manpower. One must wage war on a scale that accords with one's national resources. One must remember Frederick the Great's principles of war. The one thing that is vital is that we are ready in the North. We have no intention of attacking there. But if war broke out in the North when Japan had entered the final stage of the present conflict, we should have no prospect of victory. There is the danger that in such circumstances America and Britain would put pressure on the Soviets and act in the North.[19]

This minimum force considered necessary — 10 divisions — was only one division less than the entire force used in the southern operations (i.e. from the Philippines westwards to and including Burma). Similarly, the shipping considered necessary, 2 million tons, was almost as much as the whole quota available for the Southern operations. Of Japan's 6 million tons of shipping the Liaison Conference had in November allocated to the Army for the southern operations 2.1 million tons for four months, 1.7 million for the fifth month, 1.65 million for the sixth, 1.5 million for the seventh, and from mid-July only 1 million. This allocation could be increased only by cutting into the 1.8 million allotted to the Navy and the 3 million required to sustain industrial production. Lack of shipping had already demonstrated its restricting effect on operations. The Army component for the Java invasion force had to be scaled down because, in the event, of the 870,000 tons of shipping allocated, only 670,000 was available. (The deficiency was the result, not of shipping losses, but of the acceleration of the Java and Burma operations resulting from the unexpected ease of Japan's victories. Certain transport tasks that were to have been undertaken in sequence had, in fact, to be performed simultaneously).[20] Similarly, the reference to Russia was not added merely to strengthen the argument. To the General Staff the security of the northern frontier was at all times the primary concern. This is illustrated by the size of the Japanese Army in Manchuria, which was increased from five divisions in 1937 to eight in 1938, nine in 1939, 12 in 1940, and 13 in 1941.[21] When the Head of the Operations Section in the Operations Directorate, Col Hattori, had on January 30th briefed the Minister for the Army, Tōjō (concurrently Prime Minister), on current planning, Tōjō had commented that on the completion of Phase 1 five divisions should suffice for southern operations and had stressed that immediate thought must be given to the state of readiness in the north.[22] There were many who took with a grain of salt the General Staff's

19 *Senshi Sōsho*, 1970, p. 475.
20 *Senshi Sōsho*, 1970, pp. 345–47.
21 Hattori, 1953, vol. 1, Table 6, p. 314.
22 *Senshi Sōsho*, 1970, p. 342.

protestations that its aim was to avoid hostilities there and believed that its real purpose was to have a large uncommitted force in readiness to invade Siberia as soon as the German spring offensive in the Caucasus achieved success.[23]

When the debate between the proponents of continuing the offensive in the southern region and those who insisted on going on the defensive ended in deadlock among the planners, it was referred for resolution to a higher level — to an inter-service conference at which the Army was represented by the DMO at General Staff Headquarters (Maj.-Gen. Tanaka) and the Head of the Military Affairs Bureau at the Army Ministry (Lt-Gen. Mutō), and the Navy by the Director of the Operations Division at Naval Staff Headquarters (V./Adm. Fukudome) and the Head of the Naval Affairs Bureau at the Navy Ministry (V./Adm. Oka). This assembled on March 4th at the Navy Minister's official residence to agree on a report on the principles of future strategy for submission to the Liaison Conference. This meeting commenced with each side reiterating its established position. The Navy argued that now was the time to inflict a decisive blow against American naval forces, to destroy the bases for her counter-offensive and to act against any signs of a counter-offensive whenever and wherever appearing. The Army argued that to consider that they had reached the pursuit phase of war was complacently to underestimate America's armed strength and that to embark on strategic pursuit and seek a decisive battle with the enemy's main force would be an act of recklessness. [The Army continued], 'The scale of operations should not exceed the limits of our military and national resources. To place the enemy on the defensive and to nip his counter-offensives in the bud we must, of course, maintain our offensive stance; but we must eschew long distance attacks such as Australia or Hawaii.' The correct policy for Phase 2 operations, the Army contended, was to stand on the strategic defensive on the Pacific front and by means of necessary tactical offensives dominate the western Pacific and make Greater East Asia impregnable.

At this meeting the Navy by and large accepted the Army's arguments. A strategic policy along these lines was accordingly tendered to the Liaison Conference on March 7th and adopted by it. The Navy had abandoned its proposal for operations on the Australian continent.[24]

On March 19th the CGS tendered a report to the throne on future operations. The relevant passages read as follows:

> *Fiji, Samoa and New Caledonia.* These are important points on the lines of communication between Australia and America and important bases for the enemy's counter-offensive from the south-east. Accordingly, their capture will be extremely valuable both strategically and politically in making the Southern

23 S Takagi, *Taiheiyō Kaisenshi* (Tokyo: Iwanami, 1959), p. 48.
24 Takagi, 1959, pp. 512–13.

> Region impregnable and in progressively isolating Australia. As an extension of our existing plan of Southern operations we shall be able to take them at some suitable time after June with a force of about nine battalions under the direct command of Imperial Headquarters. This is the subject of joint study between us and the Navy.
>
> *Australia.* This is the largest base from which to mount a counter-offensive that remains in Allied hands. Its capture therefore would render our new order in Greater East Asia unshakeable and would be an effective step towards bringing Britain and America to submission. The problem, however, is whether this is possible. Its capture would require a large force and, from the Army's standpoint, to throw in such large forces could prejudice the resilience of our national defence capacity and would, in the present circumstances where the threat in the North continues unabated, be extremely dangerous. Furthermore, to throw in forces of such magnitude in the Southern area could lead to the weak points in our overall national defence being revealed. It could bring down a Soviet attack upon us. It follows that we should deal with the Australian question when necessity demands it and after our anxiety regarding the Soviets has been resolved, after the Chungking regime has surrendered, and after the situation regarding such matters has markedly improved. For the present we consider the limit of our activities against Australia to be the operations in the Fiji region referred to in the preceding paragraph and intensifying the pressure on Australia by the Navy's destruction of commerce and coastal raids and destruction. In addition we are examining whether it may be necessary, depending on circumstances, to make temporary lodgments at strategic points in northern Australia — particularly Darwin and suchlike places.[25]

These discussions and decisions were naturally handled by the Japanese with the utmost secrecy and, it would appear, did not become known to Allied intelligence organisations.[26]

---

25 Takagi, 1959, pp. 528–29.

26 The Japanese refused to to impart such information even at the highest level to their Axis partner. Allied signals intelligence intercepted and decrypted the following report of what transpired at a meeting between the German Ambassador and the Japanese Foreign Minister on April 13th:

> Otto said that he would like to ask whether Japan's future attacks were to be centered in India or Australia, and also that the recent Japanese attacks on Ceylon would indicate to him that Japan was doing this in order to interfere with British–Indian relations. Judging these operations he said he was thinking that probably the former.

In reply to this the Minister said that, although Japan had opened attacks on Ceylon and ports north of that, gradually they would extend operations to western Indian seas, and he presumed this would no doubt coincide with Germany's wishes (Assistant Chief of Staff G2, Washington, Magic Summary SRS 575, 18 April 1942, *The Magic Documents* (Washington: University Publications, 1980), reel 1, cited in DM Horner, 'Australia under threat of invasion', M McKernan & M Browne (eds) *Australia: Two centuries of war and peace* (Canberra: Australian War Memorial, 1988) p. 265)). The Ambassador's questions suggest that his Service attachés were on the ball and were receiving from their Japanese contacts in the Operations sections strong hints about what was under discussion. Whether Allied signals intelligence organisations were reading the telegrams from the German service attachés at Tokyo is not known.

In the event, anxiety regarding the northern frontier increased, the Chungking regime did not surrender, and the rapid development of the Allied counter-offensive precluded any subsequent consideration of operations on the Australian continent.[27] With her heavy losses at Midway in June, Japan lost overall sea supremacy. As a result, the forthcoming operation to capture Fiji, Samoa and New Caledonia was cancelled on July 11th. And in the weeks that followed the Allied counter-offensive commenced. On August 7th the Americans landed at Guadalcanal and Tulagi and in late September the Japanese attack on Port Moresby was repulsed at Ioribaiwa and the Australian advance to Buna begun.

The only Japanese landing in Australia was made by a small party from 19th Army's clandestine Special Operations unit in Koepang which came ashore in Admiralty Gulf in Western Australia on 17 January 1944 and spent two days reconnoitring the locality. Its purpose was to find out whether a naval base was being established there and to test the feasibility of a plan to establish a chain of about 10 permanent observation posts of about four men each to monitor enemy activity in the Australian north-west including aircraft movements out of Darwin and Drysdale airstrip.[28] Although the landing was not detected on the ground, the fact that it had taken place became known to Allied intelligence — probably through signals intelligence.[29] The plan to establish the observation posts was not proceeded with.

15 April 1997

27 Recollections by two Australian officers that at HQ 21 Bde and HQ 7 Div during the advance to Gona in December 1942 they saw among documents found on the bodies of Japanese officers 'operational orders for the occupation of Australia' (*West Australian*, 5 August 1986) are incorrect. These particular documents, which are listed and described in detail in the War Diaries of 39 Bn, 21 Bde, in *ATIS Spot Report* 34 and in *ATIS Bulletins* 45 to 51, dealt with the transport and landing of elements of 170 Regt at Basabua the previous week.

28 Nakano Kōyūkai (ed.), *Rikugun Nakano Gakkō* (Tokyo: Nakano Kōyūkai, 1978), pp. 593–98. M Yamamoto, 'Warera Gōshū Hondo ni Jōriku Suru', *Rekishi to Jimbutsu*, no. 170, 1 August 1985, pp. 112–21.

29 US Military Intelligence Service, 'The Japanese intelligence system' (typescript, 135 pp, 1945), US National Archives, Records Group 457, Special Research History no. 254, p. 41. This report has been published under its original title by Aegean Park Press in 1986 (ISBN 0894121332) and in microfilm in *Top Secret Studies on US Communications Intelligence during World War II* (University Microfilms, 1989, ISBN 1556551835), part 1, reel 41.

3

THE COWRA BREAKOUT

DCS Sissons

Editors' note

This paper is the original English text of an article that Sissons contributed to the September 1984 issue of the Japanese history magazine *Rekishi to Jinbutsu*, marking the 40th anniversary of the Cowra breakout. He presented this paper as a public lecture on 5 August 2002 to a sizeable audience at the Australian War Memorial (AWM).

Having been recruited to the Australian Army, Sissons was based at the training camp in Cowra when the breakout occurred. He was sent with a search party to capture escaped Japanese prisoners. The paper does not elaborate on his personal involvement, other than remarking on a lack of heating in the training camp, while the prisoners' huts were heated. For Sissons, however, the breakout remained a significant research topic.

Publications such as Harry Gordon's *Die Like the Carp* (1978) and Fujio Nakano's *Kaura no totsugeki rappa* (1984), as well as some survivors' accounts, reveal various details of the tragic incident. Sissons' approach to the breakout is more methodical and thorough, however, and explores the breakout from Australian and Japanese perspectives, including how it started, progressed and ended. Sissons also reviews incidents involving military personnel and local civilians that took place during the apprehension of escaped Japanese prisoners. These remain sensitive issues, but Sissons recognised the importance of addressing them in an historical context.

The official inquiry into the breakout took place soon after the incident and reported the number of Japanese deaths as 231, a figure often cited in other accounts. Sissons re-examined the records and concluded that the number should be 234, including three later deaths due to injuries received during the incident. The AWM and the Cowra Japanese War Cemetery Database (www.cowrajapanesecemetery.org) accept Sissons' conclusion and have amended their records accordingly.

The Korean's warning

On 3 June 1944 a Korean prisoner at Cowra Prisoner of War (POW) Camp told an Australian interpreter that when he arrived at Cowra three weeks earlier he had overheard Japanese members of the draft being told that plans were afoot for a breakout.[1]

At Area Command Sydney this information was regarded very seriously, and the Commanding Officer (CO) of the Cowra POW Camp garrison battalion (Lt Col MA Brown) was immediately summoned to a conference with the General Officer Commanding (Maj. Gen. EC Plant) and his staff. There, Brown argued that, if the 779 Japanese other ranks confined in his Compound B attempted a mass breakout, it was inevitable that many of them would be killed and that some would escape. He therefore urged that: (i) his battalion (which was armed only with rifles and light machine guns) be issued in addition with two medium machine guns, eight submachine guns and 100 grenades; (ii) the numbers in Compound B be reduced to 300–400 by sending the surplus to another camp.[2]

As both escapes and heavy casualties among POWs were unacceptable, Plant issued the additional weapons and sought the approval of Land Headquarters (in Melbourne) for Brown's second proposal.

The weapons arrived in Cowra on June 9th. On June 19th, Land Headquarters (LHQ) issued instructions that the number of Japanese at Cowra was to be reduced by separating the non-commissioned officers (NCOs) from the rank and file and moving the latter to Hay.[3]

1 Proceeding of [HQ NSW L of C Area] Court of Enquiry on the Mutiny at No. 12 POW Group, Cowra (National Archives of Australia (NAA) 1977/461 hereafter referred to as Christison Inquiry), Exhibit F.

2 12 POW Camp to HQ NSW L of C Area, 4583/SJ2/44, 10 September 1944 (Registry, HQ 2 Military District, S56/2/1302).

3 Adjutant-General LHQ to HQ NSW L of C Area, SM6481, 19 June 1944 (NAA MP742 255/9/435).

On August 4th notice of the move was given to the Japanese POWs in accordance with Article 26 of the 1929 Prisoners of War Convention. At 1.40 am the following day a breakout took place. The casualties were: Japanese — dead 234, wounded 105; Australians — dead four (of whom two were the crew of one of the newly arrived medium machine guns), wounded four.[4] The move to Hay had become the occasion for what it was designed to prevent. Let us examine some of the considerations that influenced Brown to make his proposal and his superiors to adopt it.

'Death is preferable to the shame of capture'

It is most unusual for POWs located thousands of miles from the war zone to attempt escape by making a frontal attack en masse on barbed wire entanglements covered by machine guns. Why then was the Korean's warning regarded so seriously?

The Australian authorities were well aware that there was no question of the Japanese being driven to desperate action by inadequate food or accommodation, by overwork, or by brutality. The Japanese POWs were provided with the same rations as their Australian guards (3,753 calories per day)[5] and consumed additional fresh vegetables that they had been encouraged to cultivate for themselves.[6] Former prisoners still remember both the quantity and quality of these rations. Takahara Marekuni in his reminiscences 'Senshisha no Kiseki' (recently published in serial form in *Eimuzu*) writes: '*Busshitsumen de wa … jūbun sugiru to itte mo kagon de wa nai*' [It was no exaggeration to say that material supply was more than enough].[7] Their standard of accommodation was similar to that of Australian troops except that their huts were heated while those of the neighbouring training brigade were not. They did no work beyond the servicing and maintenance of their own compound. The reports of the delegate of the International Committee of the Red Cross, Dr GW Morel (a neutral Swiss citizen) appear to dispose of any suspicion of brutality. After his visit to Cowra of 22–24 March 1944 he wrote:

> Nous avons pu visiter tous les Camps sans aucune escorte, et nous entretenir avec les prisonniers de guerre sans témoins …
>
> Le traitement général est excellent les rapports entre les prisonniers de guerre et la garnison sont cordiaux.

4 Christison Inquiry, pp. 13 and 14, exhibits W and AA as amended to incorporate the subsequent death of three of the wounded reported in the findings of the NSW Coroner's inquest 31 October – 15 December 1944 (NAA 1977/460).

5 NAA, War Cabinet Agendum 525/1945.

6 At the time of the break-out, the number of vegetable plants under cultivation in the Japanese other ranks' compound were as follows: Chinese cabbages 20,000, radishes 2,000, lettuces 500, cabbages 400, spinach 500, white turnips 300, cauliflower 150, onions 200 (NAA MP742 255/15/435).

7 M Takahara, 'Senshisha no Kiseki', *Eimuzu*, part 60, p. 34 (translation by Keiko Tamura).

> Les hommes de confiance ont tout specialement souligné l'attitude bienveillante et courtoise adoptée par les divers Commandants des Camps.
>
> [We were able to visit all of the camps without escort and interact with the prisoners in the absence of witnesses.
>
> The general level of treatment is excellent and relations between the POWs and the garrison are cordial.
>
> People we trust have emphasised especially the benevolent and courteous attitude adopted by the various Camp commanders.][8]

We must therefore seek elsewhere for an explanation of the breakout.

Military Intelligence was well aware that capture was regarded throughout the Japanese forces as shameful under any circumstances. This had been a recurring theme in the interrogation of prisoners in the field. Take, for example, that of Matsuoka Ryoju captured near Giruwa on 2 February 1943:

> The PW expected to be killed on capture and would have preferred that to the disgrace of being a PW. Although, as a human being, he would naturally like to see his people again, he felt at present that, like all Japanese soldiers under similar circumstances, he would not return. In any case, it had always been the case to execute men on their return and he doubted whether any allowance would be made for the fact that he was young. Although parents would be glad to see their sons again they would, nevertheless, not expect them to remain alive after disgrace or capture.[9]

They were also aware of New Zealand's experience of the dangerous consequences that could attend such feelings of extreme shame inside a POW compound. There at Featherston in January 1943 in a compound of about 300 prisoners an extremist group had urged the officers to demonstrate their leadership by committing suicide and, when the latter failed to do so, had made threats against their safety. As a result it had been necessary to place in a separate compound 32 other ranks who were resolved on suicide. At Featherston the problems involved in maintaining order and discipline among prisoners who preferred to be dead were underlined a month later when the 300 went on strike and offered resistance to an armed detail sent to extract a working party. The casualties in the ensuing mêlée were: Japanese — 48 killed, 61 wounded; New Zealanders — one dead, 17, wounded.[10]

8 NAA A989 44/925/1/140 (translation by Arthur Stockwin).

9 GHQ South-West Pacific Area, Allied Translator and Interpreter Section, Interrogation Reports, no. 161 (Australian War Memorial (AWM) 312.11).

10 Proceedings of a Court of Inquiry on the Mutiny of Japanese POWs at Featherston, 25 February 1943 (NAA MP720/663/401/634).

Information of this nature was promptly disseminated by LHQ to subordinate headquarters and to units dealing with POWs.[11] A good example of the Australian Army's conventional wisdom on such matters is the report tendered by Col JW Mitchell, the Commander of the recruit training brigade (located a mile from the Cowra POW Camp) to his Divisional Commander following a conference with Brown's second-in-command that had taken place on June 8th:

> The position was viewed by Comdr in daylight on Friday the 9 June (day following) and since all Japanese prisoners are kept in this POW Camp in Australia there wasn't the slightest doubt in his mind that these prisoners in a concerted rush, with blankets and paillasses thrown over the barb wire, would escape in some hundreds. Hundreds of course would be killed on the wire, but one has to remember that these Japs are fanatics and to die thus removes the stigma of captivity and according to their beliefs clears the way to their heaven; and to the Comdr's mind, so long as large numbers are grouped together the danger remains, and one could reasonably expect it on wet, drizzly, dark night, when immediately they clear the wire they become obscure and can then organise at a pre-contemplated place and proceed to do their mischief.[12]

Mitchell knew all about the ineffectiveness of wire in the face of an assault by a determined foe. When promoted to his current position he was by far the most experienced Regimental Commander in the Australian Army, having commanded a battalion on the Western Front for one-and-a-half years in the First World War and in the Libyan and Greek campaigns in the Second World War. (In view of his accurate appreciation of the situation, it is one of the ironies of fate that it was the Cowra breakout that cost Mitchell his job. The patrols sent out by his headquarters to recapture the escapees were unarmed. One of these was ambushed and its officer killed.)

'Firm and careful handling'

This knowledge of the ideology of the Japanese POWs and of its possible consequences led not only to the provision of strongly guarded camps, but also to the expenditure of considerable effort to remove unnecessary irritants in the prisoners' environment.

11 For example, the registration booklet of subject S56-2 at 2 Military District Registry shows that LHQ despatched information regarding the Featherson mutiny to HQ NSW L of C Area on 15 March 1943 (SM5295) and 9 April 1943 (SM7312) and that Area Command in each case forwarded this information to the POW camps at Hay, Cowra, Liverpool and Yanco and to the army hospital that treated Japanese POWs.

12 Proceedings of [First 1 Div] Court of Inquiry into the 'Search for and recapture of certain PWs ... [and] the death of Lt H. Doncaster' (Registry, HQ 2 Military District 556/2/1302), Exhibit 1: 'Alleged attempt to escape from P.O.W. camp: Report of action taken by Aust Recruiting Centre [4 July 1944]'.

The latter half of 1943 provides an illustration. On November 9th LHQ cabled to London that recently the 'truculent' behaviour of the Japanese POWs had led it to expect a repetition of the 'New Zealand riot' but that 'by firm and careful handling they have lately become more tractable'.[13]

Evidence has survived of the truculent behaviour. Late in June there had been a strike by the batmen in the Japanese officers' compound during which a Japanese officer struck the Australian Company Commander.[14] In September the leaders of the other ranks compound had tendered a list of demands that included such frivolous items as: (i) that huts be inspected only once a week; (ii) that the issue of cigarettes (suspended as a punishment for untidy kits) be resumed; (iii) that POWs sentenced to detention be released; (iv) that, for recreation, walks outside the compound be arranged. When these demands were not accepted, the whole compound refused to parade. The 'firm' element in the Australian response was the sentencing the batmen to 21 days' detention and the officer to two years' imprisonment and, when the compound refused to parade, a 'show of strength' in which the guards were ostentatiously armed with batons.[15] The 'careful' element is illustrated by a memorandum from the Deputy Adjutant-General II to the Chief of the General Staff in which 'in view of the paramount importance of maintaining discipline and yet of avoiding a repetition of the New Zealand incident' he requested that the incompetent Australian interpreter officer at Cowra be replaced by 'a skilled interpreter who understands both the Japanese and their language'. The officer in question was duly marched out and in his place came a succession of experienced linguists on loan from the Allied Translator and Interpreter Section in Brisbane. Most of these had resided permanently in Japan. Among them was Capt. RC Mann formerly of the Kobe Higher Commercial College. He served five months at Cowra[16] and it was he that conducted the interrogation of the Korean.

Once the decision had been announced that the basis of selection for movement to Hay was to be the prisoner's rank, I feel that the perceived requirement of 'firmness' would have precluded any possibility of negotiating with the Japanese leaders on this issue. On the other hand, if in the course of making the decision the Australians had felt that segregation according to rank was likely to provoke mass suicides but that segregation by some other means (by lot, for example) was not, then they may well have opted for the latter. The object of the move was to reduce the numbers in Compound B. To utilise it in order to separate the men from the NCOs appears to have been no more than an afterthought. It was felt that the men would be more tractable if not under the influence of the NCOs and that in particular they would,

13 LHQ to Aust Army Rep London, ML3792, 9 November 1943 (NAA 1973/362 P26/9 Part 10).

14 Trial of Lt M. Naka by a Military Court-Proceedings (NAA CP 337/1 POW 1).

15 'Notes from camp intelligence reports' (AWM 780/3/2).

16 War Diary 22 Australian Garrison Battalion (AWM 8/7/47).

if on their own, no longer refuse to engage in productive work such as market gardening for the Australian consumer market. (For such work the prisoners would, of course, have received remuneration in accordance with Article 34 of the POW Convention.) This, however, was merely a desirable bonus, not a vital objective.

On the other hand, the safeguarding of the lives and the health of POWs was regarded by cabinet and the Army as a very important objective. There were several reasons for this: (i) the movement to ameliorate the lot of the victims of warfare had from the period preceding the adoption of Hague Conventions at the turn of the century been widely supported by the Australian community no less than by the wider British community of which it formed part; (ii) there were no principles in the prevailing religion, philosophy or way of life of the community by which violation of the principles underlying the Conventions could be justified; (iii) it was obvious that ill-treating POWs while conferring no benefits on the captor provided the enemy with a motive and an excuse to ill-treat the prisoners that fell into his hands. This latter consideration is a factor that operates in most conflicts. Indeed, but for it, it would be very difficult to negotiate Conventions of this nature. But in the Pacific War, it was a consideration of very great weight so far as Australia was concerned. In that conflict Australia sent against Japan an expeditionary force of roughly five divisions. As a result of the disasters at Singapore, Rabaul and Ambon some 22,000 Australian troops — more than an entire division — were, from the outset, prisoners in Japanese hands. In the words of the history of its wartime activities compiled by the Directorate of Prisoners of War and Internees (DPW&I) at Land Headquarters, 'The administration of all policy matters relating to enemy prisoners of war held by us was conditioned by the strong desire to adhere to the Prisoners of War Convention standards and thus minimise the possibility of providing the enemy with pretexts for retaliation against our own men'.[17] LHQ lost no opportunity to keep this aspect in everyone's mind. Take for example the following passage in a directive issued by the Adjutant-General on 18 June 1943: 'The Commander-in-Chief attaches great importance to scrupulous adherence to the provisions of the Convention … since any breach of these provisions is bound to react on the treatment by the enemy of Allied prisoners of war'.[18] By this reasoning it was no less important that the enemy should also believe that Australia was scrupulously applying the Convention. Hence the wish to avoid another Featherston even though, to Australian eyes, the Featherston deaths were in no way the result of any act or omission by the captors.

17 AWM 780/1/6, p.vi.

18 NAA MP742 255/13/170. See also Group Comndt 12 POW Camp to HQ NSW L of C Area, 491/2, 26 July 1944 (NAA MP742 255/9/435).

No one on the Australian side, however, appears to have considered the possibility that the prisoners might regard the separation of the NCOs more seriously than the movement to another camp. To me this is not surprising. The message that I get from reading the account of the breakout written by one of the participants, Moriki Masaru, is that the separation of the NCOs was not a real issue. As Moriki says, 'It was not as if we had been together from the start. We had been thrown together by unlucky chance. We had had many separations and additions in the past'.[19] It seems to me that, with the die-hard element bent on purging their shame by death, and with the remainder having no generally acceptable philosophical or moral arguments with which to resist the die-hards' urgings, the latter group would have been successful in bringing about the breakout on that occasion irrespective of whatever method of segregation had been proposed.

The report on the incident by the Australian authorities to the Japanese Government (through the Protecting Power, Switzerland) studiously avoids the claim by the Japanese leaders that the separation of the NCOs was the cause of the breakout: *mokusatsu* [to take no notice] is a technique as well known to the English-speaking peoples as to the Japanese (although we lack a word for it). In a confidential memorandum to the Department of External Affairs, the Department of the Army explained this omission in the following terms:

> The PW leader commented unfavourably upon the proposed transfer, and it may have been a factor in causing the NCOs to execute immediately their pre-arranged plan of mutiny.
>
> Two reasons for not introducing this aspect are:
>
> a. it is not desired to cause the Japanese at this stage of the war to become unduly conscious of the fact that they have Allied and Australian officers, NCOs and men mixed together in some camps, which state of affair is greatly to the advantage of the other ranks;
> b. in a note addressed by five officers in detention to Camp Leader Kanazawa the latter was enjoined to use the impending transfer as the reason for the mutiny, although from the context of the note and from Kanazawa's own evidence it is apparent that such use of the impending transfer is a pretext.[20]

Where LHQ do appear to have come to an erroneous (but by no means ridiculous) conclusion is their belief that the consequence of continued Japanese defeats at the front would be to make the POWs in Australian camps more tractable. On 15 August 1944 they informed Area Command that 'It is considered that in view of the present state of the war the likelihood of Japanese POWs resorting to extremes is less than it

19 M Moriki, *Kaura no Shutsugeki* (Tokyo: Konnichi no Wadaisha, 1972), p. 181.

20 Secretary Army to Secretary External Affairs, TOPSEC 1906 29 August 1944 (NAA A989 44/925/1/140).

was some time ago, especially if any disobedience of orders is promptly and firmly handled from the start'.[21] (The matter under discussion with Area Command on this occasion was not the movement to Hay but LHQ's proposal that the free issue of cigarettes be discontinued so that POWs would have to end their ban on productive work, so that they could earn money with which to buy them. Nevertheless it illustrates the climate of opinion at LHQ.) Takahara's memoirs indicate that this factor could operate in quite the contrary direction — that in some of the POWs at Cowra the succession of Japanese defeats at Saipan and elsewhere evoked the response: 'We cannot sit idly by and watch Japan go down. Now is the time for us to take resolute action'.[22]

The breakout

Cowra POW Camp was a 12-sided polygon resembling a giant hotcross bun of about 650 metres diameter, divided by the arms of the cross into four individual compounds each about 7 hectares in area. The Japanese other ranks, 1,104 in number, occupied Compound B. Each compound was surrounded by three barbed wire fences about 2 metres high and 10 metres apart. Attached to the inside of the middle fence were three coils of 'concertina' barbed wire with a further coil overhanging at the top. The area between the middle and the outer fence was filled with a tangle of barbed wire to a height of about 1.25 metres.[23] At the extremity of each arm of the cross there was a sentry in a tower about 6 metres in height armed with a light machine gun or rifle. There were also sentries armed with submachine guns posted on beats along the outer fence of the polygon. The camp was guarded by the 22nd Garrison Battalion consisting of troops whose age or medical condition disqualified them from frontline service. The battalion consisted of four rifle companies. B Compound was the responsibility of B Company.

As we have already observed, the battalion received two medium machine guns (Vickers) after the Sydney conference. These were allotted to B Company and sited as shown in Figure 3.1 with each gun clamped on its tripod to fire on fixed lines along the concertina wire inside the middle of the three fences.[24]

21 SM 7500 (NAA MP742 225/9/435).

22 Takahara, part 63, p. 35.

23 Christison Inquiry, p. 4.

24 Christison Inquiry, Exhibit C.

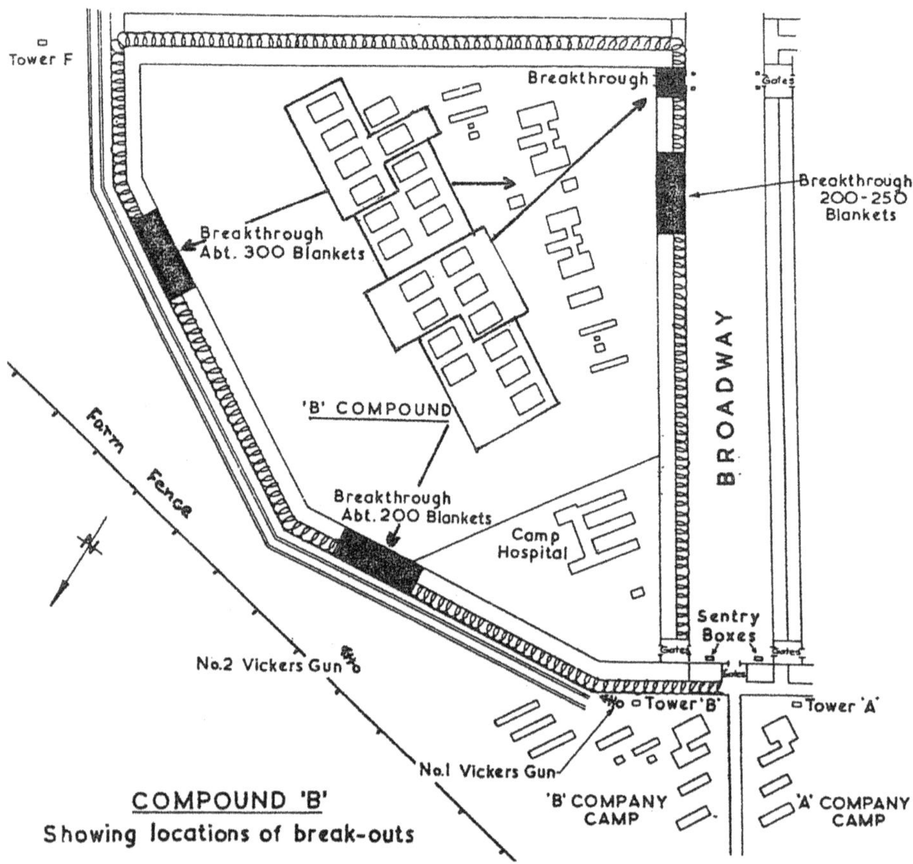

Figure 3.1. Compound B, showing locations of breakouts
Source. DCS Sissons

On the basis of the location of each man's sleeping hut, the Japanese organised themselves into four groups to breach the fences at the four places shown in black on the diagram.[25] The two groups escaping into 'Broadway' (the wide lane separating two eastern from the two western compounds) were contained there. The two breaches of the external perimeter of the polygon were, however, more successful. Those who got through the northernmost of these were able to do so before the crew of No. 1 Vickers Gun took posts. Once they were through, they were able to attack No. 2 Vickers Gun (situated only about 50 metres from the wire) and kill its two gunners before they could fire more than 85 rounds.[26] The removal of No. 2 Vickers Gun left the wire unguarded where the eastern breach occurred. The grave risks involved in leaving this gun unmanned and unprotected by covering fire so close to the wire should have been very obvious to Brown and his officers; for the escape

25 Christison Inquiry, Exhibit X (testimony of Yoshida Hiroshi, Leader of Squad 28).
26 Christison Inquiry, pp. 33–37.

of Second Lt Naka Masao the previous year had shown them the speed with which the wire could be breached. Naka had escaped at 11 pm and was not recaptured until five hours later, by which time he was 7 kilometres from the camp.[27] At the Court of Inquiry convened to report on his escape, Naka gave a demonstration in which he crossed the three fences and the intervening entanglements in 2 minutes 43 seconds 'casually smoking a cigarette throughout the performance'.[28]

The loss of the gun could easily have had even more serious consequences than the death of its crew, both of whom continued to fight the gun until overrun — a feat of supreme devotion for which they were posthumously awarded George Crosses. It seems that the gunner was still firing when he was killed and that it devolved upon his assistant to deactivate the weapon. Untrained in the mechanism of the Vickers Gun, he did this by the practical but unconventional method of removing the ammunition belt and its feed-block, thereby saving the lives of many of his comrades. Had any of his assailants, however, been experienced machine-gunners, they would merely have replaced the feed-block and belt, recocked the weapon, and opened fire.[29]

Col Brown was an experienced machine gun officer and was well aware of the basic fact that 'machine guns have only limited means of protecting themselves'[30] and must have covering fire. The concept underlying his fire plan appears to have been that No. 2 Vickers Gun would be covered by five men and a light machine gun to its right and by No. 1 Vickers Gun. (It may perhaps be for this reason that No. 2 Gun was placed so close to the wire. If it were placed further back along its own line of fire, it might have become masked from No. 1 Gun by one of the huts). Brown, however, was short of troops. At the Sydney conference he had been given the two Vickers guns, but no additional men. He allotted the guns to B Company, whose establishment of other ranks was 107. Each Vickers Gun would need a crew of three men plus five men to provide covering fire for it. To man it for 24 hours a day would thus require an additional 24 men. Thus the two guns would require an increase in the company strength from 107 to 155. And so Brown decided that the gun crews and the men covering them would take posts only when the alarm sounded. And even then he had to rely on A Company for the covering party.[31] In the event, by the time No. 1 Gun and the covering party had taken posts, No. 2 Gun had been overrun.

27 Record Book of Escapes of POWs and Internees (NAA B3813).

28 'Notes from camp intelligence reports, No. 6' (AWM 780/3/2).

29 Christison Inquiry, pp. 36–37.

30 Great Britain, War Office, *Machine Gun Training* (London, HMSO, 1925), §91.

31 Christison Inquiry, Exhibit A.

It was, presumably, because of this defective fire plan that Brown and B Company's Officer-Commanding were removed from the Active List shortly afterwards. To us with the advantage of hindsight it seems clear that Brown should have had the men sleeping in pits besides the guns instead of in their huts. He may have been disinclined to contemplate this because the men were elderly. It would, however, have been more prudent for him to have done this and then, when his medical officers complained, to have referred the matter for resolution to Area Command.

In my opinion Gen. Plant and his staff must bear some of the responsibility for the debacle. First, in providing Brown with the guns but no additional men, they were saddling him with a problem of obvious difficulty. Secondly, having done this, they appear during the eight weeks that followed to have taken no steps (such as inspections or the despatch of liaison officers) to satisfy themselves that he was coping with the problem satisfactorily.

There were, as we have stated, 1,104 Japanese in Compound B at the time of the breakout. Of these the Court of Inquiry found that 588 got through the two breaches into Broadway, 378 got outside the camp through the other two breaches, and 138 remained inside Compound B. Of these 138, 20 committed suicide before or during the breakout.[32]

The 588 who got into Broadway were in two groups. One moved north to attack the northern gates of the camp. Thirty of them were killed by rifle fire from the detail guarding A Company's offices or from the light machine guns in the towers above each gate.[33] The other group moved south. They had two objectives: (i) to force the southern gates of the camp; (ii) to release the 12 inmates of the Japanese officers' compound (D3) located at the south-west end of Broadway. Of this group, about 37 appeared to have died — including nine outside the officers' compound, seven inside it and three at the southern gates.[34] The officers' compound appears to have been effectively covered by the light machine gun in the western of the two towers at the southern entrance to Broadway. Four magazines (about 120 rounds) were fired from it.[35] The southern gates were protected by riflemen, firing into them. Some shots travelled the entire length of Broadway, injuring Australian soldiers manning a light machine gun outside the northern gates. That many of the POWs who escaped into Broadway survived is probably due to the shelter provided by the large storm-water drains there.

Of the 378 who got outside the camp, 334 were brought back by patrols — in other words they were found outside the immediate vicinity of the camp. Many got as far as 15 kilometres from the camp; some were not recaptured until eight days later.

32 Christison Inquiry, p. 120.
33 Christison Inquiry, p. 18.
34 Christison Inquiry, pp. 30, 118.
35 Christison Inquiry, p. 67. Takahara, part 67, p. 35.

Of these 334, 309 were alive and 25 were dead.[36] With, I think, five exceptions (to which I shall refer later), these 25 either committed suicide or died of gunshot wounds that they had received while getting through the wire. It seems that the bodies of the bulk of the remaining 44 (i.e. 378–334) were found in the paddock beyond the wire-netting farm fence.[37] Presumably they died of wounds received from the light machine gun and rifles hastily deployed between the compound and the farm fence, in front of B Company's huts.

Less information has survived about the location of bodies in or close to the barbed wire. We are, however, told that the bodies of 15 POWs were found at No. 2 Vickers Gun[38] and 23 in the concertina wire at the northern most breach. The casualties appear to have been lightest among those escaping through the breach to the north of Tower F. Only about four bodies appear to have been found there.[39] They were probably killed by Vickers Gun No. 2 before it was overrun. The guard in Tower F was armed only with a submachine gun (whose range was too short) and a rifle, and soon ran out of ammunition.[40]

The court of inquiry

In 1942 the United Kingdom and German governments on the initiative of the former entered into an agreement that, whenever a POW was killed or injured, the Detaining Power should immediately hold an official inquiry at which evidence should be taken from eyewitnesses (including fellow POWs) and that a statement of the facts as disclosed by the evidence should be communicated to the enemy through the Protecting Power. The agreement was enlarged to include the British Dominions at their request. There had been a number of instances where British POWs had been shot and it was felt by the British and Dominion governments that such an agreement might have a deterrent effect on German guards. This agreement in 1949 became Article 121 of the international POW Convention; but during the Second World War it was merely a bilateral arrangement between the British and the German governments. Although Japan was not a party to the Agreement, the New Zealand and the Australian authorities nevertheless decided to adopt these procedures at Featherston and Cowra. The following signal, however, despatched by the Adjutant-General to the Commander-in-Chief Australian Military Forces within 36 hours of the news of Cowra reaching Melbourne, demonstrates that LHQ was prepared to accord no more than lipservice to the principles underlying the Anglo-German Agreement:

36 Patrols from the Training brigade brought in 145 alive and uninjured, four wounded and 17 dead (Christison Inquiry, p. 92). Patrols from the POW camp brought in 160 alive and eight dead (Christison Inquiry, Exhibit S).

37 Report by the Director, War Graves Service, undated (NAA MP742 132/1/211A).

38 NAA CP337/1 POW 39, p. 27.

39 Christison Inquiry, Exhibit R.

40 Christison Inquiry, p. 79.

> Similar event occurred with Japanese PW in New Zealand last year. We have copies of governmental and diplomatic communications which clearly show policy successfully adopted by New Zealand in conjunction with United Kingdom. United Kingdom authorities then emphasized that affair should be handled normally by a military Court of Inquiry and if findings so justified charges should subsequently be laid against PW. *Essential function of Court is to produce a report which will be of maximum value diplomatically and show that shooting was fully justified and that onus entirely on PW. Local administrative aspects should not be introduced on any account.* [Sissons' emphasis][41]

(This signal in fact misrepresents in an important respect the advice given by the United Kingdom to the New Zealand authorities; the relevant cable read 'if the [court of inquiry's] findings justify, charges would subsequently be laid against Prisoners *or guards* [Sissons' emphasis].)[42]

Gen. Plant was instructed by the Adjutant-General to convene the necessary Court of Inquiry and to appoint a Col. FH Christison as its president.[43] Christison was a name unknown to the general public until 1981 when Alan Fitzgerald's *The Italian Farming Soldiers* appeared. One of the chapters of this book is devoted to the Rowville incident in which an Italian POW was shot dead by an Australian officer in March 1946 in very suspicious circumstances. Fitzgerald reveals that, in order to cover up this incident, the Army appointed a Court of Inquiry presided over by the same Col. Christison. This inquiry duly exonerated the officers involved. Times had, however, changed since 1944. By 1946 all Australian POWs in Italy had been repatriated. Furthermore, the Minister for the Army had already heard some very disquieting things about how Rowville was being run from a fellow minister who had a number of Italians in his constituency. On this occasion the Minister for the Army minuted the Court of Inquiry's report as 'the most unsatisfactory … that I can ever recollect having read' and ordered a fresh investigation by a civil judge. On the advice of the latter, several officers at the camp were court-martialled.[44] It seems reasonable to infer that by 1944 Christison was regarded by higher authority as an officer whom they could rely on not to unearth unpalatable or inconvenient truths.

On the afternoon of 5 August 1944, before he departed for Cowra, Christison was called to LHQ where he received a briefing by the Deputy Adjutant-General II and the Director of POWs & Internees. Then, on August 8th, LHQ decided to despatch to Cowra an officer from the DPW&I 'for purpose of supplementing instructions given to Col. Christison as to handling of Court of Inquiry on [lines?] similar [to?][45]

---

41 Landforces to Milbase Sydney A69531 of 6 August 1944 (NAA 1973/254 675/Rl/2).

42 Dominions' Secretary to New Zealand 46, 27 February 1943 (NAA A1608 AK 20/1/1).

43 Landforces to Milbase Sydney A69494 of 5 August 1955 (NAA 1973/254 675/R1/2).

44 A Fitzgerald, *The Italian Farming Soldiers* (Melbourne University Press, 1981), pp. 153–65.

45 As in the original text.

incident in NZ in 1943'. This officer duly arrived in Sydney on August 9th with a TOP SECRET letter for personal delivery to Gen. Plant, who was requested to arrange for his immediate movement to Cowra.[46]

The court heard witnesses at Cowra from August 8th to 15th, on which date it adjourned to Sydney to consider its findings, which it issued on September 4th.

Its principal finding was that:

> The firing was stopped at the earliest possible moment having regard to the circumstances existing. It is considered that the firing was controlled and not excessive and that the casualties among the Japanese prisoners of war were not unnecessarily heavy.[47]

It reached this conclusion after questioning a number of witnesses about the number of rounds they had fired and the time at which they had ceased fire. It also examined an analysis of the ammunition expended by the garrison battalion (Total: 11,922 rounds). But, in the years that have followed, some of the Australians who participated have come forward with credible information that there was some indiscriminate firing.[48] Nevertheless Takahara and Moriki's recollections of the hours they lay in Broadway that night lead me to the conclusion that, as an overall description, this finding is not unreasonable.[49] The fact that instead of firing on the group of 73 POWs who, having escaped through the outer perimeter, concentrated on the high ground above the Battalion Headquarters, the party sent after them were content to contain them until daylight suggests to me a high standard of discipline and humanity.

Less satisfactory is the court's finding that 'there is no evidence of ... the illegitimate use of force during the recapture of escapees by the Australian Military Forces patrols'. The *raison d'être* underlying the Anglo-German agreement was that (i) the knowledge that there must be an inquiry deterred the enemy (and one's own) forces from unlawful violence against prisoners; (ii) should this deterrent fail, the agreement enabled the Detaining Power to forestall enemy reprisals by demonstrating to the enemy by the trial of those responsible that such ill-treatment was contrary to its policy and would not be tolerated. The testimony of witnesses before the inquiry brought to light two cases of isolated shootings in circumstances which called for

46 War Diary, DPW&I, LHQ (AWM 1/1/14).

47 Christison Inquiry, Exhibit E.

48 E.g., KS Mackenzie, *Dead Men Rising* (Sydney: Angus & Robertson, 1975), pp. 265–67; H Gordon, *Die Like the Carp* (Sydney: Cassell, 1978), p. 120. Although *Dead Men Rising* is a work of fiction, its author was a member of the garrison battalion and present at the breakout. On certain matters (e.g., topography, camp-layout, and some descriptions of particular officers) the author sticks closely to the facts. There would appear to be no reason to believe that he is misrepresenting the general attitudes and behaviour of the troops.

49 Takahara, part 67; Moriki, pp. 192–94.

investigation — classical examples of the kind of incident that the Anglo-German agreement required to be investigated. The Christison Inquiry, however, in each case showed a complete lack of curiosity, and called no further witnesses.

A sergeant told the court that, in the course of collecting dead and wounded in the area south-east of the camp, he had come upon a corpse with 'his brains half out of his head'. From the evidence it seems that this was at least 300 metres (and possibly a good deal further) from the camp.[50] This seems too far from the camp for aimed rifle fire during the hours of darkness. The most likely explanation would be that this Japanese was either killed lawfully by a burst of machine gun fire from one of the towers during the night or that he was shot at close range by someone combing the area on foot in daylight. The court appears to have made no effort to narrow the possibilities by re-examining the sentries on the towers or searching the immediate vicinity for spent rounds.

Late in the afternoon of August 5th unarmed patrols from the Training Brigade were deployed in an area about 10 kilometres north of the camp, where large numbers of Japanese had been reported. They recaptured about 70. One of these patrols was ambushed on a timbered hill shortly after dusk and its leader (a subaltern) clubbed to death. His corpse was brought back about midnight, whereupon a company from the brigade was armed and sent to the hill to search for any Japanese still there. They encountered the corpses of eight Japanese who had hanged themselves. Shortly after dawn (when the company was about to leave the area) the discovery of a badly injured Japanese was reported to the second-in-command. The latter testified to the court that:

> I went down and had a look at him, and he was badly wounded. He appeared to have a wound somewhere down in the groin, and there was one in his back. He had been hit on the head, and I do not know whether he may have been shot. I could not see. He was in a pretty bad way. He was quite conscious and moving about a bit. I left him in charge of a sergeant and three men, and continued with the patrol … later on I was informed that the Japanese had died.[51]

The court pursued the matter no further. Some years later, however, the staff of the Australian War Memorial discovered that there was more that the court could have found out, had it been so minded. When working through the office files of wartime units in search of items of potential historical value, they found a file on the subject among the records of the training battalion that provided the patrol. There we may see the overall report by the Battalion Commander to brigade on the battalion's activities during that day. He refers to the incident as follows: '1 found badly wounded, subsequently died while being carried by patrol.' The Company

50 Christison Inquiry, p. 72 (testimony of L./Sgt Schafer).

51 Christison Inquiry, p. 97 (Lt. WB Atkinson).

Commander's version is: 'One Jap who died resisting arrest was found at 664 308' [the grid reference for the point at which the body of the Australian subaltern was found, Sissons]. More straightforward is the original report of the Section Commander: '1 kill 0600 hrs by rifle' to which in different handwriting has been added the words 'trying to escape'.[52] It was, no doubt, because of the presence of the latter suspicious phrase in so many of the notifications of death from German prison camps that the British Government had initiated negotiations for the 1942 Agreement.

That Japanese was killed at 6 am (Sunday, August 6th). At about 1.30 pm that day a civilian carrying a double-barrelled shotgun encountered six escapees near an outcrop of rocks on a farm named 'Claremont' about 7 kilometres from the POW Camp. He shot two of them dead. In a statement to the police he said that he had observed one of the Japanese at a distance of about 1.5 kilometres, had followed him, and was then surprised by the man and his companions among the rocks at a distance of only 6 metres. He claimed that he shot in self-defence when they moved to surround him and his son and to throw stones at them. Rumours that something of this nature had occurred reached at least one member of the Court of Inquiry the following day.[53]

Although the court's terms of reference did not empower it to compel the attendance of civilian witnesses, they did authorise it to enquire into 'the conduct of any person or persons' in connection with 'all events, matters and facts related to or any way connected with the breakout'. An incident of this nature was obviously germane to their inquiry, and the court was free to invite information about it from civil witnesses (including the police) and to demand it from the soldiers who must have collected the bodies. Had it done so, it would have discovered that, in the course of recapturing the four surviving Japanese, a Warrant Officer in charge of an armed party from the Training Brigade shot dead one more of them.[54]

It may well be that in each of these four incidents the killings were lawful; but until the court had heard evidence and examined witnesses it was in no position to say so.

The Adjutant-General could encourage his subordinates to engage in such tasks in a less than vigorous fashion only at the risk of certain deleterious consequences. As one incumbent of that office had described himself, the Adjutant-General was 'the conscience of the Army': now he was encouraging unconscionable action. It was also the Adjutant-General who was responsible for maintaining discipline throughout the Army: yet he was setting the example that offences should not be uncovered where this might prove inconvenient. Such an example must have

52 AWM 780/10/2.

53 Maj. HS Williams to Director POWs & Internees, LHQ, 8 August 1944 (Department of Defence, Archives and Historical Section, PC 264-11-1100 Item 43).

54 GOC HQ NSW L of C Area to LHQ 14235, 11 December 1955 (NAA AA 1977/460 255/6/425).

a demoralising and corrupting effect. But there was a more tangible danger. The government, the Services and the community were agreed that nothing in the treatment of Japanese POWs must afford the Japanese with a pretext for retaliating against Australian POWs. The implementation of this policy devolved primarily upon the AdjutantGeneral. As the writings of such people as Moriki and Takahara attest, he and his subordinates had carried it out with remarkable success. But they could maintain the system only by searching out its deficiencies. In order to find these and remove them, it was necessary to ascertain whether or not someone had blown out the brains of a wounded Japanese in the gully 300 metres south-east of the POW Camp: yet the court had been discouraged from doing so.

It is easy, at this distance in time, to be critical of the Adjutant-General and his advisers. But they had no legal duty to hold any inquiry at all; for Japan was not a party to the 1942 Agreement. Their object, to minimise the chance of retaliation against Allied POWs that any admission of ill-conduct might provoke, was responsible, laudable and humane. Indeed, it is hard to imagine any officer or official acting differently in the circumstances.

In so far as one of the underlying objectives of the 1942 Agreement was to lessen the possibility of retaliation, it is ironical that, in the name of this objective, liberties were taken with its procedures. I imagine that the same pressures will weigh equally heavily on those called upon to implement Article 121 of the present POW Convention, irrespective of their nationality. The strongest guarantee that Article 121 will be faithfully carried out is probably the independent right of any POW (including, of course, the eyewitness to a shooting) to complain directly to the representative of the Protecting Power. (Had this right not been already embodied in Article 42 of the 1929 Convention, the 1942 Agreement and its successor might have been difficult to negotiate.) So far as I am aware, no attempt was ever made by the Australian authorities to interfere with the operation of Article 42. Three POWs witnessed the 'Claremont' shootings. They appear to have made no complaints to the Protecting Power. They may have regarded the shootings as justified. Alternatively the shame of being a prisoner, that caused them to break out, may have prevented them from approaching the Protecting Power. Perhaps they are still alive today.

Australian attitudes to POWs

I have been asked in this article to refer to the feelings of Australians at that time towards the POWs of various nationalities held in Australia.

Excluding merchant seamen, the total numbers of POWs in Australia in the Second World War were: Italians 18,164, Japanese 5,103, and Germans 1,492.[55] All the Germans and more than a quarter of the Italians had arrived in Australia before

55 History of the Directorate of POWs & Internees, pp. 101, 106 (AWM 780/1/6).

Japan entered the war. The Japanese POWs were late arrivals. On 31 December 1942 there were 10 (of whom eight appear to have been naval airmen and two Korean *gunzoku* [civilian employee of the military]).[56] On 30 November 1943 there were 456.[57] On 1 July 1944 (one month before the breakout) the figure had reached 1,415, of whom 1,055 were Army, 122 were Navy and 238 were labour troops. (The nationalities among the latter category were: Chinese 90, Korean 82, Formosan 61, Japanese 4, Javanese 1).[58]

The Australian authorities did not regard the Italian POWs with much anxiety. In January 1941 an Australian infantry division had captured 40,000 Italian prisoners at Bardia and another 25,000 at Tobruk after battles each of only two days' duration. They regarded these Italian POWs very differently from the way they regarded the Japanese POWs. Takahara' s description of the Italian POWs could very well have been written by one of their Australian guards:

> Although we were both soldiers of the Axis Powers wearing the same burgundy PW clothing, we could not even in our most generous moments regard them as a strong military force. They were cheerful, amiable, easy-going fellows. From morning till night the strains of the mandolin, the guitar and the violin emanated from their Compound. I suppose you could say that they maintained some semblance of a military organisation; but one and all they wanted nothing more to do with the War. They were much better off than at the front. They didn't care who won or lost. They spent their time wishing for a speedy end to the war and to be reunited with their fiancées back home.[59]

In May 1943 the Australian cabinet approved a scheme for assigning Italian POWs to Australian farmers: it was argued that experience had shown that, if the Fascist agitator type were excluded, the Italian POWs were docile and, if firmly but humanely handled, good workers.[60] By this means, at virtually no risk to public safety, food production for the Allied war effort could be significantly increased. Soon the great majority of Italian POWs were living and working on Australian farms, unguarded.[61]

Even if they had been prepared to engage in work of this nature (which they were not), it is inconceivable that the Australians would have considered a similar regime for the Japanese POWs, whom they regarded as implacably hostile and ferocious. Once again Takahara convincingly portrays the atmosphere:

56 Takahara, part 49, p. 35.
57 NAA MP742 255/10/166.
58 Cable, External Affairs (Canberra) to Australia House (London), 9847, 6 October 1944 (NAA 1973/362 26/9 Part 12).
59 Takahara, part 50, pp. 38–39.
60 Fitzgerald, 1981, p. 28.
61 Fitzgerald, 1981, p. 140.

> When we passed by in our trucks, the children on the road-side stared silently at us, as we stared silently at them. Their faces were blank and hostile. But when Italians passed, the children would clap and wave and smile. The Italians in response would call out and throw them sweets. The children had been taught that short men with shaven heads were not human. Their parents, their teachers — everyone — told them spinechilling stories how 'The Japanese are beasts who if they encounter women torture them to death and if they encounter men cut off their heads'.[62]

Australian attitudes to the Japanese sprang partly from long-standing anxiety that Australia was militarily vulnerable.

In 1911 Miho, a vice-consul at the Japanese consulate in Sydney, wrote in a despatch to his government that the Russo–Japanese war had had a profound effect on Australian thinking. He argued that originally the White Australia policy had meant merely the protection of Australian workers against the competition of coloured immigrants and had been expressed in such terms. But, with the approach of Federation, those whose interests were involved had to secure the support of voters to whom coloured labour was not a threat. They therefore came to base their appeal on race prejudice pure and simple; but not, as yet, on fear of invasion. He continued:

> But with the Russo-Japanese War, fear of Japan entered into it. Today, hostility to Japan and fear of Japan is the backbone of the whole White Australia Policy. Before the war, although Japanese were kept out, this was done merely as part of the exclusion of Asians generally. Indeed, they tended to treat us with some of the indulgence that one extends to precocious children. But as soon as we were victorious they came to fear that we would invade Australia. They doubt our every deed. If they see our tourists taking photographs in the streets, they immediately think that they are spies. They fear Japan in the way that you fear a bogeyman in the dark because you cannot see natural phenomena around you.[63]

These feelings increased as the century progressed and Britain's relative naval power declined. They accelerated as Japan moved southward. They intensified with the successive news of atrocities following the Japanese advance in China,[64] Hong Kong,[65] New Britain,[66] and Papua;[67] of the execution of captured Australian airmen;[68] and of the starvation and ill-treatment of Australian POWs on the Burma–Siam Railway.[69]

62 Takahara, part 59, p. 38.

63 Japanese Ministry of Foreign Affairs, *Nihon Gaikō Bunsho*, vol. 68, pp. 548–50.

64 *Argus* (Melbourne), 15 January, 3 and 22 February 1938.

65 Great Britain, *Parliamentary Debates, Commons*, vol. 378, cols 930–31 (10 March 1942). *Argus*,11 March 1942.

66 *Sydney Morning Herald*, 10 April 1942.

67 *Sydney Morning Herald*, 16 November 1943.

68 *Sydney Morning Herald*, 6 October 1943.

69 Great Britain, *Parliamentary Debates, Commons*, vol. 396, cols 1029–30 (28 January 1944). *Argus*, 31 January 1944. In the cables received via the International Committee of the Red Cross notifying the deaths of individual Australian POWs on the railway, cholera, beri-beri and dysentery were appearing as causes of death by September 1943; *eiyo shutchosho* (i.e. malnutrition), by July 1944 (NAA 1973/362 P26/9 Parts 9–12).

There is no doubt that deep hostility to the Japanese was widespread. HBS Gullett, who commanded a company in New Guinea, writes:

> Because of the things [the Japanese] did to our dead and wounded we hated them. We never gave them a chance if we could help it. If an Italian or German were running away, one might let him go, but never a Japanese. You would kill him as you would a snake, because the next day you or a friend might not see him first.[70]

Feelings of deep hostility to the Japanese were, no doubt, present in the troops posted to Cowra. In his successful defence of the camp leader (Sgt Maj. Kanazawa) on a charge of murder, the Defending Officer in his cross-examination of the guard who discovered the bodies of the two machine-gunners had no difficulty in bringing this to the surface.

> Q. You don't like them [the Japanese] at all, do you?
> A. No.
> Q. Would you like to see them all shot?
> A. It wouldn't worry me. A dead Jap is the best Jap.[71]

To me the important thing is that as a result of a mixture of policy, discipline, humanity and tradition, it was to a large degree kept under control.

It must not be thought that hostility was unlimited in its extent. Figure 3.2 is one of a number of advertisements published in the newspapers by the Department of Information in April 1942 as part of a campaign called 'The Japanese as he is', which sought to strengthen the war effort by fomenting anti-Japanese feeling.[72] This experiment received so much criticism from the community that it was brought to a premature close and never repeated.[73] Typical of many was the protest by the League of Nations Union:

> We shall have to live in a world which contains Japanese and Germans and Italians and, while we will fight to the death to defeat Nazism and Fascism, we would still wish to fight with such chivalry as is possible in modern war and to refrain from methods (whether in fighting or propaganda) which only the Nazis could approve.[74]

70 HBS Gullett, *Not as a Duty Only: An infantryman's war* (Melbourne University Press, 1976), p. 127.
71 NAA CP 337/1 POW 39 (as quoted in Gordon, 1978, p. 211).
72 See the *Argus*, 2–14 April 1942.
73 J Hilvert, *Blue Pencil Warriors: Censorship and propaganda in World War II* (Brisbane: University of Queensland Press, 1984), pp. 115–21.
74 *Argus*, 13 April 1942.

Figure 3.2. 'The Jap as he really is', Department of Information, March–April 1942

Source. *Argus* (Melbourne), 7 April 1942, p. 4

Takahara and Moriki write of the friendship they received from a number of the Australians they encountered. Takahara speaks of the unlimited kindness (*shinsetsu kiwamari nashi*) of the drivers and guards who escorted him along the long trek from Adelaide River to Alice Springs in the bitter and dangerous days immediately following the destruction of Darwin. The guards were always smiling. They talked with them. They gave them cigarettes and chocolates. They shared their newspapers with them.[75] 'Although we were prisoner and guard, there was absolutely no feeling of tension' (*Horyo to bampei to iedomo, kinchōkan nado wa mattaku naku*).[76] Moriki writes in similar strain of his guards at the Brisbane Military Hospital: 'they were amiable men with a very human humour' (*Hitonattsukoi, ningen-mi ga jika ni furete kuru yūmoa*). He describes how these men would exert themselves and clown in order to cheer up the dispirited POW and how one of them was so appalled when Moriki told him that no Japanese could ever return to his family that he offered to take him in on his farm after the war (*Kare no wareware ni taisuru taido wa, ningen-dōshi de atte, teki mikata to iu kanjō wa mattaku nakatta*).[77]

75 Takahara, part 31, pp. 26–27.
76 Takahara, part 34, p. 26.
77 Moriki, pp. 154–55.

Nor must it be thought that hostility was felt towards the Japanese alone, among the three enemy countries. 'A dead Jap is the best Jap' is an adaptation of the phrase 'A dead German is the best German' coined during the First World War and still much in use in Australia throughout the Second World War. Nor was anti-Italian feeling: it was an Italian POW, not a Japanese, that was shot at Rowville.

As I see it, anti-Japanese feeling was not a significant factor at the Cowra breakout. Had it been a riot by German POW the consequences would have been the same.[78]

DCS Sissons
Department of International Relations
Research School of Pacific Studies
Australian National University
1 June 1984

78 At Murchison on 21 September 1942 when German POWs objecting to their blankets being dyed red advanced on their guards the latter opened fire. Nine POWs were injured (NAA A 981 Treaties 738).

4

THE AUSTRALIAN WAR CRIMES TRIALS AND INVESTIGATIONS (1942–51)

DCS Sissons

Editors' note

The National Archives of Australia (NAA) commissioned Sissons to write this seminal work on the Australian war crimes trials as part of its research guide series. A disagreement between Sissons and the NAA regrettably prevented the essay from being published on its completion in 2000. Aware of the importance of his research, Sissons sought another publisher and approached David Cohen, founding director of the Berkeley War Crimes Studies Centre at the University of California. The paper was uploaded to the internet as a PDF file after Sissons' death, however, it lacked a stable hosting framework. Finally, it has found a permanent home in this volume, with Cohen's blessing.

In the NAA research guide, *Japanese war crimes in the Pacific: Australia's investigations and prosecutions* (2019), Narelle Morris points out the difficulty faced by researchers in examining war crimes trials records prior to digitisation. Records were historically scattered across several institutional locations, which made it hard for researchers to examine them thoroughly. Sissons carried out his research in archives throughout Australia including in Canberra, Brisbane and Melbourne, as his location classifications indicate.

The paper covers comprehensive topics relating to Australia's war crimes trials and it continues to inspire researchers entering this field of investigation. As stated by the editors of *Australia's war crimes trials, 1945–51* (2016), Georgina Fitzpatrick, Tim McCormack and Narrelle Morris, in their dedication to the memory of David Sissons, he is the scholar 'upon whose shoulders all who research Australia's war crimes trials stand'.

Contents

The Australian war crimes inquiries

In January 1942 the governments-in-exile of the countries under Nazi occupation issued the Declaration of St James in which they adopted as a principal war aim the punishment of those responsible for ordering, perpetrating or participating in war crimes and resolved to ensure that they be sought out, handed over to justice and judged. The United States and British governments associated themselves with these objectives and, to facilitate their implementation, on 8 August 1942 proposed the setting up of a United Nations War Crimes Commission (UNWCC) whose functions would include the preliminary examination of charges against individual war criminals for extradition for trial by the ally laying the charges. Australia on 8 December 1942 made application to join the UNWCC as an original member.

The Allen Court of Inquiry — The Tol massacre

At 2 am on 23 January 1942 the Japanese task force for the capture of Rabaul, the *Nankai Shitai* (Maj. Gen. Horii), landed at several points in Blanche Bay. Comprising the force were the three battalions of the 144th Infantry Regiment (Col Kusunose) and supporting arms. Resistance by the outnumbered Australian garrison (2/22nd Bn and supporting arms) continued until about 5 pm, by which time the garrison had split up into small parties moving, for the most part, along two escape routes, the one in the direction of Pondo on the west coast, the other in the direction of Awul on the east coast.

As part of the mopping up operations, 3rd Bn, 144 Regt (Lt Col Kuwada) despatched a force by sea from Kokopo to intercept the escapees at Tol Plantation, a choke point where the eastern escape routes converged. It landed there on the morning of February 3rd. A party of 22 congregated around a white flag on the beach awaiting the arrival of the Japanese was spared and taken back to Kokopo. But during the day the remaining Australian troops in the area were rounded up and imprisoned in a large hut. The next day they were bound together in groups of nine or 10, marched off into the undergrowth and killed by the bayonet, one by one. The Japanese force re-embarked for Kokopo the same day.

Six of the victims left for dead managed to survive and were rescued by later groups of Australians moving along the eastern escape route. They were among the 156 escapees by the eastern route who reached Port Moresby aboard the *Laurabada* on April 12th.

This was reported to the Advisory War Council by the Chief of the General Staff (CGS) on April 28th. The Adjutant-General thereupon on May 12th appointed a Court of Inquiry (President: Brig. AR Allen) with the following terms of reference:

> To inquire into and report upon the facts and circumstances associated with the landing of Japanese forces and events subsequent thereto in New Britain, Timor and Ambon, and in particular, the facts and circumstances relating to:
>
> a. the surrender and capture of Australian troops;
> b. the treatment of Australian prisoners of war by Japanese troops;
> c. the death, after capture or surrender, of Australian troops;
> d. any acts of terrorism or brutality practised by the Japanese against Australian troops;
> e. any breaches of International Law or rules of warfare committed by Japanese forces.[1]

After examining under oath the available survivors and independent witnesses who had passed through the area, the court on July 8th reported its finding that,

> There were at least four separate massacres of prisoners on the morning of 4th February, the first of about 100, the second of 6, the third of 24 and the fourth of about 11 … All the men had surrendered or been captured and held in captivity for some time before being slaughtered.[2]

Those responsible for the Tol massacre were never brought to trial. Horii was drowned in the withdrawal down the Kumasi River on 19 November 1942. Kuwada was killed in action near Giruwa on 22 November. Kusunose after his preliminary interrogation by 2 Aust. War Crimes Section in Tokyo on 5 and 6 December 1945 fled to Takigahara and committed suicide there on December 17th.[3]

First Webb Inquiry

Following the Japanese landings in New Britain and New Guinea in 1942, evidence accumulated of the commission of atrocities. On 30 January 1943 the Commander-in-Chief (C-in-C) Australian Military Forces instructed the CGS to issue formal directions to formation headquarters to collect and submit evidence of atrocities with a view to its examination by a competent judicial authority. Such directions were duly issued on February 3rd. On March 31st the Minister for the Army at the instance of the C-in-C wrote to the Prime Minister requesting 'the appointment of a judicial authority who would take the evidence and submit a full report on this matter'. As a result the Australian Attorney-General (Dr HV Evatt — concurrently Minister for External Affairs) on 23 June 1943 commissioned Sir William Webb (Chief Justice of Queensland):

1 Australian War Memorial (AWM)226, item 1: Proceedings of a Court of Inquiry …, vol. 1, Terms of Reference.

2 AWM226, item 1, vol. 1, New Britain Report (24 pp.).

3 NAM MP742/1 336/1/1086 'Tol massacre'.

> To inquire into and report to the Attorney-General on … whether there have been any atrocities or breaches of the rules of warfare on the part of members of the Japanese Armed Forces in or in the neighbourhood of the Territory of New Guinea or the Territory of Papua and, if so, what evidence is available of any such atrocities or breaches.[4]

The inquiry heard testimony from officers and troops from Australian and United States formations that had been in action in the region up to the capture of Komiatum on the approach to Salamaua in late August (1943). To this end Webb visited and conducted hearings at places in rear areas in Papua and North Queensland where the formations were recuperating and retraining. Testimony was also taken from natives and civilians. Also tendered as evidence were captured enemy documents and the interrogation reports of Japanese prisoners of war.

Webb on 15 March 1944 tendered his report (c. 450 pp.) together with the affidavits of the 471 witnesses he had examined.[5] His findings included: (i) the massacres on 3 January 1942 at Tol and Waitavalo plantations in New Britain of at least 123 Australian soldiers and civilians; (ii) the torture and killing of up to 59 male and female natives and 36 Australian soldiers at various points in the Milne Bay area in August/September 1942; (iii) the execution of 11 missionaries (male and female) at Buna, Popondetta and Guadalcanal in August 1942; (iv) a number of cases during the Owen Stanleys campaign where individual Australian and American prisoners had been tied to trees and bayoneted; (v) mutilation of the dead and cannibalism; (vi) the execution of the bomber pilot, Flt Lt WE Newton VC, at Salamaua on 29 March 1943.

Second Webb Inquiry

The function of the UNWCC was: (i) to hear evidence of war crimes brought to it by member governments and, where it considered that a substantial case had been made out, to list the perpetrator for arrest and extradition; (ii) to make recommendations to member governments on how war criminals could be brought to trial. It held its first meeting on 20 October 1943 and in reporting this to his Minister (Dr Evatt) the Secretary of the Department of External Affairs recommended that to this end a new commission should be issued to Webb to conduct a continuous inquiry regarding war crimes against Australians and to bring before the Governments such cases as should be forwarded to the UNWCC. On 9 February 1944 Evatt issued an invitation to Webb in these terms, which Webb accepted on February 24th. The new commission was issued on June 8th.

4 NAC A3688/27, 247/R1/3.

5 Report, NAC A10943; Transcript, NAC A6236; Exhibits, NAC A6237.

In hearings that commenced on 14 August 1944 and concluded on October 20th testimony was taken from 112 witnesses. Forty-one gave evidence on the torpedoing of the hospital ship *Centaur* by a Japanese submarine off Brisbane on 14 May 1943. Twelve Australian POWs rescued by American submarines when the Japanese transport, *Rakuyo Maru*, was sunk off Hainan on 12 September 1944 gave evidence on the murder and ill-treatment of POWs on the Burma–Siam railway and elsewhere in South-East Asia. Of the remaining 59 witnesses, 35 gave additional evidence on crimes committed up to the capture of Komiatum and 14 on later crimes. On 31 October 1944 Webb tendered an interim report (104 pp.) together with the depositions of the witnesses.[6]

On the basis of these two reports Webb prepared specific cases which he presented to the UNWCC at meetings of its Facts and Evidence Committee at London on 24 and 31 January and 7 and 8 February 1945. As a result the UNWCC listed for arrest 73 individuals and all the members of 10 units, and listed for further investigation an additional 18 individuals/units not sufficiently identified.[7]

While in London Webb was invited to confer with the UK law officers on appropriate trial procedures. At his meeting with the law officers on January 22nd Webb stressed the need that in war crimes trials the rules of evidence be broadened to enable the admission of affidavits, depositions, unsworn statements etc and that where members of a particular unit had been shown collectively to have committed a war crime the onus of proof of non-participation should be shifted to the accused — a view that had also emerged in the deliberations of the UNWCC. The law officers agreed and assured him that the Royal Warrant and Regulations for UK war crimes tribunals then being drafted would contain such provisions.[8]

On his return to Australia Webb on February 27th (1945) submitted his resignation. Although Evatt on April 3rd pressed him to continue, the Premier of Queensland on April 30th notified the Prime Minister that because of the pressure of his duties as Chief Justice the Queensland Government was unable to make his services available.

Third Webb Inquiry

On May 23rd the Prime Minister replied to the Queensland Premier proposing that 'an arrangement might be made for Sir William to carry on the investigation of war crimes concurrently with his work in the Supreme Court with the aid of secretarial assistance for his work on war crimes'. This was accepted; but it was not until July 31st that the secretary was appointed.[9] Before Webb was able to resume

6 Report, NAC A10950, item 1; Transcript, vol. 1, AWM226; item 6 & vol. 2, NAC A10951, item 1.

7 NAC A10952, item 1.

8 NAC A1066, H45/580/2.

9 NAC A1066, H45/580/2.

his activities the inquiry was overtaken by events. At the four-power Conference on Military Trials which convened in London on June 26th it was agreed that in addition to conventional war crimes, planning or waging a war of aggression was also a criminal offence in international war and this was embodied in the Charter of the Nuremberg Tribunal issued on August 6th. Next, the cessation of hostilities on August 15th made the collection of evidence a more urgent and extensive task. To meet these changed circumstances a new commission was issued on September 3rd appointing Webb and two other judges, Mr Justice Mansfield of the Queensland Supreme Court and Judge Kirby of the NSW District Court as a board of inquiry. Its terms of reference were essentially the same as in the previous commission except that they were expanded to embrace war crimes against any person who was resident in Australia prior to the commencement of the War, but also 'any British subject or any citizen of an allied nation' and that in addition to the 32 war crimes previously defined there were added: (i) planning, preparation, initiation or waging of a war of aggression or a war in violation of international treaties, agreements or assurances, or participation in a common plan or conspiracy for the accomplishment of any of the forgoing; (xxxiv) cannibalism; (xxxv) mutilation of the dead.[10]

The commissioners issued a war crimes questionnaire to all Australian POWs and internees. More than 12,000 of these were completed and lodged. From these respondents 248 witnesses were selected for examination by one of the commissioners or their staff. To enable this to be done promptly before the POWs were repatriated and dispersed, Mansfield and Kirby were despatched by air to the recovery areas overseas to examine the witnesses there. The repatriation of the POWs, however had proceeded so smoothly that most had embarked before the commissioners arrived. Mansfield examined 50 at Manila, 21 at Morotai (seven Australian POWs and 10 Dutch civil internees from Ambon, four Indian POWs from Borneo), 11 at Labuan (five British internees and six Indian POWs), and seven at Macassar (four Dutch internees and three graves registration personnel). Kirby at Singapore and Kandy collected depositions regarding the murder of the Australian army nurses and the Australian official, VG Bowden on Bangka Island. En route, at Morotai he had examined eight Indian POWs recovered in the Halmaheras.

There was general agreement that there should be no delay in commencing the Australian trials. In Parliament members were demanding it and ministers were providing the required assurances. The necessary legislation, the Australian *War Crimes Act* was introduced into Parliament on October 4th and was passed by both Houses on that day. Initially it was assumed that before a war criminal suspect could be tried he had to be listed by the UNWCC. On October 6th, however, the Chairman of the UNWCC informed the Australian Minister for External Affairs (Dr HV Evatt) that

10 Report & Appendices, NAC A11049, rolls 1 & 2.

this was not necessary.[11] The procedure of listing by the UNWCC had been designed primarily to ensure that, as guaranteed in the three-power Moscow Declaration of 1 November 1943, suspects could be arrested by whichever Ally captured them and extradited to the country in which the crime had been perpetrated. Throughout the proceedings of the UNWCC the established right in international law of a belligerent to try and punish for breaches of the laws and customs of war an enemy who had come into his custody was frequently affirmed and never challenged. The US and British commanders were already exercising this right in the European theatre, and in the Far East Yamashita had been charged before a US Military Commission on September 25th without prior listing by the UNWCC. It was expected that the first Australian cases — against some 70 held in custody at Labuan on suspicion of involvement in the murder and ill-treatment of POWs in Borneo — would be ready for trial at Labuan by November 15th. In discussion with the CGS at Army Headquarters (AHQ), Melbourne, on October 15th, Webb proposed that in the Australian trials the prosecutions should be conducted by his commission — with the assistance of the best Kings counsel if the culprits and offences so warranted. The CGS agreed to this[12] and Webb cabled to Mansfield, who was at Morotai at the C-in-C's Advanced Headquarters, asking him to return to Labuan and remain there until the trials there were completed. But the CGS was promptly overruled. The following day the C-in-C (Gen. Blamey) informed Mansfield that, having perused a copy of the *War Crimes Act* and the terms of reference of the commission, he had reached the conclusion that the Australian trials were purely an Army matter and that the commission had no authority to participate in or attend them.[13] On October 22nd the Adjutant-General informed Webb that in the Australian trials the prosecutions would be conducted by the 'very efficient and experienced legal staff on the Headquarters of Commanders in the territorial areas concerned' and that the assistance of civilian counsel would not be required.[14]

As a result of these developments the task of the commission as regards the so-called 'minor' or 'conventional' war crimes (i.e. crimes against the laws and usages of warfare as distinct from the 'major' crime of planning or waging aggressive war) had undergone a change. Its task was no longer to examine witnesses for the purpose of preferring charges and presenting cases against specific individuals or units either for the UNWCC or for the Australian trials. Its task was now essentially informative — to report to the Minister the general picture — although it would continue promptly to provide the depositions to the Army authorities for use as evidence in such prosecutions as the latter might undertake. For such a report it would, Webb decided, suffice to select only about 200 witnesses for examination.[15]

11 NAC A2937, 222.

12 Webb to Minister for the Army, 15 October 1945, NAC A2937, 222.

13 Mansfield to Webb, signal of 17 October and letter of 19 October 1945, NAC A6238, 3.

14 Adjt Gen. to Chairman Aust. War Crimes Commission, 24 October 1945, NAC A4311, 752/1, Part).

15 Webb to Mansfield, 20 October 1945, NAC A6238, 3.

Mansfield returned to Australia on October 30th. There he had examined 41 witnesses (four in Brisbane, 37 in Sydney) when Evatt on December 7th dispatched him to London to present to the UNWCC an Australian list of major war crimes suspects and the charges against them. Kirby returned to Australia on November 11th and examined three witnesses in Melbourne before resigning in order to conduct a royal commission on another matter. On December 5th Mr Justice Philp of the Queensland Supreme Court was appointed to examine the remaining 33 witnesses (14 in Sydney, January 16th–21st; 19 in Melbourne, January 24th – February 1st, while Webb drafted the report.

In a letter to the Acting Minister for External Affairs dated November 29th Webb set out how he saw the task:

> The Army are dealing with the ordinary war criminals as and when they capture them. The press to-day announces the constitution at Morotai of the first Australian Military Court, which will deal with 150 Japanese accused of war crimes in the Halmaheras and Celebes.
>
> The commission's main task, however, is to ascertain the major criminals, most, if not all of whom, are in Japan.
>
> As the commission examines witnesses it obtains evidence against ordinary war criminals. This evidence is passed on to the Australian Army for use in the prosecution of such criminals.
>
> As to the major war criminals, it is necessary to show in considerable detail the type of war the Japanese have waged. For this purpose it is necessary to show how the Japanese behaved not only in battle but also out of it, not only in the field, but in prisoner-of-war camps and towards civilians …
>
> Although the case against the major war criminals should be presented in considerable detail, it does not follow that every detail is required to be stated and the report delayed until the last bit of evidence is taken. The case against Tojo will not necessarily be less effective if it does not deal with every offence committed; it will be enough to prove a large number of all kinds of offences over a long period and a wide area. But conditions in every prisoner-of-war camp where Australians were confined will, if the evidence is available, be stated in the report.
>
> I propose to make the report in two parts. The first part will disclose the serious offences committed by the ordinary war criminals and contain a tentative list of the major war criminals and the draft of a possible indictment against them on the lines of that against the major German war criminals; the second part will contain the final list of major Japanese war criminals and indicate their respective offences.
>
> At this stage I am inclined to think that the second part cannot be satisfactorily completed until we get access to Japanese records …

> No doubt we can get information from Japanese experts in Australia, but this is limited, as I discovered when the present tentative list of major war criminals was drawn up. The Japanese leaders, unlike the Germans, did not use the press or the radio to any great extent to inform the world of their individual activities.
>
> It may happen that the major war criminals prosecuted will be only those the Americans desire to prosecute. If they see fit to confer immunity on any we think guilty, it is possible they will not give us the necessary materials and facilities to prosecute …
>
> Before the report is prepared it is likely that we shall have evidence of all the serious war crimes committed by the Japanese, against Australians at all events, and also evidence of the conditions obtaining in all prisoner-of-war camps in which Australians were located. So far 208 witnesses have been examined, some at considerable length, and many documents have been tendered in evidence.
>
> More remains to be done than the making of a report. Lt.Col T B Stephens, who is assisting me to examine witnesses, has in the attached memorandum emphasized the need for a Prosecutions Bureau. This Bureau should comprise trained investigators as well as lawyers. Your Security Branch may provide the investigators. Both should be under a Commissioner, say, Mr J V Barry, K.C.
>
> The taking of evidence has been suspended for a day or two while the whole staff classify and digest the evidence already taken before proceeding to survey the remaining questionnaires, with a view to ensuring that evidence will be taken covering all serious crimes and every prisoner-of-war camp that contained Australians …
>
> I shall be disappointed if the first part of the report is not in your hands before the end of January.[16]

But within a fortnight, while Webb was still in the early stages of drafting Part 1, the commission was again overtaken by events. Webb was offered nomination as the Australian judge on the International Military Tribunal for the Far East (IMTFE). In his letter of acceptance dated December 13th he wrote that he accepted nomination 'subject to my being qualified to act. Of course, I have so far made no finding against any major war criminal. The second part of the report, dealing with the major war criminals could be completed by another Commissioner …'.[17] Thus it is that the report, which ultimately was presented on January 31st, confines itself to conventional crimes against the laws and usages of warfare, e.g.: ill-treatment of POWs in camps in South-East Asia, Formosa, Hainan, Manchuria and Japan

16 NAC A1066, H45/580/1/2.
17 NAC A1067, H45/590/3.

and on the Burma–Siam railway; the Sandakan–Ranau death-marches; and the massacres at the Alexandra Military Hospital, at Bangka Island and at Parit Sulong. It contains only one reference to the major war criminals:

> 472. The Board has not yet obtained any evidence indicating that any Japanese other than those referred to in this report and annexures was guilty of aggression, or a war in violation of international treaties, agreements or assurances or of participating in a common plan or conspiracy for the accomplishment of any of the foregoing. It may be that no such evidence is available in Australia and that it will become available only from records in Japan, including those in the custody of the American Army. Mr Justice Mansfield was endeavouring while in London to obtain evidence of the commission of this crime, that is, evidence against what are termed major Japanese war criminals and any evidence that he has secured will be included in a further report dealing with the major war criminals, if that is found necessary. However, it may be that the trials of the major war criminals will be completed before this further report can be made.

In the event, no further report appeared.

With Webb's appointment to the tribunal and Mansfield's appointment on January 10th to the International Prosecution Section, the report of the commission was written under great pressure; for it had to be completed before both commissioners left Australia to take up their appointments. Mansfield did not participate in the drafting, he did not return to Australian from London until January 20th and, together with Webb, signed the report 10 days later on January 31st before they departed that day for Tokyo. Attached to the report are the depositions of 208 of the 247 witnesses examined by the commission. Omitted are the depositions of the 39 witnesses examined by Mansfield at Morotai, Labuan and Macassar. Although copies were retained by the respective Army formation headquarters these depositions appear never to have reached the commission's secretariat. None of these witnesses are cited in the body of the report. Similarly none of the 33 witnesses examined by Philp are cited in the body of the report.

The work of the commission was brought to an abrupt conclusion when Webb was appointed to the IMTFE and Mansfield to its International Prosecution Section — before they had heard evidence on the planning and waging of aggressive war. They signed and lodged their report to the Minister (147 pp. plus affidavits) on 31 January 1946 — the day of their departure for Tokyo. Accordingly, like its predecessors, the report covers only conventional war crimes, e.g.: ill-treatment of POWs in camps in Malaya, Ambon, Sarawak, Formosa, Hainan, Manchuria and Japan and on the Burma–Siam railway; the Sandakan–Ranau death-marches; massacres of some 323 patients and staff at the Alexandra Military Hospital at Singapore, of 22 Australian nurses at Banka Island and of about 150 Australian and Indian wounded at Parit Sulong.

The indictment of the major Japanese war criminals

Australian policy to indict the Emperor as one of the major war criminals appears to have been instituted and directed by Evatt, himself. A distinguished lawyer, Evatt was a Justice of Australia's highest appeal court when he resigned to enter parliament as a Labor Party candidate in 1940.

The earliest indication of a policy in this area is a cable on 26 May 1945 from Evatt at the San Francisco Conference to his Acting Minister in Canberra admonishing him that 'Nothing should be said in Australia to indicate any weakening of our policy of bringing Japanese criminals to justice irrespective of their office or eminence of their position'.[18]

On July 17th the British Government passed on for information its comments on the US State Department's draft 'Occupation policy for Japan'. Britain suggested that instead of suspending the constitutional powers of the Emperor, as the draft proposed, and engaging in direct military government, it might be preferable for the Supreme Commander for the Allied Powers (SCAP) 'to work through those powers'. The Australian reply was clear cut: 'The Emperor as head of State and Commander-in-Chief of the Armed Forces [must] be given no immunity for Japan's acts of aggression and war crimes, which in evidence before us are shown to have been of a most barbarous character'.[19] This was reaffirmed on several occasions in the exchange of cables between the Australian and the British governments that took place between July 27th and August 18th in connection with the Potsdam Declaration and the terms of the eventual surrender. Take for example the Australian cable of August 11th:

> we must appeal to you to undertake to resist any claim of the Emperor or on his behalf to immunity from punishment, to support us in bringing him to justice and to deprive him of any authority to rule from the moment of surrender. We submit that any other course will effectually prevent the emergence of a democratic and peace-loving regime in Japan.[20]

To this the British Government replied on August 17th:

> We consider … that it would be a capital political error to indict him as a war criminal. We desire to limit commitment in manpower and other resources by using the Imperial throne as an instrument for the control of the Japanese people and indictment of the present occupant would, in our view, be most unwise.[21]

18 NAC A1838/T184, 3103/10/13/1, part 1.

19 To Dominions' Secretary, cable no. 209, 1 August 1945, NAC A5954, Box 453.

20 To Dominions' Secretary, cable no. 230, 1 August 1945, NAC A5954, Box 453.

21 From Dominions' Secretary, cable no. 303, 1 August 1945, NAC A5954, Box 453.

Meanwhile in London, at meetings of the UNWCC on August 1st and 14th, the Australian delegate urged that lists of the Japanese major war criminals be submitted to the commission for its endorsement without delay. As the Four Powers were at that moment waiting to receive the Japanese reply to the surrender terms, the American Ambassador thereupon sought the immediate assistance of the British Foreign Office to cause the Australian delegate to desist, and the following day the latter agreed for the moment to wait on American action.[22] On September 19th, however, the delegate cabled to Canberra that Evatt (who was in London at the time) wished an Australian list of major Japanese war criminals to be tendered to the UNWCC by Webb as a matter of the greatest urgency. As regards its composition:

> Presumably Chief Justice Webb will consider including Hirohito as Head of the Army, and as a knowing participant in systematic and barbaric practices in actual warfare. Presumably also the lists should include the names of leading Japanese statesmen, militarists, financiers and industrialists who were responsible for the preparation, launching and waging of aggressive war.[23]

In reply, Webb on September 26th cabled to Evatt that if he were asked to say, on the basis of his own and American reports on Japanese atrocities in the field and in occupied territory, whether the Emperor and his cabinet ministers should be placed on the list of war criminals, he would reply in the affirmative on the following grounds:

1. That as far as he is aware international law does not give immunity to sovereigns or their advisers who abet or connive at breaches of the laws of war by their soldiers and people, although this is controversial as stated by Dr Lauterpacht;
2. That the breaches committed by the Japanese were so terrible, commencing with the China Incident and continuing until February of this year and so widespread that the Emperor and his ministers must have learned of them, if not from Japanese sources then from neutral and enemy sources, through the press or broadcasts;
3. That having learned of them they must be taken to have approved of them or connived at them or abetted them, if they did not take steps to prevent them, a matter of defence for them to establish;
4. That in view of the great authority, whether spiritual or otherwise is immaterial, displayed by the Emperor in bringing about the unconditional surrender of Japan, it is clear that, if he ordered his forces or people to desist from atrocities and other violations of the laws of war, he would have been promptly obeyed; and

22 *Foreign Relations of the United States*, vol. 6 (The British Commonwealth, the Far East), pp. 902–07.

23 From Australian External Affairs Officer, London, cable no. 279, NAC A1066, H45/580/6/3.

5. That it would be a travesty of justice, seriously reflecting on the United Nations to hang or shoot the common Japanese soldier or Korean guard while granting immunity to his sovereign perhaps even more guilty than he.[24]

The task of compiling the list was entrusted to the small Post-Hostilities Planning Section of the Department of External Affairs assisted by the head of the Department of Information's Listening Post (the organisation that analysed and disseminated to ministers and departments news and information derived from the monitoring of foreign news services and broadcasts). The section commenced the task on September 24th.[25] The completed list, 64 names in all including the Emperor and 14 bankers and industrialists, was on October 22nd tendered to Webb by the Acting Head, External Affairs (JW Burton) for his approval. On October 24th Webb endorsed the list with one qualification: 'As regards the Emperor, my attitude is as stated in my cable of 26 September, but if it be within my province I suggest … need for Hirohito's case being decided at the highest political and diplomatic levels'.[26] In a memorandum to External Affairs Webb elaborated on this point:

> Out of deference to the British view-point, as indicated to me, but by no means pressed … I respectfully suggest that we omit the Emperor from this tentative list.
>
> Of course, the Emperor's immense power, as shown by the prompt way he ended the war, carried a commensurate responsibility to prevent the war, or, if he could not do that, to see that it was conducted in a civilised way. The defence that he was head of a State is negatived by the Four Power Pact of 8 August last [i.e. the Charter of the Nuremberg Tribunal], which also negatived the defence that he was a puppet, which is only the defence of superior orders. Further, any defence of ignorance must fail unless he shows he discharged his duty to inquire.
>
> But, even if he is guilty, there is a way out if one is desired on the ground of expediency, which does not concern us — a pardon for informing on his associates in war crimes. Fifty years ago in Queensland a doctor, who headed a blackbirding expedition and personally committed murders, escaped by turning King's evidence while his minions went to gaol or to the scaffold.[27]

24 To Minister for External Affairs, cable no. 261, NAC A1066, H45/580/6/3.

25 'Discussion held on 24 September, 1945', NAC A1066, H45/580/6/3.

26 To Acting-Secretary, External Affairs, teleprinter D.2158, NAC A1066, H45/580/6/3.

27 To Secretary, External Affairs, 22 October 1945, NAC A1066, H45/580/6/3.

Burton replied to Webb by teleprinter on October 25th rejecting this suggestion: 'The question of taking action for bringing to trial any person on our list will require inter-governmental decision on high level. But this is not necessary for listing of any person by commission for further investigation and position of Emperor on list is in keeping with declared Australian Government policy'.[28]

On October 26th the complete list, with the Emperor still on it, was despatched by External Affairs to the Australian delegate with instructions that it be placed before the UNWCC for consideration. Webb's fellow War Crimes Commissioner, Mansfield, was sent by air to London on December 8th to prepare and present the case against the 64 before the Evidence and Facts Committee of the UNWCC Mansfield completed a 17-page 'Excursus'[29] in support of the indictments by December 28th and lodged these to be considered by the UNWCC at its meeting on January 9th. Mansfield describes the excursus as a 'brief outline of the more important factors in the rise of Japanese imperialism' during the preceding century. It was hastily put together from whatever information Mansfield could find locally — principally, he said, 'from British White Papers'. In it 'The Position of the Emperor' receives 1½ pages plus one full page of quotation from the declaration of war rescript. Briefly, the substance of the charge is that: (i) The Emperor gave his approval to the invasion of Manchuria and the advance on Chinchow in 1931, the crossing of the Great Wall in 1935, the invasion of China in 1937, and the attacks on the Western powers in 1941; (ii) 'Under the constitution the Emperor declares war, makes peace and concludes treaties. It has therefore been necessary for him to give express approval to every aggressive military action'; (iii) 'He was not at any time forced by duress to give written approval. He could have refused to do so and supported his protests by abdication or *hari-kari* (sic)'.

On December 13th Webb accepted nomination as the Australian member of the IMTFE (Evatt's first choice, Lord Wright, the UK Appeal Court judge who had served as the Australian delegate on the UNWCC, had refused the position). As we have already noted, his letter of acceptance contains an illuminating passage — he accepts nomination 'subject to my being qualified to act. Of course, I have so far made no finding against any major war criminal. The second part of the report, dealing with major war criminals, could be completed by another Commissioner …'.[30] This shows clearly his awareness that it could (and would) be argued that his prior participation in the investigation and prosecution process should disqualify him from trying the case. When in mid-January he was asked in his capacity as Commissioner to approve an updated copy of the Australian list, he declined, stating that 'he did not feel that he should do so now that he has been nominated to

28 From Acting-Secretary, External Affairs, teleprinter, 25 October 1945, NAC A1066, H45/580/6/3.

29 'First list of major Japanese war criminals' ('Australian lists of major Japanese war criminals', NAC A2937).

30 NAC A1066, H45/590/3.

the International Tribunal'.[31] A similar anxiety seems to underlie the letter that he wrote two years later to Gen. MacArthur in response to a critical article published in *Life* magazine. In it he writes: '… at the request of the Australian Government to advise on his position, I advised that, although there was a prima facie case against the Emperor, his position should be determined at the highest level. I cabled to that effect to Dr Evatt in Washington or London towards the end of 1945. Later I told Dr Evatt that if the Emperor were indicted I would not take part in his trial.'[32]

As we have already mentioned, Webb and Mansfield's commissioners' report to the Minister of January 31st deals only with conventional war crimes and not with crimes against peace.

When on January 9th (1946) the UNWCC reconvened after the Christmas recess, the American and British delegates first adopted the tactic of at each meeting postponing consideration of the Australian list to a later date. It was just at this time that Gen. MacArthur was advising the chiefs-of-staff that if the Emperor were indicted 'It is quite possible that a minimum of a million troops would be required which would have to be maintained for an indefinite number of years'.[33] When at the meeting of the UNWCC of February 13th Australia forced the issue and demanded a vote on the proposal that the UNWCC should issue a list of key Japanese war criminals and that the Australian list should be the basis of discussion, the proposal was defeated. One of the arguments advanced against the proposal was that, now that the tribunal itself had been set up (its charter was issued by MacArthur on January 19th), the indictments could be handled more effectively and expeditiously by the tribunal's International Prosecution Section.[34]

The scene then moved to Tokyo. From there on April 6th Mansfield cabled to Evatt:

> The inclusion of the Emperor as defendant is now being discussed. There is at least a prima facie case of guilt which can be proved. This is not contested by the Allied prosecutors. When the final decision is taken, political considerations will probably prevent votes in favour of inclusion. I am pressing strongly for inclusion.[35]

31 NAC A1067, UN46/WC/1.

32 Sir William Webb to Gen. MacArthur, 11 February 1948, National Library of Australia, JG Latham Papers, 1009/32/337. Webb had a private meeting with Evatt on 20 March 1946 (NAC A5954, Box 1891, 'Japanese surrender', file no. 4, teleprinter CS 573, 20 March 1946). No record of what transpired at this meeting has been found.

33 MacArthur to Chief-of-Staff US Army, cable, 25 January 1946, *Foreign Relations of the United States*, vol. 8, *The Far East*, 1946, pp. 395–97.

34 From External Affairs Officer, London, cable no. 103, 15 February 1946, NAC A1067, UN46/WC/1.

35 From Australian Political Representative, Tokyo, cable no. 143, 6 April 1946, NAC A5954, Box 1891, 'Japanese surrender', file no. 4.

His instructions were cabled to him on April 9th:

> As previously advised to you, if you are satisfied that there is a case, it is left entirely to you to act upon considered view. At same time you should avoid any public protest if decision is against indictment or if MacArthur vetoes proposal. You are familiar with the facts and it has always been our view that if the facts warranted indictment, Hirohito is no more entitled to special immunity than the common soldier who inflicted such cruel barbarities against Allied soldiers and civilians.[36]

The matter had, however, been determined the previous day. The minutes of the April 8th meeting of associate prosecutors read as follows:

> Suggestions were invited as to any additions to the List. Mr Justice Mansfield proposed that the Emperor be included. A discussion ensued, after which it was agreed that owing to various considerations outside the Prosecution, it would be an error to indict the Emperor. AGREED not to include the Emperor.
>
> AGREED To prepare the Indictment of the 26 Defendants whose names had been decided upon.[37]

At that meeting Mansfield's was the only affirmative vote.

At the conclusion of the trial, in his supplementary opinion, Webb referred to the Emperor's part in starting the war and included the Emperor's immunity from prosecution as one of the grounds on which, in sentencing, he had, in the case of each of the accused, opposed a death sentence:

> The authority of the Emperor was proved beyond all question when he ended the war. The outstanding part played by him in starting as well as ending it was the subject of evidence led by the Prosecution. But the Prosecution also made it clear that the Emperor would not be indicted. This immunity of the Emperor, as contrasted with the part he played in launching the war in the Pacific, is I think a matter which this Tribunal should take into consideration in imposing sentences … a British court in passing sentence would, I believe, take into account … that the leader in the crime, though available for trial, had been granted immunity …
>
> The Emperor's authority was required for war. If he did not want war he should have withheld his authority. It is no answer to say that he might have been assassinated. That risk is taken by all rulers who must still do their duty. No ruler can commit the crime of launching aggressive war and then validly claim to be excused for so doing because his life would otherwise have been in danger

36 To Australian Political Representative, Tokyo, cable no. 123, 9 April 1946, NAC A1067, UN/46/WC/1.

37 International Military Tribunal for the Far East, International Prosecution Section, 'Minutes of a meeting of associate prosecutors, 4.30 pm, Monday, 8th April 1946, Room 610'. I am much indebted to Prof K Awaya of Rikkyō University for showing me this document.

> The suggestion that the Emperor was bound to act on advice is contrary to the evidence. If he acted on advice it was because he saw fit to do so. That did not limit his responsibility. But in any event even a Constitutional Monarch would not be excused for committing a crime at International Law on the advice of his Ministers.[38]

Mansfield continued as the Australian Associate Prosecutor at the IMTFE throughout 1946. Principal among his duties was the superintendence of the preparation and presentation of the 'Prisoners of war' phase of the prosecution's case, in which under Counts 52–55 of the indictment many of the accused were charged with 'ordering, authorizing and permitting' their subordinates 'frequently and habitually' to commit breaches of the laws and customs of war against the armed forces of the Allies and against 'many thousands of prisoners of war and civilians then in the power of Japan' and violating the laws of war by 'deliberately and recklessly disregarding their duty to take adequate steps to secure the observance and prevent breaches thereof'.

The *War Crimes Act, 1945*

The Australian trials were conducted by Military Courts, whose powers, composition and procedures were laid down in the Australian *War Crimes Act* (no. 48 of 1945) and *Regulations for the Trials of War Criminals* (Statutory Rules 1945, no. 164). These were modelled very closely on the United Kingdom Royal Warrant (Army Order 81/1945). They applied to these Military Courts — with certain exceptions or modifications — the provisions of the UK *Army Act* and *Rules of Procedure* (which, as applied by the Australian *Defence Act*, constituted the disciplinary code of the Australian Military Forces in time of war) governing Field General Courts-Martial.[39]

A criticism that has been levelled against this legislation is that it was discriminatory, denying a suspect, if he was Japanese, time-honoured safeguards considered vital if he was Australian.

As the war progressed it had become increasingly apparent to the legal experts in the UNWCC that, if the war crimes courts to be set up were required to follow the traditional rules of evidence of Anglo-American law (which confine evidence to the testimony of witnesses actually produced in court and subject to cross-examination), many war criminals would go free. For example, the evidence against those who killed Flt-Lt Newton was a diary found on a Japanese corpse. It contained an eyewitness account of the execution and named the executioner and the officers

38 BVA Roling & CF Ruter (eds), *The Tokyo Judgment* (Amsterdam, 1977), vol. 1, p. 478.

39 In addition to those *Rules of Procedure* excluded in the Royal Warrant, Statutory Rule no. 164 also excludes the application of *Rules of Procedure* no.s 14, 32 and 36.

who were present. But, as the writer was dead, the diary would, according to the rules of evidence, be inadmissible. Section 9 of the *Act* accordingly, following the war crimes legislation of the other Allied powers, authorises the courts to admit 'any oral statement or any document appearing on the face of it to be authentic'.

One of the basic purposes of the traditional rules of evidence is to ensure that punishment is confined to the actual offender. Apparently the highest repositories of legal rectitude in each of the Allied nations did not regard this principle as absolute. It seems to me that what they were saying was: 'It is more important that an innocent man should go free than that a guilty man should hang; but this is true only where the innocent man is one of our own side. When he is an enemy national, it is not so important'.

Among the critics of Section 9 was the Australian Judge-Advocate General (a civil appointment with quasi-judicial tenure — held from 1936 to 31 March 1946 by J Bowie Wilson, KC and thereafter by Mr Justice Simpson of the Supreme Court of the Australian Capital Territory). In his report on one of the Morotai trials (M44) Bowie Wilson expressed himself in strong terms:

> Under what are called trials under the *War Crimes Act*, none of the rules that have been considered necessary to protect accused persons apply ... would have thought that much of the evidence admitted in these proceedings even under the system of there being no rules of evidence, should not have been admitted as being relevant to the charge before the court.[40]

In the typical war crimes trial the greater part of the prosecution evidence consisted of written statements from living persons who were not produced in court. Section 9 deprived the accused and his Defending Officer of the very valuable right to confront the witness and test his evidence and his veracity by cross-examination. In one of the Labuan trials (M36)[41] the Confirming Authority (apparently on his own initiative and without any prompting from the Judge-Advocate General) withheld confirmation and ordered a retrial because affidavit evidence was used when the witnesses could have been produced in person. Such action on these grounds by the Confirming Authority appears, however, to have been quite atypical. The US war crimes courts are said to have been much less ready than the Australian courts to accept affidavit evidence when the witness himself could be produced.[42]

40 M44, Kawazumi, T et al., NAC A471 81068. See further criticism of Section 9 and other provisions of the *Act* in the article 'Japanese war crimes trials' by Maj. G Dickinson (LLB), Advisory Officer to the Japanese defence team at Manus, published in *Australian Quarterly*, vol. 24, no. 2, June 1952.

41 M36, Capt. Yamamoto, S et al., NAC A471 81663.

42 Cable from British Commonwealth Occupation Force to Department of Defence Z121, 22 December 1949, NAC A816 19/304/447.

In a calmer atmosphere in 1949 Australia and its former allies, in the amendments to the 1929 Prisoners of War Convention, renounced the option to act in this discriminatory manner in the future. Under a.85 and a.102 of the new convention, war criminals, like other POWs, can be tried only by the same courts and according to the same procedure as soldiers of the Detaining Power. These 1949 amendments also appear to close the door to any repetition of another discriminatory feature of the Australian trials. Following the generally accepted view that under international law any war crime was punishable by death, Section 11 of the *Act* empowered the courts to award the death penalty. But under the *Defence Act* the only offences for which an Australian soldier could be sentenced to death by a court martial were certain enumerated acts of treachery — even murder attracted only a life sentence under Australian military law.

The confirmation procedure was also discriminatory. A feature of Australian military law dating from the *Defence Act* of 1903 was the provision that sentences of death could be confirmed only by the Governor-General in council — i.e. by the civil authority and not by the military. When the *War Crimes Act* was enacted empowering the Governor-General to delegate this function and cabinet approved regulations delegating it to divisional commanders, FR Sinclair, the Secretary for the Army, protested to his Minister in strong terms: 'If one … takes a critical view of this procedure, (and such a critical view will, I suggest, be taken in the years to come) it might be held that any departure from the normal methods of administration and justice cannot be justified, because the motives which underlie our activities in bringing our former enemies to trial cannot be said to be altogether disinterested or unbiased …'.[43]

As a result of Sinclair's intervention, a compromise was reached whereby death sentences would be confirmed only by the C-in-C, Australian Military Forces (or, after the abolition of that appointment, by the Adjutant-General) and only after considering a report by the Judge-Advocate General (JAG) who, in such cases, was authorised to comment not only on the court's findings but also on its sentences.[44]

43 Secretary for the Army to Minister for the Army, 6 December 1945, NAC A472 W28681.

44 Secretary for the Army to C-in-C, 25 January 1946, NAC A472 W28681.

The Australian military courts

History

Initially in planning the Australian trials it was assumed that each prosecution would require the prior authorisation of the UNWCC or, at least, of its local National Office (i.e. the Webb Commission). On 12 October 1945, however, the Chairman of the UNWCC, Lord Wright, advised Evatt that it was only in the case of the major war criminals to be tried by international tribunals (or war criminals whose extradition was required) that this was necessary; trials of ordinary war criminals already in Australian custody could proceed without reference to the UNWCC; the United States was already proceeding with national trials on this basis.[45] On October 20th Webb wrote to the Secretary, Department of the Army, confirming that the Australian trials were, henceforth, purely an Army matter and that he and his fellow commissioners would confine their activities to collecting evidence and reporting to the Minister for External Affairs. On October 24th an order-in-council was issued delegating to commanders of divisions and above the power to convene Military Courts for the trial of war crimes. On November 26th orders were issued by the Adjutant-General instructing delegates to convene such courts as soon as the charges were ready for trial.[46] The first trial was convened by the General Officer Commanding (GOC) First Aust. Army that day and commenced at Wewak on November 30th.

On December 14th a small section was set up in the Adjutant-General's Branch at Army Headquarters, Melbourne (in the Directorate of Prisoners of War and Internees (DPW&I)) to exercise and administer central control and direction over war crimes investigations and prosecutions. This was headed by an Assistant Adjutant-General, Lt Col JW Flannagan (a barrister in civil life), who continued in this post until its disbandment in July 1950.

The locations and dates of the Australian trials are as shown in Table 4.1. Trials conducted under the Australian *War Crimes Act*. At Wewak, Morotai, Ambon, Labuan, and Darwin (and at Rabaul prior to March 1946) the investigations and the trials were conducted by the local formation headquarters. The accused were personnel located in the areas that came under Australian occupation at the surrender. Thereafter, under the central direction of the War Crimes section in the DPW&I, investigations and trials were administered on a continuous basis at

45 Cable from Oldham (London) to External Affairs, 12 October 1945, NAC A1066 H45/590/1.

46 Adjutant General to Adv HQ AMF and HQ 1st Aust Army 151625, 26 November 1945, NAC A1066 A45/590/1.

Rabaul and Singapore (and subsequently, Hong Kong) with investigative assistance from the Australian War Crimes sections established for that purpose in Singapore and Tokyo.

Early in 1948 the Hong Kong Government communicated to the Australian Government its wish to resume the premises occupied by the Australian war crimes court and its inability to provide alternative accommodation. At the same time the supreme Allied council, the Far Eastern Commission, had begun consideration of a draft recommendation to member governments that trials should not continue beyond 30 June 1949. In this situation the Australian cabinet on 15 June 1948 issued instructions that every endeavour be made to have the trials completed by the latter date. Representations were then made to Gen. MacArthur's headquarters (GHQ SCAP) for permission to hold the Australian trials in Japan. When these representations were unsuccessful, Darwin and Manus Island (Territory of New Guinea) were examined as possible venues, but found impractical. The Adjutant-General, accordingly, on 14 April 1949 recommended that all trials and investigations be abandoned. When this proposal was brought by the Minister for the Army to cabinet on June 28th some ministers, including the Minister for External Affairs, opposed it and agreement could not be reached: both ministers were asked to confer and present a report. In the weeks that followed, the Minister for the Army gave ground. At the cabinet meeting of September 5th he proposed that trials be held at Manus, that they be confined to cases involving 'murder or other revolting war crimes for which, on conviction of the accused involved, the sentence of death might be appropriate' (There were ready for trial 27 such cases (102 suspects), of which 22 involved murder), and that all other investigations (174 cases, 280 suspects) be terminated. But, if the Minister for the Army had been converted, there were other ministers who remained opposed to trials being held anywhere in Australia or its territories. Cabinet was deadlocked. The respective minute reads: 'It was agreed that "enquiries would be made into the possibility of making suitable arrangements for holding war trials". Meanwhile, war prisoners awaiting trial would not be released'.

Table 4.1. Statistics — Australian war crimes trials[1]

Table compiled in AG Coordination, Army Headquarters, 1958, NAM MP742, A336/1/29[2]

Place	Trials	Accused tried	Accused convicted	Accused acquitted	Death		Imprisonment				
					Hanging	Shooting	Life	25 yrs	11–24 yrs	10 yrs	Under 10 yrs
Labuan (3/12/45 – 31/1/46)	16[3]	145	128	17	2	5	5	–	56	38	22
Wewak (30/11 – 11/12/45)	2	2	1	1	–	–	–	–	–	–	1
Morotai[4] 29/11/45 – 28/2/46)	25	148	81	67[5]	–	25	–	–	10	7	39
Rabaul[6] 12/12/45 – 6/8/47)	188	390	266	124	84	3	8	2	49	22	98
Darwin (1/3 – 29/4/46)	3	22	10	12	–	1	–	–	–	1	8
Singapore (26/6/46 – 11/6/47)	23	62	51	11	18	–	6	–	10	3	14
Hong Kong (24/11/47 – 25/11/48)	13	42	38	4	5	–	4	–	12	3	14
Manus Island (5/6/50 – 9/4/51)	26	113	69	44	5	–	16	–	17	6	25
Total	296[7]	924[8]	644	280[9]	114	34	39	2	154	80	221

Notes

1. These figures incorporate the variations made to the findings and sentences by the Confirming Authority.
2. Table 4.1 is reproduced as in the original except for the addition of trial dates and explanatory footnotes.
3. The figure 16 would appear to be a clerical error. The register from which the table was compiled shows 145 accused tried at Labuan in 15 trials. The clerk may have added, in error, trial M36 (YAMAMOTO Shoichi, and 11 others, Labuan, 23–28/1/46) in which the findings and sentences were not confirmed. (This case was retried at Rabaul 21–22/5/47, R178).
4. Included here is trial of SHIROZU Wadami and 90 others (M45) which began at Ambon 2–18/1/46 and ended at Morotai 25/1–15/2/46. The figures for that trial are: accused 91, not guilty 55, convicted 34 (shooting four, 11–24 years five, 10 years two, under 10 years 25).
5. According to the register from which this table was compiled, this figure should be 66.
6. The trials at Rabaul took place over three periods: 12/12/45 – 31/7/46 (R1–167); 7/12/46 – 23/1/47 (R168–R170); and 3/4/47 – 6/8/47 (R172–R188).
7. Because of the error of one in the total of Labuan trials (See note 3) the total number of trials in which the findings were confirmed should be 295 not 296. In addition there were five trials (either aborted before a finding was made or where the finding of guilty was not confirmed) where the same accused were subsequently retried on the same charges:

   (i) YAMAMOTO Shoichi and 11 others, Labuan 23–28/1/46 (M36), not confirmed, retried at Rabaul 20–27/5/46 (R125); (ii) NEGISHI Kazue, Rabaul 12–13/2/46 (unnumbered), aborted, retried 21–22/5/47 (R178); (iii) SATO Jin, Rabaul, 25–26/4/46 (unnumbered), aborted, retried Hong Kong 3–8/12/48 (HK12); (iv) HAYASHI Eishun, Singapore 25/6/46 (S2), not confirmed, retried 10–12/3/47 (S27); (v) NAGATOMO Yoshitada and 14 others, Singapore 24–31/7/46 (unnumbered), aborted, retried 8/8–16/9/46 (S12).
8. As some were defendants in more than one trial, the total number of persons tried was 814 (not 924). For this and the additional reason that two condemned men died in custody, the total number executed was 137 (not 148).
9. According to the registers from which this table was compiled, this figure comprises:

   (i) 253 found not guilty by the court — Labuan 17, Wewak one, Morotai 65 (incl. Ambon 55), Darwin 12, Rabaul 102, Singapore 10, Hong Kong three, Manus 43; (ii) 26 whose convictions were not confirmed — Morotai one, Rabaul 22, Singapore one, Hong Kong one, Manus one.

On September 16th GHQ SCAP notified the Australian mission that, in the absence of any definite plan for their immediate trial, the 87 Japanese war crimes suspects being held in Sugamo Prison on Australia's behalf would be released on November 1st. A request for an extension of time was refused:

> G.H.Q. is unable to discover adequate grounds on which to justify their detention for a further indefinite period. More than 4 years after the termination of hostilities and after from 1 to 2 years after the original apprehension of the majority of the suspects their continued incarceration without specific charges and without even a certain prospect of eventual trial can scarcely be reconciled with fundamental concepts of justice.

On October 19th General Headquarters (GHQ) released from Sugamo all suspects held on behalf of the American authorities. On October 26th a cable was despatched to the C-in-C British Commonwealth Occupation Force conveying to him that a decision regarding the resumption of trials could be made by January 1st (a general election was to be held on December 10th and ministers would be sworn in a few days later) and instructing him to make a direct approach to MacArthur for a short extension of time. At the interview MacArthur informed him that his staff had examined the Australian cases and considered that about eight (later clarified to nine cases involving 51 suspects) 'merit trial whatever happens and … would be tried if they were offenders against the United States'. (In each of these cases the victims were Australians). In the remainder (in some of which the victims were Americans, not Australians) his staff advised that either a conviction was doubtful or the appropriate sentence was less than the period for which the suspect had been already detained. MacArthur agreed to continue the detention of the suspects until the end of the year.

At the elections the Labor government was defeated. The Menzies government took office on December 19th. The following day, at its first meeting, cabinet decided to bring these nine cases to trial 'with the utmost expedition'. At its meeting on January 10th (1950) it approved a submission by the Minister for the Army that: (i) the trials be conducted at Manus; (ii) that the trials consist of the nine cases already approved and such other cases ready for trial approved by the Minister for the Army on the recommendation of the Adjutant-General which satisfied the same criteria (i.e. cases involving Australians, in which convictions and the death sentence were likely; (iii) the Minister should determine the final list of cases within one month.

The Minister approved an additional 12 such cases. As some cases were subsequently subdivided, the actual number of trials held at Manus was 26.[47] Of the 91 persons tried there, the court sentenced 13 to death. In the case of five of these the sentences were confirmed and carried out.

Composition and procedure

The Military Courts had jurisdiction to try persons charged with violations of the laws and usages of war or war crimes against any person who was at any time resident in Australia, or against any British subject or citizen of an Allied power. They were empowered to sentence any person found guilty to death (either by hanging or shooting), imprisonment, or to a fine. A death sentence required: where the court consisted of three members, unanimity; in other cases, a two-thirds majority.

The *Act* provided that courts consist of at least three officers (including the President). The usual size was: at Morotai, Labuan, Singapore, Hong Kong and Wewak, three; at Rabaul, four; at Manus, five.

47 NAC A816 19/304/447. Department of Defence, Archives & Historical Section, unregistered files A–G Coord 218 & 219. See also NAC A2700, A2703 and A4639 (agenda and minutes of the Chifley and Menzies cabinets).

Regulation 8 of *Regulations for the Trial of War Criminals* stipulated that the Convening Officer should, so far as practicable, appoint as many officers as possible of equal or superior rank to the accused and that, where the accused belonged to the navy or the air force, the court should contain at least one member from that service, if available. This provision was virtually ignored. The best attempt to follow it was at the five 'command responsibility' trials of generals at Rabaul in April and May 1947 where the courts consisted of a major general, a brigadier, a colonel, three lieutenant colonels and a major. More typical was the trial of Lt-Gen. Ito, T in May 1946 by a brigadier and three majors. Although many of the accused were from the navy, it was only at Morotai (on two occasions) that a naval officer was ever appointed to a court.

The *Act* provided that up to half the non-presidential members could be officers of an Allied power. From time to time use was made of this provision to include a British, Indian, Dutch, American or Chinese officer on the court in cases where their nationals were among the victims.

Usually one member of the court had legal qualifications and in such cases it was rare to appoint a judge advocate. The Rabaul courts, however, almost invariably[48] had a judge advocate. Two of the Labuan and one of the Rabaul trials had no judge advocate and their transcripts do not indicate legal qualifications for any members of the court.[49]

The prosecuting officers were army officers with legal qualifications, supplemented by a civilian King's Counsel and his junior at the command responsibility trials at Rabaul and by a King's Counsel for some of the Manus trials.

The practice regarding defending officers varied according to time and place. At Morotai, Wewak and Darwin they were officers of the Australian Army Legal Corps (AALC). At Rabaul until April 1947 they were AALC officers assisted by Japanese lawyers among the troops in the area at the time of the Surrender. At Rabaul from April 1947 onwards and at Ambon, Singapore, Hong Kong and Manus they were Japanese lawyers despatched by the Japanese Government for that purpose, assisted by AALC officers (except at Singapore and Hong Kong where the assistants appear to have been British regimental officers). At Labuan they appear to have been Japanese officers without legal qualifications and there is no indication in the transcripts of the appointment of AALC officers to assist them.

The president was usually a lieutenant colonel (sometimes a major; or, at Morotai, a colonel). At Manus the president was a brigadier (a Supreme Court judge recalled to the Active List from the Reserve).

48 Trial R5, Sgt-Maj. Furukawa, T, had no Judge Advocate and there is no indication in the transcript that any member of the court had legal qualifications (NAC A471 80745).

49 M11, Capt. Nakata, T et al., NAC A471 80911; M37, Sgt-Maj. Shoji, K et al., NAC A471 80754; R5, Sgt-Maj. Furukawa, T, NAC A471 80745.

The trials

In Table 4.2. Australian war crimes trials (classified by victim) I have endeavoured to classify the trials according to the type of victim (e.g. Australian POWs, Indian POWs, natives, local Chinese, Caucasian residents, etc.).

The following are examples. In these, each trial is identified by its official trial number, in which the alphabetical prefix indicates the place of trial: M for Morotai, Wewak, Labuan or Ambon; R for Rabaul; S for Singapore; HK for Hong Kong; LN for Los Negros (i.e. Manus Island).

Massacres of surrendered troops

Laha

It is proposed to report the Laha cases in greater detail than most of the other Australian trials in order to indicate the procedure of a typical trial and to state in some detail defences common to many of the Australian trials.

Summary of events

In the course of the Japanese occupation of the island of Amboina a small force under the command of a Rear Admiral was landed at Hitoelama on the north coast of Hitoe Peninsula at 2.15 am on 31/1/42. Its task was to capture the vital airfield at Laha some 18 kilometres distant on the south coast of the peninsula. The force consisted of the HQ of 1 Bn Kure Special Naval Landing Force (Actg CO Nav. Lt Hatakeyama), No. 2 Coy of the latter (OC Sub Lt Nakagawa) and No. 10 Coy of the 228 Inf. Regt (No. 10 Coy had no involvement in the massacres that ensued, and in fact, was withdrawn from the peninsula immediately after the capture of the airfield on the morning of Feb 3rd).

At about 3.30 pm the force reached the village of Soeakodo about 4 kilometres from the airfield and there the R./Adm. established his forward base. The advanced guard continued forward and engaged the outer defences of the airfield at about 4 pm. There it encountered intense mortar and machine gun fire and at about 5.30 pm the attack was suspended and it withdrew to Soeakodo.

At about 9 pm on Feb 1st the advance guard left Soeakodo to resume the attack. During the day about 10 prisoners (most of them members of a Dutch signals section attempting to move to Paso) had been captured and evacuated to Soeakodo. There they were put to death by bayoneting shortly before the main body of the force, led by the R./Adm., moved forward at midnight to support the attack. This was the first of the four Laha massacres.

Table 4.2. Australian war crimes trials (classified by victim)

VENUE	CIVILIANS			ALLIED SERVICEMEN																	TOTAL
				Australian (including, in some cases, other) POW								UK POW		Indian POW	Chinese POW	Indonesian POW					
	Natives	Local Chinese	Caucasians	Burma/Siam (Trial S7 includes Indo-China)	Borneo	Ambon	Timor & Halmahera	Java	At Sea	New Britain	Malaya	Hainan Is.	New Britain	At Sea	New Britain & New Guinea	New Britain, NewGuinea & Bougainville	New Britain & Bougainville	Crashed Aircrew	Infiltration Parties	Cannibalism	Mutilation of the Dead	
WEWAK																						
Trials in Which Convictions Obtained																				1		1
Trials in Which No Convictions Obtained	1																					1
MOROTAI																						
Trials in Which Convictions Obtained						5												16	1			22
Trials in Which No Convictions Obtained							1											2				3
LABUAN																						
Trials in Which Convictions Obtained					15																	15
Trials in Which No Convictions Obtained																						
RABAUL																						
Trials in Which Convictions Obtained	22	12	3		4	3							2		66	20	2	1	2			137
Trials in Which No Convictions Obtained	3	5	1		2										34	2		2		2		51
DARWIN																						
Trials in Which Convictions Obtained							2												1			3
Trials in Which No Convictions Obtained																						
SINGAPORE																						
Trials in Which Convictions Obtained				18				2	1									1				22
Trials in Which No Convictions Obtained				1																		1
HONG KONG																						
Trials in Which Convictions Obtained	2		2	3								1		1				3				12
Trials in Which No Convictions Obtained	1																					1
MANUS																						
Trials in Which Convictions Obtained	1			3		3	6			1	1							3	4		1	23
Trials in Which No Convictions Obtained					1		1												1			3
TOTAL																						
Trials in Which Convictions Obtained	25	12	5	24	19	11	8	2	1	1	1	1	2	1	66	20	2	24	8	1	1	235
Trials in Which No Convictions Obtained	5	5	1	1	3		2								34	2		4	1	2		60
TRIALS: GRAND TOTAL	**30**	**17**	**6**	**25**	**22**	**11**	**10**	**2**	**1**	**1**	**1**	**1**	**2**	**1**	**##**	**22**	**2**	**28**	**9**	**3**	**1**	**295**

Source. Compiled by DCS Sissons

By about 4 am on Feb 2nd the advance guard had succeeded in penetrating at several points the wire around Tawiri at the northern edge of the airfield. Very heavy fighting ensued in which the Japanese losses amounted to about 40 killed (including the Senior Staff Officer (Cdr Ieki) and two platoon commanders) and 60 wounded. Accordingly a withdrawal to Soeakodo commenced at about noon and was completed by about 9 pm. During the day about 50 prisoners were taken, most of them Australian. Among them was the Australian Commander at Laha, Maj. Newbury, who at about 2 pm at the head of a party of 10 entered the Japanese lines under a white flag as a *parlementaire* to propose the surrender of his force. Along with the others they were taken into custody and confined at Soeakodo.

The third attack on the airfield was launched at 3 am the following day (Feb 3rd). This was successful. Resistance petered out at about 4 am and the force surrendered at 5 am. Its members, about 260 all ranks (mostly Australian but including a few Dutch), were placed in confinement in some of the barracks at the airfield.

The second massacre took place two days later, on Feb 5th, when at Soeakodo the 50 prisoners captured before the surrender (incl Maj. Newbury and his party) were killed. The Company Commander, Nakagawa, during the committal proceedings of his Japanese Naval Court Martial on 22 December 1945 testified as follows:

> We were ordered by the Admiral to kill them on the following day; for he had received a report informing him that the POWs at Soeakodo were restive. In compliance with this order, on February 5th I took about 30 other ranks to Soeakodo. I cannot recall now from which platoons these men were selected. We dug holes in a coconut plantation about 200 metres from Soeakodo in the direction of the airfield and killed the POWs with swords and bayonets. It began at 10 a.m. and took about two hours. I divided my men into three groups, the first for moving them out of the house in which they were confined, the second for preventing disorder on their way to the plantation, the third for beheading or bayoneting them. The POWs were sent to the spot one by one and made to kneel, with their eyes bandaged. Our men of the third group came out in turn one at a time to behead the POW with a sword or to bayonet him through the chest.[50]

The following day (Feb 6th) at the third massacre, the first Tawiri massacre, was perpetrated. To quote from Nakagawa's testimony once again:

> About thirty of the POW were considered especially disobedient. The R/Adm heard of this and on the evening of 5th February summoned me and Hatakeyama to his room and ordered that they be put to death. At about 3 p.m. the following day, in a coconut plantation near Tawiri about 700 metres from the airfield, I had some twenty of my other ranks kill them.

50 NAC A471 81212, part B, exhibit D, frames 75–359, 'The dossier concerning the examination of the case against Kunito Hatakeyama and Kenichi Nakagawa' (English translation), 14/6/1946.

> I cannot recall which platoons my men were from. On this occasion, too, the hapless POW were first marshalled in a nearby house and then called out in turn one by one and killed with a sword or bayonet. Their corpses were buried in the hole dug for that purpose. As previously, for most of the time I stood about midway between the house and the hole, in overall command.

It appears that on this occasion about 62 of the prisoners were killed including W./Cdr ED Scott and seven of his RAAF subordinates who had been captured at sea on Feb 4th making for Ceram in a native craft.

On February 9th the force, leaving behind a platoon to garrison Laha moved across the bay to the town of Ambon vacated by the Japanese Army, which had moved on for its next task, the capture of Timor. At about the same time the new Commanding Officer of 1 KSNLF took up his appointment, Lt Hatakeyama reverting to his former position of Adjutant. Some days later the execution of the remaining POWs took place. This was the fourth Laha massacre. To quote once again form Nakagawa's testimony at his Japanese court-martial:

> On about February 20th at our HQ in Ambon town I was told by Lt Hatakeyama that I should go to Laha to have the POWs there put to death … At about 2 p.m. that day I arrived at the quarters of the Laha detachment with about 60 men of my own coy and about 30 men of Minesweeper No. 9 who were then accommodated in my company barracks. A Reserve Officer of the minesweeper consented verbally to my taking these latter personnel. Though he accompanied us, nothing was directed or requested of him on my part.
>
> I briefed these 90 other ranks and assigned them their duties. All would participate in the digging of the burial pits. Next, they were to be divided into three parties — the first for transporting the victims from the camp to the place of execution, the second for preventing disturbances, and the third (composed of some 20 men) for doing the actual killing.
>
> The execution site was selected in a coconut plantation situated on both sides of a road running a little beyond a marsh which lies about 200 metres northeast from the detachment's barracks standing just in front of the pier. The smaller burial pit on the right side of the road was for about 30 corpses, while the larger one dug on the left side was for the remainder.
>
> According to my memory the number of POWs killed was about 220. They were killed either by sword or by bayonet, with their eyes covered. I was directing affairs from the detachment office.
>
> If I remember right, the fateful deed was commenced at about 6 p.m. and ended at about 9 p.m.

The first of these four Laha massacres did not become the subject of a war crimes trial. It appears that it was carried out by the section of Ens. Sakamoto's platoon left behind at Soeakodo by the main body, and that Sakamoto received the orders direct from the R./Adm. By the war's end both these men were dead. The other three massacres were the subject of four Australian trials. In each of these trials the defence argued, inter alia, that:

i. The defendants were acting under compulsion: they were carrying out the explicit orders of their superior officers, in the knowledge that disobedience was punishable by death under the Naval Penal Code. The prosecution argued that the commands were patently unlawful and that, accordingly, obedience to superior orders was no defence.

Whether or not international law countenanced superior orders as a defence had since the early years of the 20th century been the subject of some dispute.[51] In what became perhaps the standard work in English on public international law, LFL Oppenheim (the Professor of International Law at Cambridge) in 1906 stated that superior orders constituted a complete defence, but advanced neither reasoning nor written authority for this. This was repeated in his second edition in 1912. In 1914 when a chapter on 'The laws and usages of war on land' was added to the British Army's official text-book, the *Manual of Military Law*, Oppenheim was commissioned as the joint author and the assertion was repeated there: 'It is important to … note that members of the armed forces who commit such violations of the recognised rules of warfare as are ordered by their Government or by their commander are not war criminals and cannot therefore be punished by the enemy …'. The same view was adopted in the *Rules of Land Warfare*, the US official manual.

In the years that followed, this proposition continued to be maintained in subsequent editions of Oppenheim (including the 5th edition, by Lauterpacht in 1935). Meanwhile, however, it had been rejected by a number of other learned writers such as Phillipson (1915), Bellot (1917), Mérignhac (1917) and by the committee of distinguished experts appointed by the UK Attorney-General in November 1918 to inquire into German war crimes. It had also been rejected by the German Supreme Court, which in 1921 in the *Llandovery Castle* case held that superior orders was no justification where the act was manifestly and undoubtedly contrary to international law. By 1940, Lauterpacht had experienced a conversion: his sixth edition of Oppenheim rejects the original Oppenheim postulation. It was

51 For the history of this question see particularly: Y Dinstein, *The Defence of Obedience to Superior Orders* (Leyden: Sijthoff, 1965), pp. 38–40; JH Morgan, 'Nuremberg and after', *Quarterly Review*, April 1947, p. 318 ff; Committee of Enquiry into Breaches of the Laws of War, Interim reports — Memorandum on 'The plea of superior orders' (Cabinet papers GT7806, Public Record Office, London, CAB 24 85 Y/K 6169, pp. 32–41); H Lauterpacht, 'The law of nations and the punishment of war crimes', *British Yearbook of International Law*, 1944, pp. 58–95.

not, however, until the 1944 edition of the *Manual of Military Law*, Oppenheim's original chapter was replaced. There and in the Australian edition of that year the relevant paragraph reads:

> §443. The fact that a rule of warfare has been violated in pursuance of an order of the belligerent Government or of an individual belligerent commander does not deprive it of its character as a war crime, neither does it, in principle, confer upon the perpetrator immunity from punishment by the injured belligerent. Undoubtedly a Court confronted with the plea of superior orders adduced in justification of a war crime is bound to take into consideration the fact that obedience to military orders not obviously unlawful is the duty of every member of the armed forces, and that the latter cannot, in conditions of war discipline, be expected to weigh scrupulously the legal merits of the order received. The question, however, is governed by the major principle that members of the armed forces are bound to obey lawful orders only, and they cannot therefore escape liability if, in obedience to a command, they commit acts which both violate unchallenged rules of warfare and outrage the general sentiment of humanity.

It was also in that year that the American *Rules of Land Warfare* was similarly amended.

In March 1945 the UNWCC in its *Report to Governments on the Plea of Superior Orders* expressed the unanimous view that 'the mere fact of having acted in obedience to the orders of a superior does not of itself relieve a person who has committed a war crime from responsibility'. Three months later, in June, the International Conference on Military Trials embodied this principle in Article 8 of the Charter of the Nuremberg Tribunal: 'The fact that the Defendant acted pursuant to order of his Government or of a superior shall not free him from responsibility, but may be considered in mitigation of punishment if the Tribunal determine that justice so requires'.

Throughout the Australian war crimes trials the prosecuting officers, judge advocates and the courts consistently accepted §443 as declaratory of international law.

i. Another defence tendered was that the executions were justified by military necessity — *Kriegsraison geht vor Kriegsmanier*; the success of the operations against Java depended on the immediate and uninterrupted operation of the Laha airfield; for days after the surrender the airfield continued to be under small arms fire from bands of the enemy who had not surrendered; the POWs outnumbered their guards, were restive and likely to mutiny and recapture the airfield. The prosecution rejected this description of the situation as arrant nonsense. Furthermore it argued that, even in the 19th century, far from being consensus mundi, this maxim was no more than the view of a minority of continental writers. Following Oppenheim, the prosecution argued that any general rule that necessity in the interest of self-preservation excuses an illegal act was abrogated

> by Hague Convention IV whose Preamble expressly states that that the Hague Rules were framed with regard to military necessity. In other words, military necessity was discounted in the drawing up of the Rules.[52]

A unique feature of the Laha trials was that the prosecution was able to introduce in evidence portions of the proceedings of the aborted Japanese Naval Court Martial of Nav. Lt Hatakeyama and Sub Lt Nakagawa on charges of homicide (Japanese Criminal Code, Art. 199) at Laha. This was one of the four war crimes trials initiated by the Japanese Government in November 1945 and aborted by order of Gen. MacArthur in February 1946.[53]

Trial of Nav. Lt Hatakeyama and Sub Lt Nakagawa (R186)

The first of the Laha trials, R186, took place at Rabaul on 14, 15 & 17 July 1947.[54] In it Nav. Lt Hatakeyama and Sub Lt Nakagawa were charged with murder in respect of each of the second, third and fourth massacres and were found guilty on each charge. Hatakeyama was Acting/Battalion Commander at the time of the second and third massacres and Adjutant at the time of the fourth. Nakagawa, his Company Commander, was the Officer-in-Charge at the place of execution on each occasion.

The court sentenced Hatakeyama to death and Nakagawa to 20 years' imprisonment. On July 30th both defendants submitted petitions against the findings and sentences. The JAG in his advice to the Confirming authority dated August 28th recommended that the petitions be dismissed and reported as follows: 'I am of the opinion that none of the defences offered could properly be set up as a defence to the charge, and I see no reason why the finding and sentence should not be confirmed'. He argued, however, that the sentence awarded Hatakeyama was inappropriate:

> I find it difficult to follow the reasoning of the court in sentencing the senior officer to death and the junior officer to 20 years imprisonment. Both officers were extremely junior in rank at the time of these murders, and the actual executions were supervised by Nakagawa, while Hatakeyama was merely the conduit pipe between his Admiral and his fellow accused. Were I the Confirming Authority I would mitigate the sentence of death by hanging to 20 years imprisonment.

Despite this advice the Confirming Authority (the Adjutant-General, Maj. Gen. WM Anderson), on September 10th, confirmed both sentences and signed the death warrant. Hatakeyama, however, had lodged a further petition on September 4th and this together with a supplication by Gen. Imamura on Hatakeyama's behalf was forwarded to Army HQ by air and tendered to Adjutant-General. After

---

52 H Lauterpacht, *Oppenheim's International Law* (6th edn, 1940), vol. 2, pp. 184–85.

53 NAC A471 81212, part B, exhibit D, frames 75–359, 'The dossier concerning the examination of the case against Kunito Hatakeyama and Kenichi Nakagawa' (English translation), 14/6/1946.

54 NAC A471 81212.

considering these documents Anderson on October 7th revoked his confirmation of Hatakeyama's sentence, cancelled the death warrant and commuted his sentence to 20 years' imprisonment.

Trial of WO Yamashita and five others (LN6) — The second Soeakodo massacre

On 27 July 1950 WO Yamashita and five members of his platoon, (PO Cl 3 Shimohama, and Seamen Kamioka, Murayama, Hayashi and Miyawaki), were arraigned at Manus on the charge of murdering a number of Australian and Allied POWs at Soeakodo on or about 5 February 1942.[55]

Of the six accused all except Miyawaki admitted their presence at the execution. The only evidence implicating him was the uncorroborated testimony of the co-defendant Murayama: 'I remember that Hayashi and Miyawaki each beheaded at least one prisoner-of-war'. The court acquitted him.

The evidence for the prosecution consisted of statements made to Australian interrogating officers at Tokyo during the period 1948–49 by each of the accused and several other Japanese. Each of the accused elected to go into the witness box and gave evidence. Kamioka admitted that, under orders, he attempted to decapitate one POW but was unsuccessful. Hayashi admitted that under orders, he had finished off that prisoner with the bayonet.

In his interrogation of 4 May 1949 Yamashita stated that he had been second-in-command at the execution and in this capacity had for some minutes directed the executions during the temporary absence of the Commander.

The evidence against Shimoyama was the statement of his comrade Inazaki when interrogated on 13 September 1949, in which Inazaki stated that when, immediately after the execution, he asked whether he had executed any of the prisoners, Shimoyama replied 'Of course I did'.

The prosecution's case against Murayama consisted of allegations in a number of statements that he was present and his statement at his interrogation on 12 July 1949 that he had beheaded five of the prisoners.

Yamashita, Murayama and Shimoyama subsequently retracted the statements they made at their interrogations, claiming that the Interrogation Officer, Capt. J Sylvester, had put the words into their mouths and had obtained their signatures by offering inducements, making threats, and by torture, such as making them stand to attention for long periods, pushing them against the wall, hand-cuffing them and tugging at the hand-cuffs. (Surprisingly, the signed statements produced in court were translations in English, a language the deponents were unable to read!).

55 NAC A471 81951.

In rebuttal, the prosecution produced as a witness an Australian officer who had occupied a room adjacent to the room in which the interrogations had taken place. He testified that the interrogation room was an open-plan office occupied by six interrogating officers each of whose activities would be visible to the others and that he had never seen handcuffs anywhere in the suite of offices occupied by the Australian War Crimes Section.[56]

The court on 7 August 1950 sentenced Yamashita to 20 years imprisonment, Murayama and Kamioka to 15, Shimohama to 10 and Hayashi to eight. The JAG recommended that the finding of guilty be confirmed but commented on the severity of the sentences: 'The accused were all men of poor education and of low rank … I would, if the decision rested with me, have reduced all those sentences which exceed ten years to one of ten years imprisonment.' The Adjutant-General on 4 October 1950 confirmed the courts findings and sentences.

Trial of WO Yamashita and five others (LN12) — The first Tawiri massacre

On 8 September 1950 WO Yamashita, three members of his platoon (PO Cl 3 Shimohama, Seaman Hayashi and Seaman Murayama) together with WO Sasaki and WO Suwa, were arraigned at Manus on the charge of murdering a number of Australian and Allied POWs near Laha airfield on or about 7 February 1942.[57]

At the conclusion of the prosecution's case submissions were made by the defence that there was no case to answer against Suwa, Hayashi and Murayama — that no fact had been established by any of the prosecution's evidence that they participated in the execution or that they were on guard duty at the place of execution. These submissions were accepted by the court, and these three were thereupon acquitted.

56 It was not until some weeks later, in connection with another case, the defence team at Manus received from its Tokyo office the affidavits of two US Army sergeant interpreters who had interpreted for Sylvester. On 8 September 1950 at Tokyo Sgt FK Oshima deposed that:

> Capt Sylvester sometimes required those being interrogated by him to stand at attention before him, or against a wall or a screen; this would continue at times for as much as two hours, and was sometimes accompanied by the admonition, 'Go on standing at attention until you change your mind', or 'Continue until you regain your memory' …
>
> Four or five times I have seen Capt Sylvester produce handcuffs and exhibit them to the witness with the threat of using them, and on some occasions he also made out a warrant and exhibited it to the witness, telling him that he was going to call the police to take him to Sugamo Prison. This latter performance was repeated very often, at times when the Captain was displeased with the witness' answers; he would say on such occasions, 'You are lying, and I'm going to have you put in prison until you tell the truth' …
>
> It was Capt Sylvester's practice also to show to a witness an affidavit, or what he alleged to be an affidavit, of another person connected with the matter, saying that that affiant's testimony contradicted what the witness was saying, and that the witness had better change his statement and 'tell the truth'.

On 11th Sept 1950 Sgt T Saito swore an affidavit to the same effect:

> When a witness interrogated by Capt Sylvester answered in such words as 'it may be' or 'it might have been so', the Captain would put in the witness' statement 'it was so'. If the witness refused to sign such a statement, I have seen him threatened by the Captain, who would say that the witness would not be allowed to return home until he signed.

57 NAC A471 81952.

The evidence for the prosecution was entirely documentary. Regarding the other accused, the prosecution's case was that Yamashita was present at the execution as Commander of the guards and for a short period in the absence of a senior officer actually supervised the execution. Sasaki, it was alleged, was an executioner and he executed the first prisoner, shouting, as he did so 'I thus avenge my dead comrades'. It was alleged that Shimoyama who had been employed on sentry duty elsewhere went to the execution site of his own volition and for a short time was employed as a guard there.

The accused each gave evidence, and on their behalf their defending counsel called certain witnesses.

The defence, in part, was concerned to establish that the execution was ordered by the Commanding Admiral either for reasons of military necessity, in that he had insufficient forces to guard the prisoners or because they had made or were about to make a riot and perhaps to escape. This defence, no doubt, was raised to combat the suggestion of the prosecution that it was a cold-blooded massacre in revenge for the casualties suffered in the battle for the airfield.

Another part of the defence was that each of the accused was bound to do what he did by virtue of the direct orders of his naval superiors.

Yamashita sought to establish, in his defence, that he was merely engaged in guard duties when so ordered, and in no way participated in the execution.

Sasaki's defence was largely that he was bound to do what he did, namely, command the execution parade and actually execute some of the prisoners, by virtue of the direct orders of his military superiors.

Shimoyama's defence was that he went to the execution ground to report to his Platoon Commander that he had finished his tour of sentry duty elsewhere and while so reporting was ordered to stand guard over some of the prisoners for a period of 10 or 15 minutes.

Yamashita was sentenced to life imprisonment, Sasaki to death by hanging, and Shimohama to 10 years' imprisonment.

In his report on the trial to the Confirming Authority the JAG wrote:

> In Paragraph 11 of his petition Sasaki points out that Nakagawa, who was his immediate superior at the time of the occurrence, and Nakagawa's immediate superior, Hatakeyama, were tried and sentenced to 20 years and death respectively but Hatakeyama's sentence of death was commuted to 20 years by the Confirming Authority … [This] deserves earnest consideration by the Confirming Authority. I have not got the proceedings of the military court that tried Hatakeyama and Nakagawa before me, but I have some recollection

> of the proceedings, which I reviewed. My recollection … is that Hatakeyama was much more responsible for the murders than Sasaki was, and the Confirming Authority may well feel, if he agrees with the statement I have just made, that Sasaki's sentence should be commuted to imprisonment.

The Confirming Authority then commuted Sasaki's sentence to life imprisonment, mitigated Yamashita's sentence to 20 years, and confirmed Shimoyama's sentence of 10 years.

Trial of Sub Lt Tsuaki and two others (LN24) — The second Tawiri massacre

The evidence for the Crown was all documentary.[58] The Crown case was that Tsuaki, a reserve sub lieutenant, had been Executive Officer on a mine-sweeper which struck a mine in Ambon Bay. The explosion killed about 20 and injured about seven of the crew. The survivors were subsequently attached for duty to 1 Kure Special Naval Landing Force. On or about February 13th Tsuaki learnt that an execution of prisoners was going to take place the following day and volunteered the service of himself and his shipmates as executioners.

On Sheet 25 of the proceedings Tsuaki says: 'The Company Commander ordered me to cut the first prisoner-of-war … I cut him with a sword'.

The accused Kanamoto in a statement made by him before the trial (which was tendered as Exhibit 19 (b) of the Crown case) said:

> I could not see the faces of the men who were standing around; but I believe most of them were survivors of the sunken mine-sweeper … I heard the order was that the survivors of No. 9 Mine-Sweeper had requested and received permission from HQ to execute the prisoners-of war to revenge the death of their comrades … I sat and watched the execution. Every one of the men without exception shouted the name of his fallen comrades and cried 'in revenge of so-and-so' as he swung the sword.

As regards Kanamoto, the OC of the Pioneer Platoon, the Crown case was that at about noon he heard that executions were to take place that evening and, since he had never seen an execution, he requested permission to attend from his superior officer who, the Crown alleged, replied; 'Anyone who wants to try can try it'.

Kanamoto, the Crown further alleged, informed his subordinates of the proposed execution and offered to take with him anyone who wanted to participate in the execution.

58 NAC A471 81967.

The Crown further alleged that Kanamoto subsequently admitted that he had beheaded a prisoner, but no evidence was offered as to whether this confession was true or false. But the Crown did allege and offered evidence that Kanamoto lent his sword to one of the executioners who requested it.

The defence alleged that Tsuaki had not volunteered to participate but had been ordered to do so by his superiors and that Kanamoto had not participated in the executions.

The only evidence against Nakamura was the sworn statement of Kanamoto:

> At about 1730 hrs I went to my subordinates' quarters and said to them 'I am going to attend than execution at Laha. I shall take anyone who wants to go with me'. As a result three marines volunteered, including Seaman Cl.1 Ikezawa and, I believe, Seaman Cl.1 Nakamura. I do not recall the name of the other volunteer.

The Prosecutor referred to this in the course of his closing address:

> The law does admit as sufficient the uncorroborated testimony of one witness, even an accomplice, if the jury consider him credible; but it is now held to be the duty of the Judge to warn the jury of the danger of convicting a prisoner on the uncorroborated evidence of an accomplice and in his discretion advise them not to do so, though at the same time pointing out that it is within their legal province to convict upon it if they so choose … So what this really means is that there is sufficient evidence to convict Nakamura if you are satisfied that Kanamoto's statement is true, but you must approach this task with the utmost caution, being at all times mindful of this danger.

The court acquitted Nakamura and sentenced Tsuaki to death by hanging and Kanamoto to life imprisonment.

The JAG, in his report to the Confirming Authority, wrote:

> In my opinion there was ample evidence from which the court could arrive at the conclusion which it did arrive at, that both these accused were guilty of the charge of murder. Tsuaki by virtue of the fact that he himself took part in one of the 'executions' and Kanamoto as a principal of the second degree, that is one who is present at the commission of this offence and aided and abetted its commission. I see no reason why the findings and sentences should not be confirmed.

On 2 May 1951 the Adjutant-General did so. Tsuaki was hanged at Manus on June 11th.

The Parit Sulong massacre

On 22 January 1942 about 100 Australian and 40 Indian soldiers were captured by 4 Konoe Division in the fighting at Parit Sulong. They were inspected by the Divisional Commander, Lt Gen. T Nishimura, who thereupon issued verbal orders through his Assistant Divisional Commander (ADC) that they be executed. They were killed that evening by machine gun and rifle fire. In trial LN2 Nishimura was sentenced to death; the ADC, to six months imprisonment.[59] Nishimura had already on 2 April 1947 been sentenced to life imprisonment by a British court in connection with the massacre of Chinese civilians in Singapore following the surrender.

POW camps and work-places

Borneo: Sandakan and Ranau

In World War II the Australian Army lost 18,000 men. Of these, about 1,650 perished in or about Sandakan in British North Borneo during 1945. At Sandakan in August 1944 the Japanese had about 2,200 POWs They had brought them there to build airfields from which the Japanese hoped to stem the Allied advance on the Philippines and on Java. About three-quarters were Australian; the rest, British. Within 12 months all but six were dead. Some 1,200 died in Sandakan Camp itself; the rest on the two death marches to Ranau, 260 kilometres to the west — about half of them on the march and half at Ranau. Of the total 2,200, at least 150 were shot, either when, exhausted, they fell out on the march, or in the executions of the last survivors — 23 at Sandakan and 33 at Ranau — in July and August. The rest died of starvation and its grim attendants, malaria, beri-beri and dysentery.

In R176[60] the first and second Sandakan–Ranau marches and the massacres at Ranau were the basis of the charge against the Corps Commander, Lt Gen. Baba, of 'unlawfully disregard[ing] and fail[ing] to discharge his duty as … Commander to control the conduct of the members of his command whereby they committed brutal atrocities and other high crimes against people of the Commonwealth of Australia and its allies'. He was sentenced to death.

The ill-treatment of the POWs in Sandakan Camp in the period preceding the marches was the subject of two trials: the Commandant was sentenced to death (M28)[61] and three of the Formosan guards were sentenced to 15 years (M35)[62].

59 LN2, Lt-Gen. Nishimura, T et al., NAC A471 81942.
60 R176, Lt-Gen. Baba, M, NAC A471 81613.
61 M28, Capt. Hoshijima, S, NAC A471 80777.
62 M35, Hayashi, Y et al., NAC A471 80779.

The first Sandakan–Ranau death march

The first Sandakan–Ranau march was the subject of three trials. In R125[63] the march Commander (Capt.) and 10 of his subordinates (eight officers, two other ranks) were charged with: (i) murder of numerous POWs in their charge; (ii) (alternative charge) ill-treatment of POWs in compelling them 'to march long forced marches under difficult conditions when sick and underfed as a result whereof many of the POWs died'.

In this trial the accused pleaded 'superior orders' as a defence. This defence was rejected by the court.

The march Commander and the Commander of the rear group (the group whose task included shooting the stragglers from the groups preceding it) were sentenced to death; the other officers, to 10 years. The other ranks were acquitted.

The other two trials arising out of the first Sandakan–Ranau march were R102[64] and R151[65]. In the former a Formosan guard was sentenced to death for bludgeoning to death with a rifle butt a POW who fell behind; in the latter three Formosan guards were sentenced to death for torturing to death over a period of four days a recaptured escapee.

The second Sandakan–Ranau death march

The second Sandakan–Ranau march was the subject of five trials. The Commander and second-in-command were sentenced to death (M17)[66], as was a sergeant who on his own initiative had shot two POWs who fell behind (M16)[67]. Twenty-one guards (mainly Formosans) who, as ordered, shot those who were unable to continue marching were charged with murder (M18).[68] Of these, two were acquitted and the remainder were sentenced to periods ranging from eight to 20 years.

In R122[69] a Formosan guard was charged with the murder of one of the POW after his arrival at Ranau. At a parade of a working party when a sick POW (who also had badly ulcerated leg) failed to march off, the guard had knocked him to the ground and repeatedly kicked him on the head and body, as a result of which he died some hours later. The court found him guilty and sentenced him to death. Confirmation was, however, withheld, on the ground that the accused had been acquitted on the same charge by an earlier court.

63 R125, Capt. Yamamoto, S et al., NAC A471 81029. This was the retrial of M36 in which the findings and sentences were not confirmed.

64 R102, Hayashi, Y, NAC A471 81015.

65 R151, Kitamura, K et al., NAC A471 81213.

66 M17, Capt. Takakuwa, T et al., NAC A471 80771.

67 M16, Sgt Hosotani, N, NAC A471 80714.

68 M18, Nagahiro, M et al., NAC A471 80772.

69 R122, Fukushima, M, NAC A471 81218.

In these death marches cases, where other ranks under orders killed POWs who were unable to march, the courts did not award death sentences. And in these circumstances the JAG recommended that the sentences be mitigated — in most cases to three years imprisonment. The Confirming Authority, however, with rare exceptions confirmed the original sentences.

Massacre of survivors at Ranau and Sandakan

The final massacres of survivors at Ranau[70] and Sandakan[71] were the subject of five trials of non-commissioned officers (NCOs) and rank-and-file (including Formosans) in which eight were acquitted and 33 were sentenced to terms ranging from five years to life imprisonment.

Sarawak: Kuching and Miri

At Kuching in Sarawak the POW camp held about 1,250 persons (mostly UK other ranks, but including 160 Australian POWs and some UK civil internees). Of these 592 died — most of them from starvation.

The CO (Lt Col) committed suicide in custody. The 2 I/C (Capt.) (who controlled the general affairs of the camp), the Quartermaster (Capt.), the Labour Officer (Lt) and the MO (Lt) were charged with ill-treatment of POWs and internees by: (i) authorising and permitting assaults; (ii) denial of sufficient food and medical supplies and attention; (iii) forcing the sick and starving to do heavy manual work. They were found guilty on all charges (with the exception of 'medical supplies and attention' in the case of the 2 I/C and the Labour Officer) and sentenced to death (M11)[72]. The JAG recommended that in the case of the Quartermaster and Labour Officer the findings be not confirmed: he argued that they were subordinate officers who were unable to obtain supplies and that they were not responsible for the conduct of the guards or the provision of medical attention. The Confirming Authority confirmed all the findings, but for these two officers commuted the sentences to five years imprisonment.

Among the camp guards six NCOs, two interpreters and 37 rank-and-file (mostly Formosans) were charged with assaulting POWs and internees in violation of the laws and usages of war. The court acquitted three of the rank-and-file and sentenced the remainder to terms of imprisonment ranging from one year to life (M37)[73]. The JAG was very critical of this trial — the use of affidavits, thereby denying the

70 M19, Sgt Iwabe, S et al., NAC A471 81216; M22, Goto, T et al., NAC A471 81970; M21, Sgt Okada, T et al., NAC A471 80705; M25, Sgt-Maj. Beppu, Y et al., NAC A471 80913.

71 M24, Sgt-Maj. Murozumi, H et al., NAC A471 80776.

72 M11, Capt. Nakata, T et al., NAC A471 80911.

73 M37, Sgt-Maj. Shoji, K et al., NAC A471 80754.

accused the opportunity to test the evidence by cross-examination, the failure of the court to produce individual POWs sought by the accused as defence witnesses, and the manner in which the prosecution presented the case:

> It was alleged by the prosecution that the serious death rate amongst prisoners of war during the last few months of their internment was due to the ill-treatment of the guards. There was no evidence to support such statement and there was no evidence to show that the ill-treatment had increased during the last few months and in fact most of the incidents referred to in the statements occurred well before that time and I think it is clear that the increased mortality was due chiefly to the shortage of food and medical supplies.

He recommended that the sentences be reduced — for the 28 sentenced to 10 years or more, to three years; for the remainder, to one year. The Confirming Authority disregarded these recommendations and confirmed all the sentences unaltered.

On 10 June 1945, in consequence of Allied landings in other parts of Borneo and the imminent threat of a landing in the Miri area, a labour detachment of 51 POWs at Cape Lobang were disposed of by shooting and bayonetting. The sergeant-major in charge was sentenced to death (M2).[74] Of the guards (M3,[75] M4[76]), four were acquitted and the remaining 20 were sentenced to death (commuted to 10 years imprisonment).

The Burma–Siam Railway

Twenty-one of the Australian trials (18 at Singapore[77], three at Hong Kong[78]) were in connection with the ill-treatment of POWs on the Burma–Siam Railway. Of the 44 accused, four were acquitted, 16 were hanged and 24 sentenced to imprisonment (life, seven; 11–20 years, eight; 10 years, two; less than 10 years, seven). The typical charge was 'inhumanely treating POWs'. The accused were for the most part NCOs and guards in close contact with the POWs and the typical crimes were assaults and forcing the sick to work. In only five of the 21 trials were officers (Lt Col one, Capt. five, Lt four) charged. Among the 44 accused, 15 were Korean guards. Of the 16 hanged, six were officers, three were NCOs, one was a private, and six were Korean guards.

The principal railway trial was S12[79], in which Lt Col Nagatomo (CO of No. 3 POW Branch), five officers, two NCOs, one interpreter and six Korean guards were charged with committing a war crime in that between 25 October 1942 and 1 May 1944 in the construction of the Burma–Siam Railway between Thanbyuzayat and

74 M2, Sgt-Maj. Sugino, T, NAC A471 80716.

75 M3, Matsumoto, H et al., NAC A471 81214.

76 M4, Hirota, S et al., NAC A471 81204.

77 NAC A471 81201–3, 81242–4, 81246–8, 81250–1, 81300–1, 81639–41, 81655, 81659.

78 NAC A471 81638, 81660, 81662.

79 S12, Lt-Col Nagatomo, Y, NAC A471 81655.

Niki they 'illtreated POWs thereby causing deaths of many of them and bodily injury, damage to health and physical suffering of many others of the said POWs'. Nagatomo and two of the officers were also charged on six additional counts of ordering the shooting of recaptured POWs. Nagatomo, two officers, one NCO and four Korean guards were sentenced to death; three officers, to life imprisonment; two Korean guards, to 20 and six years respectively. The interpreter and one Korean guard were acquitted. The court made specific findings of fact against each of those convicted. For example against the Korean, Hirahara (sentenced to death): '(i) Frequent brutal assaults on POWs including Ebaugh, Zummo, Tims, Ritchie, Gibbons, Collins, Hall and Lt Hard; (ii) Forcing sick PsW to work; (iii) Frequently assaulting many sick POWs including Trim, Joyner, Williams, Reed, Smith, Forgey, Bray, Ward and Hall'.

Tan Toey Camp, Ambon

Trial M45[80] commenced at Ambon on 2 January 1946 and ended at Morotai on February 15th. In this trial 91 persons were charged with ill-treatment of Australian and Dutch POWs at Tan Toey Camp, Ambon, during the period February 1942 and August 1945. There were 15 separate charges covering the following general categories: (i) assaults; (ii) withholding of adequate food, medical supplies and medical treatment; (iii) imposition of unreasonably heavy and dangerous labour. In addition to numerous individual attacks, the assaults included two large-scale protracted beatings: in July 1942, 33 Dutch POWs were beaten for some two hours for conveying messages to their families without permission; in November 1942, 25 Australian POWs were systematically beaten and tortured (some for as long as 11 days) for procuring food from the native population. In each of these incidents deaths and serious injuries resulted. Of the 548 POWs in the camp in October 1942, 379 died of illness, 17 were executed, 13 escaped and in August 1945 there were only 139 survivors.

Of the 91 accused, the court acquitted 55. It sentenced four to death — a naval captain (the Commander of the garrison unit), a naval lieutenant (the Deputy Commander), a sub lieutenant (the Commander of the camp guard company), the camp manager (a civilian). The garrison Medical Officer (a lieutenant commander) was sentenced to 18 months imprisonment. Of the 31 other ranks found guilty, the sentences were: 12–20 years, five; 5–10 years, 11; less than five years, 15.

Hainan Island

In November 1942, 263 Australian and about 240 other Allied POWs were moved from Ambon to a POW camp on Hainan Island controlled and staffed by 4 Yokosuka Special Naval Landing Force (SNLF), where they remained for the rest of the war.

80 M45, Nav. Capt. Shirozu, W et al., NAC 471 81709.

Their rations were inadequate and were progressively reduced (in February 1945 the daily rice ration was 450 grams; by May they were receiving less than 170 grams), they were denied medical supplies and assistance, they were compelled to engage in heavy labour (including the construction of defence works) even when sick, and assaults and ill-treatment by the guards were common. Of the 263 Australians, 72 died. Among the POWs as a whole, there were 626 cases of the deficiency disease, beri-beri, resulting in 26 deaths in 1943, and there were 67 deaths, principally from malnutrition and starvation, between March and August 1945.

This was the subject of trial HK3[81] in which 17 members of 4 Yokosuka SNLF were charged with being 'concerned in the inhumane treatment of … POWs thereby contribution to the deaths of some and causing bodily injury, damage to health and physical and mental pain and suffering to many of such POWs'. The 17 accused consisted of the following: (i) Force HQ officers — the three successive commanding officers (Nav. Capt.), their two successive senior medical officers (SMO), and their two successive principal supply officers (Nav. Lt); (ii) camp HQ staff — the Camp Adjutant (Nav. Lt), the two successive camp supply officers (CSO) (Sub Lt) and one of their Supply Assistants (Ldg. Seaman); (iii) camp guards — three CPO and one civilian: (iv) Force AA Regt. — the commanders (Nav. Lt) of two AA Bty to which POWs were assigned for construction work.

The case for the prosecution was, inter alia, that each of the CPOs had himself assaulted POWs as well as permitting their subordinates to do so, that both Bty Cdrs had failed to control the conduct of their subordinates in charge of working parties and that one of the Bty Cdrs had himself inflicted cruel beatings, and that the Supply Assistant had assaulted POWs, had diluted the rations with floor sweepings, and had confiscated the POWs' scales to prevent their recording the amounts issued.

The sentences (after commutations and mitigations by the Confirming Authority on the recommendation of the JAG) ranged among the other ranks from 14 to one years and among the officers from 20 years (the SMO from 1942 to March 1945) to six months (the CO from November 1944 to January 1945 — acquitted on the principal charge but convicted on the second charge of employing POWs on 'work having connection with the operations of war'). The other two CO and the other SMO received 12 years. The two principal supply officers received 10 and four years. Of the two camp supply officers one was acquitted, the other (regarded by the POWs as well-intentioned but ineffective in securing compliance with his instructions among his staff) received one year which was remitted after he had served five months.

81 HK3, Nav. Capt. Tahara, S et al., NAC A471 81950.

Indian POWs

During 1943 several thousand of the Indian troops captured at Singapore were brought to New Guinea, New Britain and Bougainville as labourers. Ninety-nine of the Australian trials (about one-third) arose out of their subsequent ill-treatment there. In 66 of these (including the 'command responsibility' trials of the theatre Commander Gen. Imamura[82] and the Army Commander Lt Gen. Adachi,[83] in which the ill-treatment of Indian and Chinese labourers was among the principal charges) convictions were obtained. Thirty-six of those accused were sentenced to death.

In these cases not only the elements of the charge, but also the jurisdiction of the court depended on the truth of the affidavits of the prosecution witnesses. If (as the Japanese claimed and the Indians denied) the latter had joined Japan's Indian National Army, then it is arguable their ill-treatment became a matter for a Japanese and not an international tribunal.

The following are some examples of the Indian cases.

In R72 two subalterns received death sentences for executing without trial at Arigau (Bougainville) in April 1945 15 Indians apprehended deserting with arms and food.[84] In R90 a captain and two subalterns were sentenced to 10, five and two years for the execution in similar circumstances of 12 Indians at Tenin-Bau-Bau (Bougainville) in January of that year.[85]

R41 arose out of the shooting of two Indians at Parom (New Guinea) in August 1944. In a quarrel, the two Indians beat another, who complained to a guard. Thereupon a sergeant-major, a corporal and a lance-corporal beat the two Indians senseless and bound them. Half-an-hour later they were joined by another sergeant-major who shot the two Indians on the orders of the Platoon Commander. The latter was sentenced to death; each of the other four, to 15 years.[86]

A number of the Indian trials involved ill-treatment of individual POWs resulting in death.

In R142 a sergeant-major was convicted on 13 counts of murder and sentenced to death. Each charge involved beatings that he had administered to Indians working in the vicinity of Parom (New Guinea) as a result of which, it was alleged, each had died within a few days.[87]

82 R175, Gen. Imamura, H, NAC A471 81635.
83 R173, Lt-Gen. Adachi, H, NAC A471 81652.
84 R72, Lt Hironaka, T et al., NAC A471 80985.
85 R90, Capt. Ikeba, T et al., NAC A471 81007.
86 R41, Lt Mitsuba et al., NAC A471 80787.
87 R142, Sgt-Maj. Kaminaka, T, NAC A471 81040.

In R33 two NCOs received death sentences for the murder of an Indian at Bitawanas (New Britain) in January 1945. They had forced a sick Indian to carry a heavy load, causing him to collapse. They then kicked and beat him, causing him to vomit blood. He died two days later.[88]

In R38 L./Cpl Maeda was sentenced to death for the murder of an Indian at Kurringe (New Guinea) in February 1945. In an affidavit jemadar Chint Singh deposed that he saw Maeda severely beat the deceased with a big stick so that he bled and became unconscious; the deceased said that he was beaten because he had not cleaned Maeda's boots perfectly; Maeda forced him to work while still suffering from the beating as a result of which he became progressively weaker and died three weeks later.[89]

Chinese POWs

Late in 1943 some 1,500 Chinese troops were brought as labourers to the New Britain – New Guinea theatre from the region of China under the control of the puppet, Wang Ching-Wei regime. Their ill-treatment was the subject of 22 of the Australian trials, in 20 of which convictions were obtained. In R55 two NCOs and seven Formosan guards were on 16 April 1946 sentenced to death by a court consisting of three Australian and two Chinese officers for in March 1943 shooting 30 of the sick among some 800 Chinese POWs working for the 26 Field Supply Depot at Rabaul. The sentences were confirmed on June 28th and the two NCOs and two of the Formosans hanged on July 17th.[90] The execution of the other five Formosans was deferred so that they could testify as crown witnesses in the 'command responsibility' trial of Maj. Gen. Hirota, the GOC supply depots in Rabaul, on the charge of 'failing to control the members of his command whereby they committed brutal atrocities …'. On 3 April 1947 a court consisting of a major general and six other officers sentenced Hirota to seven years imprisonment.[91] It also addressed a memorandum to the District Commandant strongly recommending that the transcript of the Hirota trial be closely examined with a view to quashing the convictions against the five surviving Formosans:

> After carefully examining the evidence submitted to the Military Court which tried these Formosans, the present Court has very grave doubts whether such evidence is sufficient to establish their guilt. In forming this opinion, the Court has the advantage of observing the demeanour of the five Formosans while in the witness box. While the Military Court by which they were tried

88 R33, Sgt-Maj. Hasegawa, J et al., NAC A471 80732.

89 R38, L./Cpl Maeda, B, NAC A471 80784.

90 R55, Sgt Matsushita, T et al., NAC A471 80915.

91 R172, Maj.-Gen. Hirota, A, NAC A471 81653.

> had a similar advantage, this Court had the additional advantage of hearing the evidence of Maj Gen Hirota, which was, for some reason, not called by the Defending Officer at the original trial.

The proceedings of the original trial were accordingly re-examined by the JAG. He reported that he remained of the opinion that there was ample evidence to justify the original court in its decision and that he was therefore not prepared to recommend a review of the case and a quashing of the convictions. He suggested that 'in all the circumstances' the CA commute the death penalty to a long period of imprisonment. He expressed astonishment that men should be kept awaiting execution for such a long period. This alone, he considered, more than justified commutation. In forwarding the JAG's recommendation to the Adjutant-General the DPW&I added his own recommendation:

> whereas these Formosans and many others, have been sentenced to death for crimes committed while under the command of Maj-Gen Hirota, the Court in sentencing this Japanese General, saw fit to impose 7 years' imprisonment. Therefore, as this officer has only been awarded this light sentence after being found guilty of the responsibility for the crime committed by his subordinates, it is not considered the death penalty should be carried out in this case.

The Adjutant-General on 27 June 1947 commuted the death sentences to life imprisonment.[92]

United Kingdom POWs

A working party of 599 UK POWs arrived in Rabaul in October 1942. Of these, 517 drowned in Rabaul harbour when the Japanese ship taking them to the Solomons was sunk by American aircraft. Of the 82 who remained in New Britain only 18 survived. Two of the deaths were the subject of Australian trials. In R62 a Japanese private was on 7 May 1946 sentenced to death for the murder on Wattom Island in May 1945 of a British officer who was bedridden with malaria, beri-beri and a tropical ulcer. The officer had spilt a bed-pan, whereupon the accused beat him severely on the ulcer causing it to bleed profusely. He died four days later. Apparently the court did not believe the evidence of the Japanese Medical Officer who had written the death certificate. He testified that the cause of death was black-water fever and that the corpse bore no signs of a beating.[93] In R65 the same Japanese was, the following day, sentenced to five years imprisonment for at the same time repeatedly beating another sick POW and for reducing his rations. This POW, too, had died.[94]

---

92 Regulation 19 of the Australian *Regulations for the Trial of War Criminals* (which is similar to *Army Act* §57(2) and AO81/1945 §12) enabled a confirmed sentence to be mitigated, remitted or commuted by a General Officer holding a command or rank not inferior to that of the original Confirming Officer.

93 R62, L./Cpl Tokawa, M, NAC A471 80908.

94 R65, L./Cpl Tokawa, M, NAC A471 81069.

The command responsibility trials

In July 1946 when the first series of trials at Rabaul ended, Flannagan sought from the Adjutant-General a policy direction regarding trials of more than a dozen generals (commanders and staff-officers) held as war crimes suspects but against whom specific charges had not yet been formulated:

> It appears that all or most of these officers were in command or were staff officers in areas where most shocking and brutal atrocities were carried out. Such atrocities having been proved in Aust War Crimes Courts and appropriate action taken against the actual perpetrators or others directly concerned with the crime it is considered that all or most of these officers should have knowledge of the conduct of the personnel of their command and therefore can be held responsible accordingly.

He argued that 'when atrocities were consistently committed in their commands and in justice to their subordinates who have been punished … these seniors must at least be arraigned before a court'.[95] The matter was referred to the Director of Legal Services (DLS) at Army Headquarters and, after examining the dossier against Lt Gen. Adachi (GOC 18 Army), he advised that on the basis of evidence presented at certain of the trials of his subordinates for the ill-treatment of Indians a charge would lie of 'disregarding and failing to discharge his duty as Commander by permitting the members of his command to murder prisoners of war'.

On September 4th the Adjutant-General authorised the trial of Adachi and the other senior officers on such charges wherever there seemed to be 'a reasonable chance of conviction'. By December the preparation of the cases had been completed for three such trials: Gen. Imamura (GOC 8 Army Group), Lt Gen. Adachi (GOC 18 Army — in New Guinea) and Lt Gen. Kanda (GOC 17 Army — in Bougainville). In each case the victims were Indian or Chinese or Indonesian POWs brought as labourers to their areas of command. In each trial, there were to be charged jointly with the GOC his two principal staff officers. In January (1947), however, the DLS advised that there was no case against the staff officers: 'Although an army commander, being charged under the law of war with the duty of preventing the troops under his command from committing violations of the law of war, may be charged with personal responsibility for failure to take steps to prevent violations, I know of no authority or principle which fastens a similar responsibility on his staff officers …'. Staff officers, he advised, could be properly charged only with violations in which they had personally participated or which they had expressly permitted. (This is similar to the view taken by an Allied tribunal in Germany in the High Command trial: 'In the absence of participation in criminal orders or their execution within a command, a Chief-of-Staff does not become criminally responsible for criminal acts occurring therein …').

95 DPW&I to Actg Adjt-Gen., 9 July 1946 (NAM MP742/1 336/1/1205).

In the evidence assembled for these cases the DLS could see no basis for any charges against any of the staff officers named except Lt Gen. Kato (Chief of Staff, 8 Army Group), who he considered could be charged with 'unlawfully employing prisoners of war on work having a direct connection with the war' contrary to the provisions of the Hague Convention. As regards the commanders, he considered that charges lay against Imamura and Adachi (but not against Kanda as the atrocities in question had occurred very shortly after he assumed command and in a location distant from and out of communication with his headquarters).

The outcome was that, in addition to Imamura and Adachi, Maj.-Gen. Hirota, the GOC supply depots in Rabaul, was charged with command responsibility regarding the ill-treatment of Indian and Chinese POWs and Lt Gen. Baba, the Corps Commander in North Borneo, with command responsibility regarding the Sandakan–Ranau death marches. In each case the wording of the charge was identical with that on which Gen. Yamashita had been arraigned before an American military tribunal at Manila: 'While a commander … unlawfully disregarded and failed to discharge his duty as such Commander to control the conduct of the members of his command whereby they committed brutal atrocities and other high crimes against …'.

Kato was tried on the charge recommended by the DLS These five trials took place at Rabaul during the period March to June 1947 before courts consisting of a Major General and six other officers (in the Baba trial, five other officers), the President and the same four of the other members participating in every trial. Except for the Baba trial the prosecution was conducted by a civilian KC and his junior.

On this question of a commander's responsibility to prevent the commission of war crimes by his troops there had been among international lawyers two schools of thought. According to one view he was responsible only when he 'ordered or, with knowledge thereof and with power to intervene, abstained from preventing or taking measures to prevent … violations of the laws or customs of war'. This was the doctrine accepted by the Allied Commission on Responsibilities which reported to the Paris Peace Conference in 1919. It is reflected in the wording of Count 55 of the IMTFE indictment: 'deliberately and recklessly disregarded their legal duty to take adequate steps to secure the observance and prevent breaches …'. According to the other, his responsibility went further and included a duty to take steps to see whether offences were being committed. The Australian courts convicted each of the commanders, the sentences being: Baba, death (R176);[96] Adachi, life (R173);[97] Imamura, 10 years (R175);[98] Hirota, seven years (R172).[99] Imamura's conviction coupled with a substantially lighter sentence than Adachi's suggests that the court subscribed to the latter doctrine and believed that Adachi was aware that crimes were

96 R176, Lt-Gen. Baba, M, NAC A471 81631.
97 R173, Lt-Gen. Adchi, H, NAC A471 81652.
98 R175, Gen. Imamura, H, NAC A471 81635.
99 R172, Maj.-Gen. Hirota, A, NAC A471 81653.

being committed but that Imamura as a result of culpable negligence was unaware. The JAG accepted the wide responsibility doctrine. In his report on the Imamura case he argued that 'the laws and usages of war impose a responsibility upon commanding officers to take all possible measures to prevent violations of those laws by troops in their command'. Some months later the IMTFE, approaching the subject from a slightly different angle, arrived at a similar result: 'An Army Commander must be at the same pains to ensure obedience to his orders in this respect as he would in respect of other orders he has issued on matters of the first importance'.

The court acquitted Kato (R174).[100] The case against him was that an 8 Army Group order stating that 'The Indians and Indonesians of the Special Duty Coys are to be retained and employed until the end as a part of the Army strength …' bore his signature. The defence he tendered was that: (i) in the Japanese Army every order originating from a GOC is drafted in its final form by a Staff-Officer and bears the latter's signature; (ii) the Indians and Indonesians were no longer POWs but Japanese volunteers. The acquittal is difficult to justify in logic. The first proposition does not amount to a defence: his signature was proof of participation in the illegal act. The second proposition the court had rejected in the Adachi trial. On the other hand the acquittal is not difficult to explain. Enough was enough. They had just sentenced Adachi for the Indian POWs and Imamura's turn was coming. Kato was a lesser link in the chain and they ruled their line under the commanders.

Murder and ill-treatment of natives

Ocean Island

The execution of the entire population of Ocean Island on about 20 August 1945 on the orders of the Commander of the local Naval Garrison Unit (Lt Cdr.) was the subject of five trials, R51, 52, 53, 68, 70.[101] The day after the natives were informed by the Japanese of the war's end they were assembled, divided into about five groups, marched to different sections of the cliffs overlooking the sea, bound, blindfolded and shot. The bodies were weighted and dumped at sea. The Lieutenant-Commander, the Supply Officer (who had separated the victims into groups for execution), the four company commanders (Lt) and three of the platoon commanders (Sub Lts) were sentenced to death (on the recommendation of the JAG the Supply Officer's sentence was reduced to 20 years). Among the remaining platoon commanders: six sub lieutenants and one Sub Lieutenant (junior grade) received 20 years imprisonment; three (Sub Lts, junior grade), 15 years; and one (Sub Lt, junior grade) was acquitted. Two other ranks received seven years and one was acquitted.

100 R174, Lt-Gen. Kato, R, NAC A471 81065.

101 R51, Lt-Cdr Suzuki, N et al., NAC A471 80796; R52, Nav. Lt Sakuma, W et al., NAC A471 80797; R53, Nav. Lt Sakata, J et al., NAC A471 80798; R68, Nav. Lt Miyasaka, D et al., NAC A471 81071; R70, Nav. Lt Yamaguchi, N et al., NAC A471 80983.

Nauru

In July 1943 the Commander of the naval garrison at Nauru (Lt Cdr) issued orders to his Adjutant (WO) that as, in the air raids then taking place, there was the danger that the lepers (about 20 in number) in the isolation hospital would escape and infect the rest of the population, they were to be embarked in a small boat which was to be towed out to sea and sunk by gunfire. Any that survived the sinking were to be shot in the water by rifle fire. In November 1948 the Adjutant, a Petty Officer and a Seaman were tried for the murder of the lepers (the Lieutenant Commander had in 1946 been sentenced to death and executed for the murder of the five Caucasian residents of Nauru in March 1943 (R93)).[102] The Petty Officer and the Seaman were on the towing vessel, the former in charge of the gun crew which fired the shots, the latter as lookout. The Adjutant and the Petty Officer were sentenced to life imprisonment, the Seaman to four years. On the recommendation of the JAG the conviction and sentence of the Seaman were not confirmed.[103]

At Nauru in September 1944 a native employed by the Japanese in producing an essential foodstuff, toddy, was detected diluting and stealing it. He was sentenced by the naval officer in charge of native affairs (Sub Lt) to three days imprisonment during which period he was to receive 10 strokes of the cane daily. During those three days he was kept tied to a tree and was repeatedly beaten in turn by this officer's subordinates (four sub lieutenants and a Warrant Officer) using such instruments as a walking stick and a heavy pole. In R54 all five were convicted of torture. The sub lieutenant in charge was sentenced to 20 years. Of his subordinates, two were sentenced to death, one to 20 years and two to 15 years.[104]

New Britain

At Vunarima in New Britain in September 1944 the local Military Police detachment arrested 17 natives and one half-caste suspected of acts of sabotage, possession of firearms and conspiracy to assist the Allies, and secured a partial confession from the suspected leader, the half-caste. The detachment Commander (a subaltern) then held a conference with his two sergeant majors at which it was decided that all 18 were guilty of offences and to execute them. They were bound together, blindfolded and decapitated. In R26 the two sergeant majors (who also took part in the decapitations) and five of their subordinates were charged with murder. (The detachment Commander had not been apprehended.) The court acquitted the five subordinates and sentenced the two sergeant-majors to life imprisonment. The JAG recommended mitigation since, although their conduct constituted a war crime, they were acting within the scope of Japanese military law. The Confirming Authority reduced the sentences to two years.[105]

102 R93, Lt-Cdr Nakayama, H, NAC A471 81010.
103 HK10, Sub Lt Sakata, T, et al., NAC A471 81661.
104 R54, Sub Lt Sakoda, H, et al., NAC A471 80799.
105 R26, Sgt-Maj. Ohashi et al., NAC A471 80750.

At Ramale in New Britain on four occasions during 1945 a Sergeant Major and Sergeant of the Military Police in the course of interrogating natives in custody to secure confessions used two of the Military Police's well known torturing techniques: (i) making the victim kneel, inserting a pole behind his knees and placing heavy weight on it; (ii) placing him on his back and pouring water down his throat. In R8[106] and R7[107] they were convicted of torture and sentenced to 30 and 25 years (reduced in each case by the Confirming Authority to 10 years).

Murder and ill-treatment of local Chinese

New Ireland

During 1944 and 1945 on a number of occasions the Lieutenant General in command in New Ireland authorised the Lumburua detachment of Military Police to execute Chinese, half-castes and natives held by them on charges of war treason. On the ground that such killings were executions without prior trial as required by the Hague Rules, nine persons who at various levels participated in the process — the Lieutenant General, his Legal Staff Officer (Lt Col), the Assistant Provost-Marshal (Capt.), the detachment Commander (WO) and the four NCOs who were the actual executioners — were charged with murder. In R127[108] the court acquitted the two most junior NCOs (corporals) but found the rest guilty of murder and sentenced them to death. The Confirming Authority, however, quashed all the convictions. In so doing he followed the advice of the JAG, who argued that the court had been misdirected by its Judge-Advocate when he instructed it that the presence of the accused before the 'tribunal' and his ability to speak on his own behalf and call witnesses were essential elements of a trial. According to the JAG:

> A trial within the meaning of the Hague Rules is the ascertainment by a competent authority of the truth or otherwise of allegations made against the accused person where such competent authority applies its mind fairly and impartially to the matters at issue … . I see no reason why the accused must be present before the tribunal which decides upon the verdict and sentence … . The test is not what does British jurisprudence understand by a trial, but what does a trial mean applying the principles of the laws of nations derived from the usages established among civilised people from the laws of humanity and from the dictates of public conscience.

Witnesses had testified that the procedure in force had been that in each case the charge was investigated and the Lieutenant General, on the basis of the investigation report, made a decision upon the guilt or otherwise of the person charged. The JAG

106 R8, Sgt-Maj. Kitada, Y, NAC A471 80741.
107 R7, Sgt Tagai, T, NAC A471 80743.
108 R127, Lt-Gen. Ito, T, et al., NAC A471 81030.

advised that if these witnesses were believed, then the essential elements of trial were present and, in so far as in international law war treason was a crime punishable by death, the executions were lawful.

In some other cases involving the execution of natives (in New Guinea and New Britain) and the essential elements of prior 'trial', either the accused was acquitted (R29),[109] or on the advice of the JAG either the findings of guilty were not confirmed (R31)[110] or the sentences were substantially reduced (R26).[111] It may be noted that the decisions of some other Allied tribunals (e.g. a US Military Commission in *Lt-Gen Isayama and others* and the Norwegian Supreme Court in *Latza and others*) indicate that they interpreted the Hague Rules to go further and to require, in addition to fair and impartial investigation, adequate opportunity to the accused to defend himself and present counter-evidence.

In January 1945 the Military Police detachment at Loguramau (New Ireland) interrogated a Chinese woman suspected of providing assistance to a crashed airman. In the course of the interrogations the detachment Commander (a warrant officer), another Warrant Officer and a Sergeant on separate occasions instructed native police to insert bananas into her vagina. The detachment Commander struck her more than 40 times with a cane. In R35 all three were found guilty of torturing and sentenced to death.[112]

New Britain

Two trials arose out of the execution of Woo Chin Kiong at Massowa in New Britain in October 1944. Woo had been arrested on a charge of illegal possession of dynamite and inciting the natives against the Japanese. After interrogating him and two native witnesses, the Sergeant Major in charge of the Massowa Military Police Detachment decided that he was guilty and sent a report to this effect to the Provost Marshal at Rabaul (a colonel). The latter replied ordering his execution. The Sergeant Major himself decapitated Woo. Two of his subordinates were present at the execution, one escorting the prisoner, the other blindfolding him. In so far as Woo had been executed without trial, the Sergeant Major and his two subordinates were charged with murder. The court on 18 December 1945 sentenced all three to death. In his advice to the Confirming Authority, the JAG expressed 'grave doubts' whether the actions of the two subordinates constituted a crime and suggested that he quash the convictions against them. The Confirming Authority on February 15th confirmed the finding of guilty against all three and in the case of the two subordinates commuted the sentence to two years imprisonment. The Sergeant Major was hanged on March 20th.[113] The Provost Marshal was tried for

109 R29, Lt-Gen. Kawakubo, S, NAC A471 80736.
110 R31, Capt. Shinohara, E, et al., NAC A471 80734.
111 R26, Sgt-Maj. Ohashi, S, et al., NAC A471 80750.
112 R35, WO Matsumoto, T, NAC A471 80782.
113 R3, Sgt-Maj. Inagaki, M, NAC A471 80731.

the same offence on March 28th, found guilty and sentenced to death (R30). This was confirmed by the Confirming Authority on June 11th. Subsequently, however, the Confirming Authority received a plea for leniency on the Provost Marshal's behalf from the Roman Catholic Bishop of Rabaul and other priests who stated that during their internment at Vunapope and Ramale they had been well treated and that this they attributed to his efforts. In the light of this, the Confirming Authority on July 8th commuted the sentence to seven years imprisonment.[114]

Late in 1944, in order to exact her consent to sexual intercourse with him, a Military Police Sergeant at Massowa (New Britain) tied a Chinese woman to a tree for three hours and put ants on her face and body. She consented only when he threatened to execute her husband. This was the subject of the first of the Rabaul war crimes trials. On 12 December 1945 the Sergeant was convicted of rape and torture and sentenced to death by hanging.[115] It is one of the very few cases in which the accused did not exercise his right to submit a petition to the Confirming Authority against the verdict and sentence.[116] According to one of the Japanese Defending Officers, the C-in-C, Gen. Imamura, regarded rape by a military policeman as such a heinous crime that he forbade the condemned man to appeal.[117]

Nauru

In R69 a paymaster Warrant Officer and six petty officers were sentenced to death for the murder of a Chinese gardener, Lee, on Nauru in December 1944. At a time of acute food shortage, Lee was suspected of stealing pumpkins, the staple foodstuff. He was beaten, immersed in a well and again beaten. During the second beating boiling water was poured over his legs. While undergoing this he died.[118]

Murder and ill-treatment of Caucasian residents

New Ireland

When in March 1944 the intense Allied air attacks commenced there were in Kavieng (New Ireland) under Navy control about 23 Australian planters and about nine Roman Catholic priests (one was a Luxemburger; the remainder, German, i.e. Axis nationals) housed in two internment camps in the vicinity of Kavieng No. 1 Airfield. On about March 17th, some days after the commencement of the air raids, these two groups were told to pack their belongings for a move to Rabaul. They were then escorted by a party headed by the senior Platoon Commander of the local security detachment to a spot about 50 metres from Kavieng South Wharf, where two barges loaded with cement sinkers had been moored. There they were

114 R30, Col Kikuchi, S, NAC A471 80735.
115 R1, Sgt Yaki, Y, NAC A471 80747.
116 Australia, *Statutory Rules*, 1945 no. 164 (Regulations for the Trial of War Criminals), section 17.
117 Rabauru Keiykai, *Rabauru* (privately printed, 1980), p. 164.
118 R69, WO Hatakeyama, Y, NAC A471 80982.

blindfolded and, one by one, led to the edge of the wharf and required to sit. Sailors then placed a noose over each victim's head and strangled him. The bodies were weighted with the sinkers and dumped in Steffen Strait.

After the surrender in August 1945 the perpetrators of this crime and their superiors at Fleet Headquarters at Rabaul stated that these internees had been evacuated from Kavieng on 17 February 1944 on the *Kōwa Maru*, a vessel sunk by Allied aircraft on February 21st. This was not believed — particularly as, at the time, there had been rumours among the local population that they had been executed. Furthermore — a fact of which Fleet Headquarters was unaware — the US Navy had rescued some survivors from the *Kōwa Maru* and the reports of their interrogations showed that it had taken no POWs or internees on board.

In HK 1 the Naval Officer in Command in New Ireland (a captain) and five of his subordinates were charged with the massacre of the 23 Australians in this group and found guilty. At the trial the Captain testified that, when the air raids had become intense and the Executive Officer of the Naval Garrison Unit sought instructions regarding the internees, he had ordered that in the event of an enemy landing they were to be killed. The prosecution argued that the order was manifestly criminal and that accordingly those who at each level issued it and carried it out were guilty. The court sentenced the Captain to death and the others to terms of imprisonment ranging from 20 years in the case of the Executive Officer to four years in the case of the executioner.[119]

New Britain

In November 1943 Father Mayrhofer, a Roman Catholic missionary at Ramale in New Britain (a German national) was arrested by the Military Police on suspicion of assisting the Allies. In the course of his interrogation by a Sergeant Major he was blindfolded, tied to a tree, prodded with a pistol and told that he would be shot. He was then held on the ground and a towel was placed over his face. Water was then poured over the towel. This continued for more than an hour, during which time he swallowed much water and nearly suffocated. He was kept handcuffed for more than a month and interrogated twice daily — always with attendant beatings. He was required to sleep in the open, in irons. In R5 the Sergeant Major was convicted of torturing and sentenced to death. This was commuted by the Confirming Authority to 15 years imprisonment. In this trial there was no Judge Advocate and none of the members of the court had legal qualifications. As a result, a procedural irregularity disadvantageous to the accused occurred: the Defending Officer's closing address, instead of following that of the Prosecuting Officer, preceded it.[120]

119 HK1, Rear-Adm. Tamura, R, et al., NAC A471 81645.

120 R5, Sgt-Maj. Furukawa, T, NAC A471 80745.

Infiltration parties

Nine trials arose out of the execution or torture of captured members of infiltration parties.[121]

The Otakwa party

In November 1944 a patrol of five Australian other ranks and two natives was disembarked from a Dutch minesweeper into a small boat in the Eilanden River in Dutch New Guinea to conduct a three-day patrol to ascertain whether there were Japanese troops in the Otakwa area. The party was ambushed and all but the Australian signals sergeant were killed in the encounter. He was taken to the Japanese outpost at Kaparapoka (which consisted of two Japanese subalterns, two NCOs and about 16 native troops) and was confined there until executed by firing squad in mid-March. In M23 the outpost Commander, a glass-moulder in civil life, aged 27, stood trial for murder. In his defence he claimed that he received orders by wireless from 5 Division at Kai to execute the prisoner. The court sentenced the Subaltern to death. The JAG did not recommend mitigation: '[He] should have known that it is illegal in International Law to execute a prisoner without trial and the fact that he had received orders from superior authority to carry out the execution is not considered of itself to be a defence, more particularly when the accused is the senior officer in charge of the party'.

He was executed at Morotai on 3 March 1946.[122]

The Ainbai party

In January 1943 a party of 'M' Special Force consisting of a Dutch NCO, an Australian signals Sergeant and two Indonesians was despatched to establish a long-term intelligence post in the Hollandia area of Dutch New Guinea. By September they had reached Ainbai in the vicinity of Aitape. The Dutch NCO was killed in an ambush on October 4th. The remainder of the party retreated but were betrayed to the Japanese by natives about a fortnight later. They were executed at Aitape on October 24th. When the Americans captured Hollandia in April 1944 photographs of the execution were found on the dead body of a Japanese officer and natives identified as the executioner of one of the Indonesians, Yunome, a member of the Navy's native affairs detachment at Aitape, which consisted of four Japanese civilians (of rank equivalent to sub lieutenant) and half-a-dozen Formosan other ranks. Yunome was one of a number of Japanese sick captured by the Americans at Hollandia on April 25th. Among his belongings was his diary in which he described the interrogations (at which he was the interpreter) and the execution. In R143

121 M23 (NAC A471 80774), D1 (NAC A471 80708), R143 (NAC A471 81041), R183 (NAC A471 81210), LN5 (NAC A471 81945), LN9 (NAC A471 81947), LN20 (NAC A471 81964), LN21 (NAC A471 81961).
122 M23, Capt. Kato, K, NAC A471 80774.

he was charged with the murder of the Indonesian. The case advanced for the defence was that in decapitating the prisoner he was acting under the command of his Detachment Commander who, in turn, was carrying out an order received by wireless from the Commander, 2 Special Base Force at Wewak (Rear Admiral Kamada), to execute the prisoners. Yunome was sentenced to death on 28 June 1946. With this the JAG concurred: 'In my opinion the finding and sentence are valid. It was within the knowledge of the accused that the victim of his sword had had nothing in the way of a trial'.[123] The carrying out of the sentence was, however, deferred in case Yunome should be required as a prosecution witness in other trials.

The detachment Commander, Yasuno (who himself executed one of the prisoners), and the other executioner appear not to have survived the war. Rear Adm. Kamada was in Dutch custody awaiting trial for murders in Borneo (for which he was sentenced to death and executed on 18 December 1947). In July 1947, in R183, Kamada's Senior Staff Officer at Wewak (Captain Noto) and Watanabe, the Chief Petty Officer in charge of the garrison platoon at Aitape, were charged jointly with the murder of the three prisoners. At this trial the defence tendered an affidavit from Kamada that he had ordered the executions and that his order was pursuant to the finding and sentence of a Military Punishment Tribunal consisting of himself, his Chief-of-Staff and a civilian lawyer (convened in accordance with Combined Fleet Confidential Ordinance no.s 68 and 69 of 1941), which had examined the interrogation reports and on that basis found the prisoners guilty of espionage. Noto testified that he had received the order verbally from Kamada and had conveyed it verbally to Watanabe through a Warrant Officer in charge of a barge departing from Wewak for Aitape at that time. Watanabe testified that he had received the order in this manner and that the prisoners were in his custody, but that, when Yasuno represented to him that since his detachment had captured the prisoners and conducted the interrogations it should provide the executioners, he had consented to this. In addressing the court the Judge Advocate advised that: (i) if there had been a trial of the three prisoners the actions of Noto and Watanabe would not amount to murder; (ii) although in international law the presence of the accused was not mandatory, among the essential ingredients of a trial were that the accused should have the opportunity of knowing the charge and the evidence adduced against him and of putting forward his defence. The court found Noto and Watanabe guilty of murder and sentenced them to 20 and seven years respectively. The Legal Officer reporting on the case recommended some mitigation of sentence in the case of Noto because of: (i) the sentences imposed in other cases in respect of officers holding similar appointments; (ii) Noto's having taken up his posting only a few days previously; (iii) the fact that there had been some form of prior investigation.

123 R143, Nav.-Civ. Yunome, K, NAC A471 81041.

The JAG concurred in the finding and expressed the view that 'any form of trial which does not give the prisoner an opportunity of knowing that he is being charged or being heard in his defence cannot properly be called a trial under Public International Law'. (These are more rigorous criteria than the JAG enunciated in his advice the previous year in reviewing the case arising out of the execution of Chinese civilians in New Ireland. There, although there was no suggestion in the evidence that any of these requirements had been met, he had advised that the findings of guilty should not be confirmed — presumably because in that case the Judge Advocate had, in his opinion, misdirected the court in stipulating that an essential element of 'trial' was the presence of the accused and the right to speak and call witnesses). He suggested that Noto's sentence be mitigated to seven years. The Confirming Authority, however, confirmed both sentences unchanged.[124]

The Legal Officer reporting on the Noto trial suggested that, in the light of the evidence tendered and sentences imposed in that trial, the death sentence on Yunome should be reconsidered. The matter was referred to the JAG who on 29 September 1947 suggested commutation of Yunome's sentence to 10 years. This was effected by the Adjutant-General on October 9th.

The Batavia escapees: Operation 'Ki'

Another case revolving around the essential requirements of 'trial' for persons accused of spying or war treason was S11, Maj. Katsumura et al., in which the Commander of the Bogor Detachment of the Military Police (Maj. Karsumura) and five of his NCOs were charged with the unlawful execution of a group of three escaped POWs (two Australian, one Dutch) in hiding and a woman member of the Dutch underground who had been harbouring them. The POWs had escaped from a POW camp at Batavia in May 1942 and had remained at large for more than a year. The Bogor Detachment on 12 August 1943 captured the three hiding in a concealed cellar in the house of a Dutch resident and on September 5th executed them and the woman by decapitation. Katsumura, the NCO in charge of the execution party, and the four executioners were tried by an Australian court at Singapore in September 1946 on a charge of 'committing a war crime in that they at or near Bogor on 5/9/43 in violation of the laws and usages of war were concerned in the unlawful killing' of the four victims.

The prosecution contended that the victims had been executed without trial in contravention of Article 30 of the Hague Rules 30 which provides that 'a spy taken in the act shall not be punished without previous trial'.

124 R183, Nav. Capt. Noto, K, et al., NAC A471 81210.

The defence case was that the men had engaged in anti-Japanese activity, had obtained and passed on Japanese military information, were in possession of arms and incriminating documents and had resisted arrest and that the woman had aided them and conveyed military information to them. The defence further contended that trial had actually taken place in accordance with the procedure laid down in a directive titled *Ki Operation* issued by the C-in -C 16th Army in July 1943. Witnesses testified that the gist of the directive was as follows: (i) Instead of being referred to a court martial as in the past, each case of obstruction of military operations or the possession of arms will be reported to higher authority and sanction for the execution of the culprit requested on the prescribed form, to which will be attached photographs and all the evidence; (ii) When the sanction of the C-in-C has been received, execution by beheading will be performed by the Military Police detachment in whose custody the prisoner is held.

Katsumura testified that following the arrest of the prisoners he had despatched the completed pro forma and the attached testimony to Military Police HQ at Batavia which on September 3rd notified him that the C-in-C's sanction had been obtained and instructed him to perform the executions.

The defence argued that that in these circumstances the accused was entitled to believe that 'a trial by documents' had been performed which satisfied the requirements of Hague Convention Article 30.

The Australian court made the following finding: 'The Court finds you not guilty. The court in its finding is guided by the amendment to Para 443(as amended), Manual of Military Law, Page 288, Australian Edition'.

In the context of the court's finding the operative portion is the phrase 'not obviously unlawful'. Accordingly, the finding of the court means that it decided that the defendants had reasonable grounds for concluding that the *Ki Procedure* for trial in absentia constituted a trial as required by the Hague Rules and that the procedure had in fact been faithfully carried out.

The court made its finding on 30 September 1946. On reading it, 1 Aust. War Crimes Section, the unit at Singapore administering the trials and directing the prosecutions, the same day cabled Army HQ Melbourne seeking guidance on two points: (a) whether proceedings in absentia without any representation constitutes a trial under Hague Convention Article 30; (b) whether superior orders constitutes a legal defence where the order is unlawful but not obviously so. Whether, in fact, the prosecution must prove that the accused knew or should have known that the order was unlawful.

With the assistance of the Director of Legal Services, the DPW&I (a barrister in civil life) despatched an opinion on November 13th in which he cited the recent ruling of the JAG in case of Lt Gen. Ito et al., R127. The gist of the DPW&I's opinion is as follows:

> a. For a trial under Article 30 of the Hague Convention, it is not necessary that the accused be present or represented before the tribunal which determines the verdict and sentence. If, however, on account of the special status of the accused or for any other reason any Convention additional to the Hague convention becomes applicable to the case it must further be determined whether or not such additional Convention prohibits the trial in absentia of persons subject thereto.
>
> b. The principle applicable to the defence of 'superior orders' is that stated in MML Para 443 (as amended) … The onus is on the prosecution to prove that the order was obviously unlawful … or that the nature of the order and/or the facts known to the accused were such that he should have known that the order was unlawful or would raise such doubts in his mind as to his legality that he should refuse to carry it out.[125]

The Tambisan party

In February 1944 a Subaltern and two sergeants, members of an Australian reconnaissance party that had been introduced by submarine were captured in the vicinity of Tambisan in the Sandakan district in Borneo. On the completion of the investigation by the local Military Police they were in August sent to Jesselton for judicial examination preliminary to trial by court martial on a charge of espionage. The trial took place at Jesselton in December. They were sentenced to death and hanged. In LN15 the Corps Commander who convened the trial, the officer who conducted the preliminary examination and who prosecuted, and the two surviving members of the court were charged with murder and (as an alternative charge) with unlawfully disregarding their duty to try the three accused persons in accordance with the rules of International Law. The Australian court found all the accused not guilty. Although, as is the custom with military tribunals, it did not state its reasons, these are apparent in the frequent questioning addressed to the Prosecuting Officer by the President that are a feature of this case. There were two key issues — judicial immunity and whether the Australians were wearing uniform or had disguised themselves as civilians. In the words of the President: 'I take it that the question for us is not merely whether we consider the decision of the court-martial to be wrong, either in law or in fact, but surely there must be some evidence — if there is jurisdiction in that court — there must be some evidence of a wicked mind in the court and, of course, the Convening Officer, the Prosecutor also — if the Prosecutor can be said to have had any part in it'.

125 AWM226 18.

The prosecution argued that there was evidence of a wicked mind on the part of all concerned in that the evidence before the court martial that the men were not spies was so overwhelming that no reasonable man could honestly arrive at a contrary conclusion. The relevant provision of the Hague Convention provided that a person could be considered a spy only if he were acting clandestinely or on false pretences and that a soldier not wearing a disguise could not be considered a spy. The three Australians were wearing the regulation 'jungle-green' Australian Army uniform and were openly carrying arms, yet at every stage of the Japanese investigations and trial it was stated that they were not wearing uniforms. This was either deliberately accepting a palpable falsehood or being maliciously remiss in making no attempts to ascertain from informed sources what the Australian Army's combat uniform was. But among the evidence adduced at the Japanese investigations was testimony that the Australians were wearing neither their badges of rank nor their identity disks. Here again, the attitude of the Australian court and the importance which it attached to this issue can be gauged from the President's questioning:

> Now it is a matter of common knowledge … that Australian soldiers were required to wear at all times identity discs and were also required to carry a pay-book … . Also they were required to wear the badges of rank to which they were entitled … . Would not each of the accused be entitled to say to himself: I know that normally an Australian soldier wears an identity disc, that normally an Australian officer or N.C.O. wears his badges of rank?[126]

Captured air crews

Of the RAAF airmen shot down in New Guinea (excluding New Britain) and the Netherlands East Indies 66 were executed and only 15 (of whom 12 were from the same aircraft) survived the war.[127]

Tandjong Priok

The three survivors from a RAAF Catalina were beheaded at the execution ground of the Judicial Section, 16 Army HQ at Tandjong Priok on 5 February 1945. This was the subject of trial S14[128] in which the court passed the following sentences: on the GOC 16 Army who ordered that they be executed secretly without trial — death; on his Staff Officer Intelligence (Lt Col) who recommended this and conveyed the order — death; on his Chief Legal Officer (Lt Col) — 15 years; on the officer in charge of jail, who conducted the execution (Lt, judicial branch) — 10 years; on the executioner (Sgt Maj.) — seven years. The conviction and sentence of the Chief Legal Officer was not confirmed, the JAG advising that mere knowledge that the GOC had ordered the execution and failure to take any steps to prevent it was insufficient to sustain the charge.

126 LN15, Lt-Gen. Yamawaki, M, et al., NAC A471 81956.
127 'History of the Directorate of PW & Internees', pp. 446–47, AWM 780/1/6.
128 S14, Lt-Gen. Harada, K, et al., NAC A471 81632.

Ambon

In M43[129] three naval personnel were sentenced to death for the execution of four survivors from a RAAF Mitchell bomber at Ambon on 16 August 1944. Sub Lt Katayama had been in charge of the execution party and had himself executed one of the airmen. Sub Lt Takahashi had beheaded another. They were officers of the Volunteer Reserve aged 25 and 21 at the time of the offence. WO Uemura had been in charge of the escort and burial party. The JAG advised that the findings and sentences against Takahashi and Uemura should not be confirmed, since Takahashi could not be expected to know that the order for execution was illegal and Uemura's mere presence did not amount to participation in the crime. As regards Katayama, he advised that the fact that he was ordered to carry out the executions by a senior officer should be considered in mitigation. Despite this advice, the Confirming Authority confirmed the findings and sentences against all three. In the case of Takahashi and Uemura this seems a clear breach of Australian Military Regulation 575(10) which bound all members of the Australian Military Forces to follow the rulings of the JAG on questions of law. Uemura was executed on 3 March 1946. The executions of Takahashi and Katayama were deferred so that they could appear as prosecution witnesses at the subsequent trials of superior officers. In his report on the latter trials to the DPW&I, the Prosecuting Officer on 1 October 1947 advanced three grounds on which Takahashi and Katayama's sentences should be reconsidered. First, the reasons given in the JAG's original advice; second, their 19 months in the condemned cells; third, the need for some 'uniform standard of punishment according to the degree of guilt'. He noted that sentences passed in early 1946 were severe by 1947 standards — e.g. (Naval) Captain Noto's recent sentence of only imprisonment. But despite the JAG's recent recommendations for reprieves following that trial and the Hirota trial the matter was not resubmitted either to him or to the Confirming Authority; and Takahashi and Katayama were executed at Rabaul on October 23rd.

Failure on some occasions to provide overall uniformity of punishment proportionate to guilt is a disturbing feature of the Australian trials. It was foreseen and criticised from the outset by some senior officers involved in the trials. Brig. WAB Steele, the Commander of the force that reoccupied Ambon, urged that unless the officers who had ordered executions were tried, their subordinates who struck the actual blows should not be tried. In June 1946 the Area Commander at Rabaul, Maj. Gen. BM Morris, urged that confirmation should be deferred until all trials relating to the one incident were completed. It appears to the author that, in so far as the power to confirm (and at the same time to mitigate) sentences and the power to mitigate a sentence already confirmed were centralised at a high level, the means were there to do more in this direction than was done.

129 M43, Nav. Lt Katayama, H, et al., NAC A471 80918.

Double jeopardy

It is a rule of the common law that a person must not be put twice in peril ('double jeopardy') for the same offence. This rule is specifically applied to courts-martial by *Rules of Procedure* no. 36, which enables an accused to offer a plea in bar autrefois acquit on the ground that he has been previously convicted or acquitted of the offence. In the Australian *Regulations for the Trial of War Criminals*, however, Regulation 4 directs that Rule no. 36 shall not apply and Regulation 9 provides that 'an accused shall not be entitled to offer any plea in bar'. At Rabaul in May and June 1946 the GOC 8 Military District availed himself of Regulation 4 to order retrials of defendants on charges on which they had already been acquitted.

On May 29th a court at Rabaul found Fukushima, a Formosan guard, not guilty on the charge of 'Murder in that he at Ranau, Borneo, on or about 4 Jul 45 murdered Pte Richard Bird of the Australian Imperial Force'. At the trial (R121), two of the survivors of the Sandakan death march went into the witness box and testified that they had witnessed Fukushima at the parade of working parties knock Bird to the ground, repeatedly kick him on the head and body and leave him where he lay, that they had found Bird severely injured lying in the same position when their working party returned to camp in the evening, and that Bird died during the night. The Judge Advocate in his closing address explained that in law 'A person is guilty of causing death even if he merely accelerates the other's death, and it is no excuse that the person here killed must have died very shortly from some other cause'. The court, nevertheless found Fukushima not guilty. (Presumably they either doubted the witnesses' veracity or believed that Fukushima's assault had not accelerated Bird's death or that someone other than Fukushima had assaulted Bird while he lay unattended). The GOC immediately convened another court (of different members) which on May 31st found Fukushima guilty on the same charge and sentenced him to death (R122). At the second trial the prosecution produced a third Australian witness who testified that he had witnessed the assault by Fukushima, that on return to camp he had observed the injuries on Bird's face and the congealed blood in one ear and that the following morning he had seen Bird's body stripped for burial and observed extensive bruising on the trunk.

As the second trial resulted in a conviction, its proceedings had to be sent to the Judge-Advocate General for his report and advice to the Confirming Authority. On examining these the JAG noticed a remark by the Defending Officer in his opening address that 'the accused was tried yesterday on this charge and acquitted'. As a result, on July 24th he advised the Confirming Authority that the second court 'had no jurisdiction and that the proceedings cannot be confirmed'. He argued that the common law rule of autrefois acquit could be abrogated only by statute and that, since the Australian *War Crimes Act* did not do so, any regulation made under its authority that so purported was *ultra vires*. The Confirming Authority, following this advice, on September 3rd minuted the proceedings 'Not Confirmed'.

The JAG's advice to the Confirming Authority on R122 is dated July 24th. The following day he recommended that the finding and sentence of trial R137 should be confirmed, unaware that the defendant had been found not guilty on the same charge in an earlier trial.

On June 8th a court at Rabaul had found Sgt Maj. Karube Saburo not guilty on the following charges: (1) Ill-treatment of a POW in that he at Komareya, New Britain, about 7 February 45 ill-treated a number of Indian POWs; (2) Ill-treatment of a POW in that he at Komareya ill-treated 2/Lt Hari Kishan Das of 1 Bn Hyderabad Inf, a POW. The prosecution case consisted of two affidavits. The first was by the victim, 2/Lt Hari Kishan Das dated 3/10/45 stating inter alia that Sgt Maj. Karube had beaten him with his hands, hit him twice on the temples and then kicked him. The second was by Abdul Hashin, a mess cook, dated 16/11/45 identifying a photograph of the defendant as that of a person known to him as Karube Saburo. The trial Judge Advocate accordingly advised the court as follows: 'There is no evidence of the identification of the accused with the person referred to in this statement presented by the prosecution and my advice to the court is that there is no case to answer', whereupon the court on June 8th entered a finding of not guilty. On June 11th the prosecution interrogated Karube who, in the course of the interrogation, stated inter alia that he was Sgt Maj. Karube Saburo of 2 Special Land Service, that he was with the Production Unit at Komoriyama from January to March 1945, and that he knew an Indian 2/Lt named Das. On June 12th the GOC convened a court of three (including two members of the previous court) to try Karube on the same charge. The court assembled on June 13th (R137). The prosecution tendered, in addition to the two previous affidavits, the transcript of the June 11th interrogation. The Defending Officer made no mention of the fact that the accused had already been acquitted on the same charge and put him into the witness box as a defence witness. In the course of the cross-examination by the prosecution that ensued, Karube admitted to having beaten 2/Lt Das. The court found him guilty and sentenced him to three years imprisonment.

As Karube's first trial resulted in an acquittal its proceedings were not tendered to the JAG. For this reason and because there was no reference to in the proceedings of R137 the JAG was unaware that the latter was a retrial. Accordingly on July 25th he advised the Confirming Authority as follows: 'The proceedings appear to me to be in order. The evidence tendered was all admissible under the War Crimes Act and there was evidence from which the court could be satisfied of the guilt of the accused. In the circumstances I see no reason why the finding and sentence of the court should not be confirmed'. Confirmation was signified on September 3rd. Karube served his sentence and was released on 12/6/49.

Serving of prison sentences: Locations and eventual remissions

Those convicted by the Australian courts at Singapore and Hong Kong served their sentences in the same prisons as those convicted by the British courts until transferred with them to Sugamo Prison in Tokyo in August 1951. Those convicted by Australian courts elsewhere were confined first at Rabaul (until March 1949) and then at Manus until transferred to Sugamo in July 1953. The Australian authorities carried out no systematic review of prison sentences like that in the United Kingdom where in 1949 the length of all sentences being served was reviewed by the War Crimes Sentences Review Board — Far East, which adopted a standard scale of punishment according to the relative gravity of the offence (eight grades ranging from 'ill-treatment causing death' to 'minor torture … not sufficient to cause severe injury') and the relative degree of responsibility of the accused (three grades: major, intermediate, minor) and initiated action under AO 81/1945 §12 for the reduction of all sentences that exceeded this standard. In 1951 the Australian Government enacted Statutory Rule no. 11 authorising good conduct remissions of one quarter of the sentence for those serving sentences of 5–25 years and after 30 years for those serving life sentences. The first to gain such remissions, those sentenced at Labuan to 12 years on 9 January 1946, were released on 8 January 1955. In April 1955 following the practice in other Commonwealth countries this was amended to authorise release after serving 10 years or one third of the original sentence — whichever was the less. In 1957 this was further amended and the last prisoners (including those sentenced to life imprisonment in 1951) were released on 4 July 1957.

Crimes not brought to trial

A number of the crimes investigated were not brought to trial. The following are a few examples.

On 16 February 1942 at Banka Island 22 Australian Army nurses, survivors from the *Vyner Brooke*, who had surrendered, were put to death. They were marched into the sea in line and machine-gunned. The Commander of the unit responsible was serving in Manchuria at the war's end and was not repatriated by the Russians until 1948. He was arrested and gaoled in Sugamo Prison on 6 June 1948 but committed suicide two days later.[130]

130 NAM, MP742/1, 336/1/1976.

In August 1942 a group of nine Australian civilians (men, women and a child) were executed on the beach at Buna and at Popondetta, nearby, two women missionaries were bayoneted to death beside a prepared grave. The Commander of the unit responsible was killed in an air raid at Salamaua in August 1943 and most of the unit perished in the course of the New Guinea campaigns.[131]

On 18 March 1943 an Australian bomber was shot down while making an attack on the Japanese positions at Salamaua. Two members of the crew, Flt Lt WE Newton and Flt Sgt J Lyon swam ashore and were captured by 5 Sasebo Special Naval Landing Force. In July the diary was captured of an eyewitness of Newton's execution at Salamaua a few days later. This described the execution and named the executioner. Newton's body was recovered the following October when Salamaua was recaptured. Lyon's body was recovered at Lae in July 1948. The autopsy showed that he had been bayoneted while his hands were tied. Newton's executioner was killed in action in the Philippines. The Area Commander (Rear-Adm.) and his Chief-of-Staff (Cdr), suspected of ordering the executions, committed suicide in April and May 1947 respectively.[132]

On about 16 March 1943 the destroyer *Akikaze* en route for Rabaul took aboard about 26 civilian internees (for the most part German priests, Brothers and nuns and their leader, the Roman Catholic Bishop of Central New Guinea; and two small children) at Kairiru Island. The following day it embarked another 20 (Dutch nuns and priests; Australian and German planters; Protestant missionaries) at Lorengau (Admiralty Island). At sea between Kavieng and Rabaul they were executed one by one. In the course of his interrogation in December 1946 one of the ship's officers describes the slaughtering (which, he said, took 2 hours 50 minutes) as follows:

> Each internee passed beneath the forward bridge on the starboard side and came upon two waiting escorts. Here they were blindfolded with a white cloth and supported by each arm. By this time the interrogation of the second person was begun. Meanwhile, beneath the bridge of the quarter-deck on the starboard side, both wrists of the first person were firmly tied and he was again escorted to the execution platform. On the execution platform, they were faced toward the bow, suspended by their hands by means of a hook attached to a pulley, and at the order of the commander, executed by machine gun and rifle fire. After the completion of the execution the suspension rope was slackened and it had been so planned that when the rope binding the hands was cut, the body would fall backwards off the stern due to the speed of the ship. Moreover, boards were laid and straw mats spread to keep the ship from becoming stained … Thus, in this way, first the men and then the women were executed. The child going on toward five years old was thrown alive into the ocean.[133]

131 NAM, MP742/1, 336/1/1055.
132 NAC A705 166/1/102.
133 NAM, MP742/1, 336/1/1444.

As there were US nationals among the victims, the Australian War Crimes Section in Tokyo, having completed its investigation, on 18 July 1947 handed the matter over to the American authorities, who appear to have taken no further action.

The ill-treatment of UK POWs on Ballale Island was one of the cases ready for trial in December 1949. In December 1942 527 UK POWs were sent to Ballale Island (off Bougainville) to construct airfields there. They were forced to remain in their huts during an air raid and as a result about 280 were killed. Another 147 died as a result of ill-treatment. The remainder were bayoneted to death. Although the senior Japanese officer throughout was in custody and, among the 42 cases ready for trial, it was one of the 17 cases listed as murders in which a conviction was likely and a death sentence appropriate, it was not proceeded with when cabinet in January 1950 decided to confine the trials at Manus to cases in which there were Australian victims. The War Office in London had informed the Australian authorities that it did not intend to bring the case to trial but would have no objection if Australia did so.[134]

Among the cases under investigation in January 1950 were several arising out of executions of a total of about 30 Australian and US airmen and POWs by 18 Army in the Madang and Wewak areas at various times between June 1943 and late 1944. Some of these cases were ready for trial but did not satisfy cabinet's criteria on two grounds in so far as in each case a death sentence was considered 'possible' rather than 'likely' and the weight of the evidence indicated that the victims were Americans rather than Australians.[135]

Similarly a number of executions at Rabaul did not come to trial. At the site of the Japanese Navy's cemetery at Matupi an Australian war graves unit in May 1946 found the bodies of 24 Caucasians, all bearing signs of execution, buried in seven contiguous trenches. Four could be identified: two American airmen, an Australian naval telegraphist and an Australian civilian. In June 1949 a Japanese rating testified that he had witnessed the execution of 12 Allied airmen there in November 1943 in the presence of high-ranking naval officers whom he named. In the course of the investigations that followed, one admiral committed suicide and a number of other ranks and officers admitted to participating in, or witnessing, executions at that location between August 1942 and April 1944. On at least two occasions some of the victims were civilians — six Australians in October 1942; some Australians, a Swiss and a Finn in April 1944. After cabinet's decision to terminate all war crimes investigations, the task of casualty identification and reburial continued. The Imperial War Graves Commission in June and July 1950 searched 12 acres at the foot of Matupi crater. They found five graves containing the bodies of 15 Australian airmen, 12 American airmen and one Australian civilian, all bearing signs of execution. It would appear that, over all, at Matupi the Navy executed upwards

134 NAM, MP742/1, 336/1/1460.
135 NAC A705 116/1/400.

of a hundred Caucasians (including at least 19 civilians).[136] On the basis of these new discoveries the Minister for the Air in October 1950 (while the Manus trials were still in progress) proposed to cabinet that the suspects for the Madang and Rabaul executions be re-arrested and brought to trial. Cabinet, however, reaffirmed its previous decision.[137]

Abbreviations

AALC	Australian Army Legal Corps
AHQ	Army Headquarters, Melbourne
C-in-C	Commander-in-Chief
CGS	Chief of the General Staff
CO	Commanding Officer
CSO	Camp Supply Officer
DLS	Director of Legal Services
DPW&I	Director[ate] of Prisoners of War & Internees
GHQ	General Headquarters
GOC	General Officer Commanding
HQ	Headquarters
IMTFE	International Military Tribunal for the Far East
JAG	Judge-Advocate General
NAB	National Archives of Australia, Brisbane Office
NAC	National Archives of Australia, Canberra Office
NAM	National Archives of Australia, Melbourne Office
NCO	non-commissioned officer
POW	prisoner(s) of war
SCAP	Supreme Commander for the Allied Powers
SNLF	Special Naval Landing Force
UNWCC	United Nations War Crimes Commission

136 NAC A703 (Department of Air), 614/1/7. NAM, MP742/1, 336/1/1955 & 336/1/1965.

137 NAC A4639, vol. 1, agendum 2B.

Select bibliography

Location symbols

Documents referred to in this bibliography are held at the following locations: where the series number bears an A prefix, at the Canberra office of National Archives of Australia (NAC); where the Series number bears an MP or B prefix, at the NAA Melbourne office (NAM); where the series number bears a J prefix, at the NAA Brisbane office (NAB); where the series number bears an AWM prefix, at the Australian War Memorial, Canberra.

File titles

File titles may be ascertained by logging into *RecordSearch*, the National Archives of Australia database, at recordsearch.naa.gov.au.

Principal sources

The following collections constitute the principal sources used in the preparation of this paper.

Trial proceedings

(Series A471)

The original proceedings of each trial contain the following: (i) convening order; (ii) stenographic record; (iii) exhibits tendered; (iv) findings and sentences; (v) report on trial to Convening Officer by formation Legal Officer; (vi) petitions to Confirming Authority against finding/sentence; (vii) Judge-Advocate General's advice to Confirming Authority; (viii) confirmation; (ix) certificate of promulgation; (x) where death sentence is confirmed, execution warrant and death certificate. Proceedings vary in length from some 30 folios (Hidano A471, item 83839) to 23.5 cm of shelf space (Nagatomo A471, item 81655).

On completion the proceedings were sent for custody to the Commonwealth Attorney-General's Department, where each, on arrival, was allotted its six-figure item number in Series A471, the series containing the proceedings of all courts-martial of the three Australian armed services. The proceedings of the war crimes trials are interspersed among these in small clusters between items 80713 and 81969. Each item number can be ascertained from A3193/XM, an alphabetical index to Japanese defendants. Alternatively, each item number is indicated in the registers of proceedings for each trials series.

A digital image of the proceedings (unabridged) of each trial is available in the NAA database, *RecordSearch* (recordsearch.naa.gov.au).

Registers of proceedings

Series AWM226 Items 15, 16 & 17

The original registers of proceedings of each of the six trial series comprise three ledgers (35 cm width x 29 cm height):

Vol. 1 (AWM226, item 15)

- M Series — Morotai, Ambon, Wewak, and Labuan (Trials M1–29, 31–32, 34–35)
- D Series — Darwin (Trials D1–3).

Vol. 2 (AWM226, item 16)

- R Series — Rabaul (Trials R1–188 plus two aborted trials)
- Dates and places of execution (or death in custody) of each accused sentenced to death at: (i) Morotai, Labuan and Darwin; (ii) Rabaul; (iii) Singapore; (iv) Hong Kong; (v) Los Negros (i.e. Manus Island).

Vol. 3 (AWM226, item 17)

- S Series — Singapore (Trials S2–14, 16–18, 20–24, 26–28 plus one aborted trial)
- HK Series — Hong Kong (Trials HK1–13)
- LN Series — Los Negros (i.e. Manus Island) (Trials LN1–26).

On the arrival of each transcript at Army Headquarters from the court, a trial number (e.g. M1) would be allocated, beside which would be entered vertically at the left-hand edge of a verso page the names of each accused. Thereafter there would be entered at the appropriate times, in a series of vertical columns extending across the verso and recto page, precise details of the findings, sentences confirmations, dispositions and file movements, including the following: (i) name, rank, Australian War Criminal Registration Number; (ii) charge (omitted in M Series); (iii) place and date of the trial; (iv) sentence of court; (v) dates to and from Directorate of Legal Services (HK and S series only); (vi) dates to and from Judge-Advocate General; (vii) dates to and from Confirming Authority, name and appointment of Confirming Authority, date and details of confirmation; (viii) date of promulgation of sentence; (ix) date to and from 2nd Echelon; (x) date proceedings transferred to Attorney-General's Department; (xi) six-figure item number in Series A471; (xii) item number of corresponding 'Court correspondence' file in Series MP742/1 (LN series only); (xiii) remarks column (here from time appears such information as next-of-kin informed, date and cause of death in custody, date of transfer to custody of another Allied power, date of outwards correspondence with Department of External Affairs, etc.).

Department of the Army Central Registry files

(MP742/1 Items 336/1/)*

The correspondence files of the war crimes section of the DPW&I that passed through the Central Registry, Department of the Army, were registered, for the most part, in the 336/1/ [War Crimes] block of Series MP742/1. The appropriate Registration Booklet,

Series B1801, registers in chronological sequence 2,168 papers of this description (336/1/1 to 336/1/2196) and records the subsequent movement of each, including the combination of papers on the same matter into files bearing the registration number of the latest of the constituent papers. Some 560 such files are extant. Their titles and registration numbers are listed on the NAA database, *RecordSearch*, www.naa.gov.au/the_collection/recordsearch.html. Of these files the bulk fall into two categories designated by DPW&I as 'Investigation files' (209 extant items) and 'Court correspondence' files (some 250 extant items). A catalogue of the former according to the place where the crime was committed and an alphabetical listing of the latter by name of the accused are available in MP742/1 Item 336/1/2125. Another useful finding aid for the 336/1/* files is the list, 'W.C. files P/A in Central Registry and Archives on 21 June 62' available in AWM226 Item 37.

First Webb Inquiry

(Commissioned 23/6/43; Reported 15/3/44)

- Report, NAC A10943, item 2
- Transcript, NAC A6236 (whole series)
- Exhibits, NAC A6237 (whole series)
- Address by Counsel Assisting, NAC A10948, item 1, parts 1–6
- Office files, NAB J1889, items NAM BL43895/1 – 19, 22–25; NAC A10952, item 3 (part of); NAC A10953, item 1 (part of).

Second Webb Inquiry

(Commissioned 23/6/44; Reported 31/10/44)

- Report, NAC A10950, item 1
- Transcript, vol. 1, AWM226, item 6 & vol. 2, NAC A10951, item 1
- Office files, NAC A10952 (whole series); NAC A10953, item 1 (part of); NAC A6328, item 10; NAB J1889, items B43895/26 & 27.

Third Webb Inquiry

(Commissioned 3/9/45; Reported 31/1/45)

- Report (incl appendices), NAC A11049, rolls 1 & 2
- Office files (numbered), NAC A6238 (whole series)
- Office files (unnumbered), NAC A10953 (whole series); AWM226, items 91–94.

Other sources

Additional sources are indicated in the individual footnotes.

5

OBSERVATION AND CORRESPONDENCE

Editors' note

The following sections in this chapter will shock most readers with their descriptions of the appalling and inhuman savagery that modern warfare can generate. How human beings can treat other human beings in the callous ways described is simply beyond belief, and yet modern history reveals many similar examples from other wars.

In the immediate aftermath of the Second World War, strong anti-Japanese sentiment was reflected especially in the popular press. Part of this was the result of Australia having been threatened and attacked by a powerful and determined enemy, but most significantly it focused on the gross ill-treatment of Australian and other Allied prisoners, as well as of civilian populations in the western Pacific. David Sissons served as an interpreter in three of the Australian war crimes trials on the island of Morotai, and in his much later researches into these trials he became aware of episodes where Australian forces also ill-treated Japanese prisoners, mostly in forced marches when the prisoners were in poor physical shape. As a researcher deeply concerned with issues of legality, he sought to apply military law as the supreme arbiter in the cases he examined, whether the accused were Japanese or Australian.

One area that caused him particular concern was what he regarded as discrepancies in the degree of punishment meted out by Australian courts against Japanese servicemen accused of war crimes. He regarded some of the decisions of earlier trial courts as excessive. He researched extensively about the Katayama case, which concerned a Japanese naval junior officer who was ordered by his superior officer to execute an Allied air crew who had crash landed. Katayama personally executed one of the crew members, for which he was condemned to death by an Australian military court. At that time, the death penalty remained an accepted part of judicial punishment in Australia. Despite subsequent representations from Australian and Japanese quarters (including Church representatives, as Katayama was a Christian), the Australian authorities refused to commute the sentence, and he was duly executed.

The Katayama case, amongst others, raises difficult questions of law in cases where subordinates commit atrocities on the orders of a superior officer. According to earlier editions of the leading textbook on military law in the first half of the 20th century, the receipt of orders from a superior officer was sufficient to exculpate a serviceman who had committed atrocities. Editions from the late 1930s, however, reversed this position, placing responsibility onto the person who had committed the atrocity. In the Japanese case, however, the consequences for defying orders from superior officers were extreme and almost certainly resulted in execution.

As the war concluded, and the postwar international system, based on Cold War polarities, was established, Australian attitudes towards Japan gradually softened. By the early 1950s, most of those sentenced to long prison terms had been transferred to Japan and they were eventually released. At the time when Sissons was writing about war crimes, mainly in the 1980s, democracy had become a major premise of the Japanese political system, and a close political relationship between the two countries was developing.

This raises a profound question that is almost impossible to answer in a satisfactory manner: the Asia-Pacific war that began with the Japanese war against China from July 1937, through Pearl Harbor, through the creation of a huge Japanese empire in East and South-East Asia, the atomic bombing of two Japanese cities and fire-bombing of many others, leading to ultimate defeat for Japan and seven years of foreign occupation, caused immense human suffering and physical destruction across the region. Atrocities and war crimes were just one horrible aspect of this history. The war was followed by the establishment of international relationships and institutions that have ensured *relative* peace for three quarters of a century (though they may now be under threat). Our question is the following: in order to create peace and understand its value and opt for a better way to order the world's affairs, is it necessary first to experience the horrors of war?

DUNTROON LECTURE, JULY 1978[1]

DCS Sissons

The Australian war crimes trials

Introduction

Under the Australian *War Crimes Act*[2] a total of 296 trials was held. The first began at Morotai on 29 November 1945; the last ended at Manus Island on 9 April 1951. Table A gives the dates and statistics regarding the number of trials held and the findings and sentences given at each place.[3]

I have found that nowadays[4] when I mention Australian war crimes trials, most Australians think of Manus. There could be several reasons for this. To the best of my knowledge only the Manus trials were the subject of articles in Australian learned periodicals.[5]

1 When David Sissons wrote this lecture, he provided approximately 10 abbreviated footnotes and in-text references to sources. Georgina Fitzpatrick (GF) has extended these and has provided extra footnotes; in particular, to the specific trials discussed in the text. For a full list of the Australian-run trials, see 'Appendix 4: Trials list with National Archives of Australia series and item number', in Georgina Fitzpatrick, Tim McCormack & Narrelle Morris, *Australia's War Crimes Trials, 1945–51* (Brill, 2016, pp. 826–30).

2 *War Crimes Act 1945* (C'th). No. 48 of 1945. An Act to provide for the Trial and Punishment of War Criminals [Assented to 11th October 1945].

3 GF: There was no Table A attached to the lecture but it is likely to be similar to a later published version. See Table A, in David Sissons, 'Sources on Australian investigations into Japanese war crimes in the Pacific', *Journal of the Australian War Memorial*, 30 (April 1997), www.awm.gov.au/articles/journal/j30/wcrimes (accessed 11 January 2019).

4 GF: 'Nowadays' being 1978. Forty years later only a small group of historians and lawyers know that the trials occurred.

5 Two articles in the *Australian Quarterly* and the *Journal and Proceedings of the Royal Australian Historical Society* written by GA Dickinson, the Sydney barrister who served there as the Australian legal advisor to the Japanese defence lawyers. GF: These are G Dickinson, 'Manus Is trials', *Journal and Proceedings of the Royal Australian Historical Society*, vol. 38 (June 1952), no. 1, pp. 66–77; and G Dickinson, 'Japanese war trials', *Australian Quarterly*, vol. 24 (June 1952), no. 2, pp. 69–75.

Another reason may be that the question of whether or not to hold them (an issue on which the Chifley government was deadlocked) was the subject of a debate in the House of Representatives in February [GF: March] 1950 soon after the Menzies government took office.[6] That debate is relevant to our present discussion in that the remarks of some of the participants indicate that the hatred that had so characterised popular attitudes towards the Japanese in the years immediately following the surrender had by 1950 begun to erode. In 1946, as I propose to demonstrate, there were few people who wished to stand in the path of the clamour in the press urging a none-too-reluctant Confirming Authority to cease dawdling and get stuck into the hanging. In the 1950 debate, however, there was diversity of opinion on both sides of the House. On the Labor front bench Ward wanted the trials to continue while Chifley wanted to call it a day. Among the Labor backbenchers, Tom Burke (the Member for Perth) felt that the trials brought us down to the inhuman level of those whom we were trying. Among the ministerialist backbenchers Squadron Leader Graham (who held the Sydney seat of St George) in the course of a speech that was nothing if not anti-Japanese came down on the same side as Chifley. The crux of his argument was that there had been illegal acts on both sides. He described as an atrocity the action of American and Australian planes when they machine-gunned Japanese in the water as they tried to scramble on to life rafts. He considered that it was a reflection on us that, during the war, we had shown to our school children the newsreel, *Bismarck Convoy Crushed*, in which Damien Parer recorded such exploits in faithful detail. (I have yet to see this film. It is preserved in the National Library's film archives.)[7]

The Menzies government had no alternative but to face up to the issue at which its predecessor had balked. It promptly released 71 suspects against whom sufficient evidence had not yet been collected and ordered the trials to resume. It was in fact more than a year since the last Australian trial. This decision flew in the face of the recommendation of the representatives of the Allied powers that the trials of all Japanese should if possible be completed by the end of September 1949. The British Government (which had ended its own trials in 1948) and the American Government (which overshot the deadline by a mere 10 days) felt that their own interests required them to disassociate themselves from Australia's policy. The British would not allow us to continue to hold trials in Hong Kong. The Americans would not grant us facilities to hold them in Tokyo. And so they were held at Manus — from June 6th 1950 to April 9th 1951.

6 GF: Menzies made a ministerial statement on 24 February 1950 concerning the release of war criminal suspects and the number of cases to be tried at the last set of trials held on Manus Island, *Commonwealth Parliamentary Debates* (CPD), 24 February 1950, vol. 206, pp. 99–102. For the debate on the statement, see *CPD*, 16 March 1950, vol. 206, pp. 881–990.

7 GF: This is now preserved as part of a compilation of videorecordings; see *At the Front, 1939–1945*, National Film and Sound Archive, 1995.

Imprisonment for long periods while awaiting trial was one of the features of the totalitarian rule that the Allies had been much given to criticising. Furthermore, America and Britain, with greater experience of international politics than Australia, were more interested in preparing against future problems than in fighting old battles. Presumably what weighed heavily with the Menzies cabinet was the manifest injustice that men like Nishimura, the Divisional Commander who had personally initiated the massacre of the Australian prisoners at Parit-Sulong, should escape just when, after years of patient effort, the keystone of a convincing indictment was ready to fall into place. Lower down the line — among the men who worked on nothing but the investigations and the trials — the majors and captains with law degrees in the former Directorate of Prisoners of War and Internees — the men who analysed the transcripts and petitions and wrote the first draft of the submissions to the ministers — this argument was reinforced by another: it would be a travesty of justice if we let the big fish escape when in the months that immediately followed the surrender we had convicted and executed subalterns who had carried out — reluctantly and with no additional barbarities of their own — [executions of] individual prisoners, solely as the result of specific orders from high-ranking superior officers.

To illustrate this and other issues underlying the Australian trials let us look at some of the early cases heard under the *War Crimes Act*. You will see from Table A that, for early trials, there are two groups to choose from. Those held at Morotai and those held at Labuan. My choice fell on the former. There were two reasons for this:

1. For some years, until an enlightened Attorney-General, Mr Enderby, cut through pettifogging bureaucracy and opened the proceedings of the trials to public inspection, the only material I had to work on was Japanese material. This referred to two Australian trials — both of them at Morotai.
2. The Morotai trials contain more variety. Those at Labuan dealt almost exclusively with the ill-treatment of prisoners in POW camps. The Morotai trials as you will observe from Table B[8] contain much about this subject; but in addition they deal with other important matters such as the execution of captured airmen and the doctrine of the formation of Commander's criminal responsibility for acts done by his troops without his knowledge — subjects barely touched upon in the Labuan trials.

8 GF: No Table B accompanied the lecture and it does not appear to be the same as Table B: Australian war crimes trials (classified by victim), included in David Sissons, 'Sources on Australian investigations into Japanese war crimes in the Pacific', *Journal of the Australian War Memorial*, 30 (April 1997). The figures in that table refer to cases involving prisoners of war and, separately, 'Crashed aircrew' but do not marry up with his text above.

The Morotai courts

The effect of the Australian *War Crimes Act* was that except in certain respects (We shall refer to the more important of these later) each war crimes court was — in the way it was selected, in its composition, and in its procedure — essentially a copy of that workhorse[9] of British and Australian military discipline at the front line — the Field General Court Martial. The important difference between the Field General Court and its peacetime counterpart, the General Court Martial, is that the former is smaller (a minimum of three[10] members instead of five[11]), the minimum rank of its presiding officer is captain instead of full colonel,[12] and its members may be junior in rank to the accused. Like the United Kingdom Royal Warrant, the Australian War Crimes Regulations sought to moderate the lack of these differences by providing that 'the Convening Officer should, so far as is practicable, but shall be under no obligation so to do, appoint as many officers as possible of equal or superior relative rank to the accused'.[13] Similarly they provided that where the accused was a sailor or an airman the Convening Officer should appoint as a member at least one officer from that service if such officers were available.[14] At Morotai the Convening Officer appears to have taken neither of these provisions very seriously. The court that tried Major General Endo[15] (who commanded a brigade) consisted of two colonels who had held only staff appointments, a Lieutenant Colonel who had not been given command of a battalion until after the Armistice, a Captain and a Flight Lieutenant.

There is obvious merit in the philosophy underlying *Australian Military Regulations and Orders* (AMR&O) 503 (2) which provides that, for the trial of a Commanding Officer of a unit, as many members of the court as possible must hold or have held an equivalent command. Endo was charged, in effect, with culpable negligence. It could be argued that only men who had themselves commanded a brigade could assess whether the evidence adduced amounted to this. In 10 of the 25 Morotai trials the accused were naval personnel. In only two of these was there a naval officer on the court.[16] Vice Admiral Ichise was tried by two lieutenant colonels and a major.[17] The absence of naval officers from the courts, however, may not have been

9 GF: Sissons pencilled beside this 'WW1 statistics'. It is unclear what he would have inserted here.

10 AA 49 (1) (b). GF: The *Army Act* is an Imperial one from 1881 used by the Australians as modified by the *Defence Act* 1903 to 1945 (Cth).

11 AA 48 (3).

12 AMR&O 80 503. GF: *Australian Military Regulations and Orders.*

13 RP 21 (b). GF: This could be Rules of Procedure.

14 SR 164 (8) AO 81 (5). GF: The first element could be Statutory Rules. AO may mean Army Order.

15 GF: Maj. Gen. Endo Shinichi was tried at Morotai (M38). For the trial transcript, see National Archives of Australia (NAA) A471 80977.

16 GF: Sissons is referring to the trials of Lt Yunomura Fumio (M14) and Rear Adm. Hamanaka Kyōho (M20). Commanders Jack Donovan and Oliver Jones sat on the respective courts. See the trial transcripts at NAA A471 80770 and NAA A471 80773 respectively.

17 GF: For the trial of Vice Adm. Ichise Shinichi (M41), see NAA A471 81644.

as serious as at first sight appears. None of the Morotai trials involved fighting ships or the laws and usages of war at sea. All the naval personnel on trial were charged with offences against prisoners of war ashore.

In providing trial by Field General Court Martial the *War Crimes Act* was certainly providing a less elaborate standard of justice than that afforded in 1902 to Morant and Handcock who, so far as I am aware, are the only Australians ever to have stood trial for war crimes.[18] The British General under whom they were serving ordered them to be tried by General Court Martial — not by Field General Court Martial.

At Morotai there were in operation four courts — essentially of three members each. In effect the president and next most senior member in each were permanent and there was some turnover with the third member. The four presidents were a full colonel and three lieutenant colonels. Occasionally (for example, for the trials of the Admiral and the General) a court was augmented to a total of five. For the Admiral, a brigadier was brought in as President.[19]

In Table B[20] I have designated the courts A, B, C, and D respectively. A purist would, of course, argue that there were 25 Morotai courts, each separately convened; but I don't think anyone who goes through the composition of each carefully will disagree violently with my classification.

As with courts martial, the Convening Officer was free virtually to choose any officers he pleased to serve on the courts. It would have been relatively easy, by selecting known fire-eaters, to make a conviction and the sentence of death foregone conclusions. Most of the Morotai trials were convened by Major General Milford, the General Officer Commanding the Seventh Division. The rest were convened by Brigadier Woodward, the Deputy Adjutant (DA) & Quartermaster General (QMG) at Advanced Headquarters. I have seen no evidence at all of any attempt to stack the courts. Whatever the backgrounds of the members, it can always be argued that from the standpoint of the accused they were inappropriate for ensuring justice in his particular case. If a Staff Officer is selected, it is argued that only someone with extensive experience of command in the field can appreciate the realities of the situation in which the man on trial had to operate. If on the other hand a fighting soldier is selected, it is argued that his rough and ready forthright approach make him impatient of the subtleties of the Defending Officer's argument.

18 GF: Sissons is referring to a notorious and controversial trial under the British military justice system. Australian lieutenants Harry Morant and Peter Handcock were tried during the Second Anglo-Boer War for executing South African civilians.

19 GF: Sissons is referring to Hamanaka's trial (M20) over which Brig. Eric Woodward presided. See NAA A471 80773.

20 GF: See note 8 about his reference to a Table B. Also by 'courts' Sissons is referring to the personnel constituting the members of the court rather than a physical and separate hut acting as a court space.

One of Yamashita's defending officers in his book on that trial[21] noted that the court (which, of course, was American) consisted entirely of Regular Army generals and that such people are accustomed to their own dictatorial power and prone to regard legal rules as pettifogging technicalities that they must brush aside. From the Morotai transcripts it seems to me that the judges were patient men eager to play by the rules. Of the four presidents,[22] two of the lieutenant colonels were regulars.[23] The third Lieutenant Colonel was a citizen soldier first commissioned in 1935.[24] The full Colonel was also a citizen soldier. He had served in the ranks in the First World War.[25] In the Second World War he had served as Chief Signals Officer on various formation headquarters overseas. Of the three lieutenant colonels, one, the citizen soldier, had commanded a pioneer battalion overseas for the last four months of the war.[26] The second had commanded an armoured regiment at home.[27] The third had held staff positions at home.[28]

By contrast for the four-man court at Wewak, General Robertson selected three of his battalion commanders, all of whom had commanded battalions overseas for some years. Their frontline knowledge of conditions did not however result in their passing a lenient sentence. The case before them was cannibalism — a Japanese officer in a half-starved condition eating the flesh of an Australian killed attacking his position.[29] The court condemned him to death by a 3:1 verdict. The *Sydney Sun* correspondent filed a report which merely recorded the trial and sentence but at the same time sent a report to his news editor not for publication in which he argued that the sentence was outrageous and suggested that the court was packed. He noted that one of the lieutenant colonels was known as Jap Happy Jack while another member of the court had stated openly that he did not intend to allow the little yellow bastard to escape. The news editor conveyed the letter to External Affairs who took it seriously and passed it to the Attorney-General who also took it

21 GF: General Yamashita Tomoyuki was tried by an American military court in the Philippines soon after the war. It is not possible to identify the book to which Sissons refers.

22 GF: There were actually six presidents. Col George W Watson presided over only one Morotai trial (M14) and so did Woodward (M20). The four main presidents at Morotai were Col James L McKinlay who presided over 11 trials, Lt Col Edward B Ellison who presided over four trials, Lt Col Edward F Aitken who presided over four trials and Lt Col Francis Costello who presided over three trials. In the light of Sissons' earlier division of the Morotai trials into four different courts, these are probably the four men he meant.

23 GF: They were Costello and Ellison.

24 GF: This is Aitken but his 1935 enlistment date into the Citizen Military Forces (Militia) cannot be verified. His service file has not been found in the NAA database.

25 GF: This is McKinlay, who fought at Gallipoli and the Western Front during the First World War, receiving a Military Medal (MM). See his digitised service file at NAA B883 WX3379.

26 GF: This is Aitken. He commanded 2/33 Pioneer Battalion. See his Nominal Roll, Dept of Veterans Affairs online at nominal-rolls.dva.gov.au/ (accessed 16 November 2018).

27 GF: This is Costello who commanded 13 Armoured Regiment, Nominal Roll entry, Dept of Veterans Affairs online at nominal-rolls.dva.gov.au/ (accessed 16 November 2018).

28 GF: This is probably Ellison, whom Sissons identified in Box 32: Morotai as 'Regular Staff'. At the time of his discharge, he was Commanding Officer of 63 Battalion, Nominal Roll entry, Dept of Veterans Affairs online at nominal-rolls.dva.gov.au/ (accessed 16 November 2018).

29 GF: This is Wewak (MW1). For the trial transcript, see NAA A471 80713.

seriously and passed it to Army.[30] The Commander on the spot, the Acting General Officer Commanding (GOC) 6 Division also thought the sentence unduly severe and recommended it be commuted[31] — Sturdee reduced it to five years.

Unlike the Yamashita court there were lawyers among the members of all the Morotai courts. Although not required by any regulation to do so, on each court the Convening Officer always put one (and often two) members with legal qualifications.[32] The Staff Officer (Civil Affairs) at Advanced Headquarters, a full Colonel, was a barrister in civil life.[33] He was a member of Court A throughout. The junior legal officers from various neighbouring headquarters — captains and majors who were solicitors in civil life — were rotated as prosecutors, defending officers and members of the courts. After a couple of weeks they were reinforced by three members of the junior bar from the mainland.[34] One had been in khaki since 1942; the other two were specially enlisted for the purpose. Two of these and the Staff Officer (Civil Affairs) later became Supreme Court judges.[35]

In terms of legal requirements there seems to have been no parallel in the Australian legislation to Regulation 5 Paragraph 2 of AO 81/1945 that there should be one member of court with legal qualifications: that, if not, there must be a Judge Advocate.[36]

From Table B you will observe that each court tended to specialise. Court A, for example, was given all eight cases arising out of the Talaud atrocity.[37] This, of course, has obvious advantages from the standpoint of efficiency: the background and much of the evidence is the same for each case. But where the decision of life and death rests with laymen such as jurors or soldiers it weakens the position of the accused, because men may be influenced against a particular defendant by information about the event that would be inadmissible in his own particular trial. This is one of the

30 GF: The original letter by Noel Ottaway, Sydney *Sun* to John Goodge, 3 December 1945 and official responses may be found in NAA A472 W18153 PART 2 and A1067 UN46/WC/8 PART 1. These were files consulted by Sissons. See the Papers of DCS Sissons, Box 34: Wewak, National Library of Australia.

31 GF: This was conveyed to Sturdee by Brig. Alan Lloyd, the Director of Legal Services. See NAA A471 80713, p. 8.

32 GF: Sissons pencilled in a question mark beside this statement but it can be confirmed by this researcher.

33 GF: Col Malcolm P Crisp. Crisp became a judge of the Supreme Court of Tasmania.

34 GF: Sissons pencilled in the margin at this point two of the three names: Travers and Campbell. Capt. John L Travers was Prosecuting Officer for M31 and M38, Defending Officer for M39 and M41 and a member of the court for M44. He became a judge in the Supreme Court of South Australia. Capt. Douglas M Campbell was Prosecuting Officer for M40, Defending Officer for M42, M43 and M44 and Reviewing Officer for M41. He became a Supreme Court judge in Queensland. The third recruit from the junior bar was Capt. Kenneth R Townley (later president of the court for all the Manus Island trials in 1950–51). He was Judge Advocate for six of the early Morotai trials and Reviewing Officer for six more. He also became a judge in the Supreme Court of Queensland.

35 GF: In fact, all four became Supreme Court judges.

36 GF: This is a requirement for the British military courts conducting war crimes trials. The legal instrument is Army Order 81 of 1945 promulgated by Great Britain War Office (1945), Royal Warrant 0160/2498, 18 June 1945.

37 GF: The trials related to the Talaud Island garrison were M6, M7, M8, M9, M10, M12, M13 and M26.

reasons why a person is ineligible to serve on a jury if he has prior knowledge about the case to be tried. Later I shall refer to one of the Ambon cases where I think this may have cost one of the defendants his life.[38]

Now let us look at the trials. The Talaud atrocity[39] is a good place to begin. It includes the very first of the Australian trials of Captain Iwasa Tokio and, since the defendants comprised the participants in the crime at each successive level from the other ranks who struck the blows to the Brigade Commander who failed to prevent it, it provides plenty of scope for us to consider the problem of superior orders which naturally emerges as a defence in every war crimes trial.

The facts, for the most part, were not disputed. The airmen had crashed and been taken prisoner. Colonel Koba Shigeru,[40] the officer in charge of Japanese troops on the island, in the middle of March 1945 summoned a conference at which he announced that the airmen were to be executed and that the execution was to take place on March 23rd after a formal parade at which new colours were to be presented. These orders were passed on to company commanders before the parade. After the parade each company was marched off under its Company Commander to the place of execution, one prisoner was allotted to each company. Each Company Commander then called out one man from the ranks and ordered him to kill the prisoner with his bayonet.

Iwasa, one of the company commanders was the first to be tried. The transcript of his trial gives an indication of some of the disadvantages under which defendants laboured.[41]

In an attempt to ensure equality, Australian Military Regulations require that when the prosecutor is a lawyer the Defending Officer must be a lawyer also. They do not, however, say that they must be men of equal attainments. The prosecutor in Iwasa's trial was a Lieutenant Colonel[42] with eight years more professional experience behind him than the Defending Officer (Captain John C Brown). This disparity continued throughout most of the Morotai trials. The opportunities for Iwasa and Brown to prepare a defence were scarcely more extensive than those of the dock brief: at Morotai prisoners were first informed of the specifications of the charges against them by their defending officers. Brown was allotted to Iwasa only three days before the trial. In 1949, when the nations of the world assembled at Geneva

38 GF: This is probably referring to Katayama's case (M43).

39 GF: The murder of four prisoners of war at Karakallan; Beo, in the Talaud islands; and Celebes, in March 1945 was the matter being prosecuted in several related trials held at Morotai.

40 GF: His trial was M10. See NAA, A471, 80719.

41 GF: For the trial of Capt. Iwasa Tokio (M9), see NAA, A471, 80718.

42 GF: Lt Col Lyle Byrne.

to revise the 1929 Prisoners of War Convention, they determined on three weeks as the minimum interval between charge and trial (including a period of two weeks for the Defending Officer to prepare his case).

When the trial opened Brown drew the court's attention to the fact that it was a case of first impression and that his defence would involve arguments on the interpretation and constitutional validity of a new statue. The library available to him at Morotai was totally inadequate for the preparation of such a defence and he accordingly applied for a change of venue to the mainland. The court heard counterarguments from the prosecutor and refused the application. Let me quote from the prosecutor's argument:

> the fact that this Court is called on to adjudicate upon grave charges makes it no different to the position of any court martial which may be called upon in some outpost of Empire without any more facilities than we have, to adjudicate on an equally serious charge, and to impose possibly an equally serious punishment … . In this case the ultimate protection is given to the accused by review. The proceedings leave this area to go into the calm and elevated area of thought where library facilities are available, and the possibilities of a mis-carriage of justice are very, very remote in the long run.[43]

The prosecutor's suggestion that Iwasa's position was just the same as that of any Australian soldier being tried by court martial was ridiculous. Iwasa was being tried for murder, and the likely penalty under the *War Crimes Act* was death. The maximum penalty permissible for an Australian soldier charged with the same offence was life imprisonment. Admittedly in the one or two capital offences in the Australian military code for which a court martial could sentence an Australian soldier to death — mutiny and certain acts of treachery — the review process, in which the matter had to go before cabinet, was so effective that over a period of 40 years and two world wars no Australian soldier had ever been executed.

What then was left of 'the process of review' on which the Morotai prosecutor set such store as 'the ultimate protection' of the accused? In fact, the latter's only safeguard was as we have seen that, under the regulations implementing the *War Crimes Act*, when the prisoner under sentence appealed, the Confirming Officer had to refer his petition and the proceedings of the trial to the Judge-Advocate General (who was a civilian and a King's counsel for advice and report. He was not, of course, bound either to follow that advice, or, when he ignored it, to give his reasons. Nor was the atmosphere in which the review process was carried out as calm as Iwasa's prosecutor made out. The Australian press was howling for blood. The Judge-Advocate General[44] was working through the transcripts while the *Argus*

43 GF: See NAA A471 80718, p. 16.

44 GF: This was J Bowie Wilson.

was carrying headlines like 'No condemned Japs executed yet'[45] and commenting on the considerable time he was taking. While Gen. Sturdee was reading the Judge-Advocate General's reports and deciding between life and death *Smith's Weekly* was asking why our military authorities were delaying executions 'where butchers and sadists have been found guilty by court martial'. 'The Jap,' it argued 'won't take our court martials [sic] very seriously until he sees the condemned men at the rope's end.'[46]

One other important safeguard denied to the Japanese defendants was one we have referred to already — the protection afforded by the exclusion of evidence from witnesses not available for cross-examination in court. Section 128 of the *Army Act* provides that the rules of evidence to be adopted in proceedings before courts martial (including Field General Courts Martial) shall be the same as those which are followed in civil courts in England. The rule excluding hearsay is part of those rules. The relevant passage from the *Manual of Military Law* explains the extent of this exclusion and the reasons underlying it:

> the term 'hearsay' is primarily applicable to what a witness has heard another person say with respect to facts in dispute. But it is extended to all statements, whether reduced to writing or not, which are brought before the court, not by the authors of the statements, but by persons to whose knowledge the statements have been brought. The reasons for excluding such statements are first that they are not made on oath; and, secondly, that the person to be affected by the statement has no opportunity of cross examining its author.[47]

In another passage the manual commended this rule as preventing jurors (and members of courts martial) 'from being misled by statements or documents the effect of which, through the prejudice which they excite, is out of all proportion to their true weight'.[48] But Section 9 (1) of the Australian *War Crimes Act*, in words identical with those of the United Kingdom Royal Warrant, abandoned this safeguard. It reads:

> At any hearing before a military court the court may take into consideration any oral statement or any document appearing on the face of it to be authentic, provided the statement or document appears to the court to be of assistance in proving or disproving the charge, notwithstanding that the statement or document would not be admissible in evidence before a field general court martial.

45 GF: 9 January 1946, p. 1.

46 GF: 'Condemned Japs are still alive. Australian or army policy?', *Smith's Weekly* (Syd), 2 February 1946, p. 1.

47 MML, p. 91. GF: This is probably: Australian Military Board, *Manual of Military Law*, Commonwealth Government Printer, 1941. The 1941 edition was used at the trials.

48 MML, p. 75.

Having failed in his application for a change in venue, Brown, rather surprisingly did not ask for more time to prepare his case. As far as I can see, the only occasion when the defence did this was in the Shirozu case.[49] There, the accused had exercised the right to be defended by Japanese lawyers. The junior counsel were legal officers from the Japanese naval headquarters at Ceram. Senior counsel (private practitioners) were brought from Tokyo. These arrived by air at the end of the first day of the trial. They then sought and were granted an adjournment of one and a half days. (You will remember that in the Yamashita trial the American tribunal rejected a very reasonable request from the defence for more time to prepare the case.)

Iwasa was found guilty of murder. So were the others in the Talaud cases — from Colonel Koba to the other ranks who struck the blows. There was one exception. Asaoka, the only one of the platoon commanders to be charged, was acquitted.[50] His defence was that he was not in any way involved. The company commanders had selected the executioners, called them out and shouted the commands direct to them. The only fact in dispute in the Talaud trials was whether Koba had, as he alleged, received a signal from Lieutenant Colonel Komura, the Staff Officer at brigade headquarters at Menado 300 miles [480 kilometres] away, ordering the executions. Koba's cipher clerks testified to this effect and as a result Komura, too, was found guilty of murder.[51] In the Talaud cases each of the officers was sentenced to death; each of the other ranks to 10 years imprisonment. Endo, the Brigade Commander (who had been charged with neglecting to take proper steps to ensure that prisoners were treated in accordance with the laws and usages of war) was sentenced to five years imprisonment. Critics of the American Yamashita trial have vigorously attacked the doctrine of the international criminal responsibility on the part of superior commanders for atrocities committed by their troops. It may be that in that trial the court behaved as if it were absolute responsibility and not a responsibility to exercise reasonable care and that they failed to consider evidence of the magnitude of the tactical and administrative problems with which Yamashita as Commander of an entire army group in retreat was dealing. Yamashita was a very busy man facing problems that were superhuman. The Endo trial was quite different. First the prosecutor did not ask for a heavy sentence. Secondly the evidence of both Endo and his Staff Officer indicated that if he wished to give oversight to the treatment of prisoners he had plenty of leisure in which to do so. He had a comfortable house in the hills overlooking Menado and spent most of his time there reading his books.[52] He left the running of the brigade to his Staff Officer and in fact visited his headquarters only twice between February 1945 and the end of the war.

49 GF: Naval Captain Shirozu appeared in two trials — M41: NAA A471 81644 and M45: NAA A471 81709, parts 1–5. However, as the latter is the mass trial of 91 accused where Shirozu is merely one of such a large number of defendants, Sissons' discussion probably concerns M41.

50 GF: Lt Asaoka Tosho was tried at Morotai (M6). For the trial transcript, see NAA A471 80717.

51 GF: Lt Col Kōmura Takeo was tried at Morotai (M26). For the trial transcript, see NAA A471 80753.

52 GF: The prosecutor, Travers, referred to this in his closing address, NAA A471 80977, p. 111.

But let us return to the first trial. When, on November 30th, the court found Captain Iwasa guilty of murder, this was a very important decision — not only for the defendants in the other Talaud trials but for all war criminal suspects in areas where Australian prisoners had been. It meant that an Australian court had decided against them a vital point of law — whether or not superior orders constituted a good defence. In theory, of course, it mattered only to Iwasa; for a court martial is not a court of record and its decisions do not have the force of legal precedent. Theoretically the same three judges were at liberty to take the contrary view on the same point when they tried Asaoka the following week; and then to revert to their initial view when they tried Misumi.[53] But in fact there was no chance of this; for men hearing capital charges are eager to avoid giving the impression that they are lunatics. Similarly, being human, the members of courts B, C, and D would tend to follow suit (particularly those of them who were laymen and therefore not confident of their own mastery of the opposing views on the merits of this defence held by the legal experts).

In the Iwasa trial then, the defence of superior orders was an issue of great importance. It was a point that merited every effort that the Defending Officer could put into it. For although, as you all know, in British criminal law, superior orders have never been a defence, the proposition that superior orders were a defence in *international* law, was certainly arguable. In fact there it was in black and white in the only official textbook of the British and Australian armies — the *Manual of Military Law* — a copy of which lay on the table in front of each judge and in every orderly room throughout the Australian Army. At page 288 in the chapter on the laws of war it read:

> members of the armed forces who commit such violations of the recognised rules of warfare as are ordered by their Government, or by their commander, are not war criminals and cannot therefore be punished by the enemy.[54]

That sentence had been there in the manual, unchallenged in every edition since 1914. But now, pasted to the margin was a slip of paper — one of the 1944 amendments — which said the reverse: (I quote)

> The fact that a rule of warfare has been violated in pursuance of an order of the belligerent Government or of an individual belligerent commander does not deprive the act in question of its character as a war crime; neither does it, in principle, confer upon the perpetrator immunity from punishment by the injured belligerent …

53 GF: Capt. Misumi Michiaki was tried at Morotai (M8). For the trial transcript, see NAA A471 80769.

54 GF: This passage was cited by J Bowie Wilson with the same page reference in his review of the case for the Directorate of Prisoners of War & Internees (DPW&I), 15 January 1946, in relation to the trial of Lt Tanaka and Pte Fujisaki (M7). See NAA A471 80768, p. 5. Wilson referenced it as the Australian edition.

> The question … is governed by the major principle that members of the armed forces are bound to obey lawful orders only and that they cannot therefore escape liability if, in obedience to a command, they commit acts which both violate unchallenged rules of warfare and outrage the general sentiment of humanity.[55]

Despite what the *Manual of Military Law* said on the subject, the issue remained open for the court to decide. For while the appendices to the manual, i.e. the *Army Act* and the *Rules of Procedure* have statutory force, the manual is nothing more than what its authors consider to be the state of the law — a commentary. Superior orders is one of the many gray [sic] areas of international law. It is not covered by written agreements such as the Hague Rules or the Geneva conventions. It was therefore open to the defence to dispute whether there had been a change in international law between 1940 and 1944 and indeed whether there could be such a vital change in such a short period. Why had the War Office changed its mind (and the Americans too — for in the same year they had made a similar volte face). The defence could have pointed out that two things had happened. The first was that Britain's principal academic writer on the subject, Professor Lauterpacht, had changed his stand on the subject. As a later writer has put it, between the 1935 and the 1940 editions of his standard work on international law, Professor Lauterpacht suddenly like Saul on the way to Damascus saw the light. The other thing was that after the end of 1942, when it was becoming increasingly apparent that the Allies were going to be at the administering (rather than receiving end) of international law, a number of conferences of Allied lawyers and Allied officials were held at which views similar to those of Professor Lauterpacht prevailed.

Iwasa's Defending Officer put this argument well — very well for a man with only three days warning and with only a handful of standard textbooks to work on.

In the time that remains to us perhaps we can consider the sentences handed down by the Morotai courts, the advice tendered on each by the Judge-Advocate General and the action taken on that advice by the Confirming Authority, the Acting Commander-in-Chief, Lieutenant General Sturdee.

The Judge-Advocate General (JAG) was Mr John Bowie Wilson, a barrister. He was one of that interesting group who joined the old Australian Intelligence Corps before the First World War. He appears to have transferred to the Legal Corps in 1920. He was appointed JAG in 1935 on retirement from the Citizen Military Forces at the age of 60. He had never served overseas.

55 GF: This passage was cited by Bowie Wilson as a change; see NAA A471 80768, p. 5. The change can be cited as *Amendment 34 of 1944 on superior orders*.

The pattern of the sentences is that the Morotai courts, in the cases where prisoners of war were killed without court martial, followed the doctrine of the 1944 amendment to the manual and found all persons directly involved guilty of murder. They then considered the question of superior orders as a mitigating circumstance when deciding the degree of punishment appropriate. Where the accused was an 'other rank' their practice appears to have been that, provided that it was not he that had urged his superior to issue the order, superior orders were a mitigating factor sufficient to reduce the appropriate punishment from death to imprisonment. Thus in the Talaud cases the court sentenced to 10 years each the sergeants and the privates ordered from the ranks to bayonet the prisoners. Wilson went further and suggested that they should not be punished. Sturdee reduced the sentences to five years.[56] Where the accused was an officer the attitude of the courts appears to have been that superior orders were no ground for mitigation. In *principle* Wilson took the same view. Take for example his advice on Iwasa's petition:

> I am of the opinion that such a flagrant breach of international law as the execution of prisoners of war without proper trial and conviction of an offence should be known to be illegal by all commissioned officers and I therefore cannot advise that the death penalty in the case of Capt Iwasa is too severe.[57]

By using this word 'flagrant', however, Wilson left himself some latitude. He was able to see the situations confronting the five junior officers carrying out the executions[58] as quite different from those which the company commanders at Talaud faced. The Morotai courts had sentenced these five officers to death.[59] Wilson advised that they should be acquitted.

> I am of the opinion that before an accused can be found guilty of a war crime by obeying an order of a superior officer, there must be something, either from the nature of the order or the circumstances surrounding it, from which the accused should know, or at least be put on enquiry, that such order was illegal.[60]

56 GF: See the cases of Sup Pte Suzuki and Pte Ōishi (both M6), Pte Fujisaki (M7), Sup Pte Gotō (M8) and Sgt Uchino (M12).

57 GF: J Bowie Wilson to DPW&I, AMF minute paper: 'Trial of Japanese war criminal — Capt. T Iwasa', 14 January 1946, NAA A471 80718, p. 5.

58 GF: It is unclear as to which junior officers Sissons refers.

59 GF: The only junior officers who received the death sentence for one set of Talaud killings were Lt Tanaka (M7), Lt Yabe and Lt Nomura (both M12) all executed on 6 March 1946 on the first day when death sentences were carried out. Lt Yunomura was also given the death sentence for executing another group of prisoners, but this was commuted (M14). A possible fifth junior officer, Lt Katagiri (M40) involved in the same incident as Lt Yunomura, was never sentenced to death but given a 10-year sentence. Five more senior officers were also executed — Capt. Misumi (M8), Capt. Iwasa (M9), Col Koba (M10), Maj. Tamura (M10) and Lt Col Kōmura (M26), all on 6 March 1946, except for Kōmura.

60 GF: This quote comes from the trial of Naval Lt Yunomura whom he discusses below and not one of the initial set of Talaud cases discussed up to this point. See, J Bowie Wilson (JAG) to DPW&I, 16 January 1946, in the trial transcript for M14, NAA A471 80770, p. 4.

One of the differences that carried weight with Wilson was that the airmen at Talaud were the battalion's own prisoners and the company commanders must have known that they had not been court-martialled. In the other three cases the prisoners were held by another unit. The officers were told that the sentence had been lawfully imposed by higher authority. In the absence of any suspicious circumstances, that, in Wilson's view, was sufficient for an acquittal. He considered that it was not possible to credit junior officers with sufficient knowledge of either international law or Japanese naval law to make them enquire further.

Sturdee confirmed all five findings and sentences. But changed his mind on one, Naval Lieutenant Yunomura, in the interval between the signing of the confirmation and the issuing of the execution warrants. During that interval Wilson had sent on to him the transcript of the trial of Yunomura's senior officer, Rear Admiral Hamanaka and his advice on it.[61] The Admiral had been sentenced to death for authorising the execution that Yunomura had been ordered to carry out. In the case of the Admiral, however, the court had added a recommendation to mercy. Wilson did not oppose the recommendation to mercy for the Admiral; but used it to reiterate his plea for clemency for Yunomura (someone had conveyed to him that Sturdee had rejected it). The Admiral, he argued, was much more responsible for the execution of the two prisoners than was Yunomura and it would be unjust if Yunomura was executed while the Admiral was reprieved.[62] Sturdee commuted the Admiral's sentence to 15 years and Yunomura's to five years.

Wilson was on occasion more lenient to junior officers than his own rule. In the trial of Vice Admiral Ichise[63] Court B, accepting evidence that the Admiral's Staff Officer and not the Admiral had issued the execution order, acquitted the latter. They also acquitted the two petty officers who had struck the blows. They sentenced to death the naval captain, the lieutenant and the sub lieutenant through whom the execution order was passed down along the chain of command. Wilson argued that the two junior officers, although technically guilty, might be acquitted. He conceded that they knew that no court martial had taken place and that as officers they *ought* to have known that a court martial was necessary. As junior officers, however, he had extreme doubt whether their knowledge of law was of sufficient standard to know this.[64]

Sturdee confirmed the death sentences on all three.

61 GF: This is Morotai (M20), NAA A471 80733.

62 GF: He made this point when reviewing Hamanaka's case (M20). See Bowie Wilson to DPW&I, 11 February 1946, NAA A471 80773, pp. 4–5.

63 GF: This is Morotai (M41), NAA A471 81644. Ichise was tried with five others – Capt. Shirozu, Lt Miyazaki, Sub Lt Shimakawa, PO Tanaka and PO Kakuda.

64 GF: Bowie Wilson to DPW&I, 14 March 1946, NAA A471 81644. pp. 5–6.

I have said that Wilson was on occasion more lenient to junior officers than his own rule — sometimes but not always. In the case of Naval Lieutenant Katayama[65] although he was not opposed to mitigation, he did not press for the verdict of guilty against Katayama to be set aside although Katayama's position was very similar to the lieutenant in the Ichise trial. Wilson did advise that the finding of guilty and death sentence against another defendant in this trial, Warrant Officer Uemura, be set aside. Uemura had merely been in charge of the escort at the execution.[66] The only explanation I can give for Uemura's death sentence is that the same court at another trial had heard evidence that he had played a more active part in other atrocities. Sturdee let both sentences stand.

So far as I know Sturdee never commuted a death sentence on his own initiative.[67] It is ironical that in the only Morotai trials where he commuted the death sentences, Hamanaka and Yunomura, it was of no avail. They were both tried by the Dutch in 1948 and shot.

65 GF: This is Morotai (M43), NAA A471 80918.

66 GF: Bowie Wilson to DPW&I, 15 March 1946, NAA A471 80918, p. 5.

67 'Check this. I now think he sometimes did in Rabaul cases', 10/6/82.

'THE TRIALS: WERE THEY JUSTICE OR VENGEANCE?'

DCS Sissons,
Sydney Morning Herald
(16 August 1985)[1]

A few months ago, a visiting Japanese author brought me a photograph of a monument erected on Mt Sangane near Nagoya in 1981. It commemorated the men sentenced to death by Australian war crimes courts.

She asked me whether I agreed with the following sentence in the Japanese inscription carved on it: 'These trials were nothing more than vengeance, the proud victors exercising arbitrary judgment over the vanquished.' The question called for a 'yes' or 'no' answer. I am afraid my reply must be more complex.

As a result of the Australian trials, 139[2] Japanese were executed and 450 served prison sentences. As she was only an infant when the war ended, my visitor was rather vague about the details of the crimes with which these men were charged. The following are some examples.

There was the ill-treatment of prisoners-of-war. At Sandakan camp in Borneo, out of 2,400 prisoners more than 1,000 died. The principal cause was malnutrition but there were no deaths among the guards. At Tantoei camp on Ambon, of 548 only 139 survived. On Hainan Island there were 181 survivors out of 263.

1 This is the original manuscript of an article that was published in the *Sydney Moring Herald*, on 16 August 1985. The notes to this version have been prepared by Georgina Fitzpatrick.

2 David Sissons corrected this figure to 137 individuals in Table A, 'Sources on Australian investigations into Japanese war crimes in the Pacific', *Journal of the Australian War Memorial*, 30 (April 1997), www.awm.gov.au/articles/journal/j30/wcrimes (accessed 11 January 2019).

There were the massacres. About 1,300 set out on the Sandakan–Ranau death marches: only six survived. About 200 members of 2/20[3] Battalion were put to death after their surrender on Ambon. The entire native labour force on Ocean Island (about 150 people) were shot some days after the war ended.

There were the executions of survivors from aircraft that had been shot down. It seems to have been the common practice to interrogate these airmen for some weeks and then execute them.[4] The same fate usually befell any members of long-range reconnaissance parties that were captured.

There was the ill-treatment of local inhabitants. At Nauru, 34 patients at the leper hospital were taken out to sea and drowned. At Tobera in New Guinea, when one native resisted a Japanese overseer five were clubbed to death.[5]

These crimes shocked not only the Australian man in the street but also the distinguished legal authorities formulating Allied policy on war crimes trials. When the Lord Chancellor (Viscount Simon) read the evidence collected by Sir William Webb on the atrocities at Tol Plantation and Milne Bay and on the execution of Flight Lieutenant Newton at Salamaua he was so disturbed that he spent a sleepless night. All were agreed that to allow the perpetrators to escape would be to mock the living and insult the dead. To what extent this is a demand for justice and to what extent a demand for vengeance is difficult to determine.

To the citizens of the Tokyo suburb of Mitaka when their homes were burning, it was unthinkable that the pilots of the planes raining bombs on them should go free. In order to prevent the unthinkable from happening, when an airman parachuted they tied him to a post in the town square so that each citizen could club him until he died.

In choosing war crimes trials, the Allies chose the path of punishment 'through the channel of organised justice'. Therein lay some difficulties. As the war progressed, it had become increasingly apparent to the legal experts in the United Nations War Crimes Commission that, if the courts to be set up followed the Anglo-American rules of evidence, many war criminals would go free. For example, the evidence against those who killed Flight Lieutenant Newton was a diary found on a Japanese corpse. It contained an eye-witness account of the execution and named the executioner and the officers who were present. But, as the writer was dead, the diary would, according to the rules of evidence, be inadmissible.

3 In his reference to the Laha massacre, Sissons gave the wrong battalion. It was 2/21. See Lionel Wigmore, *The Japanese Thrust*, Australian War Memorial, 1957, p. 420. This matter was tried at two trials at Manus (LN12 and LN24). For the trial transcripts, see National Archives of Australia (NAA) A471 81952 and A471, 81967 respectively.

4 Sissons himself interpreted at three trials concerning the execution of captured airmen. They were held at Morotai in early February 1946. For the trial transcripts of M32, M29 and M34, see NAA A471 80722, NAA A471 81059 and NAA A471 80778 respectively.

5 This was tried at Rabaul (R4), NAA A471 80748.

Australia, accordingly, followed the lead of the other Allies and, in the legislation setting up the courts, authorised them to admit 'any oral statement or any document appearing on the face of it to be authentic'.[6]

One of the basic purposes of the traditional rules of evidence is to ensure that punishment is confined to the actual offender. Apparently the highest repositories of legal rectitude in each of the Allied nations did not regard this principle as absolute. It seems to me that what they were saying was: 'It is more important that an innocent[7] man should go free than that a guilty[8] man should hang; but this is true only where the innocent man is one of our side. When he is an enemy national, it is not so important.'

In a calmer atmosphere in 1949, the same governments by their amendments to the 1929 Prisoners of War Convention renounced the option to act in this discriminatory manner in the future. Under a.85 and a.102 of the new convention, war criminals, like other prisoners of war, can be tried only by the same courts and according to the same procedure as soldiers of the detaining power.[9]

These 1949 amendments also appear to close the door to any repetition of another discriminatory feature of the Australian trials: whereas the *War Crimes Act* empowered the courts to award the death penalty to enemy troops,[10] under the Defence Act the only offences for which an Australian soldier could be sentenced to death by a court martial were certain enumerated acts of treachery — even murder attracted only a life sentence under Australian military law.

The headlines of Australian newspapers in the weeks preceding the first executions certainly indicate a widespread thirst for vengeance: 'No room for mercy here' (*Herald*, January 21, 1946), '20 Japs to die immediately' (*Argus,* February 1, 1946), 'Condemned Japs are still alive' (*Smith's Weekly*, February 2, 1946). There is also evidence that some people even saw political prestige accruing from promptly stringing up a few guilty Japanese. Some weeks earlier, on November 16, Dr Evatt, our Attorney-General, had cabled from Washington: 'Cannot understand why first trials of Japanese war criminals have not commenced … The Americans have already commenced trials and it is a matter for comment that we should not also already have done the same in view of the initiative we took in the field of Japanese criminals.'[11]

6 The regulation he cites here may be found in *War Crimes Act 1945* (Cth), Section 9 (1).

7 Sissons must have meant guilty.

8 Sissons must have meant innocent.

9 For the conventions cited, see *Convention Relative to the Treatment of Prisoners of War*, Geneva, 27 July 1929 online at ihl-databases.icrc.org/applic/ihl/ihl.nsf/INTRO/305?OpenDocument and *Convention (III) Relative to the Treatment of Prisoners of War*, Geneva, 12 August 1949 at ihl-databases.icrc.org/applic/ihl/ihl.nsf/Treaty.xsp?documentId=77CB9983BE01D004C12563CD002D6B3E&action=openDocument (both accessed on 8 November 2018).

10 See *War Crimes Act 1945* (Cth), Section 11 (1).

11 Cable from HV Evatt, NAA A1066 H45/590/1.

If, however, one looks deepen there is much evidence of participants at each level endeavouring to operate the war crimes system with restraint.

With one possible exception there are no indications of any attempts to pack the courts. In the case in question, the court had sentenced to death a Japanese officer who, in a starving and fevered condition, had eaten flesh from the corpse of an Australian soldier killed attacking his position.[12] The reaction that this sentence produced in a number of places and the rapid corrective action that ensued is something in which Australians may take some pride.

Noel Ottaway, a Sydney journalist covering the trial, was shocked by the severity of the sentence and, on the ground that the anti-Japanese attitudes of two members of the court were well known, prevailed upon his editor to intervene. The response of the Attorney-General's Department was prompt and sympathetic.[13]

Action was put in train to raise the matter at ministerial level. This, however, proved unnecessary. Quite independently, the Divisional Commander had recommended that the sentence be commuted to imprisonment and the Confirming Authority had acted in accordance with that advice.

The transcripts of the trials suggest that the presidents of the courts were conscientious men eager to play by the rules. Of the 819[14] Japanese who appeared before them, 230 were acquitted on all charges.

Here are a couple of examples. In January, 1946, when the cries for retribution were at their loudest, a court at Morotai acquitted the Commander of a military police unit in the Celebes that had on a number of occasions executed captured air crews. The suspicion against him was very strong, but the actual evidence was inadequate.[15]

At Manus in October, 1950, a court acquitted the members of a Japanese court-martial who had sentenced to death as spies members of a *Z* Special Force patrol in Borneo and had thereby, it was alleged, unlawfully disregarded their duty to try the prisoners in accordance with the rules of international law. In this Manus trial most of the legal debate with the Prosecuting Officer was conducted, not by the Defending Officer, but by the President of the court, who laid great stress on the fact that the members of the patrol were wearing neither their badges of rank nor their identity discs.[16]

12 This was tried at Wewak (MW1), NAA A471 80713.

13 For a copy of the initial letter from Noel Ottaway to John Goodge, 3 December 1945, which initiated the subsequent consultations between government departments, see NAA A1066 H45/590/1.

14 In Table A, Sissons corrected this figure to 814 individuals. In that table he enumerated the acquittals at each set of trials, arriving at a total of 280. However, he did not calculate the number of individuals.

15 For the trial transcript for Morotai (M15), 14–16 January 1946, see NAA A471 80756.

16 This was Manus (LN 15), 16–18 October 1950, NAA A471 81956.

There were many cases where the Confirming Authority (initially the Acting C-in-C; for the later trials, the Adjutant General) exercised clemency. In this manner the 225 sentences of death passed by the courts were reduced to 148.[17]

This was usually the result of a recommendation by the Judge-Advocate General (JAG), a civilian King's Counsel with quasi-judicial tenure, to whom proceedings were required to be sent before confirmation. The latter requirement was the result of a hard-fought battle by an enlightened civil servant, FR Sinclair, the Secretary for the Army.

A feature of Australian military law dating from the *Defence Act* of 1903 was the provision that sentences of death could be confirmed only by the Executive Council. When the War Cabinet passed regulations delegating this power in war crimes trials to divisional commanders, Sinclair protested to his Minister in strong terms: 'If one … takes a critical view of this procedure (and such a critical view will, I suggest, be taken in the years to come), it might be held that any departure from the normal methods of administration and justice cannot be justified, because the motives which underlie our activities in bringing our former enemies to trial cannot be said to be altogether disinterested or unbiased …'[18]

As a result of Sinclair's intervention; a compromise was reached whereby death sentences would be confirmed, not by divisional commanders, but by the Acting C-in-C, who would in all cases seek the views of the Judge-Advocate General (JAG) on both the court's verdict and its sentence.

The public demand for the trial of war criminals continued longer in Australia than in Great Britain and America. For example, while the House of Lords debate in May 1949[19] demonstrated a strong and widespread feeling that the time had come to rule off the ledger, in the Australian House of Representatives in March 1950 the Menzies government was subjected to strong criticism for releasing 71 of the 91 suspects still awaiting trial.[20] Nevertheless, in the 1950 debate there was evidence of new attitudes appearing. The Labor Member for Perth, Tom Burke, argued that war crimes trials reduced the victor nation to the level of the war criminals.[21] The Liberal Member for St George, Sqn Ldr BW Graham, argued that Australia must follow the lead of the Dutch, who in the interests of prosperity and their future security, had put recollections of the bombing of Rotterdam behind them. Graham was one of

17 See note 1. Several men received more than one death sentence. This accounts for the final figure of 137 individuals executed.

18 FR Sinclair to F Forde, Minister for the Army, 6 December 1945, NAA MP 742/1 336/980.

19 United Kingdom. House of Lords, *Debates*, 19 May 1949, (columns) cc. 858–904.

20 Menzies made a ministerial statement on 24 February 1950 concerning the release of war criminal suspects and the number of cases to be tried at the last set of trials held on Manus Island, *Commonwealth Parliamentary Debates (CPD)*, 24 February 1950, vol. 206, pp. 99–102. For the debate on the statement, see *CPD*, 16 March 1950, vol. 206, pp. 881–990; in particular, see the criticisms voiced by Mr E Ward, Labor Member for Sydney, pp. 881–83.

21 *CPD*, 16 March 1950, vol. 206, p. 892. For Burke's complete speech, see pp. 891–93.

the first in Australia to argue publicly that war crimes were committed by the Allies as well as by the Japanese. He recalled how in 1943 Australian parents had not been ashamed to take their children to see newsreel films of RAAF and USAF planes repeatedly strafing unfortunate 'sub-human Japanese wretches' as they climbed onto life rafts, in the Battle of the Bismarck Sea.[22]

Forty years later one is certainly appalled at the double standards of the Allies whereby MacArthur in his communique after that engagement could announce that 'barges and rafts still afloat were strafed and sunk', yet three years later the captain of U-852 and three of his subordinates were executed for machine-gunning the survivors of the Peleus in their life-boats.

A characteristic of the debate in the Lords was the belief expressed by many members (particularly those with service backgrounds like Lord Hankey and Admiral of the Fleet, Lord Cook) that young subordinates ordered to commit unlawful acts by their commanders were being treated more harshly by the courts than they deserved. Although there was no similar voice in the Australian parliament, there were people of similar views within the Australian system who tried to do what they could for these unfortunate young men.

As early as November 1945, Brigadier WAB Steele, the Commander of the Australian force that reoccupied Ambon, urged that unless the officers who had ordered executions were tried, their subordinates who struck the actual blow should not be tried.[23]

Obviously, this principle could not be adopted in its entirety or most crimes would have gone unpunished. It is unfortunate, however, that the problem underlying this suggestion was not given more thought.

A more practical proposal came in June 1946 from Major General BM Morris, the Area Commander at Rabaul. He urged that the trials should not be delayed, but that confirmation should be deferred until all trials on the one incident were completed.[24] This proposal was not adopted either. The following are examples of the kind of problems that occurred.

On April 16, 1946, an Australian court sentenced to death a Japanese Sergeant, a Japanese Private and seven Formosan labourers for shooting 30 sick Chinese prisoners-of-war at Rabaul.[25] The Confirming Authority on the advice of the JAG confirmed the sentences, and the sergeant, the private and two of the Formosans were hanged on July 16.[26]

---

22 *CPD*, 16 March 1950, vol. 206, p. 891. For Graham's complete speech, see pp. 888–91.

23 This source cannot be identified.

24 This source cannot be identified.

25 This is Rabaul (R55), NAA, A471, 80915.

26 The sentence was promulgated to the men on 16 July but the hangings were carried out early on the morning of 17 July 1946. See the four warrants of execution that were not cancelled, NAA A471 80915, pp. 45–48.

The execution of the other five Formosans was deferred so that they could appear as prosecution witnesses at the trial of Major General Hirota, who, it was alleged, had issued the order to kill the Chinese.[27] In April 1947, Hirota was found guilty of this and other crimes and sentenced to seven years' imprisonment. The President of the latter court, Major General JS Whitelaw, thereupon wrote to area headquarters urging that the five Formosans be reprieved. This was referred to the JAG who, while defending the original sentences, urged that such long detention of men condemned to death justified commutation. The Confirming Authority accordingly mitigated the punishment to life sentences.[28]

Another case was even less satisfactory. On February 28, 1946, three naval personnel were sentenced to death for the execution of four Australian airmen at Ambon.[29] Sub Lieutenant Katayama had been in charge of the execution and had himself beheaded one of the airmen. Sub Lieutenant Takahashi had beheaded, another. Warrant Officer Uemura had merely been in charge of the escort and burial party.

The JAG advised that the findings and sentences against Takahashi and Uemura should not be confirmed since Takahashi could not be expected to know that the order for the execution was illegal and Uemura's mere presence did not amount to participation in the crime. As regards Katayama, he advised that the fact that he was ordered to carry out the execution by a senior officer should be considered in mitigation.[30]

Despite this advice the Confirming Authority confirmed both findings and sentence for all three. In the case of Takahashi and Uemura, this seems a clear breach of Australian Military Regulation 575 (10) which required all members of the military forces to follow the rulings of the JAG on questions of law. Uemura was executed on March 3, 1946. The executions of Takahashi and Katayama were deferred so that they could appear as prosecution witnesses at the subsequent trials of their superior officers.[31] In his report[32] to the Head of the War Crimes Section on the latter trials

27 This trial (R172) was one of the 'command responsibility' trials held in 1947. See NAA A471 81653 PARTS A–D.

28 In R55 the death sentences of five of seven Formosan guards found guilty with two Japanese non-commissioned officers (NCOs) of shooting 30 sick Chinese prisoners of war at Rabaul were delayed. While the other four were hanged on 17 July 1946, the five were kept alive to give evidence in the 'command responsibility' trial of Major General Hirota (R172) held in March and April 1947. Although the JAG, WB Simpson, on reviewing the original case of R55 did not agree that their sentences should be quashed, he did agree that making them wait for their executions for so many months justified commuting their death sentences to life sentences.

29 This was M43. See NAA A471 80918.

30 J Bowie Wilson to Directorate of Prisoners of War & Internees (DPW&I), AMF minute paper: 'Trial of Japanese war criminals', 15 March 1946, NAA A471 80918, p. 5.

31 For example, they appeared as witnesses at the trial of Naval Captain Kawasaki (R184), 30 June – 4 July 1947. For the trial transcript, see NAA A471 81067.

32 Maj. HF Dick to DPW&I, AMF minute paper: 'Sub Lt Katayama Hideo and Sub Lt Takahashi Toyoji', 1 October 1947, NAA MP742/1 336/1/1737. The existence of the report to the DPW&I was cited by Lt Col JT Brock, the Reviewing Officer, in his report on R184, dated 14 July 1947. See NAA A471 81067, p. 22.

(which ended on July 4, 1947), a Legal Officer[33] at Army headquarters advanced three grounds on which Takahashi and Katayama's cases should be reconsidered: one, the reasons already given in the JAG's original advice; two, their 19 months in the condemned cells; three, the need for some 'uniform standard of punishment according to the degree of guilt'. He noted that sentences passed in early 1946 were severe by 1947 standards — recently a naval captain had received only 20 years for ordering the deaths of all prisoners at Aitape.[34]

Despite the JAG's recent advice in the Formosans' case, the matter was not referred *to* him. Takahashi and Katayama were shot at Rabaul on October 23, 1947.

The inscription on the monument at Mt Sangane speaks of arbitrary justice. In the light of these examples I cannot deny an arbitrary element. But that the trials were nothing more than vengeance, I do contest.

Throughout the British Commonwealth it is unusual for a court martial to state its reasons when passing sentence. At the first of the Morotai trials, the President, Colonel JL McKinlay (a citizen soldier who in the First World War had served in the ranks and won the Military Medal), felt it appropriate to depart from this tradition. When passing sentence, he said: 'We are not taking our vengeance, but protecting society from the ravages of cruelty and imposing a sentence to act as a deterrent to others who, in the years to come, may be like-minded.'[35]

He spoke sincerely. I trust that the labours of men like McKinlay, Sinclair and Whitelaw were not in vain and that the Second World War trials will be the subject of careful study not only at our own service academies but also, if this is possible after My Lai, by those in Asia.

**D.C.S. SISSONS, who as a young soldier attended some of the war crimes trials at Morotai, is now a specialist in international relations at The Australian National University.*

33 This is Major Herbert Dick with whom Sissons had a long correspondence about Katayama. See, for example, NLA, Papers of DCS Sissons, Box 22: Ambon: Major Dick.

34 This refers to the trial of Naval Capt. Noto Kiyohisa who, with CPO Watanabe Teruo, was accused of ordering the executions of one Australian and two Indonesian prisoners of war. Noto got 20 years and Watanabe seven years. For the transcript for R183 (9–10 July 1947), see NAA A471 81210.

35 The first trial at Morotai was M9 which began on 29 November 1945. For the President's statement, see the trial transcript, NAA A471 80718 p. 71.

SOME OBSERVATIONS ON AUSTRALIAN WAR CRIMES TRIALS INVOLVING CANNIBALISM/ MUTILATION OF THE DEAD

DCS Sissons

A Military Court convened under the Australian *War Crimes Act 1945* sat at Wewak on 30 November and 1 December 1945 to try Lt Tazaki on the following charges:

> First Charge
>
> Mutilation of the dead in that he at Soarin No. 1 on or about 19 July 1945 mutilated the dead body of Q148482 Pte John Kraut an Australian soldier.
>
> Second Charge
>
> Cannibalism in that he at Soarin No. 1 on or about 20 July 1945 ate portion of the dead body of Q148482 Pte John Kraut an Australian soldier.

The court consisted of four officers. Their last postings before the cessation of hostilities had been, respectively, Commanding Officer 2/2, 2/3 and 4 battalions and Staff Learner (Major) HQ 6 Division.

The accused pleaded not guilty but was found guilty on each charge. There was evidence (including the accused's own confession) to support the finding.

The court by a majority of 3:1 sentenced the accused to death by hanging. This was a valid sentence under Section 11 of the Act which gave statutory embodiment to the widely accepted view that in international law 'all war crimes may be punished with death or with any more lenient penalty' (*History of the United Nations War Crimes Commission*, p. 31).

Even in the atmosphere of December 1945 there were those who regarded the sentence as unduly severe. For example, the officer administering command of 6 Division, in forwarding the proceedings to the Confirming Authority, recommended commutation of the sentence to imprisonment, giving the following as his reasons:

1. the act was an isolated one so far as the accused was concerned and there is no suggestion of a system or practice on his part;
2. the offence of cannibalism, though disgusting and degrading, is not a crime under English criminal law, and does not represent a violation of any specific prohibition in any international convention, save to the extent that it constitutes maltreatment of the body of a dead enemy;
3. the conditions under which the accused was living afford some sort of palliation of his crime.

Another example was Noel Ottaway, the *Sydney Sun*'s war correspondent covering the trial. He wrote privately to his news editor urging him to take up with the federal government the 'impossible severity' of the sentence. The *Sun* immediately passed on his letter to External Affairs who contacted the Deputy Adjutant-General by telephone on December 17th. The memorandum from the Director of Legal Services (the direct subordinate of the Deputy Adjutant-General) conveying to the Confirming Authority 6 Division's recommendation of commutation was signed on December 18th (although it may have been drafted at an earlier date). On December 19th the Confirming Authority (Lt Gen. Sir Vernon Sturdee) commuted the sentence to five years imprisonment.

It is sometime since I last read the Tazaki transcript (National Archives of Australia (NAA) A471 80713). My recollection is that the Defending Officer (an Australian Army Legal Corps captain) put all his energy into a defence of insanity and did not raise the question whether cannibalism is a war crime. At first sight this would not appear to be capable of denial. Section 3 of the *War Crimes Act* defines 'war crime' as: (a) a violation of the laws and usages of war; (b) any war crime within the meaning of the instrument of appointment of the Board of Inquiry appointed on 3 September 1945 (i.e. the third Webb Inquiry). That instrument lists 35 crimes or groups of crimes including: (xxxiv) cannibalism, (xxxv) mutilation of the dead.

The source of an Australian military court's authority to try a Japanese war criminal is, however, international and not municipal law and is limited to the trial of breaches of international law. An Australian statute cannot create an offence in international law: whether or not cannibalism is a crime in international law cannot be determined merely by the *ipse dixit* of the Australian legislature. This was an argument raised by the Japanese counsel for the defence in the trial of Lt Gen. Adachi (General Officer Commanding (GOC) XVIII Army) at Rabaul in 1947 (transcript NAA A471 81652).[1] This is good law and much easier for Australian judges, trained in a federal system, to accept than for their UK brethren weighed down by the shibboleth of the omnipotence of parliament. At the International Military Tribunal for the Far East in Tokyo it took its Australian president, Sir William Webb, three years to extract from his colleagues the reluctant admission that, if their charter — the product of MacArthur's HQ — sought to create *ex post facto* crimes, then they must disregard it and not be parties to judicial murder.

Adachi's counsel pointed out that the list of 35 crimes in the instrument of 3 September 1939 was the list of 32 crimes produced by the Commission on Responsibilities at the Paris Peace Conference in 1919 to which three additional crimes had been superimposed: (i) planning or waging a war of aggression, (xxxiv) cannibalism, (xxxv) mutilation of the dead. He noted that the instruments appointing Webb's two earlier inquiries (issued on 23 June 1943 and 8 June 1944 respectively) contained the original list of 32 items without these additions. Hence, he argued, the addition had no authority in international law.

At the Adachi trial the Judge Advocate (Lt Col JT Brock) in his summing-up before the court retired to consider its verdict, accepted the argument that the Australian parliament cannot create an offence in international law. He did not, however, accept the proposition that cannibalism was not an offence in international law. There were no grounds for regarding the list drawn up by the 1919 Commission on Responsibility as exhaustive or immutable: Article 3 of the Red Cross Convention of 1929 recognised the duty of belligerents to protect the corpses of enemy dead against pillage and maltreatment.

Brock's argument that maltreatment of the dead is a crime in international law is convincing. It does not, however, convince me that cannibalism was a crime in international law other than as a manifestation of maltreatment. Nor does Webb seem to have regarded it as an independent crime. For at p. 89 of his second report (dated 31 October 1944) he concludes the section on cannibalism with the following sentence:

> These further cases of cannibalism will, with your approval, be placed, with other cases dealt with in the Japanese Atrocities Report, before the United Nations Commission in the form desired, as a breach of the Red Cross Convention against *mutilation of the dead* (DCSS emphasis).

Where the prosecution charged a Japanese with cannibalism as well as with maltreatment, I feel the onus was on it to establish the cannibalism itself was regarded as a crime in international law. With some research from the Attorney

1 The issue of cannibalism arose indirectly in the Adachi trial, as he was charged with 'unlawfully disregard[ing] and fail[ing] to discharge his duty as commander to control the operations of the members of his command, permitting them to commit brutal atrocities …'.

General's Department in Canberra and from legal historians at the universities they might well have been able to do so. They might have unearthed say a couple of medieval cases where, at the end of a long and terrible siege in which the besieged had eaten the occasional member of the attacking force whose corpse they had managed to capture, and the victor lord had executed the lord of the castle for this crime. With one or two cases like this behind them, the prosecution could have argued (and I should have found it convincing) that the only reason why the prolific 19th and early 20th century writers on international law (including the 1919 Commission) failed to include the crime of cannibalism in their catalogues was, not that they did not regard it as a crime, but that for a couple of centuries conditions had been such that in the wars between civilised powers its occurrence was very rare.

The privations suffered by XVIII Army were conducive to cannibalism. Of its 120,000 members only 20,000 were alive at the war's end. Almost all of these had travelled the entire 2,000 kilometres from Buna to Aitape on foot. Of these 20,000 survivors 70 per cent were hospitalised on their repatriation to Japan. The American landings at Aitape and Hollandia in April 1944 had cut off all supply from the rear and at that time stocks were sufficient only for four months at one-third rations. No regular rations were available after September 1944.[2] Cannibalism was sufficiently widespread to cause considerable demoralisation. Consequently it was one of the offences for which, in an Emergency Punishment Order issued in October of that year, Adachi prescribed capital punishment.[3] In the following five months 70 Japanese were executed after summary investigations by their formation commanders pursuant to this order. In 40 of these cases the charge was desertion or refusal to carry out orders; in the remaining 30 the charge was cannibalism.[4] But although the prosecution at Adachi's trial did not raise this point, there are grounds for believing that these summary trials for cannibalism were confined to cases where the victim was a fellow Japanese. On 31 December 1944 Australian troops in an engagement on the Danmap River (near Aitape) captured a directive on discipline issued by the GOC of the infantry component of 41 Division (one of the formations comprising Adachi's command). This contained the following clause:

> Notwithstanding that there is no provision in the criminal law to this effect, the death penalty shall apply to any person who knowingly eats human flesh (other than that of the enemy) — a most serious crime against humanity.[5]

2 Australian War Crimes Trial (AWCT) R173, Lt Gen. H Adachi, transcript (NAA A471 81652), exhibit 5: 'Lt Gen Adachi's statement (no. 5)'.

3 (AWCT) R173, exhibit 3: 'Lt Gen Adachi's statement (no. 3)'.

4 (AWCT) R173, sheet 105, Lt Col K Tanaka (defence witness).

5 GHQ, SWPA, Allied Translator and Interpreter Section, *Research Reports*, no. 72, supplement no. 2 (23 January 1945), pp. 4, 5, 75. The International Military Tribunal for the Far East also refers to this document on p. 1067 of its judgment.

It is reasonable to suppose that in this directive the subordinate Commander was reproducing either the text or the intent of the Emergency Punishment Order. If so, this would explain why, in his trial, Adachi's counsel never tendered the actual text of the latter.

Other Australian trials involving cannibalism or mutilation of the dead are listed in Table 5.1.

Besides Australian cases, the only trial mentioned in the United Nations War Crimes Commission's *Law Reports of Trials of War Criminals* involving cannibalism was that of Lt Gen. Y Tachibana and others by an American Military Commission in the Marianas in August 1946 (vol. 13, p. 154). In this trial, 14 of the accused were convicted of murdering eight prisoners of war. Some of these accused were also charged with 'preventing an honourable burial due to the consumption of parts of the bodies of the prisoners-of-war by the accused during a special meal in the officers' mess'. They were found guilty of these charges and received sentences ranging from death to five years. To me the avoidance of the word, 'cannibalism', in framing the charges is significant.

18 October 1984

Table 5.1. Australian war crimes trials involving cannibalism/mutilation of the dead

Venue	Accused	Trial & transcript no.	Charges	Finding and sentence of court	Confirmation
Wewak 30/11 – 1/12/45	Lt T Tazaki	M1 80713	1. Mutilation of the corpse of an Australian soldier at Soarin No. 1 about 19/7/45. 2. Cannibalism in connection with same.	Guilty on both charges.	Commuted to five years.
Rabaul 28/5/45	L/Cpl H Mena	R101 81048	Same charges as M1 above	Not guilty on both charges.	
Wewak 11/12/45	Sgt Maj. Y Hidano	M5 (No transcript. Summary in A1067 UN46/WC/8, part 1)	1. Murder of a NG native at Kunjama about January 1945. 2. Cannibalism in connection with same.	Not guilty on both charges.	
Rabaul 2/4/46	Lt H Tomiyasu	R36 80783	1. Murder of several unknown Indian POW at Sowam at intervals between May and October 1944. 2. Cannibalism in connection with same.	Guilty on both charges. Death by hanging.	Finding confirmed against advice of the JAG. Sentence commuted to 15 years.

Source. DCS Sissons

THE FATE OF THE JAPANESE GARRISONS AT NAURU AND OCEAN ISLAND

DCS Sissons[1]

The Japanese Navy occupied the small phosphate islands, Nauru (0°32'S, 166°55'E) and Ocean Island (0°52'S, 169°55'E) in 1942 and held them throughout the war with garrisons numbering about 4,000 and 500 respectively. From early 1944 they were effectively blockaded and deaths from malnutrition were occurring daily. By the beginning of 1945, however, the troops were managing to survive — on pumpkins they grew and toddy made from the sap of coconut palms. Deaths from dysentery, however, continued.

On Japan's surrender in September 1945, the task of reoccupying these islands and removing the Japanese to concentration areas to await repatriation devolved upon the First Australian Army. Along with the Japanese Army units in Bougainville these troops were moved to a staging camp at Torokina (6°14'S, 155°03'E) while the permanent concentration area in the Fauro group of islands (6°55'S, 156°05'E) was being prepared.

On September 20th about 2,000 of the troops from Nauru were disembarked at Torokina and were marched the 10 miles to the staging camp. They were followed by another 1,250 the next day. These were base troops unaccustomed to marching and debilitated by malnutrition and disease. The temperature was 95°–100°F. They were pressed to maintain marching speed by Australian guards at the rear of each squad. A number succumbed to heat stroke. Exactly how many dead is not known; but survivors estimated the number as 'about 50' or 'a few dozen'.

1 This essay is the original English text for 'Nauru shubihei no "shi no kōshin"' [The 'Death March' of Japanese soldiers on Nauru and Ocean Island] in I. Hata et al. (eds), *Sekai sensō hanzai jiten* [Encyclopedia of war crimes in modern history] (Tokyo: Bungei Shunjū, 2002).

The remaining 700 from Nauru and the 513 from Ocean Island were disembarked and marched to the staging camp on October 8th. The war diary of the Australian guard unit (9 Battalion) records that this time 12 died on the march.

The misfortunes of the Nauru and Ocean Island garrisons did not end at Torokina. As was well known to the Australian Army, both islands are malaria free. Accordingly these troops had no immunity to the disease and carried with them no suppressive atebrin or quinine. At the end of October they were moved to the concentration area in the Fauro group, a highly malarial region, and were located there alongside the Japanese troops from Bougainville, many of whom were infected. The Australians did not provide them with any suppressive drugs. The inevitable outcome is related by the Director of Medicine at Australian Army Headquarters, Brig. N Hamilton Fairley, in an article in the *Medical Journal of Australia*:

> 799 Japanese prisoners-of-war from Nauru, a non-malarious island, with their own medical service, were sent to Fauro on 30 and 31 October 1945, after a brief period of staging at Torokina. The first case of malaria occurred on November 8, and was followed by an epidemic involving almost every man. On November 26, four weeks after entering the malarious area, 530 patients were in hospital undergoing anti-malarial treatment. By December 5, thirty-five days after movement to Fauro, 212 deaths [26.5%] had occurred … . Their enormous death rate again indicated the terrible fate awaiting any group of non-immunes not protected by atebrin or other effective anti-malaria suppressant.

Fairley's figures, however are incomplete; for they deal with only one group numbering 799 of the approximately 4,400 Japanese troops from Nauru and Ocean Island moved to the Fauro area. These 4,400 were distributed among areas 10, 11, 12 and 14. His figures probably refer to Area 11. Furthermore the deaths continued after December 5. The war diary of the Australian guard unit (7 Battalion) records the total deaths each week among all Japanese naval personnel in the Fauro concentration areas. It shows that these peaked at 164 in the week ending December 9 but were still as high as 46 in the last week of that month. According to the Commander of the Ocean Island garrison, during the period of two months from November 20 the deaths among his troops numbered 78 and those among the Nauru garrison exceeded 600.

References

Hamilton Fairley, N, 'Malaria in the south-west Pacific', *Medical Journal of Australia*, 3 August 1946.

Katayama, H, 'Rabauru Sempan no Shinsō', in *Dokyumento Nihonjin: 8 Anchihyūman*, Tokyo: Gakugei Shorin, 1969, pp. 262–68.

SISSONS' CORRESPONDENCE

Editors' note

We include two sets of correspondence in this chapter to show how Sissons approached research topics and prospective informants. The first set is between Sissons and Major Herbert F Dick, whose interesting personal and career backgrounds are described in a short biography, compiled by Georgina Fitzpatrick. In his letter to Dick as a prospective informant, Sissons outlines the details of what he knew and what he wanted to find out. Reading Sissons' comprehensive descriptions triggered Dick's memory and the outcome is his 'random recollections'. Some of Dick's terminology is offensive by contemporary standards, however, we chose to include Dick's response in its entirety in order to elucidate various issues of the postwar period.

The second set of correspondence is between Sissons and his brother, Hubert, a distinguished medical practitioner working in New York. It gives a graphic illustration of Sissons' extraordinary ability to conduct research in areas far removed from his own expertise. In this case, he was concerned to establish the causes of a high death rate among a group of Japanese prisoners, which is described in Section 5.4 'The fate of the Japanese garrisons at Nauru and Ocean Island'. The group was forcibly marched considerable distances in a debilitated state in conditions of extreme heat, and Hubert concluded that David's research gave him a superior knowledge of the effects of extreme heat on the human body than he had himself.

The other aspect of Sissons' correspondence that is worth noting is his deep concern to consider evidence that not only the Japanese, but also the Australian side in the conflict, were capable of gross mistreatment of prisoners, thus putting himself at odds with the overwhelming majority of Australian opinion in the aftermath of the war that saw Japanese behaviour as uniquely reprehensible under international and military laws.

MAJOR HERBERT FRANCIS DICK

Georgina Fitzpatrick

David Sissons began looking for the former Major in the early 1970s as part of his hunt for anyone who had anything to do with the Katayama case.[1] Dick signed a minute paper in November 1946, when working at Victoria Barracks Melbourne, concurring with the view of Judge-Advocate General William Ballantyne Simpson that Katayama's death sentence should be reviewed, stating: 'I am of opinion that there has been a miscarriage of justice in this case.'[2] Perhaps it was this intervention that endeared Dick to Sissons.

It turned out that Dick's experience in relation to war crimes was both as a victim and as a Legal Officer in the Australian war crimes trials apparatus after his recovery from prisoner-of-war camp. It is therefore not surprising that, once Sissons had located his whereabouts in the 1970s,[3] he wanted to pick Dick's brains, not just for the Katayama case but also for a wide range of his research interests.

Dick, who was born on 2 March 1908 in Melbourne, was already an established lawyer when he enlisted in May 1940.[4] He went as an officer to Malaya at the end of July 1941, four months before the Japanese attack on Pearl Harbor. Wounded in action on 12 February 1942 as the Japanese forces moved down the Malayan peninsula towards Singapore, he spent the rest of the war as a prisoner. He was 'recovered' from Changi on 5 September 1945 and repatriated from Singapore. He had recovered sufficiently by 9 January 1946 to be 'allotted for duty with HQ

1 Sub Lt Katayama Hideo was tried, found guilty and sentenced to death by firing squad for his part in the execution of captured Allied airmen. For the trial transcript of M43, see NAA A471 80918. See Chapter 1 in this volume for my discussion of Sissons' obsession with this particular case.

2 Report on submission, 20 November 1946, NAA MP742/1 336/1/1737. So significant was this that Sissons listed it as a point to be made in his 1978 Duntroon lecture, Papers of David Sissons, NLA MS 3092, Box 32: Morotai: Duntroon lecture.

3 There is a telegram, dated 20 September 1973, from Bronwen Sissons to her husband (he might have been on a research trip away from Canberra) letting him know that Dick was a solicitor in Rochester, in rural Victoria, Papers of David Sissons, NLA MS 3092, Box 22: Ambon.

4 See his Attestation form, NAA B883 VX16481.

Vic L of C as [a] Legal Officer' with the rank of Captain.[5] He was sent to Singapore in May 1946 to work on war crime trial files and, in August 1946, he was appointed Staff Captain in the Directorate of Prisoners of War and Internees in Melbourne. Until the end of 1949, he worked in Rabaul, Tokyo and Hong Kong as a Legal Officer on war crimes trials.

5 See his Officer's Record of Service, NAA B883 VX16481.

DCS Sissons: Letter to Herbert F Dick, 5 August 1976

Department of International Relations

5 August 1976

H.F. Dick, Esq.,
Lindsay Street,
Rochester, Vic. 3561.

Dear Mr. Dick,

Please excuse this long letter from a complete stranger. As a member of the academic staff of this Department I am doing some historical work on the Australian war crimes trials.

Although, thanks largely to the articles written by George Dickinson (of the Sydney Bar) in the Australian Quarterly (June 1952) and the Journals and Proceedings of the Royal Australian Historical Society (Vol. 38, 1952/53) there is available to the public a general record of the Manus Is trials of 1950-1951, little is known about the more numerous and more important Australian trials of 1945-48.

From the details of your service as set out in the Army List your experience in this field as a regimental officer, as a P.O.W., as a DAAG in DPW & I and as an AALC officer participating in some of the trials themselves must be virtually unique.

I wondered whether it might be possible for me to call on you and hear some of your recollections of the Directorate of P.O.W. and Interness and of the trials.

During the War I heard no shots fired in anger, but as a 20-year old sergeant I was attached to the Defending Officers as an interpreter at some of the Morotai trials in January 1946.

At the time I was quite sure that the trails were a necessity and that as a result of them prisoners and civilians were more likely in future wars to be treated with humanity. I thought, however, that some of the Morotai courts were unduly severe in imposing the death penalty on very junior officers and other ranks who had carried out death sentences as a result of specific orders from superior officers and had not aggravated the offence by additional barbarities or indignities.

Now, like Telford Taylor (one of the Nuremberg prosecutors), I am, as a result of Vietnam, less certain.

My interest in the trials as an academic dates from four or five years ago when I translated for my own use part of Gen. Imamura's autobiography. It was there that I first came upon your name. At page 450 he writes:

> Finally the last of the Rabaul trials, my own, arrived. Several days after the sentence was handed down, one of the three prosecuting officers, Maj Dick, visited me.

He said that he was unlucky to be involved in the trial. Personally he had no feeling of hostility towards the Japanese Army. He had been seriously wounded in Singapore but had recovered thanks to a Japanese doctor and good treatment by the camp commandant. As a result of his testimony, prosecutions against both had been stopped. He wished to go to Japan.

I told him that I was very disappointed that Cpl "Y" had got twenty years. [On the previous page Imamura related how "Y" had been sentenced to death on several counts including killing an Indian officer, "CHAMURATTO". "Y" had done so because the latter had drugged and then sexually assaulted him. From feelings of shame "Y" had witheld this information from the court. Imamura informed the District Commandant, "ARUPIN" who then had "Y" interrogated by Capt. Backhouse of the ALLC. As a result "Y's" sentence was reduced to 20 years].

I suggested to Dick that he get Cpl "Y" for his servant for the month he was in Rabaul, and see for himself. He did so and promised to recommend remission.

Imamura also devotes seven pages to the case of Lt (Naval) Hideo KATAYAMA. For a couple of years I had to content myself with a Japanese translation of the transcript of Katayama's trial given to me by the Japanese Lutheran clergyman who in 1958 published the diary and the letters written by Katayama in prison at Sugamo, Morotai and Rabaul. Last year, however, the Attorney-General, as a result of representations by Prof. Geoff Sawer and myself, opened to the general public the case files of all the Australian war crimes trials. These contain the full transcript of proceedings, the advice tendered by the Judge-Advocate General and other officers to the Confirming Authority, and the latter's decision.

You will probably remember the facts of Katayama's case because the same ground was covered in the later trial of Capt. (Naval) Kawasaki in which you were Prosecuting Officer. To refresh your memory, however, I am enclosing a copy of my translation of the Japanese translation of the transcript.

In the original trial the court sentenced all three accused to death. The JAG (Bowie Wilson) advised that in the case of Takahashi and Uemura the finding should not be confirmed and that in the case of Katayama "the fact that he was ordered to carry out the execution by a much superior staff officer should be taken into consideration in mitigating the death penalty".

Sturdee nevertheless confirmed the death sentences against all three. Most junior of them, a warrant-officer (who was at the execution but, unlike the other two accused, had not been one of the executioners), was executed at Rabaul a month later. The execution of the other two, however, was postponed for over a year so that they could give evidenee in the trial of Kawasaki (who was not in custody at the time of the first trial).

The Kawasaki trial took place at Rabaul at the end of June 1947. On May 7th Kawasaki's Japanese Counsel had approached the Australian authorities and asked their assistance to procure details of Kawasaki's service record from the Japanese Navy Ministry to establish that he was at Manila at the time Katayama said that he was in Ambon ordering the executions. Some months earlier (10 July 1946) Katayama, presumably after Kawasaki's apprehension, had facilitated this by retracting his own confession and swearing that, far from participating in the executions, he, Katayama, had not even heard about them until after the War.

The Court were satisfied with Kawasaki's alibi and acquitted him.

In a minute to the DPW & I that you wrote on 1 October 1947 (three weeks before Katayama's execution) you said:

> 7. I entirely concur in the acquittal of Kawasaki, but this acquittal does not necessarily mean that Katayama and Takamashi took no part in the execution. It means merely that they did not get their orders from Kawasaki. Having seen and heard them give evidence and also considering all the other evidence, I am of the opinion that they did take part in the execution.

You may be interested to know that there is now additional information confirming your opinion. Gen. Imamura in correspondence with Katayama's next-of-kin some years later said that Katayama repeated the original account to him at their first meeting in May 1946. Imamura never doubted it and considered that Katayama departed from it as a result of very bad advice from his naval superiors. Katayama's next-of-kin were also told by Katayama's room-mate in the Rabaul compound (Cdr. Hatakeyama) that his second account was concocted on the advice of Vice Adm Kusaka, the senior naval officer in the compound. Hatakeyama was sentenced to death at Rabaul on 17 July 1947 for war crimes at Ambon in 1942. The JAG (Simpson) advised that the sentence was excessive insofar as Hatakeyama was only a lieutenant at the time and 'was merely the conduit pipe between his Admiral and his fellow accused'. Despite this, the Adjutant General (Anderson) signed a warrant for Hatakeyama's execution on September 10th. On October 7th, however, he had second thoughts and commuted the sentence to 20 years). Hatakeyama said that they had tried to get Chibaya (the Ambon witness who established Kawasaki's alibi) to concoct an alibi for Katayama; but Chibaya had refused to do this.

Your minute of 1 October 1947 continued:

> 10. It may be argued that Uemura, the least guilty of the three, having been executed, these two criminals should suffer the same fate. I, however, am of opinion that mitigation is desirable for the following reasons:
>
> (a) I concur in the opinion of the J.A.G. and his reasons.
>
> (b) I consider it desirable that there should be some uniform standard of punishment according to the degree of guilt. To cite one example only - Capt. Noto was awarded only 20 years' imprisonment for ordering the deaths of "All prisoners on Aitape". These accused were much junior in rank to Noto, and their degree of guilt was, in my opinion, less.
>
> 11. Although it is perfectly lawful to keep condemned men alive to appear as witnesses, I think that some notice should be taken of the lapse of time in this case - 19 months.

There is a memorandum by the CLO HQ 8MD Rabaul (Brock) dated 14 July 1947 and minuted by the Brig Comdt 8MD (Neylan) which contains the suggestion that they too felt that the death sentences against Katayama and Takahashi should be commuted.

Naturally I concur whole-heartedly with your minute. You and the other members of your profession in khaki served your country and humanity well. You in your prosecution of Kawasaki and Capt. Williams (presumably J.M. Williams, now a Judge in the N.S.W. Workers' Compensation Commission) in his prosecution of Katayama appear to have been falling over backwards to ensure that the accused had fair trials.

I am amazed that on this occasion, two years after the cessation of hostilities, your recommendation was not accepted. The next item on the file is the bleak signal from the DPW & I to HW 8MD dated 9 October 1947: "I am directed by the Adjt-Gen to refer to our 34958 of 18 Apr 46 advising confirmation of the finding of guilty and sentence".

Imamura at page 468 of his autobiography writes how, before dawn on the morning of the execution (23 October 1947), he roused Backhouse and Upson and asked to be paraded before Neylan, and how at 7.30 a.m. the latter received him and told him that, having already on his own authority delayed the executions for a week in response to the representations of everyone in the compound, he could delay them no longer.

One of the things that now worries me about our War Crimes Act 1945 is its authorization of the Governor-General to delegate his responsibilities as the Confirming Authority. Under this authority Cabinet delegated this power first to the Commander-in-Chief and then, when the Military Board was reinstituted, to the Adjutant-General. In the case of the United Kingdom this provision was not so objectionable since, there, it did not deprive a Japanese prisoner of a right enjoyed by a British military offender under sentence of death. But as I understand it, one of the important points in which Australian and British military law differed, was the provision in the Australian Defence Act, jealously guarded by Cabinets irrespective of their political complexion, that in the case of an Australian serviceman the death sentence could be confirmed only by Cabinet. If it was thought improper for the military to possess this power even in time of war, then I can see no legitimate reason for their conferring on the military such a power in peacetime. In fact this delegation by Cabinet of the confirming function appears to me to be rather sordid. The Labor Cabinet, by the ALP Platform and by years of practice, was committed to the principle that all death sentences should be commuted; but they wanted to hang the war criminals - and so they passed the buck to the C in C. It is particularly in the light of this background that I am surprised that the C in C (and later the Adjutant-General) treated the advice of the JAG so lightly.

It also seems discriminatory that the War Crimes Act made capital, offences which, if committed by Australian servicemen overseas, under Australian military law could only be punished by imprisonment. For as I understand it, under Australian military law the only capital offences were mutiny and certain acts of treachery (Defence Act, Section 98).

During the Occupation of Japan, the U.S. 8th Army in the administration of its war crimes jurisdiction appears to have taken very seriously the role of the Confirming Authority in ensuring - to use your own phrase - 'that there should be some uniform standard of punishment according to the degree of guilt'. Enclosed is a reference to this in an article on the Yokohama War Crimes Trials which appeared in the American Bar Association Journal. 8th Army's second review in 1950 of all the cases tried, 'with the view of equalizing by reduction of the sentences of some of the early cases that are unduly severe by comparison with those of later cases' seems particularly appropriate.

Kawasaki though acquitted in the trial involving Katayama was, you will remember, found guilty of the murder of Pte Schaefer in a similar trial held earlier in June 1947. Here it was established that Kawasaki knowing that no court-martial had been held, passed on the orders for Shaefer's execution to the Garrison Commander. In 1947 the punishment thought appropriate for this was 10 years. Eighteen months earlier the penalty for the very much junior officer, who merely struck the blow, was death.

Sir William Webb in his judgment at the Tokyo trials the following year took into consideration in reducing the sentences of some of the major war criminals the fact that their superior, the Emperor, went unpunished. Katayama's case suggests to me that we were mistaken in proceeding with the trials of junior officers, like Katayama, until their superiors (e.g. Kawasaki) had been tried.

Although certain aspects of it are informative, the case of Katayama as a whole is of no particular significance to my research. It just happens that, because of the material available about it in Japanese, it was the only one that I could study in detail before the Australian archives were opened. Thanks to Imamura and Katayama's friends in high places among the Japanese Christian churches, it is the case best known in Japan. There are, no doubt, other cases that merit even greater sympathy. Katayama chose to be sworn on the bible and then, at his second trial, perjured himself. Personally I regard this as no more serious than if an Australian P.O.W. in similar circumstances lied to a Japanese military tribunal. He did the same in his open letter to 'Dear Christians in Japan' in which he likens himself to the Christian martyrs. As this was part of efforts to secure a remission of sentence, this too is understandable. Very unwisely, however, his family published this letter in serial form in the Japanese Christian weekly, Kirisuto Shimbun, in June 1956 and later in 1958 as an appendix to his diary. They thereby, quite unnecessarily, made it difficult for later writers to confine themselves to his misfortunes without also dealing with his perjury.

If you could spare me a couple of hours I should very much like to pay you a visit and discuss the trials with you. I see from our membership list that you, too, are a member of the Naval & Military Club. Do you come to Melbourne from time to time? If so, could we talk over a meal there? If on the other hand you are too busy during your Melbourne visits, I could easily make the journey to Rochester. The Tourist Bureau here tell me that, because of bad communications between here and Deniliquin, the best way to get to Rochester is via Melbourne. My recollection is that there used to be a bus service from Melbourne to Echuca. Does this still exist, or is rail the best way from Melbourne?

Possibly you might like to make further enquiries about the bona fides of anyone working on such a topic. There are two members of your profession who know me well and who have discussed such matters with me on many occasions over the years. One is John Wright (Prosecutor's Chambers, County Court, Melbourne). He used, I think, to appear on the Bendigo circuit. Perhaps the best Japanese linguist in the AMF, he was the official interpreter in several of the Morotai trials. The other is Sir Peter Crisp, who until his recent retirement, was a Supreme Court judge in Hobart. He sat on several of the Morotai courts.

Once again I do apologise for burdening you with a letter of this nature.

Yours sincerely,

D.C.S. Sissons,
Fellow.

Herbert F Dick: Letter to DCS Sissons, 26 August 1976

STEWART & SONS

BARRISTERS & SOLICITORS FOR VICTORIA & NEW SOUTH WALES
COMMISSIONERS FOR ALL AUSTRALIAN STATES
INCORPORATING H. W. RALEIGH ROBERTS & DICK. MYLES O'BRIEN & SON

Tel. Stewart & Sons 22 or 28 139

I. M. STEWART LLB
D. J. FINDLAY LLB
~~W. R. M. BLACKWELL~~
~~R. A. McDONALD~~
K. A. APPLEYARD LLB
ASSOCIATE
~~P. R. CLEELAND LLB~~
CONSULTANTS
H. F. DICK MA LLB
~~G. L. ROBERTS~~

Please Reply to Rochester Office
Our Reference HFD:FP
Your Reference

235 ANSTRUTHER STREET,
ECHUCA 3625
P.O. BOX 267
ECHUCA 8 2222
GILLIES STREET,
ROCHESTER 3561
P.O. BOX 57
ROCHESTER ~~22/68~~ 3561
KING GEORGE STREET,
COHUNA 3568
P.O. BOX 40
COHUNA 56 2504

26th August 1976

D.C.S. Sissons Esq.,
Box 4,
CANBERRA. A.C.T. 2600

Dear Mr. Sissons,

I must apologise for the delay in answering your letter of the 5th instant. I had not looked closely at the envelope, and had assumed that it was just another of the numerous circulars that come in the mail.

On opening it a few minutes ago I realized that courtesy demanded an immediate reply. As, however, I am leaving for Melbourne tomorrow and have some loose ends to tidy up I can do no more now than to acknowledge it and to assure you that when I return next week I will read it carefully and write a considered reply.

Yours sincerely,

H F Dick

H.F. Dick

Tel. 223

Herbert F Dick: Letter to DCS Sissons, 17 September 1976

STEWART & SONS

BARRISTERS & SOLICITORS FOR VICTORIA & NEW SOUTH WALES
COMMISSIONERS FOR ALL AUSTRALIAN STATES
INCORPORATING H. W. RALEIGH ROBERTS & DICK MYLES O'BRIEN & SON

I. M. STEWART LLB
D. J. FINDLAY LLB
W. R. M. BLACKWELL
R. A. McDONALD
K. A. APPLEYARD LLB
ASSOCIATE
P. R. CLEELAND LLB
CONSULTANTS
H. F. DICK MA LLB
G. L. ROBERTS

Please Reply to Rochester Office
Our Reference HFD:FP
Your Reference

235 ANSTRUTHER STREET,
ECHUCA 3625
P.O. BOX 267
ECHUCA 8 2222
GILLIES STREET,
ROCHESTER 3561
P.O. BOX 57
ROCHESTER 22/28
KING GEORGE STREET,
COHUNA 3568
P.O. BOX 40
COHUNA 56 2504

17th September 1976

D.C.S. Sissons Esq.,
Box 4,
CANBERRA. A.C.T. 2600

Dear Mr. Sissons,

As promised in my letter of the 20th ultimo, I read your letter carefully when I returned to Rochester. While I would be very pleased to discuss the matter with you, it would be unfortunate if you were to take the time and trouble to travel over here and then find that I have nothing of interest to tell you. It is therefore better that you should have some advance information about the matters within my knowledge.

I gathered from your letter that you are interested in obtaining background information that does not appear in the official records. I was somewhat astonished by the number and variety of the memories that your letter brought to my mind. It is only natural that after three decades many of the names have escaped my memory, but I am quite clear on the essential points.

The attached random recollections are restricted to matters unlikely to be mentioned in official documents. If, after reading them, you are of opinion that further discussion would assist your research, I will be very pleased to see you.

Against that possibility I advise that I will be in Melbourne during the weekend 2nd and 3rd October next, and could meet you at the Naval & Military Club at a time convenient to yourself. If that does not suit you, and if you still consider a personal visit to be worth your time, some alternative arrangement may be made by correspondence.

I omitted from the recollections details of the precise method by which the Emperor was allowed to escape responsibility, as

l.....

these may already be known to you. On the other hand, however, the story is so discreditable that even the masochistic Americans may have concealed it. If that is the case I will be pleased to advise you.

Even if the attached recollections are of no value from the angle of research, they should provide some light entertainment, and I will look forward to hearing from you in due course.

Yours faithfully,

H.F. Dick

Random Recollections

I became involved in war crime trials because legal firms were reluctant to employ one who had been away for so long and who was considered to be inferior to those who had carried on in the profession.

This led me to transfer to AALC in order to keep the pot boiling. Then, in or about May 1946 GOC 8 Div. asked me to return to Singapore to represent him at discussions with British officials concerning 8 Div. scholarships for Chinese nurses.

My main recollection of these is that I had great quantities of drinks at public expense. For the purpose of the exercise I was attached to 1 Aust. War Crimes Section.

I took no part in the trials, and did not even attend a court as a spectator. I did, however, look over affidavits relating to Changi camp. Many of these were made by officers on whose evidence I would not hang a pariah dog, and I marked them accordingly. These men had not conducted themselves well in action or as prisoners, but I had noted that when TEC took over they made big fellows of themselves, and I suspected that they would go to the extent of giving false evidence from a safe distance. One of my few victories in my many arguments with military brass was the abandonment of proceedings against Capt. Takahashi and some of the guards.

The courts were turning out death sentences like sausages out of a machine. A scaffold was built in Changi gaol to accommodate three victims at a time, and on Tuesday mornings four batches went through the trap.

This was a great tourist attraction, and there were some quite amusing incidents. One that comes to mind was an American girl posing alongside a swinging corpse while her companion photographed her. In another case a tourist started to pull a pair of elegant boots from a suspended admiral, but the hangman's assistant stopped him, saying: "Zorry, Zur, them boots is bespoke".

When I returned to Australia I was shunted to DPW & I and was told to help a major in the preparation of the cases against the generals at Rabaul. It seemed to me incredible that, with so many AALC officers twiddling their thumbs, such a job should be given to an unqualified person. He had the combination of qualities that Ludendorf considered most dangerous. He was stupid and industrious.

I tried to see the Director to point out the absurdity of the situation, but had no success. Whenever I grumbled about this the other officers would say: "Well, the Colonel's got a fair bit to do, you know." The point of this did not become apparent until some time later.

I accordingly spent a lot of hours with other idle officers at a pub in St. Kilda, I think it was called The George, until the Directorate was thrown into a panic by the news that the trials of the Generals were due to begin, and that Badham KC and McKay of the New South Wales Bar were briefed to lead the prosecution.

On finding that no effective preparation had been made the Director called me in, and after a brief discussion a satisfactory arrangement emerged. I would be promoted to the rank of major immediately, and after the completion of the Rabaul trials I would be posted to Japan, and my wife would accompany me. I regarded the sending of families to Japan as a fraud on the taxpayer, but I could not stop the racket, so I considered that I might as well be in it.

My part of the bargain was that I completed the preparation of the cases and briefed the civilian prosecutors. I went to Sydney and conferred with Badham and some Crown Law officers. I naturally had lunch with them, and claimed the cost of this as a travelling expense. The Paymaster, however, refused it on the ground that I should have taken a cut lunch from Marrickville. After a lot of argument, and several months later, I received more than my original claim.

These were the first Australian trials under the new doctrine of Command Responsibility. The senior army officers in Australia did not like the idea, as they considered, with very good reason, that it could operate against them if they were later to be on the losing side.

I did not give it much thought until after I had met and talked with Imamura Hitoshi, whom I consider to have been the most truly noble man I ever knew. His men venerated him as a god.

I remember Ogata, the batman whom he commended to me. While changing for mess I would tell him of the day's events, and if I mentioned that I had seen or spoken to the General he would leap to his feet, stand to attention facing the compound, salute, and shout: "Imamura Taisho! Hai!"

It was his authority that kept the prisoners under restraint, and the civilians used to refer to the Australian Commandant as General Imamura's 2 I/C.

He appeared, always wearing his MC ribbon, as a defence witness at the trials of his subordinates, claiming that as Commander in Chief he was responsible for everything that happened.

This brought home to me the absurdity of the doctrine. The

evidence showed that by reason of allied activity his communications were cut and he did not have the means of knowing what was happening in other sectors.

It was also clear that if he had been able to do so he would have prevented such things from happening.

I remained at Rabaul to prosecute Baba for the Sandakan-Ranau affair, and also acted variously as prosecutor or judge-advocate in sundry other trials.

The form of the oath administered to Coons who testified in person may be of interest: "Longtime mi gat tok-tok long dispela Court mi tok-tok tru. Mi noken gaimon. Long Deo antap mi tok-tok tru. Emtasol."

When summing up to the members I used to start with the blurb about the Court deriving its jurisdiction from the War Crimes Act, but always had a doubt about it.

When I reached Japan I had plenty of time to think further about it. For days, and sometimes weeks, there was nothing to do except read or solve cryptic crossword puzzles.

I read Real's book on the trial of Yamashita. His argument was that MacArthur hated him for having defeated him in the Phillipines, and was determined to hang him through the agency of a hand-picked court. Even allowing for an anti-MacArthur bias this appeared to be substantially right. Yamashita was not directly responsible for any war crimes. His conduct after the fall of Singapore was beyond reproach. In the Phillipines his position was similar to that of Imamura in New Guinea. By reason of allied activity he could not exercise effective command, and he certainly had no control over the forces that carried out the so-called rape of Manila. The only way in which his execution could be given a colour of legality was through the doctrine of command responsibility.

I then remembered a remark made in private conversation by Gen. Yajima. He commented that their real crime had been to lose the war. The significance of this did not strike me until I had read Real's book.

It then occurred to me that we had all the time been confusing jurisdiction with authority.

A war crime is, by definition, a violation of the laws and usages of war, and these are part of the public international law. Jurisdiction to try and punish war criminals must therefore spring from the law that has been violated, namely, international law.

On that basis, therefore, any nation, and certainly any that had ratified the various conventions, has jurisdiction to deal with any war-crime suspect, regardless of nationality or the place of the alleged crime.

But jurisdiction without effective power is of no value. Taking a contemporary example, the New South Wales courts have jurisdiction to deal with the Bartons, but their power to do so depends on the will of a foreign country.

The various courts therefore derived their authority, and not their jurisdiction, from the respective governments of countries that had been on the winning side.

But all governments were bound by the principles of international law, and could not unilaterally declare new categories of war crimes.

It was not possible, even for a Philadelphia lawyer, to make commanding officers responsible for crimes which they could not prevent. Nothing in the conventions even remotely suggested it. Accordingly, the Americans were themselves guilty of a war crime when they hanged Yamashita, and the Australians were likewise guilty when they imprisoned Imamura.

That, however, brings us back to the comment of Yajima Shosho. They had not lost the war, and so there was no power to punish them.

I was on very friendly terms with Carr K.C., chief of the U.K. prosecution team, and during a walk in a forest near Tokyo near the end of 1947 I put this to him. He listened in his customary courteous way, but as he made no comment I thought that he was not impressed. However, at breakfast on the following morning, he remarked that he had stayed awake for part of the night thinking about it, and finally concurred.

By then, however, the question was of academic interest only. It did not arise in the political trial with which he was concerned, and the only general, Nishimura, with whom I was thereafter concerned, had personally ordered the Parit Sulong massacre.

It is an interesting postscript, however, that when the question of command responsibility later arose in connection with the Vietnam activities the doctrine was expressly repudiated by the American army authorities.

I had a personal interest in the Parit Sulong affair, as I had gone over the bridge in an ambulance truck only a short time before it happened, and many of the victims were from my brigade.

Nishimura was already convicted of crimes, I think in China, and was serving a 20 year sentence. Our last chance of pinning the Parit Sulong affair on him appeared to have gone when we found that Maj. Morioka, to whom he gave the order, had been killed in an air crash in China in 1943. However it later appeared that Lt Fujita had been present when Nishimura gave the order to Morioka. He made an affidavit to that effect, and Nishimura was subsequently hanged.

It is an interesting commentary on the influence of the Japanese military families that on the morning after he made his statement Fujita was found floating in the Sumida River with a knife between his shoulders.

The cuttings from the American Bar Association Journal gave me my best laugh since the Prime Minister delivered his policy speech late last year. Both the Courts and the reviews were quite funny from my point of view. The situation was well summarized when a newly arrived American lawyer asked for a copy of Whigmore, and one of the older hands told him that it would be no use to him as it was Rafferty's rules there. This had an amusing sequel when, a few days later, the newcomer said that he had looked everywhere, but could not find any book on evidence by any guy called Rafferty.

These matters are outside your line of research, but, as you acted as interpreter, the following incident may interest you. In a case in which there were five accused, one of the court members recorded six findings of guilty. The sixth, to whom he gave the longest term of imprisonment, was the Court interpreter. When asked the reason, he said that he had admitted to more offences than any of the others.

The Australian army brass, always wanting the limelight, were not content to have cases involving our troops heard by the American courts, and moved to have their own courts established in Japan. This came to a head about the middle of 1949. MacArthur agreed, but laid down conditions too stringent for Australia to meet.

It was accordingly announced that the trials of all the remaining accused involving Australian troops would be held at Manus , and I returned to Australia in or about November 1949 with two large boxes filled with fully-prepared prosecution briefs, and then proceeded to while away my time at Albert Park.

The Government, however, had in fact decided to discontinue the trials altogether. Before there was any formal announcement someone leaked the decision, and there was so much protest that Menzies denied it and unblushingly announced that the trials would proceed as scheduled.

The real decision, however, was to hold only a few trials to satisfy the public, and to drop all the other cases. The AG and DPW & I had to decide which cases should go on. The Director knew little, if anything, of the briefs in the boxes, so the selection was just a lottery. Whether they drew the names out of a hat, or whether they used a pin in the dark, will never be known. In the event, many of the worst of the cases were dropped, and some of the least blame-worthy accused were prosecuted.

I seldom allowed my personal views to affect my judgment, but I was very anxious to hang Nakahara Tokio, whom I regarded as the most vicious of the accused. One charge on which we had conclusive evidence was that of raping a 10 year old Coon girl. On his orders two of his men held her legs apart while he did so. When I learned that he was set free I declined to have anything further to do with the trials.

Looking back from this distance of time it seems that the punishments suffered by the Japanese accused depended on when and where they happened to be tried.

As I remember it, the early trials were held at Darwin, and the blood-thirsty press complained about the allegedly light sentences.

Then, bowing to pressure, CGS convened courts further away and detailed tougher-minded officers for the job. I remember one officer who had a collection of rings and other ornaments taken from dead Japanese. He said that he used to hack their fingers off with a machete. The dead men would not have felt it, but the attitude of mind disclosed tends to support my view. In another instance a court member said that he was not concerned with evidence. It was enough that the accused were Japs. Some of them delighted in watching executions. Later on, when I was prosecuting in Rabaul, I was always able to avoid being nominated as mandatory witness by ensuring that one of these was in court when I anticipated a death sentence. When the President asked me the inevitable question I had my nominee present.

That was the era of quick trials and severe sentences, and those accused who were tried then were unlucky. Many of them would have escaped death, and some may have been acquitted, if they had been tried later. This applies particularly to those who did no more than carry out orders. Many of Noto's subordinates were executed for carrying out his orders, while he escaped death. In his case, however, I think there was diplomatic pressure.

The trial of the generals brought on the scene a different type of officer. Maj.-Gen. Whitelaw was, I think, the finest

Australian officer I met in the whole of my army experience, and Brig. Neylan and Col. Tinsley were also very fair-minded. They set a standard that endured after they had returned to Australia.

I noticed also that in late 1948, when I crossed briefly to Hong Kong to prosecute a few outstanding cases, the attitude of the court members in 1 Aust. War Crimes Section was one of judicial responsibility.

It appeared to me that some general guide lines should be laid down, and just before I returned to civilian life I wrote a memo suggesting that some matters should be raised by the Australian delegates to a convention to be held at Geneva later in 1950. I forget the details, but the question of command responsibility was one of them and also a uniform set of rules and procedures to be followed at future trials.

In this latter regard I was particularly concerned bythe application of the domestic law of the nations conducting the trials. Take, for example, the question of superior orders. Under British law it was no defence at all. Dicey saw nothing odd in writing that a soldier was liable to be shot by a court martial if he refused an order or hanged by a judge and jury if he carried it out. This attitude places on a subordinate, sometimes illiterate, the duty of evaluating the legality of an order and facing the consequences if he decides to refuse it. Clearly some further thought should be given to this subject.

I wrote it more in hope than in any real expectation of action being taken on it. I learned later that it did not get beyond the Director's table.

In the long run this did not matter. Events in Vietnam indicated that the Americans, the self-righteous upholders of the laws and usages of war three decades ago, had then thrown them to the winds. And this had the approval and blessing of the true-blue Tories in Australia.

They appear to justify it on the basis of the proposition that the Right must always be right. That has no validity. The nature of an act does not change according to the politics of the nation by which it is perpetrated. I certainly have not derived any satisfaction from the knowledge that the bullets that shattered parts of my carcase were fired from the extreme Right.

DCS Sissons: Letter to Hubert A Sissons, 25 June 1979

Department of International Relations
Research School of Pacific Studies

25 June 1979

Dr H.A. Sissons
Department of Laboratories
Hospital for Joint Diseases
1919 Madison Avenue,
NEW YORK. N.Y. 10035
U.S.A.

Dear Hubert,

In my letter to you from the coast, I said that when I returned to Canberra I should write to you in detail about what I had learnt regarding the heavy death-rate among the Japanese garrisons after their movement to the Bougainville area.

To refresh your memory I am enclosing a copy of my letter to you of September 15th.

The Malaria Epidemic

The weight of opinion among the Japanese M.O.s with whom I talked was that the troops from Nauru and Ocean Is did not become infected at Bougainville - but only after their movement to Piedu and Masa Masa Is. This view is based on: (i) their local experience of the incubation period for MT malaria; (ii) their recollection that the PW compound at Torokina was virtually free of mosquitoes. The implication of this for my own argument is that HQ 2 Corps and not (as I previously thought) HQ First Army was the guilty party. There is nothing criminal in sending troops directly from one malaria-free area to another. The responsibility lies with HQ 2 Corps who moved them without drugs into a malarious area already occupied by infected troops.

The 'Death Marches'

When I wrote to you about these, I was thinking about beri-beri as a contributing factor. Before the War the Administration at Nauru was always worried about it and kept up the supply of vitamin B1 artificially with Vegemite.

In Tokyo my first contact on this particular matter was Dr M. Hirao. He was not present at any of the marches, but as an officer on Fleet HQ at Bougainville, he heard about them from participants in the months that followed. He said that there was no doubt among those whom he spoke to that the cause of death was heat stroke.

Katsuki's letter (enclosed) confirms that heat disorders certainly caused some of the casualties on October 8th. I have also spoken to a Japanese officer, Paymaster Sub.Lt. Shiono, who participated in the march of September 20th. He has no doubt that the cause of death on that day was heat-stroke. He attributes his own survival to the fact that he kept half the water in his bottle for the afternoon. He felt very close to collapsing and remembers that his vision was temporarily disturbed - everything he saw looked purple. In Tokyo I discovered that there was a third 'death march': on September 23rd 4 out of 700 men from Buka Is collapsed along the same stretch of road and died. This was after a journey lasting 24 hours in open landing barges that were so over-crowded that the men had to take shifts to sit down. The sea was choppy (If there was sea-sickness would this strengthen the likelihood of salt depletion and therfore of secondary dehydration? D.C.S.S.). Their bottles were empty when they arrived at Torokina and there was no water for them there. They tried to drink from streams along the route, but the Australian guards would not let them.

The point of the discussion in the following paragraphs is to make sure that I get my terminology right and to find out whether I should be explaining the deaths specifically as heat-stroke or, more cautiously, as heat-effects, and whether I should be seeking the causes in the standards of accommodation, messing, ventilation, and water supply on the ships before disembarkation, as well as in the absence of water-trucks along the route.

Two Australian M.O.s (who according to the 1978 edition of the Medical Directory of Australia are still in practice) may be able to help me, if I go about it in the right way. One, Dr P.L. Jobson, was the S.M.O. of the Australian expedition to Nauru. He was on the vessel from which the first group of Japanese from Nauru disembarked at Torokina on September 20th. This, however, is pretty delicate ground. If the A.A.M.C. was working to R.A.M.C. standards, he should have been very busy throughout the voyage monitoring wet and dry bulb temperatures, testing urine for salt with potassium chromate and silver nitrate, and putting pressure on the ship's captain for every ounce of drinking water that the ship's condensers could produce. If, instead, he was taking the attitude, 'the bloody Japs can look after themselves', and was spending his time playing deck tennis, then he will not welcome my enquiries and will not provide informative answers. The other person who could be helpful is Dr D.R.L. Hart, who set up a Camp Dressing Station at the Torokina PW Compound on September 19th and remained in charge of it until October 3rd. If he kept the prescribed Admission and Discharge Book, all our uncertainties will be at an end.

In order to prepare myself for correspondence with these two men, I have read what I can about heat disorders.

The most relevant discussion that I have so far come upon is in the 'Preventive Medicine' volume of the medical series of the Official History of the Indian Armed Forces in the Second World War. This follows closely H.L. Marriott's Croonian Lectures (reported in British Medical Journal, 1947, Vol. 1, pp. 245, 285, 328). In fact it may well have been written by Marriott, who appears to have been the Indian Army's principal expert on this subject during the War. Also useful was W.S.S. Laddell's 'Disorders due to Heat'. (Royal Society of Tropical Medicine and Hygiene - Transactions, Vol. 51 [1957], p. 189, ff).

I realise how very dangerous it is for a layman to dabble in matters of this nature on the basis of highly specialized articles which he has not the basic physiological background knowledge properly to understand. But I haven't much choice. I can only barge in and rely on you to stop me making a fool of myself.

On reading the sources that I have mentioned, it seems to me that heat disorders can be broken down into three categories: heat-syncope, heat-stroke and heat-exhaustion and that, in the situations that we are considering, cases of each of these could have occurred. In what follows, each sentence should be prefaced 'Am I right in thinking that ...'

It appears that unlike heat-exhaustion, heat-syncope and heat-stroke are not caused by dehydration. Let us take each of these three in turn.

Heat-Syncope

The classic example of heat-syncope is the guardsman collapsing during the Trooping of the Colour.

> The physiology is simple: if the circulating blood volume is too small for an expanded vascular bed, there is a poor venous return, and the end result is a rapid pulse, very low blood pressure and syncope ... [It is] an acute condition seen in unacclimatized men and, with no treatment other than rest and removal to a cooler atmosphere, a patient quickly recovers completely (Laddell).

Even if the Japanese on the River Glenelg and River Burdekin had enjoyed adequate sleep, ventilation, food, water and salt, some cases of heat-syncope might well have occurred. The men would have fainted as they marched. No-one besides an M.O. could have distinguished them from heat-stroke cases. If left to themselves they would quickly recover; but if placed at the bottom of a stack of other casualties they would, because unconscious, die of suffocation.

Heat-Stroke

Heat-stroke is overheating from cessation of sweating

caused by a breakdown in the heat-regulating mechanism. Its essential characteristic is a temperature of 107°F or above. The skin is hot and bone-dry to the touch. This dryness of the skin is absolute and distinguishes heat-stroke from any other heat disorder.

Heat-Exhaustion

According to the Indian official history, 'in the majority of cases heat-exhaustion is an expression of dehydration due to the deficiency of water and salt in the body'. The writer divides dehydration into two types: primary dehydration, where only water is lacking; and secondary dehydration, where there is also salt depletion.

It is in connection with heat-exhaustion that I am most confused. How quickly does it produce acute symptoms? The length of the voyage was only 4 days at the most (3 days for the troops from Nauru).

In the situation under study, I should expect the dehydration to be primary, rather than secondary. 'Sweating without water drinking produces effects mainly of water loss, because sweat is much more dilute than extracellular fluid. Hence in men lost in deserts, and without water, the effects of water depletion overshadow the effects of salt depletion' (Marriott). Furthermore, the ration of salt available to the Japanese for cooking purposes on board was the Australian tropical scale, which was more than adequate. But they may, perhaps, have not been using it all. By Australian standards Japanese put very little salt in their rice. There is also one isolated piece of evidence that perhaps suggests salt depl tion. A Japanese engineer officer of the Ocean Is garrison gives the following description of how the man marching beside him collapsed: 'His front foot became locked and he fell forwards on the ground on his instep'. The word he used for 'locked' was hikitsuru, the word commonly used for muscular cramp. According to Laddell, cramps are almost an inevitable consequence of a low concentration of sodium in the extra-cellular fluid. When someone faints from heat-syncope or heat-stroke, would one expect him to fall in a more relaxed fashion?

Assuming, however, that their systems were not deficient in salt, one should expect that, with sweating, the extracellular fluid would become hypertonic and, by osmosis, would replenish its volume by withdrawing water from the cells. The quantities involved sound fantastic to a layman. If I under tand them correctly, the writers of 'Performance in Relation to Environmental Temperature' (Johns Hopkins Hospital Bulletin, Vol. 76, [1945], p. 25, ff) found that, with the temperature at 90°F and the relative humidity 95%, when unacclimatized men carrying 20 pound packs marched 2¼ miles at a speed of 3.2 m.p.h., some produced 1310 gm of s eat and the average was 725 gm! How rapidly would this be replaced with water from the cells and what sort of immediate effects would this produce? Laddell writes that 'the vital processes demands the integrity of the intracellular fluid: intracellular dessication means death'.

Can we make any deductions about which heat disorders were involved from the speed of the patients' recovery? Katsuki says that almost all the cases were able to leave hospital within one or two days. In cases of primary dehydration the patient's condition, according to Marriott, improves within a matter of minutes after water ingestion. In heat-stroke, the authorities appear to be conflicting. According to Laddell, once the temperature is reduced by wet sheets and fanning, convalescence is rapid. But the experience of Austin and Berry in their 'Observations on One Hundred Cases of Heat-stroke' (Journal of the American Medical Association, Vol. 161, [1956], p. 1525, ff), was that, although the greatest threat to life is in the first 24 hours, 'the next 7 days present a constant threat to the patient's life'.

Earlier in this letter I made the assertion that heat-stroke was not caused by dehydration. In this I was relying on the suddenness with which it sometimes appears and on the following comment in the Indian official history: 'In the majority of cases heat-exhaustion is an expression of dehydration due to the deficiency of water and salt in the body ... The mechanism of theproduction of heat stroke is quite different, it is an acute failure of the heat regulating mechanism of the body'. But the steps taken by the Directorate of Medical Services in London after the two troopships incidents referred to in my letter to Dr Katsuki (enclosed) indicate that they, not unreasonably, felt that there was a correlation. Do you think that Fabricant in his article 'Heat Stroke' (U.S. Armed Forces Medical Journal, Vol. 9, [1958], p. 1106, ff) may have hit the mark:

> The degree of hydration may be an important variable in predisposition to heat stroke. Lichton, working with subjects acclimatized to heat for two weeks, demonstrated that there was a rise in the threshold for sweating and also a fall in the rate of sweating in acute water deprivation. The rectal temperature in the dehydrated subjects reached high levels at much lower effective air temperatures than was the case in normally hydrated subjects. Dehydration is said to set the hypothalmic thermostat at a higher than normal level, therefore adding to the vicious circle of hyperpyrexia.

Exhaustion unconnected with Environmental Heat

Katsuki in the last paragraph of the first page of his letter says: 'The causes of death were probably exhaustion and heat-stroke'. The word he uses for exhaustion is *hirō*, which according to the dictionary means 'fatigue, weariness, exhaustion'. The order of words in his sentence suggests that more of the deaths were from this than from heat disorders. What is the mechanism involved in succumbing from exhaustion unassociated with environmental heat? Would such a person faint or would he just sink to the ground and say 'I don't care whether you do prod me with your bayonet, I just can't march another step'? Presumably, provided that he doesn't faint, if he is put onto the back of a truck and an insensible person is thrown on top of him, then he will be able, no matter how exhausted he is, to roll the insensible man off him and, by grabbing the side of the truck, raise himself from the floor and thereby prevent more people being tossed on top of him.

I'm sure that Hart would not have bothered to do autopsies on Japanese. Without autopsies, would he have been able at a glance to tell which corpses in the back of a truck were caused by heat-stroke, which by dehydration, which by simple (i.e. 'non-heat') exhaustion, and which by suffocation?

I do apologise for inflicting a letter of such length upon you. Any comments that you can make to stop me making an ass of myself - particularly in the letters I am preparing for Dr Jobson and Dr Hart - will be very much appreciated.

Hubert A Sissons: Letter to DCS Sissons[6]

New York,
August 23rd 1979

Dear David,

A belated reply to your letter of 25th June about your further enquiries with regard to the Japanese deaths following troop movements from Bougainville.

I have been through your letter several times and find the questions hard to answer with any certainty: *your reading has made you much more familiar with information on 'heat effects' than I am* [editors' emphasis].

My finding is that Katsuki is probably correct in ascribing the deaths simply to exhaustion and heat. In a debilitated group of people under the conditions prevailing, it would, I think, be difficult to distinguish between heat stroke and other heat effects; from what you write, one doubts whether a great deal of effort would have been put into either the prevention of the problems (water, etc.), or to a check of what actually went wrong. I expect that all the factors you mention — accommodation, ventilation, supplies of food and water, previous nutritional conditions — all played a part. I really doubt whether, in the end, you will be able to say more than that. But it all makes interesting and absorbing reading.

Love to all,
Hubert

6 Arthur Stockwin transcribed Hubert Sissons' handwritten reply.

6

DAVID SISSONS, POLITICAL SCIENTIST AND WRITER ON POSTWAR JAPANESE POLITICS: AN INTRODUCTION

Arthur Stockwin

When David Sissons joined The Australian National University in 1961 and became my doctoral thesis supervisor, from my point of view, he was a political scientist. I remember he told me that he spent every Thursday working on the history of relations between Australia and Japan, but this seemed much subordinate to his principal interest, which was contemporary Japanese politics. It was not until the late 1960s, during a period of sabbatical in Japan, that he definitely switched the focus of his interests towards the history of Japan–Australia relations, and became the great specialist in that area of international history for which he is known.

He spent the years between 1956 and 1960 attached to the Institute of Social Science (Shaken) of Tokyo University, in part funded by a Saionji Memorial Scholarship. During that period he researched a number of political issues then current. Japanese politics in the late 1960s was highly polarised, as the democratic and peace-oriented 1947 constitution was still in its early stages of operation, and the broadly conservative Liberal Democratic Party (LDP, only founded in 1955) was in power but confronted by the Japan Socialist Party (JSP), which at the time commanded wide support, mainly in urban areas. From 1957 the LDP prime minister was Kishi Nobusuke, grandfather of the prime minister at the time of writing, Abe Shinzō. Kishi, who was a major figure in Japanese wartime governments, as well as in the Japanese-run government of Manchukuo, was classified as a class-A war criminal by the postwar Allied occupation, but was never brought to trial. His appointment as prime minister in 1957 raised the political temperature and led eventually to the most serious political crisis of the postwar period, over-revision of the Japan–US Security Treaty in 1960.

In 1958 the Kishi government introduced into the National Diet a bill designed to strengthen the powers of the police to handle demonstrations and other activities that the government regarded as disorderly behaviour. This led to a major expansion of 'disorder', as opposition parties (particularly the JSP), labour unions and many other bodies, supported by much of the mass media, protested, sometimes violently, against the bill. David analysed the course of the conflict in his 1959 essay 'The dispute over Japan's police law'.[1] The controversy was fought out with much reference to the arrogant behaviour of the police in the prewar period where, for instance, policemen had the right to enter inns in search of 'undesirable elements', engage in what David described as 'peeping Tom activities', and demand to be fed for their pains. The article bore the hallmarks of his meticulous research methods, often with a legal focus, including detailed comparisons of Japanese police powers with those in the United Kingdom. The political issue of police powers in Japan has not gone away in the period between publication of David's article and the present time.

An article that greatly helped me and influenced me in my doctoral research on the neutralist policies of the JSP was David's 'Recent developments in the Japanese socialist movement'.[2] This long article in two parts covered the period of the late 1950s that culminated in the Security Treaty revision crisis, which came to a head in June 1960. The 1950s were a period of deep division within the socialist movement but also, from 1955, of a coming together of the various factions, so that the Socialist Party was able to mount a serious challenge to the right-wing policies of the Kishi government. Even though they did not succeed in defeating him on the Security Treaty, that crisis ushered in a calmer period in the politics of Japan, which coincided with rapid economic growth. That growth itself, however, tended to undermine the appeal of left-wing agitation. David's analysis of socialist factions and trends in the 1950s was prescient about what was to come in the 1960s.

The new constitution, introduced under occupation auspices, that came into force in 1947, has never been revised in the smallest particular, but it has remained a matter of endless controversy. The successive Abe governments from 2012 have regarded constitutional revision as their most important long-term political objective. Of all the articles of the constitution, article 9, the 'peace clause', has always been the number one target for revision. One of the relatively early and most informative articles on this subject was David's 'The pacifist clause of the Japanese Constitution:

1 *Pacific Affairs*, vol. 32 (March 1959), no. 1.
2 *Far Eastern Survey*, March & June 1960.

Legal and political problems of rearmament'.[3] A highlight of the article was David's analysis of the circumstances whereby article 9 was originally drafted, then revised, and subsequently gone through various phases of interpretation. He homed in on the 'Ashida amendment', officially meant to strengthen the pacifist content of the article but in fact cunningly designed to permit military activity for the purposes of self-defence (defence of Japanese territory), but not for aggressive activities overseas. On the final page of his article David drills down into this distinction with the ironic comment: '[T]hen, as now, it was also well known that there is no form of defensive potential that cannot be utilized for aggression'.

David continued his research into the Japanese Constitution well into the 1960s, as shown in: 'Human rights under the Japanese Constitution'.[4] This was then, and has continued to involve, a highly controversial set of issues dividing the right-wing government forces from their critics on the left.

He also wrote a lengthy article on a constitutional issue that remains highly controversial in the 2010s, namely whether a prime minister has the freedom to dissolve the House of Representatives at will, or whether conditions need to be met: 'Dissolution of the Japanese lower house'.[5] Once again, he highlighted the divisive character of this problem between left and right.

David published several political science articles in the 1960s as shown in his publication bibliography. While most of those in the major academic journals are now available digitally, the two articles mentioned above were published at The Australian National University as a collection of Japanese politics articles in two volumes. They are included in the following two chapters to showcase his academic contributions to the field of political science. In his work as a political scientist focused on political, and especially constitutional, issues in Japan, David combined great legal and technical expertise with an ability to pick issues that mattered centrally and would continue to matter over the decades to come.

3 *International Affairs*, January 1961.

4 'Human rights under the Japanese constitution', *Papers on Modern Japan*, 1965, Research School of Pacific Studies, The Australian National University (reproduced in this volume).

5 'Dissolution of the Japanese lower house', *Papers on Modern Japan*, 1968, Research School of Pacific Studies, The Australian National University, Canberra (reproduced in this volume).

HUMAN RIGHTS UNDER THE JAPANESE CONSTITUTION

'Human rights under the Japanese constitution', *Papers on Modern Japan*, 1965, Research School of Pacific Studies, The Australian National University, Canberra.

HUMAN RIGHTS UNDER THE JAPANESE CONSTITUTION

by

D. C. S. Sissons

(Department of International Relations, Institute of Advanced Studies, Australian National University)

At the time of the Surrender in 1945, Japan was governed under the Meiji Constitution which came into effect in 1889 and had not subsequently been amended. Among the features of this constitution regarded as unsatisfactory by the Occupation authorities was the absence of an effective bill of rights; for although it conferred on Japanese subjects certain rights such as freedom of association and freedom of religion, it stated explicitly that such rights could be abridged by legislation.

It was well known that the Occupation authorities desired substantial constitutional revision. The period immediately following the Surrender saw the emergence of a number of draft constitutions sponsored by the major political parties (both ministerialist and Opposition) and by interested citizens. Some of these sought to provide judicial review and hard guarantees of fundamental rights. For example, the draft produced by the ministerialist party, the _Nihon Shimpōtō_, sought expressly to confer on the Supreme Court the power to examine the constitutionality of all laws and regulations,[1] and to require that legislative restrictions on specified rights should be within the limits necessary for maintaining public order.[2] Similarly the draft produced by the other conservative party, the _Nihon Jiyūtō_, although it did not expressly confer the power of judicial review, nevertheless contained a prohibition against legislation which arbitrarily restricted specified rights.[3] The draft produced by the Japanese Government, however, followed the Meiji Constitution in these, as in most other, respects: it made such rights subject to abridgment by

1. 'Nihon Shimpōtō no Kempō Kaisei Mondai', (24 February 1946), a. 22.

2. _Ibid._, a. 12.

3. 'Nihon Jiyūtō no Kempō Kaisei Yōkō', (21 January 1946), Ch. 3, a. 1.

legislation and did not provide judicial review.[4] The story is now well known how MacArthur, exasperated at the Government's lukewarm attitude to constitutional revision, then instructed his staff urgently to prepare 'for the instruction of the Japanese Government' the 'MacArthur draft'[5] constitution which became the basis for the famous thirty hours' continuous 'negotiations' between the Japanese and the Americans from which an 'agreed' draft emerged which, with a few minor amendments agreed to by the Americans, was adopted by the Diet.[6]

The Courts and Human Rights

One of the sections of the Constitution on which, during the negotiations with the Americans, the Japanese cabinet and draughtsmen attempted considerable resistance, was the section on human rights. They tried, unsuccessfully, to insert into practically every Article which established an important right, an express safeguard such as 'to the extent that they do not conflict with public peace and order', or 'as provided by law'.[7]

With all written constitutions, one of the most difficult problems in interpretation is the degree of consideration to be given to public order and the public welfare when determining the constitutionality of

---

4. See 'Kempō Kaiseian (Otsu An)' translated in Supreme Commander for the Allied Powers, Political Reorientation of Japan - September 1945 to September 1948, Washington 1949, Appendices Volume, pp. 607 ff.

5. The 'MacArthur draft' is reproduced in its original English in T. Miyazawa, Nihon Koku Kempō, Tōkyō, Nihon Hiyōron Shinsha, 1955, Appendices Volume, pp. 40-60.

6. The fullest account of the origins, drafting and enactment of the Japanese Constitution is Kempō Chōsakai, Kempō Seitei no Keika ni kansuru Shōiinkai Hōkokusho [Commission on the Constitution, Report of the Sub-committee on the Process of Enactment of the Constitution] (Tokyo, 1961). The fullest account in English is R. E. Ward, 'Origins of the Present Japanese Constitution', American Political Science Review, December 1956.

7. See the 'First Government Draft of Constitution, 4 March 1946' which is reproduced in full in Political Reorientation of Japan, Appendices Volume, p. 625 ff.

statutes which would limit the exercise of rights and freedoms guaranteed in the Constitution. That in Japan this problem is even greater than elsewhere is partly the result of bad drafting. In the Constitution as finally enacted, a. 12 states that: 'The freedoms and rights guaranteed to the people by this Constitution shall be maintained by the constant endeavour of the people, who shall refrain from any abuse of these freedoms and rights and shall always be responsible for utilizing them for the public welfare' (D. S. underlining). Article 13 states that: 'All the people shall be respected as individuals. Their right to life, liberty, and the pursuit of happiness shall, to the extent that it does not interfere with the public welfare, be the supreme consideration in legislation and in other governmental affairs' (D. S. underlining). In the articles dealing with specific rights, however, only a. 22 (choice of residence and occupation) and a. 29 (property rights) are expressly made subject to the public welfare. This has led to controversy whether a. 12 and a. 13 constitute a general authority to legislate restricting, in the public interest, all the rights conferred by the Constitution, or whether they are merely hortatory, in which case only a. 22 and a. 29 would be subject to such restriction.

The courts were quick to decide that the Constitution does not prohibit legislation which restricts, in the interests of public welfare, other rights besides those provided in a. 22 and a. 29 - among them freedom of expression. Article 21 provides that: 'Freedom of assembly and association as well as speech, press and all other forms of expression are guaranteed. No censorship shall be maintained, nor shall the secrecy of any means of communication be violated'. Many famous cases have arisen involving this provision.

Take for example the following. In 1951 in trying to find the whereabouts of eight Communist leaders suspected of engaging in illegal political activities, the police installed a microphone in the room adjoining that occupied by another Communist (he was not a suspect; nor was membership of the Communist Party an offence) and overheard his private life for several days. Discovering what was going on, he removed the microphone; whereupon the police, instead of feigning ignorance, actually charged him with theft of the microphone. At a later stage, the Procurator, rather understandably, dropped the charge; but the Communist brought an action against the police for abuse of their powers as public officials. In deciding this case, the appeal court held that freedom of communication may be limited in the public interest, and that where the police suspect crime they may, notwithstanding this constitutional guarantee, use any methods of enquiry which do not involve the use of force and which are not prohibited by legislation.[8] This is a case where many had hoped that the courts would devise some proper standard to circumscribe eavesdropping of this nature.

The limits of freedom of expression became the issue in the Lady Chatterley case. The case arose out of the prosecution of the publisher and translator under the Obscene Publications Law. Here the Supreme Court decided (1957) that, although undoubtedly a work of art, the book contained passages which were 'bold, detailed and realistic beyond the limit permitted by the collective conscience of the community and which accordingly outraged the feeling of shame which distinguished mankind from the beasts and which acted as a brake on licence'. The maintenance of a minimum standard of sexual morality was, the Court argued, part of the public welfare. Hence freedom of expression could be restricted to restrain obscenity.[9]

Next among the a. 21 cases let us deal with freedom of assembly. In 1945 all legislation restricting public meetings and demonstrations was repealed at the behest of the Occupation authorities. In 1948, however, some demonstrations by Korean residents turned into riots and the Occupation authorities began to encourage local government authorities to enact what are called 'Public Safety Regulations'. Such regulations require the local Public Safety Commissions to be informed in advance of processions and the like, and empower them to refuse permission in certain circumstances. By 1952 some hundred prefectures and municipalities covering most of the country had enacted such regulations.

In 1954 the Supreme Court had to rule on the constitutionality of the Niigata prefectural regulations which required notice to be given of processions and demonstrations on roads, and other public places where traffic passed, and which empowered the local Public Safety Commission to refuse permission where there clearly was a danger to public safety. The Court, in dealing with the case, laid down the following principles: (i) processions and demonstrations, to the extent that they do not use improper methods or do not have an objective

8. Decision of Tōkyō High Court 17 July 1953, Hanreijihō, No. 9, 1 October 1953.

9. J. M. Maki, Court and Constitution in Japan, Seattle, 1964, at p. 3 ff.

contrary to the public welfare, are part of the essential freedoms of the people, and therefore cannot be made subject to a general licensing system; (ii) they may, however, be made subject to a system requiring prior notification, or to restrictions based on a clear standard as regards place and method. On examining the Niigata Regulations in detail, the Court decided that they did not constitute an overall licensing system. In particular the Court laid stress on the provision in the regulations that stipulated that where, twenty-four hours before the procession was due to commence, no answer had been received from the Public Safety Commission permission could be assumed.[10]

More recently in Tōkyō Prefecture, regulations were enacted which apply to meetings in public places, and to demonstrations in any place whatsoever, and which, unlike the Niigata regulations, contain no provision to the effect that permission can be assumed if no decision has been given by twenty-four hours before the procession etc., is due to start. In 1960 the Supreme Court handed down a decision in a case involving demonstrators charged with a breach of the Tōkyō regulations. In this case the Court held that demonstrations and the like differ from expression stricto sensu in that underlying them is potential force and in that they can always lead to violence. Hence it is inevitable, the Court argued, that the authorities should pass regulations to enable them to know of such activities in advance and take 'the necessary minimum steps to prevent unforeseen occurrrences'. Somewhat surprisingly, the Court came to the conclusion that, although the Regulations apply to demonstrations 'in any place whatsoever', and although they contain no '24 hours clause' this nevertheless does not amount to a general licensing system.[11] Thus, in effect, the Court now threw overboard the standard it laid down in the Niigata case. And so, the situation has been reached where even people hiring halls for class reunions or film evenings apply for permission, to be on the safe side. This decision is very unpopular among Japanese academic lawyers. The basic objection to it is that, whereas the Constitution suggests that freedom of expression is so important that it should have special protection, the Court in the Tōkyō case has in effect decided that, because demonstrations involve expression, they are liable to special restriction. Moreover the Court, having said that the minimum restriction necessary is

---

10. Maki, op.cit., p. 30 ff.

11. Maki, op. cit., p. 84 ff.

permissible, then proceeded to permit the widest conceivable restriction.

Another important case involving the restriction, in the public interest, of a right guaranteed by the Constitution, arose in connection with the Passport Law and its relationship to a. 22 of the Constitution which provides that: 'Every person shall have freedom to choose and change his residence and to choose his occupation to the extent that it does not interfere with the public interest. Freedom of all persons to move to a foreign country or to divest themselves of their nationality shall be inviolate'.

In 1952 Hoashi, an economist and former Left-Socialist Member of the House of Representatives prominent in the movement in favour of trade with Communist countries, applied for a passport to attend the International Economic Conference to be held in Moscow. In reply, Hoashi was notified that the Minister had refused to issue him with a passport, by virtue of the powers conferred on him by a. 19 1 iv of the Passport Law which provides that 'Where the Minister deems it necessary for the protection of the person or the property of the bearer to prevent the journey, he may order the passport to be surrendered'. No one really thought that the Minister was worried about the safety of his Socialist opponent, but it probably seemed a safe clause to apply. Hoashi and his friends, however, drew attention to the fact that the Soviet authorities had guaranteed all travel and living expenses, as well as the personal safety of the delegates. At this, some bureaucratic faces must have reddened, for four days later Hoashi received a further communication from the Ministry informing him that, due to a clerical error, the previous letter had failed to notify him that the Minister was also acting under a. 13 1 v of the same law which empowered him to refuse a passport where he had reasonable grounds for considering that the applicant might act in a manner markedly and directly harmful to Japanese interests.

Human ingenuity and enterprise being what it is, Hoashi later in the year applied for and received a passport to visit Denmark. Although this was endorsed as not valid for the Communist countries, he nevertheless visited Moscow and Peking *en route*, though after the Conference had ended.

Subsequently Hoashi sued the State for damages for loss of professional opportunities in not being able to attend the Conference, and for loss of reputation resulting from the Minister's action which, it was contended, was contrary to the Passport Law and a. 22 of the

Constitution.

In evidence the reasons tendered on behalf of the Minister for his refusal were as follows: First - participation in the Conference would weaken Japan's bargaining position in the hitherto unsuccessful negotiations with the Soviet for a peace-treaty and the liberation of Japanese prisoners-of-war and fishermen. Secondly - the purpose of the Conference was to weaken the United Nations embargo on trade with the Communist countries, which was necessary to restrain Communist aggression in Korea; it was also aimed at sowing dissention among the nations of the Free World of whom Japan by signing the Peace Treaty was about to become a member. Thirdly - although SCAP had placed the issue of passports completely under Japanese control, Japan was still under U. S. Occupation; it would, accordingly, have been unwise to issue a passport when participation in the Conference was obviously inimical to U. S. policy. Lastly, for good measure, they added that in the light of the history of Japanese-Soviet relations the Soviet's guarantee of Hoashi's personal safety was quite unreliable.

The Supreme Court handed down its decision in 1958.[12] Although in a. 22 the express provision safeguarding the public interest obviously applies only to the first sentence whereas the freedom to move to a foreign country is dealt with in the second sentence, the Court, nevertheless, held that freedom of foreign travel should not be interpreted as being permitted without limit, but subject to reasonable restriction in the public interest. The restrictions imposed by the Passport Law it considered reasonable. Many found this decision alarming in that, despite the constitutional guarantee of freedom of movement to a foreign country, this can be interfered with for no better object than strengthening the Government's hand in current diplomatic negotiations!

Last among the 'public interest' cases let us consider the courts' interpretation of a. 28: 'The right of workers to organize and to bargain and act collectively is guaranteed'. The *volte face* in labour policy is well known whereby General MacArthur, having initially conferred on Japanese labour the right to strike, in 1948 instructed the Japanese Government to legislate prohibiting strikes among Government employees.[13] In 1949 at Hirosaki, engine-drivers of the Government railways went on strike and were accordingly charged

---

12. Maki, *op. cit.*, p. 117 ff.

13. *Political Reorientation of Japan*, Appendices Volume, pp. 581-3.

under this legislation. In deciding the case the Supreme Court held that it followed from Constitution a. 13 (quoted supra p.52) that the rights guaranteed by a. 28 must necessarily be subject to limitation for the sake of the public welfare.[14]

So much for cases where the courts have countenanced restriction of rights on the grounds of 'public interest', or 'public welfare'. Next let us consider 'equality under the law'.

Article 14 (i) provides that: 'All of the people are equal under the law and there shall be no discrimination in political, economic or social relations because of race, creed, sex, social status or family origin'.

The Supreme Court in 1947 in the Fukuoka Patricide Case rejected the contention that, by reason of this provision, the section of the Criminal Code is unconstitutional which provides a heavier penalty for inflicting bodily injury resulting in death on a 'lineal ascendant' than on others.[15] More recently it has, like the American courts in similar American cases, refused to upset, under this provision, electoral legislation under which there is a considerable discrepancy between the value of the vote in different constituencies.[16]

The implications of the principle of equality for inheritance are made clear in a. 24 (ii): 'With regard to property rights, inheritance, ... laws shall be enacted from the standpoint of individual dignity and the essential equality of the sexes'.

In Japanese law a person may bequeath only portion of his estate by will. For example, where he is survived by his wife or lineal descendants, half of his estate must be inherited according to the provisions of the Civil Code dealing with succession;[17] where he dies intestate (wills are uncommon in Japan),[18] the whole is inherited

14. Saikosaibansho Hanreishū (Keiji), Vol. 7, No. 4, p. 775 ff.

15. Maki, op. cit., p. 129 ff.

16. Supreme Court decision of 5 February 1964 (Case "O" 422 of 1963.)

17. Civil Code (1947), a. 1028

18. Wills are, however, becoming more popular. See the evidence of Professor Y. Nakagawa in Kempō Chōsakai, Kempō Chōsakai Dai 1 Iinkai Dai 27 Kai Gijiroku, pp. 12-13.

according to such provisions. The prewar Civil Code applied to this 'legally secured portion' of the estate the principle of primogeniture. The revised (1947) Civil Code, however, makes, in the first instance, the spouse and the lineal descendants the successors, the spouse receiving one-third and the lineal descendants two-thirds.[19]

In conformity with Constitution a. 24 (ii), it further provides that where there are more than one successor in the same degree (e.g. sons and daughters) their respective shares shall be equal.[20] Since the typical farmer in Japan is the peasant[21] working a minimal family holding which is incapable of subdivision into smaller viable units, there was from the outset considerable apprehension that equal inheritance would ruin the peasantry - some 40% of the nation. In 1946 the Special Committee of the House of Peers appointed to report on the proposed legislation to revise the pre-war Civil Code resolved that 'Whereas we approve the system of equal inheritance required by the new Constitution, we nevertheless believe that the new Constitution does not prohibit the addition of suitable regulatory measures to maintain and develop agriculture. It therefore behoves the Government expeditiously to devise the legislative measures necessary to prevent arable land's being atomized by reason of succession'.[22] The Government in 1947 and again in 1949 introduced a bill[23] to provide that, in the case of succession to agricultural land, the agricultural capital should not be divided among the children but should pass to a single successor whom the testator, the successors jointly, or, in the case of disagreement, the courts, considered the most suitable for conducting agriculture. According to the 1947 bill this person would be obliged to pay compensation to the other successors only where the value of the agricultural capital amounted to more than half the estate plus an equal share in the remainder. The bill was not proceeded with, as it was unacceptable

19. Civil Code (1947), a. 900 (i).

20. Ibid., a. 900 (iv).

21. According to a national survey carried out in 1950,as against 61,700,000 farmer households there were about 13,000 non-family units engaged in agriculture (Evidence of T. Ogura in Kempō Chōsakai, Kempō Chōsakai Dai 1 Iinkai Dai 31 Kai Gijiroku, p. 2.).

22. Quoted, Ibid., p. 2.

23. The title of the bill was in each case Nōchi Sōzoku Tokurei Hōan. For descriptions of each bill see Ogura, op. cit., p. 3-4.

to MacArthur's headquarters.[24] According to the 1949 bill, the inheritor of the agricultural capital would be obliged to pay compensation (over a long period at a very low rate of interest) to the other successors, equal to the amount by which the value of such agricultural capital exceeded what his share would have been if the estate had been equally divided. It further provided that in each case the amount of compensation should be fixed at a level that would not prejudice the stability of the agricultural operations of the inheritor of the agricultural capital, and that whereas non-agricultural assets should be valued at current market price, agricultural assets should be valued on the basis of yield (about 50-60% of market price). Although the 1949 bill managed to pass the Lower House, there was considerable opposition to it both among scholars and society at large on the grounds that it was unnecessary, that it might revive the evils of the prewar family system, and that it contravened the principle of equality as provided in Constitution a. 14 and 24.[25] In fact little subdivision has occurred as a result of succession: in many cases sisters and younger brothers renounce their succession, often receiving in exchange a trousseau or the cost of their higher education.[26]

Articles 31 to 40 of the Constitution deal with safeguards in criminal procedure.

Article 37 (which in the drafting process the Japanese attempted to omit[27]) guarantees speedy trial in criminal cases. In 1948 the Supreme Court handed down an interesting decision involving this

---

24. Meyer, Grajdanzeo and Hughes, officers of MacArthur's headquarters, on 16 July 1947 handed to a meeting of the Permanent Heads of the Japanese ministries concerned a memorandum criticizing the bill. A Japanese translation of the memorandum is given in Kempō Chōsakai, Kempō Chōsakai Dai 1 Iinkai Dai 31 Kai Gijiroku, pp. 58-60. Note, however, the testimony of Professor T. Kawashima (who was closely associated with the revision of the Civil Code) that the Americans were not unsympathetic regarding the question (ibid., p. 41).

25. See for example the joint statement (11 April 1949) of various professors of law at Tōkyō, Waseda and Meiji universities attacking the bill on constitutional grounds (Hōritsu Jihō, 1949, No. 5, p. 55).

26. Ogura, op. cit., p. 5.

27. Note its absence in the 'First Government Draft of Constitution, 4 March 1946', Political Reorientation of Japan, Appendices Vol. p. 625 ff.

article.[28] A prisoner had appealed against a conviction on the ground that there had been undue delay in hearing his case. The Supreme Court, properly, no doubt, dismissed the appeal on the ground that irrespective of the delay the verdict was correct. But it went on to say that there was little that it could do about delay since this was due to a lack of court staff and since the only remedy it could give - a retrial - would merely serve to increase the backlog of cases and delay justice even further. The answer to this line of reasoning is pretty obvious: if the courts were to order retrials in such cases the legislature would be forced to take action to provide the facilities for more efficient and speedy justice; but in the absence of such a prod from the courts they will, of course, do nothing. The situation today is much worse than in 1948. The first instance trial of participants in the May Day riots of 1952 has, to the best of my knowledge, not yet ended. A good deal of this delay appears to be due to a cumbrous system of detection and of preparing indictments by the police and the procurators. The delay in justice is also partly due to the slowness of the judges in making up their minds. For example, in the Sunakawa case the fifteen Supreme Court judges were reported to have conferred twenty-five times between the end of the hearings and the handing down of their judgments. The delay is also partly attributable to what many consider a violation of a. 39 - 'No person... shall... be placed in double jeopardy'. The courts have decided that the latter guarantee does not prevent the State from appealing against an acquittal [29] (During the drafting the Japanese unsuccessfully tried to word the provision in this manner).[30] But if it is not a safeguard against this, it is a safeguard against very little. Such appeals by the State against acquittals are in fact very common. This means that large periods of a person's life may be blighted by criminal proceedings.

Similarly the courts have undermined the guarantee which restricts entry and search. Articles 33 and 35 provide as follows:
a. 33. 'No person shall be apprehended except upon warrant issued by a competent judicial officer which specified the offense with which the person is charged, unless he is apprehended, the offense being committed'.

---

28. Maki, op. cit., p. 207 ff.

29. Maki, op. cit., p. 219 ff.

30. 'First Government Draft of Constitution, 4 March 1946', Political Reorientation of Japan, Appendices Vol. p. 626, a. 31.

a. 35. 'The right of all persons to be secure in their homes, papers and effects against entries, searches and seizures shall not be impaired except upon warrant issued for adequate cause and particularly describing the place to be searched and things to be seized, or except as provided by Article 33 . . . . '. This is obviously an attempt to provide the principle to which we are accustomed, namely, that entry and search must be by warrant except at the moment of arrest. The Japanese Excise Offences Law is a prewar statute still in force. It authorises search and seizure by excise officers without warrant where an offence is occurring or has occurred. The court found such search constitutional even though made independently of an arrest. It held that 'except as provided in a. 33' did not mean 'except where a person is apprehended while he is committing the offence' but that it meant 'except where an offence is being committed'. In the case in question the mere presence of an illegal still on the man's property constituted the crime in process. He was arrested after the search, as a result of it.[31]

Article 34 of the Constitution provides that no person shall 'be detained without adequate cause' and that 'upon demand of any person such cause must be immediately shown in open court in his presence and the presence of his counsel'. In the words of Professor Walter Gelhorn (the celebrated U. S. constitutional lawyer) after his visit to Japan, this constitutional requirement has degenerated almost into a 'ceremonial formality', instead of growing into a strong bulwark against the possibility of oppression.

The Japanese Habeas Corpus Law of 1948 provides that a person whose physical freedom has been restricted other than by a lawful and proper procedure may apply for a writ of habeas corpus. Unfortunately the Supreme Court has, under its rule-making power, made a rule which gravely constricts this statute. Article 4 of the Habeas Corpus Rules provides that an application for habeas corpus may be made only where the restraint is either patently without authority or patently and seriously violates a form or procedure established by law. A rule framed in this manner badly undermines the effectiveness of habeas corpus as a means of discovering by judicial process whether restraint is proper. Restraint may often seem to be entirely lawful. But, as Professor Gelhorn says, 'when no other suitable appellate procedures remain available, an application for habeas corpus has in some other countries been the way to summon the courts to their historic mission of delving below the

31. Maki, op. cit., p. 165 ff.

surface'.[32]

In 1952 the Supreme Court refused to entertain a *habeas corpus* application made on behalf of war criminals who were held in Sugamo prison in accordance with the terms of the Peace Treaty.[33] The applicants contended that the Treaty could not be enforced as against them, because it conflicted with the Japanese Constitution. The Court refused to consider the matter saying that since the Governor of the prison was acting in accordance with the Treaty and the related statutes he was not imposing *obviously* improper restraint on the prisoners. The dissenting judges pointed out very effectively that this all but nullified the Habeas Corpus Law. The prisoners had no means, other than *habeas corpus*, of testing the validity of their imprisonment.

A similar disinclination to give *habeas corpus* its proper breadth was evident in a deportation case in 1956. A three-year-old Korean child born in Japan was about to be deported to Korea with her mother. The deportation order against the child was alleged to be invalid. The Court said bluntly that invalidity was not patent and hence no further judicial examination of the matter was appropriate.[34]

It would be unfair to give the impression of complete gloom regarding the judicial enforcement of rights guaranteed by the Japanese Constitution. Admittedly in its seventeen years of existence the Supreme Court has never once found a statute unconstitutional, despite what some people would consider the considerable temptation provided by the legislature. Nevertheless in the case of two articles, the Court has given some encouraging decisions. It has set aside convictions which rested on confessions made under duress (a. 38).[35] It has also, in interpreting statutes giving effect to a. 17 ('Every person may sue for redress as provided by law from the State or a public entity, in case he has suffered damage through illegal act of a public official'), bent the wording of the statute considerably in the interests

---

32. W. Gelhorn, Comment on the Constitution of Japan (Kempō Chōsakai, *Kenshi Sō Dai-32-Gō,* January 1959), pp. 19-20.

33. *Saikōsaibansho Hanreishū (Minji)*, Vol. 8, No. 4, p. 848.

34. *Ibid.*, (Minji), Vol. 9, No. 10, p. 1453 ff.

35. E. G. Maki, *op cit.*, p. 191 ff.

of the private citizen. Take, for example, the following case.[36] A policeman, wearing his uniform, but not on duty, trumped up a charge against a person so that he might search him and in so doing rob him. During the search he collected all the man's belongings including his purse and then made as if to escort him to the police station. En route, he attempted to abscond. His victim pursued him shouting 'Stop thief' and was shot dead by the policeman. His widow sued the municipality for compensation under the State Compensation Law whereby it was liable for 'damage inflicted unlawfully by public officials, deliberately or by negligence, in the execution of their duty'.[37] Although the policeman was certainly not acting in the execution of his duty the Court argued that his actions had the externals of an execution of duty and that compensation was therefore payable.[38]

In the Case of acquisition of private property by the State, however, the courts have weakened the guarantee of 'just compensation'. Constitution a. 29 (iii) provides that 'Private Property may be taken for public use upon just compensation therefor'. In the land reform carried out in 1946 on the initiative of the Allied Powers whereby more than one third of the agricultural land was acquired and redistributed, the compensation provided was contemptuous - equivalent to about half the value of the annual crop which it produced. The Supreme Court sustained the legislation, reasoning that compensation was fair if it were 'a proper sum rationally calculated on the basis of a value which could be considered to exist under current economic conditions; it need not always conform completely to such value'.[39]

Administrative Machinery for the Protection of Human Rights[40]

In 1948 in the endeavour to ensure that the rights specified in the Constitution were not merely guaranteed, but also enjoyed, adminis-

36. Saikōsaibansho Hanreishū (Minji), Vol. 10, No. 11, p. 1502 ff.

37. Kokka Baishōhō (Law 125 of 1948), a. 1.

38. For similar reasoning see also Saikōsaibansho Hanreishū (Minji), Vol. 9, No. 14, p. 2047 ff.

39. Ibid., Vol. 7, No. 13, p. 1523 ff.

40. Except where the contrary is indicated, the information in this section is derived from the evidence presented to the Commission on the Constitution by S. Suzuki, Director of the Human Rights Protection Bureau on 2 November 1960. (Kempō Chōsakai, Kempō Chōsakai Dai 1 Iinkai Shōiinkai Dai 1 Kaigi Gijiroku, pp. 1-19, 49-58).

trative machinery was set up, charged with the protection of human rights.

Presumably under the influence of MacArthur's headquarters, on 15 February 1948 (shortly after the new Constitution came into effect) a Human Rights Protection Bureau was set up in the Ministry of Justice. Although those responsible for this innovation were probably influenced by the existence of a Civil Rights Section in the United States Department of Justice, the matters the Japanese bureau deals with are somewhat different and include the investigation of violations of human rights, the collection of information on human rights problems, the promotion of the protection of human rights in the community, matters relating to the Human Rights Protection Commissioners (v. infra), habeas corpus, legal aid to the needy etc.[41] It has (1960) a central staff of 16[42] together with an additional 200 in the Human Rights Protection Sections in the regional offices of the Ministry. The head of the bureau is traditionally a lawyer from private practice.

Also dating from 1948 are the honorary Human Rights Protection Commissioners in cities, towns and villages. Their functions as described in the relevant statute[43] are roughly parallel to those of the Bureau. These Commissioners are nominated by the mayor (after consultation with the municipal council) from 'inhabitants entitled to vote at municipal elections (for which there is universal franchise - D. S.), of high character, knowledge and judgment, conversant with social reality, and knowledgable about the protection of human rights, who are social workers, educationalists, journalists, etc. or are members of a lawyers' association or of an association of women, workers youths etc. whose immediate object is the protection of human rights or which supports human rights'.[44] Selection is then made from among such nominees by the Minister after consultation with the respective Prefectural Governor, Bar Association and the Prefectural Council of Human Rights Protection Commissioners. Commissioners serve for a term of three years but are frequently reappointed. Their occupational break up (1960) is as follows: agriculture and fishery, 26%; religion, 14%; trade, 10%; civil

---

41. Homushō Setchihō, a. 11.

42. Cf. a central staff of 25 when originally established in 1948.

43. Jinken Yogo Iinho 1949 (as amended by Law 319 of 1959), a. 11.

44. Ibid., a. 6

service, 9%; lawyers, 7%; educational, 7%; clerical, 7%; officials of organisations, 4%; journalists, 2%; others, 13%. Of these, women constitute only 7.5% but this proportion is on the increase. The Minister after consulting the appropriate Prefectural Council of Human Rights Protection Commissioners, may terminate the appointment of a Commissioner for action contrary to the responsibilities of his office, neglect of duties, physical or mental incapacity, or conduct unbecoming a Commissioner.[45]

The Commissioners are grouped into some 300 Regional Councils which in turn are organised into 49 Prefectural Councils. There is also a national council of Commissioners which is convened by the Minister annually.

The finance provided for these activities is small in comparison with the task. For example, the amount allocated in the 1960 national budget was ¥32m (¥1,000=£sg 1), of which ¥8m was for legal aid and ¥15m was for the activities of the Commissioners (mainly travel and out-of-pocket expenses). Many municipalities, however, provide some financial assistance for the activities of the Commissioners. Such local assistance probably amounts to more than that provided by the central government.

The Commissioners are very active in the field of propaganda, organizing meetings, lectures and discussions etc. on human rights problems.

Legal aid to the needy is adminstered by the Bureau. In the two years 1958-59 such assistance was given in 677 cases.

The Bureau is also in close touch with the Human Rights Committee of the United Nations Economic and Social Council to whom the Director periodically reports on Human Rights in Japan.

The types of complaints arising, and the manner in which they are brought to the Bureau and disposed of by it, are shown in the following table:

---

45. Ibid., a. 15.

Activities of Human Rights Protection Bureau 1948-59

Status of Accused and Nature of Violation Alleged	Allegations Received by Bureau												Origin of Allegations Received in 1959					Manner in Which Allegations Disposed of during 1959 (includes cases carried forward from preceding years)									
	1948	1949	1950	1951	1952	1953	1954	1955	1956	1957	1958	1959	Notoriety	Complaint	Commissioners	Notified by a Government Department	Transferred from a Government Department	Prosecution	Disciplinary Warning	Ordinary Warning	Violation established but no action taken *	Brought to attention of appropriate Department	Transferred to another Department	Legal aid provided	Not proceeded with	Dismissed: violation not substantiated	Pending
Public Officials:																											
Police Officers:																											
Arrest							97	96	44	27	38	40	2	33	2		3				19		1	5		24	25
Detention							16	8	11	10	11	9	1	7			1				1			1	1	4	9
Search and Seizure							44	28	19	12	14	11	1	9	1						3				1	3	10
Forced Confession							97	94	59	28	64	53	4	44	2		3			1	13		5	5	1	20	36
Violence and Indignity							139	112	77	58	89	66	11	48	3		4			2	33	3	4	4	8	23	47
Use of Weapons							4	1	4	1	6	2	1	1													
Other							276	193	124	122	186	128	13	98	12	1	4				43	5	9	23	10	69	45
Other officials engaged in the investigation of crimes								90	73	48	77	71									9	6	3	18	1	34	34
School Teachers:																											
Corporal Punishment							114	119	122	139	127	111	87	16	8					5	103			1		6	51
Other							48	36	40	43	40	31	11	17	3					1	11			2	3	10	16
Prison Officers							32	22	20	25	29	43	1	31	1		5				8		5	4	5	19	15
Tax and Excise Officers							58	47	26	21	14	28	3	21	3		1				10	1	1	3	1	5	15
Other Public Officials							323	263	203	161	203	212	20	163	27		2				68	5	4	52	9	74	74
Total: Public Officials	29	88	385	932	917	1324	1248	1109	822	695	898	805	159	554	66	1	25			9	324	20	32	118	40	300	379
Private Citizens																											
White Slavery							225	228	272	350	156	47	7	21	5	6	8				36	5	7	3	3	12	18
Cruelty; driving people hard							427	476	443	402	554	593	20	379	185	2	7				207	5	7	297	23	65	59
False Imprisonment							298	447	343	241	201	256	8	201	40	3	4			1	81	1	7	86	9	66	53
Mura-hachibu (Village Boycott)*							119	152	128	134	126	81	14	60	6		1			1	54			2	4	13	91
Private punishment of transgressors of local mores							217	193	151	114	82	172	14	87	70		1				43		2	107	6	10	13
Discriminatory treatment							515	356	262	239	173	380	8	231	138		3				65	1	5	236	9	38	54
Violation of right to the franchise							24	77	20	29	22	32	6	16	10						6	2	1	12	6	7	4
Defamation							1202	1207	852	744	714	993	9	736	244	1	3			2	262	6	6	506	40	135	125
Violation of freedom of expression, religion or association							46	47	60	76	47	153	5	97	40	1	1				25	2	2	104	5	13	12
Violation of right to education							67	33	108	102	54	119	16	62	40	1					30	2		72	2	8	10
Violation of rights of labour							301	315	351	390	400	585	18	459	106		2				130	28	4	337	7	71	62
Violation of security of habitation							718	734	1300	992	1071	1198	16	853	329						259	11	1	820	15	86	76
Coercion							960	963	1684	1255	1468	1664	60	1266	323	6	9				591	15	9	722	68	231	291
Other							1494	1536	1964	1835	1724	2012	39	1423	539	1	10				367	20	15	1469	34	126	212
Grand Total	40	178	1,075	3,227	5,383	7,959	7,861	7,872	8,760	7,598	7,680	9,090	399	6,445	2,150	22	74			13	2500	118	98	4900	271	1,179	1,459
Consultations by citizens with the Bureau on matters involving their Human Rights	8	4,898	3,718	12,362	15,374	22,085	34,426	41,033	54,928	66,462	75,903	92,055															

* V. infra p. 67

Only two of the categories in the Table call for elaboration:

Mura-hachibu is a boycott by the village of one of their number for such acts as causing a fire, immorality, non-participation in village working parties or levies, breaches of village agreements or regulations, failure to accept arbitration by the village, reporting the crimes of villagers to the central authorities, engaging in litigation disadvantageous to the village, failing to vote for the hamlet's candidate in a village election, etc. The boycott may include withholding the offender's food ration, his supplies of fertilizers and seeds; refusal to sell him daily necessaries or to let him use communal tools and the communal rice mill; exclusion from the local youths' or women's society and from local ceremonials. The offender's family is also likely to be similarly treated.

'Violation established but no action taken' is defined as follows: 'The facts of a violation of human rights are established, but, taking into account the personality, age and circumstances of the offender, the lightness of the offence, and the circumstances surrounding it, and the offender's subsequent attitude of mind, the matter is disposed of without prosecution, warning or other action'.

In addition to the roughly 100,000 consultations per annum between individual citizens and the Bureau there would be about twice this number of consultations between individual citizens and Commissioners.

An interesting recent trend is that whereas the annual number of complaints against public officials is decreasing,those against private citizens are on the increase. Numerous among the latter are complaints of defamation and invasion of privacy by the press and radio, group violence attending labour disputes, and public nuisance. There are many instances where the local Commissioners have been able to solve public nuisance problems where all other approaches have failed. A good example of this occurred in the town of Bizen in Okayama prefecture. The smoke from a local factory was so bad that the inhabitants could not hang out their washing and were unable to open their windows even in heat of mid-summer. Complaints to the Department of Health, the police, and the municipality brought no relief. The local Human Rights Protection Commissioners then took the matter up with the owner of the factory and induced him to replace his existing coal furnace with an oil furnace, the Commissioners using their good offices locally to secure him a low interest loan to finance the conversion.

The Bureau has no power of compulsion in its investigations. On the other hand, there are no legal restrictions as to when it should institute an investigation. It acts mostly on the basis of individual complaints but also acts where it notices in the press or on the radio cases meriting investigation. Unlike the U. S. Civil Rights Division (which uses officers of the F. B. I. for its investigations) it relies solely on its own central and regional staff, frequently assisted by the Commissioners. As the above Table demonstrates, the object of the Bureau is not the punishment of offenders; it is rather the abatement of the violation, the prevention of its repetition, at the provision of relief. The Bureau claims that, for this reason, it generally receives the cooperation of those involved, and finds it much easier to arrive at the truth than is the case in criminal investigations. The prior consent of the Minister of Justice is required before the Bureau may issue a warning to, or prosecute, a public servant.[46] It will be noted from the Table above that such action is rare.

The Bureau also frequently investigates violations of human rights at the request of Standing Committees of the Diet.

It is hard to assess the impact on the Japanese of the idea of human rights embodied in the Constitution. The words of the Director of the Human Rights Protection Bureau (1960) are, however, worth quoting:

> As I see it from the Bureau, respect for fundamental human rights is as a concept widely diffused among the nation, as are the words, 'human rights' and 'respect for human rights'. Respect for human rights, however, cannot yet be said to have become part of people. I am afraid that among the intelligentsia and the classes which provide leaders there is a tendency for violation of human rights and human rights problems to be used as a stick with which to beat one's adversary or the organisation to which he belongs. One example of this is, as everyone knows, where in labour disputes, etc. one union is fighting another. In such circumstances, whereas one's adversary's violations of human rights are listed with neurotic precision, one is

---

46. Jinken Shimpan Jiken Shorikitei (Hōmushō Kunrei No. 1, 21 June 1956), a. 17.

almost indifferent to the violation of human rights by members of one's own union. There is not yet a wide feeling that protection of human rights means that while protecting one's own human rights one takes care not to transgress another's. On the other hand, there are many people who are completely ignorant regarding human rights. We have a mixture of undue sensitivity to human rights on the one hand and complete indifference on the other.[47]

47. Evidence of S. Suzuki, pp. 11-12.

DISSOLUTION OF THE JAPANESE LOWER HOUSE

'Dissolution of the Japanese lower house', *Papers on Modern Japan*, 1968, Research School of Pacific Studies, The Australian National University, Canberra.

DISSOLUTION OF THE JAPANESE LOWER HOUSE

by

D.C.S. Sissons

(Department of International Relations, Institute of Advanced Studies, The Australian National University)

'Dissolution' is considered a worked out lode by United Kingdom, Commonwealth, and European political scientists: the *International Bibliography of the Social Sciences - Political Science* lists only five articles on this subject over the period 1951-63 and two of these were by Japanese writers. As will become apparent from the present paper, these latter constitute but a small proportion of the spate of articles written by Japanese scholars on the subject during this period. Furthermore, the few United Kingdom and Commonwealth writers who find dissolution worth considering tend now, as in the past, to concentrate on the single question, under what exceptional circumstances if any may the Crown refuse a Prime Minister's request for a dissolution.[1] But in the Japanese articles and the political controversies which gave rise to them the discussion was much wider - the entire case for and against a power of dissolution on the part of the executive was argued in painstaking detail. Moreover, in Japan dissolution appears to be regarded, by observers and participants alike, as important politically.

As a case-study let us consider the most recent dissolution, that of 27 December 1966, as it appears in the pages of the *Asahi shimbun* newspaper (and hence, no doubt, as it appeared to the *Asahi's* four million daily readers). At some risk of tediousness we shall sometimes quote the *Asahi* and the principal participants in some detail; for we are dealing with a political culture which is strange to all of us and the atmosphere is often best conveyed by the actual words used.

1. E.g. E. Campbell, 'The Prerogative Power of Dissolution: Some Recent Tasmanian Precedents', *Public Law*, 1961, pp.165-79. Among recent British writers who consider that under certain circumstances the Crown may properly refuse a Prime Minister's request for a dissolution are Sir Ivor Jennings, *The British Constitution*, Cambridge U.P., 1950, p.114, N.H. Gibbs, *Keith's British Cabinet System*, London, Stevens, 1952, p.301-3, and Lord Atlee, 'The Role of the Monarchy', *The Observer*, 22 August 1959.

The 'Black Mist' Dissolution, 27 December 1966

The House of Representatives had been elected on 21 November 1963 and in the absence of a dissolution the tenure of Members would have terminated by effluxion four years later. In Japan, as in Great Britain, it is customary to terminate a Parliament by dissolution rather than suffer it to end by effluxion[2] and in recent years such end-of-term dissolutions have usually occurred at about the end of the third year. Accordingly by September 1966 the *Asahi* was reporting that 'the autumn wind of dissolution' was blowing daily through the political world, that Members had deserted the capital to electioneer in their constituencies and, in contrast with other years, were not volunteering for junkets overseas.[3] Despite statements by the Prime Minister and those close to him that dissolution was not contemplated,[4] the Prime Minister was himself touring the country. According to the *Asahi*, the Ministerialist leaders were unable to decide whether to dissolve before the New Year or not. Some felt that if they delayed they would be adversely affected by the deterioration of the situation in Vietnam, by increased co-operation between the Opposition parties and by further increases in consumer prices. Others argued that a dissolution before the New Year would create a political vacuum at an inopportune time (The preparation of the annual budget is usually completed in December) and that more time was required for recent scandals to die down, for improving the Prime Minister's image, for coping with the price spiral and for the effects of economic recovery to permeate beyond big business.[5]

In October the Socialists succeeded in organising a united front of the four Opposition parties, whose purpose was to force a dissolution by acting in concert in the Diet to keep the Government under constant attack for its responsibility for the 'Black Mist' (the rich crop of scandals which

---

2. Four Japanese Parliaments have terminated by effluxion - in 1902, 1908, 1912 and 1942.

3. *Asahi shimbun*, 11 August & 3 October 1966.

4. *Asahi shimbun*, 11 August; 3, 6 & 24 September; 5 October 1966.

5. *Asahi shimbun*, 4 September 1966.

commenced with the prosecution of a Ministerialist backbencher, TANAKA Shooji, in August and the forced resignation of the Minister for Transport, Arafune, in September). The Government, accordingly, was faced with the prospect of mounting pressure from the Opposition parties - in the remaining Committee sessions of the current Session, in the forthcoming Session convened to pass a supplementary budget and in the regular Session commencing in late December in which the annual budget is brought down. The Asahi predicted that, since the Government, faced with such pressure, could not hope to weather the regular Session, the Prime Minister would reconstruct the cabinet immediately after his re-election as Party president at the beginning of December and go to the country later in December, or in January; the prospect of office in the reconstructed cabinet might restrain some members of the Party from voting for Satoo's rival in the presidential election.[6] Activity in the constituencies had now reached such a height that the Prime Minister on November 2nd besought both the office-bearers and the rank-and-file of his party not to indulge in any statements regarding dissolution. On November 5th he replied to a questioner that he neither was, nor should be, thinking of dissolution.

In the Diet Steering Committees negotiations between the Government and the Opposition parties on the time-table of the forthcoming Session broke down. The Opposition parties required that the Session should be long enough to ensure adequate discussion of the 'Black Mist'. The Government, however, insisted that the Session should be short and that the supplementary budget must have priority. The Opposition then announced their intention to boycott the Session.

Satoo was re-elected as Party president on December 1st and on December 3rd reconstructed his cabinet. At a press conference on December 5th in answer to questions he stated that with the reconstruction of the cabinet the situation had changed since his previous statement and he had now to consider dissolution; he would not dissolve during the present session but would determine the timing of the dissolution before the term of Members expired the following November in the light of public opinion and the progress of Diet proceedings. He deplored the tendency to make dissolution a tool in the party struggle: 'The people are the sovereign. To say 'We shall

6. Asahi shimbun, 24 October 1966.

force a dissolution', or for me to say 'I will not dissolve' is likely to produce an argument in which from first to last the essence of the dissolution problem is misconceived'. When asked whether he was considering fixing the date of dissolution by agreement with the Opposition he replied that this would be improper and that dissolution must be carried out in an open manner (The Socialists had already stated that they would have nothing to do with any agreement to dissolve in January[7]). When reminded that the Opposition would try and prevent the passage of the supplementary budget, Satoo replied 'Can't they wait ten days or a fortnight' [sc. for an announcement of the date of dissolution - D.C.S.S.].

The Asahi interpreted the Prime Minister's answers as indicating his feeling that 'depending on the attitude of the Opposition dissolution may take place this year and that, in view of the increasing demand of public opinion, if he does not dissolve this year he must do so very early in the New Year'. It saw in his remarks 'the feelings of a Prime Minister who is wrestling with the question how, in the midst of a very serious political situation, he can snatch an opportunity to dissolve on the basis of his own initiative'.

Although in the past the Socialists had contested the legality of measures passed by the Diet while they were boycotting proceedings, the Government calculated that they would not do so on this occasion, since the principal measure in the forthcoming Session was a supplementary budget to enable higher wages to be paid to public employees. The Government therefore opened Diet proceedings on December 15th. The Opposition did not attend. The following day the Speaker offered to mediate between the parties in order to 'normalise' Diet proceedings and a conference of the Secretaries-General of the parties was held on December 17th. The _Asahi's_ report (18 December 1966) of this conference is as follows:

> At this conference the Socialists and the Democratic-Socialists demanded that the date at which the dissolution would take place should be stated plainly. The Socialists in particular insisted that the Government should promise to dissolve the House, if not this year, then immediately the Diet resumes after the New Year recess at the latest.

7. _Asahi shimbun,_ 22 November 1966.

The Liberal-Democrats on the other hand insisted that they could not state plainly when they would dissolve. They accepted, however, the position of the Speaker's mediation proposal which read: 'The Ministerial party shall carefully examine and take into consideration the contentions of the Opposition parties regarding resolving the political situation'. According to the Secretary-General of the Liberal-Democratic Party, Mr Fukuda, 'Our party does not regard this sentence as making it clear that we intend to have an early dissolution. The Opposition parties, however, are free to interpret it as suggesting an early dissolution. It can be interpreted either way'.

It is inevitable that it will be taken as suggesting an early dissolution.

At the conference some progress was made with a proposal to append as a confidential note to the Speaker's proposal the Speaker's opinion that: 'In my opinion it is a plain fact that dissolution will take place either when the supplementary budget is passed, at the beginning of the regular Session of the Diet, to be convened on the 27th, or just after the New Year recess (about January 20th). When, however, Mr Fukuda consulted the Prime Minister on this point, the latter instructed him to add the sentence 'The Opposition parties may interpret it in this fashion if they like'.

One can say therefore that the conference broke down because of the Prime Minister's firm resolve to preserve to the end his leadership in the matter of dissolution. Nevertheless one can say that in the course of the discussion between the parties the Liberal-Democrats did try to suggest that they were thinking of an early dissolution, although they would not say so directly.

Insofar as Diet proceedings, as a result of the breakdown of the conference, have become completely bogged down, the opinion has become strong in both the Ministerialist and the Opposition parties that, even though the present session of the Diet may somehow be weathered out with the Liberal-Democrats alone participating, there is almost no prospect of normal proceedings at the regular session and that in fact an early dissolution has become unavoidable.

The *Asahi's* explanation (17 December 1966) of the Government's attitude was that 'Among the Ministerialist leaders the view has been pretty firm that they should dissolve in January after the New Year recess when they had passed the supplementary budget and prepared the annual budget. But, even though it would achieve this result, they are strongly opposed to a dissolution in the form of a 'dissolution by agreement' or a 'dissolution forced on us'. Accordingly at this juncture they wish to avoid stating plainly the date of dissolution'.

The supplementary budget was passed on the last day of the Session, December 20th. For the first time in Japanese history, the Opposition had boycotted the entire Session. The following day, in response to a request by his colleague, Mr Fukuda, 'to tell us your intentions regarding dissolution as frankly as possible since members of the Party are on tenterhooks over the issue' (21 December 1966; evening edition), the Prime Minister made a long statement to a meeting of Liberal-Democrat Members of both Houses. The following extracts are from the summary of it which appeared in the *Asahi* (21 December 1966; evening edition).

> What are the reasons for the Opposition parties' refusal to participate in Diet proceedings? They say that we should tell them the date on which we shall dissolve and that we should give them a definite promise regarding it. It is this demand by the Opposition and not the Session just ended that should be called 'extraordinary'. In the past there have been instances of dissolution by agreement between the parties. News and information about these, however, slipped out inadvertently. They were the outcome of behind-the-scenes deals. An Opposition has never before openly demanded an explicit statement of the date of dissolution. This is the issue ....
>
> My attitude has been that after passing the supplementary budget we should begin to prepare the annual budget and that I should decide the question of dissolution in the light of public opinion and the progress of proceedings in the Diet. Yesterday (December 20th) I decided my basic attitude regarding the preparation of the annual budget. We have now come to the stage where I must think seriously about dissolution. Dissolution should be carried out after ascertaining public opinion - in accordance with the popular will, not as a result of the machin-

> ations of the Opposition parties .... A dissolution is a serious matter. We should not yield before the plots and pressures of the Opposition parties. We have now reached the stage where we should think seriously about the question of dissolution together with and at the same time as the preparation of the annual budget. The time is drawing near when the Liberal-Democratic Party must stand at the bar and be judged by the people.

Most of this statement was, however, an attack on the Opposition for boycotting the Session: 'The way of parliamentary politics is to participate in parliamentary proceedings and appeal to the people by one's votes in the House'. The Ministerialists thereby sought to make this the issue for the election campaign.

According to the Asahi (22 December 1966) this statement appears to have been generally accepted as an indication that dissolution would take place at the beginning of the regular session of the Diet commencing on December 27th (In Japan to dissolve when the House is not in session would be unprecedented[8]). It was greeted by a statement by the Vice-Chairman of the Socialist Party that 'the Satoo Cabinet has capitulated in the face of the contentions of the four Opposition parties centred on the Socialist Party, and in the face of public opinion'.

Satoo then asked the leaders of the Opposition parties for the 'normalisation' of Diet proceedings (i.e. the attendance of their parties) at the forthcoming Session. To this end they met on December 24th. The following is from the account of this meeting given in the Asahi (24 December 1966;

---

8. It is a precedent unbroken to the present day that dissolution shall take place only when the Diet is in session. The dissolution of 1930, for example, was delayed until the Diet reassembled, because there were doubts as to the propriety of dissolution other than during session. This custom arose no doubt because dissolution, over the formative period, was regarded as the abnormal way of terminating a Diet - the result of a dispute; otherwise a Diet terminated naturally by efflux of time as happened in 1902, 1908, 1912 and 1942. Ex hypothesi such a dispute could occur only during session.

Compare this Japanese convention with Fox's assertion on 12 January 1784, in support of his famous Motion, that dissolution during a Session is unconstitutional (The Parliamentary History of England from the Earliest Period to the Year 1803, London, Hansard, 1815, vol.24, p.281). Fox supported this assertion with a reference to a pamphlet by Lord Somers in which the latter 'supported his opinion on an Act of King Richard II'. I have not, however, been able to track down this pamphlet although reference was also made to it by Lord Holland and Lord Howick during the debate in Parliament on the dissolution of 1807 (Cobbett's Parliamentary Debates, vol.9, pp.587 & 619). Hearn points out in support of Fox that for the eighty years before 1784 Parliament had died a natural death either by effluxion of time or by the demise of the Crown (W.E. Hearn, The Government of England: Its Structure and its Development, Melbourne, 1886, p.160).

evening edition) under the headline 'Understanding Reached that Dissolution will take place on 27th'.

Tsuji (Koomeitoo). Will dissolution be on 27th as reported?
Satoo. It is unreasonable to expect me to speak clearly on this matter. Even within the Liberal-Democratic Party all I have said is that we have come to the time when we must think seriously of dissolution.
Sasaki (Socialist Party). The Prime Minister's utterance at the Liberal-Democratic Party caucus meeting has been accepted in the Liberal-Democratic Party and by public opinion to mean dissolution at the beginning of the Session. Cannot the fact that the Prime Minister doesn't deny this be taken to mean that he accepts this? Satoo is not the kind of man who would do such a thing as dissolve by agreement with the Opposition parties.
Nishio (Democratic-Socialist Party). Even though he won't speak as clearly as that isn't it enough that he has said that there will be a speedy dissolution? The Prime Minister recently said that, as regards dissolution, he would watch and consider public opinion. The trend of public opinion is that there will be a dissolution on 27th and it accepts this. The three of us are certain that the Prime Minister has decided on 27th. As regards the dissolution, isn't this enough for us?
Satoo. During the special Session it was remarks about dissolution that led to the breakdown in communication between us. This being the case, isn't it sufficient that I say no more than I have said now? I can't say clearly when. However, at yesterday's press conference with overseas correspondents, when asked the date of dissolution I said 'Almost all the Japanese newspapers say 27th'. Please judge from this.

The Prime Minister smiled at these remarks by the Socialist Party and Democratic-Socialist Party leaders but showed no particular disagreement with what they said.

After twenty minutes' discussion, the Prime Minister said 'We shall next meet on the battlefield' ....

The dissolution duly took place on December 27th.

To United Kingdom and Commonwealth readers the above case-study may reveal some unexpected features.

It was Churchill who spoke of 'the odour of dissolution' being in the air in the months preceding it.[9] But the Asahi's 'autumn wind of dissolution' blowing daily through the political world some three months before the event is something much more pervasive. Indeed the 70% of the Members of the Lower House whom, the Asahi tells us (30 October 1966), it caused to return to their electorates and squander their campaign funds in early October, call to mind those 'oozy woods' which, on encountering a more celebrated West Wind of autumn, 'tremble and despoil themselves'. It will be argued elsewhere in this paper that, because of the high cost of electioneering in Japan, once dissolution is in the air very strong pressure is exerted on a Prime Minister to name the day by Members of the Diet who have jumped the gun and whose pockets, accordingly, are running empty. An indication of such pressure in the present case was Fukuda's appeal to the Prime Minister on December 21st (v. supra, p.96).

Another unusual feature is the great significance which both the Prime Minister and the Opposition parties attached to creating the impression that the dissolution was the product of their initiative. In effect it appears to have been extracted from the Government by the Opposition parties under the threat of continuing the boycott into the regular Session. The Prime Minister availed himself of several devices to save face: he suggested that he was dissolving because, the annual budget having been prepared (It had not, in fact, been prepared) there was no urgent task outstanding; he did not actually announce the date of dissolution until the day preceding it; he made the somewhat surprising suggestion that the actual timing was in response to public opinion which, paradoxically, wished for dissolution on December 27th rather than another date but at the same time was satisfied with the Government's record.[10]

---

9. Parliamentary Debates, Commons, vol.404, col.667, 31 October 1944.

10. Strange to say, Japanese public opinion pollsters do trouble the citizen with technical questions in such a field. Probably the most recent information available to the Government would have been the poll conducted by the Asahi on November 21st and 22nd (published on November 30th and December 1st). The results, as one might expect in a poll of this nature, were rather strange. Although a plurality of 49% gave the Liberal-Democrats as their favourite party, a plurality of 46% favoured a general election, a plurality of 44% (in answer to a separate question) wished the cabinet to resign, and only 25% (in answer to a separate question) supported the Satoo Cabinet (cf. 38% who did not support it)!

That on December 21st Satoo coupled his virtual decision to dissolve with an attack on the Opposition for boycotting proceedings is hardly surprising. Most Prime Ministers would enjoy an issue of this nature, rather than just their policies, on which to fight an election. Utilisation of an issue of such a nature does, however, accord with the preoccupation of Japanese Prime Ministers in recent years with the need for a 'just cause' for dissolution - a subject which we shall touch on later in this paper.

Let us briefly trace these and other influences in the history of dissolution in Japan since the inauguration of the Diet in 1890.

Dissolution under the Meiji Constitution

The classic occasion where a unilateral dissolution of a representative body by the executive is permissible in terms of democratic theory is where a hostile majority in the former is impeding the implementation of the latter's policies and where at the same time there are reasonable grounds for believing that the electorate will support the executive.[11] In such circumstances it is a device whose function is to ensure that the representative organ remains truly representative. A corollary of this function is that, should the election precipitated by the dissolution return a majority hostile to the cabinet, the latter should resign: it should not be able to dissolve the representative body a second time.[12] Nevertheless,

11. A similar justification would apply to a dissolution carried out on the return to normalcy after a war (e.g. the Shidehara Cabinet's dissolution of 1945), on the adoption of fundamental constitutional changes (e.g. the 1st Yoshida Cabinet's dissolution in 1946 following the enactment of the New Constitution), or where cabinet appeals to the electorate in the face of obstruction by a non-elective upper house (In fact, however, the occasions when the Japanese Government and the Lower House were, together, at loggerheads with the Peers were such that the Government always chose to modify its policies and give way).

12. In the ferment of ideas preceding the drafting of the Meiji Constitution this was the stand of Ookuma and some of the liberals (C. Fukase, 'Shuugiin no kaisan - hikakuhoo shiteki koosatsu' in J. Tanaka, *Nihonkokukempoo taikei : miyazawa toshiyoshi sensei kanreki kinen*, 1962, vol.4, p.187). It was not, however, the philosophy of the officials who drafted and then operated the Constitution. Its spirit was not popular sovereignty but, as Professor Miyazawa has succintly put it, 'A strong flavour of divine right, superimposed on the principle of constitutional monarchy characterising the nineteenth century German constitutions' (quoted *ibid*., p.186). ITOO Miyoji, who as an assistant to his famous namesake Prince Itoo was closely associated with the drafting of the Constitution, expressed himself at that time (1891) as follows:

> In a constitutional monarchy the Diet is empowered to give its sanction in only one section of the task of administration. It follows that even though cabinet should not receive the assent of the Diet in this single sphere cabinet is not prevented, in its task of assisting the Emperor, from carrying out other tasks of administration. Bismarck, for example, continued in office for a long period without a majority in the Lower House and, having once dissolved the latter, he did not consider it inconvenient for the cabinet to remain in office even though the newly assembled House did not change its attitude. Moreover, for the reason stated above, there was no one in the whole country who denounced his conduct or considered it illegal. *A fortiori* in Japan if cabinet dissolves the Lower House because of a disagreement with the Diet on a financial matter, and cabinet knows that at the new election the people will agree with the outgoing Diet, then it can dissolve it again - two, three or four times. This is because the administration of this country comprises many things besides finance. Who, because of the part, would abandon the whole field of administration to the majority party in the Lower House? (Quoted *ibid*., p.186).

when Prince Itoo in 1893 dissolved the Lower House (in order to silence discussion prejudicial to current treaty negotiations) and the resultant election returned a hostile majority, he dissolved againly only nineteen days after the new House assembled. Again in 1898 he dissolved a newly elected House only twenty-one days after it had assembled, when it rejected a Government proposal to increase taxation.

Under the British system the Crown might well refuse a dissolution to a Prime Minister from whom the Lower House is withholding Supply: the Lower House can hardly be expected to make possible a dissolution by granting Supply to a minority Government if there is a potential majority Government available.[13] In Japan, however, the situation was very different. Article 71 of the Meiji Constitution empowered the Government, should the Diet fail to pass the Budget, to repeat the Budget of the previous year. As the table on the following page demonstrates, only in one of the sixteen pre-War dissolutions (that of 1937) had Supply been voted. On the remaining fifteen occasions the Government acting under Article 71 repeated (or had already repeated) the Budget of the preceding year.[14] In the absence of financial worries the Government was able to dissolve as early in the Session as it wished - usually in the first month.[15]

The typical dissolution was a peremptory reply to a hostile House. With the single exception of that of 1919 all the pre-War dissolutions were performed by minority Govern-

---

13. Spencer Walpole considers that it would be a breach of convention for the Commons to withhold Supply in order to prevent a dissolution. He supports this with the claim that they have only once since 1784 acted in this manner [S. Walpole, Todd's Parliamentary Government in England (1892 ed.), vol.2, pp.127 & 215. For the means by which public monies were expended in 1784 and 1807 see the Chancellor of the Exchequer's statement of 26 June 1807 in Cobbett's Parliamentary Debates, vol.9, p.631]. Nevertheless as recently as 1950 the Governor of Victoria refused a dissolution to a Premier who was unable to obtain Supply from a newly elected House (Round Table, vol.40, 1950, p.383). The Governor's action in this case was generally accepted as eminently proper. Note, however, in support of Walpole's contention, that the House of Commons in 1919 unanimously, by agreement between the Government and the Opposition, and deliberately enacted legislation renouncing an additional power to prevent dissolution by its control of the purse strings which had been inadvertently conferred upon it by a provision of the Representation of the People Act 1918 to the effect that the cost of Returning Officers, which hitherto had been borne by the candidates, should be paid by the Treasury out of moneys provided by Parliament. In moving its repeal the Joint Financial Secretary to the Treasury criticised this provision as 'putting it in the power of the House of Commons, by refusing the Estimate, to prolong its own life and to do away with the old constitutional practice in this country that the right of dissolving Parliament rests with the Crown on the advice of his Ministers' (Parliamentary Debates, Commons, vol. 112, col.1334, 21 February 1919).

14. Hoorei zensho, Naikaku insatsu kyoku, passim. The testimony on this point given before the International Military Tribunal for the Far East is misleading (See the testimony of C. Okada in International Military Tribunal for the Far East, Proceedings, p.17715).

15. As mentioned in footnote 8, above, a dissolution when the Diet was not in session would be unprecedented.

Elected	Session Began	Dissol-ution	Months Since Elected	Date and Method of Acquiring Supply	Cabinet	Circumstances of Dissolution
1/ 7/90	26/11/91	25/12/91	17	17/ 3/92*(a.71)	1st Matsukata	The Lower House had refused money for naval construction.
12/ 2/92	28/11/93	30/12/93	22	6/ 2/94 (a.71)	2nd Itoo	To silence discussion in the Lower House which the Minister for Foreign Affairs considered prejudicial to current treaty negotiations.
1/ 3/94	15/ 5/94	2/ 6/94	3	Not applicable	2nd Itoo	The Lower House had carried an address censuring the Government.
1/ 9/94	24/12/97	25/12/97	39	7/ 2/98 (a.71)	2nd Matsukata	To forestall a vote of censure by a hostile majority.
15/ 3/98	19/ 5/98	8/ 6/98	2	Not applicable	3rd Itoo	Rejection of a Government proposal to increase taxation.
10/ 8/02	9/12/02	28/12/02	4	5/ 2/03 (a.71)	1st Katsura	To forestall the defeat of a Government proposal to increase taxation.
10/ 3/03	10/12/03	11/12/03	9	2/ 2/04 (a.71)	1st Katsura	The Lower House had passed the Address-in-Reply, not realizing that the President had inserted a phrase condemning the Government's foreign policy. Since a hostile majority was forming, the Government used this as an excuse for a dissolution.
15/ 5/12	7/12/14	25/12/14	19	28/12/14 (a.71)	2nd Ookuma	The Lower House had deleted provision for two infantry divisions in the Estimates.
25/ 3/15	27/12/16	25/ 1/17	22	20/ 2/17 (a.71)	Terauchi	A hostile majority had presented a motion of censure.
20/ 4/17	26/12/19	26/ 2/20	34	16/ 3/20 (a.71)	Hara	To expedite an election under a newly enacted electoral law advantageous to the Government.
10/ 5/20	27/12/23	31/ 1/24	44	28/ 2/24 (a.71)	Kiyoura	To forestall a vote of censure by a hostile majority.
10/ 3/24	27/12/27	21/ 1/28	46	15/ 3/28 (a.71)	Tanaka	To forestall a vote of censure by a hostile majority.
20/ 2/28	26/12/29	21/ 1/30	23	10/ 3/30 (a.71)	Hamaguchi	The Government was in a minority and clearly unable to face the Lower House.
20/ 2/30	26/12/31	21/ 1/32	23	14/ 3/32 (a.71)	Inukai	The Government was in a minority and clearly unable to manage the Lower House.
20/ 2/32	26/12/35	21/ 1/36	47	23/ 3/36 (a.71)	Okada	A vote of censure had been moved by a hostile majority.
20/ 2/36	26/12/36	31/ 3/37	13	Budget passed both Houses 29/ 2/36	Hayashi	The Government whose legislative programme had been obstructed by a hostile majority sought a mandate for non-party Government.
Post-War						
30/ 4/42	27/11/45	18/12/45	42	26/ 3/46 (a.71)	Shidehara	'First G.H.Q. Dissolution'. After the passage of SCAP-inspired legislation extending the franchise.
10/ 4/46	28/12/46	31/ 3/47	11	Budget passed both Houses 25/ 3/47	1st Yoshida	'Second G.H.Q. Dissolution'. In compliance with General MacArthur's letter to the Prime Minister.

* The maximum length of a Diet was fixed at four years by the Electoral Law

ments confronted by an actively hostile majority.[16] Only half the pre-War dissolutions provided the Government with a decided majority - 1894, 1914, 1917, 1920, 1932 and 1936. In 1894 the Government's success was partly due to patriotic feeling caused by the outbreak of war between the date of dissolution and the resultant election; in 1914 and 1920, to Government interference with the elections.

Though he did not abide by this in practice, Prince Itoo in his semi-official Commentaries goes as far as saying that 'The dissolution of the House of Representatives is a mode of ascertaining the public opinion from the tone of the newly elected House'.[17] To fulfil this role it is necessary that there be a clear issue presented to the electors for their decision and that the Opposition have the same opportunities as the Government to put its case. This requirement was not satisfied in the following dissolutions. In 1893 no reason was stated for the dissolution. In 1894 the reason given was so vague as to be meaningless. In 1897, 1903, 1917, 1920, 1924, 1928, 1932 and 1936 the Government gagged the Opposition by dissolving either to forestall a vote of non-confidence or before the Opposition could state its case. In fact the only occasion where a cabinet, having decided on dissolution, deferred this until the Opposition had had its opportunity to speak, was the Hamaguchi cabinet in 1930.

The first two post-War dissolutions (1945 and 1947) took place under the old Constitution. This was a revolutionary period and almost nothing was done except at the suggestion (or at least with the approval) of General MacArthur, the Supreme Commander for the Allied Powers (SCAP). Accordingly, they do not merit close study. The purpose of the 1945 dissolution was to replace the tainted wartime Lower House as soon as possible with new men elected under the SCAP-inspired legislation extending the franchise.[18] The 1947 dissolution was

---

16. It may be argued that the dissolutions of 1924, 1928 and 1936 could, in view of the age of the respective Diets, be more fairly described as 'efflux of time' dissolutions. More important, however, is the fact that they were peremptory, punitive acts by minority Governments.

The 1919 dissolution was purely tactical. The Government was keen to dissolve in order to reap the benefits of the newly enacted electoral law, the provisions of which could be expected to work to its advantage. It made the occasion of the dissolution an unacceptable Opposition bill which it could easily have outvoted (T. Watanabe, Tooshu to seitoo, Koobundoo, 1961, p.175).

17. H. Itoo, Commentaries on the Constitution of Japan, Second English Edition, Tokyo, 1906, p.14.

18. It is somewhat ironical that SCAP, in delaying the resultant election after the 1945 dissolution so that its directive on 'Removal and Exclusion of Undesirable Personnel from Public Office' could be sufficiently implemented to exclude ultranationalist candidates, caused considerably longer periods (16 and 28 weeks respectively) to elapse between dissolution and the election and between dissolution and the convocation of the new Diet than had ever been the case previously. The supreme Allied body, the Far Eastern Commission, would have had SCAP delay the election even further. This delay also meant that on this occasion the Government had to resort to the notorious Article 71 of the Meiji Constitution for Supply.

carried out in compliance with General MacArthur's letter to the Prime Minister (Mr Yoshida) of February 16th instructing him to dissolve so that 'a new legislative body may initiate and synchronize with the introduction and effectivation of the new Constitution ...'[19]

Dissolution under the New Constitution

The Drafting of the Constitution

On 7 January 1946 a paper prepared in Washington entitled 'Reform of the Japanese Government System' was approved by the State-War-Navy Coordinating Committee and forwarded to MacArthur 'for his information'.[20] This paper noted that although '... resolutions of no confidence by the Lower House prior to 1931 frequently led to the resignation of a cabinet or of ministers thus censured, such resolutions have also frequently led to the dissolution of the House and a new election which, although it supported the House against the government, was not followed by the latter's resignation'. It concluded that 'The Supreme Commander should indicate to the Japanese authorities that the Japanese governmental system should be reformed to accomplish the following general objectives: .... an executive branch of government deriving its authority from and responsible to the electorate or to a fully representative legislative body ...' If the Emperor Institution were retained a necessary safeguard was that 'the Ministers of State, chosen with the advice and consent of the representative legislative body shall form a Cabinet collectively responsible to the legislative body ...'

The story is well known how in February 1946 MacArthur, dissatisfied with the Shidehara cabinet's half-hearted attitude to constitutional reform, caused the Government Section of his headquarters to prepare a complete draft constitution which, with minor amendments, they forced the cabinet to accept.[21] This is known in Japan as the MacArthur Draft.[22] As

19. Political Reorientation of Japan: Report of Government Section, Supreme Commander for the Allied Powers (hereafter referred to as PRJ), Washington, Government Printing Office, 1949, Appendices Volume, p.721.

20. This document is reproduced in Kempoo choosakai jimukyoku, Kenshi soo dai-30-goo, January 1959, pp.1-15.

21. C. Whitney, MacArthur - His Rendezvous with History, New York, Knopf, 1956, pp.246-55.

22. The text of the MacArthur Draft is available (in the original English) in T. Miyazawa, Nihonkoku kempoo, Nihon hyooron shinsha, 1955, Appendices Volume, pp.40-60.

regards relations between the legislature and the executive it followed 'Reform of the Japanese Governmental System' fairly closely. Whereas the role that it gave to the Diet was 'the highest organ of state power', cabinet was merely the repository of the executive power. It reduced to seventy days the maximum period which could elapse between the end of one Diet and the convocation of the newly elected one (cf. seven months under the Meiji Constitution). It required cabinet to resign on the convening of a newly elected Diet, whereupon the latter would proceed to elect the new Prime Minister. This in effect would prevent the same cabinet's dissolving the House a second time.[23] For, like 'Reform of the Japanese Governmental System', it did give cabinet the option of dissolution as an alternative to resignation. It enjoined cabinet within ten days of the passage of a resolution of non-confidence either to resign or dissolve.

On receiving the MacArthur Draft, the cabinet was required to prepare a Japanese draft embodying its essential features. Cabinet did so and these requirements stand part of the present Constitution which on enactment by the Diet came into effect on 3 May 1947. The Articles in the Constitution as finally enacted (and as it stands to-day) that are relevant to dissolution are the following:

> Article 7. The Emperor, with the advice and approval of the Cabinet, shall perform the following acts in matters of state on behalf of the people: ....
> (iii) Dissolution of the House of Representatives.
> Article 40. The Diet shall be the highest organ of State power ....
> Article 54. When the House of Representatives is dissolved, there must be a general election of members of the House of Representatives within forty (40) days from the date of dissolution, and the Diet must be convoked within thirty (30) days from the date of the election ....
> Article 65. Executive power shall be vested in the Cabinet.
> Article 69. If the House of Representatives passes a non-confidence resolution, or rejects a confidence resolution, the Cabinet shall resign en masse, unless the House of Representatives is dissolved within ten (10) days.

23. This was one of the few points on which the Shidehara Cabinet had considered the Meiji Constitution required revision. PRJ, Appendices Volume, p.607.

Under the new Constitution the following dissolutions have taken place:-

Elected	Session Began	Dissolution	Popular Nickname given by Japanese Press	Months Since Election*	Cabinet
25/ 4/47	1/12/48	23/12/48	'NAREAI' ('Collusion')	19	2nd Yoshida
23/ 1/49	26/ 8/52	28/ 8/52	'NUKIUCHI' ('Sudden Swoop')	43	3rd Yoshida
1/10/52	8/11/52	14/ 3/53	'BAKAYAROO' ('Bloody Fool')	5	4th Yoshida
19/ 4/53	21/ 1/55	24/ 1/55	'TEN NO KOE' ('Vox populi vox dei')	21	1st Hatoyama
27/ 2/55	20/12/57	25/ 4/58	'HANASHIAI' ('Agreement')	37	1st Kishi
22/ 5/58	18/10/63	24/10/60	'YOYAKU' ('Promised')	29	1st Ikeda
20/11/60	17/10/63	23/10/63	'MUUDOO' ('Mood')	35	2nd Ikeda
21/11/63	27/12/66	27/12/66	'KUROI KIRI ('Black Mist')	37	3rd Satoo

* The Maximum length of a Diet is fixed at 4 years by Constitution a.45.

The 'Nareai'[24] ('Collusion') Dissolution, 23 December 1948

The first dissolution under the new Constitution took place on 23 December 1948.

On 7 October 1948 the Ashida cabinet resigned. As a coalition of three parties (Democrats, Socialists and People's Cooperatives) it had from the outset lacked stability: it needed only the involvement of some of its members in the Shoowa denkoo scandal[25] to bring it down. Yoshida, the leader of the Democratic-Liberal Party, became Prime Minister. The coalition parties went into Opposition.

Yoshida, leading a minority Government, was eager to go to the polls while the Opposition's involvement in the Shoowa denkoo scandal was still fresh in the minds of the electorate. He stated his intention to dissolve as soon as the amendments to the Public Servants Law should have been enacted (SCAP had required these amendments). The Ministerialists, with the support of eminent constitutional lawyers,[26] claimed that cabinet

24. The nicknames used in these headings are the standard titles used by Japanese newspapers and popular histories.

25. Sixty-four officials, Members of the Diet and ministers including eventually Ashida himself were charged as a result of allegations of bribery and corruption by a firm which had received large-scale loans from a Government credit institution.

26. See for example the views of T. Miyazawa (Professor of Constitutional Law at Tokyo University) in the Asahi shimbun, 8 November 1948 and Y. Suzuki in the Jiji shimbun, 14 November 1948 and Yomiuri shimbun, 15 November 1948.

had this power by virtue of Constitution a.7(iii) (v. *supra* p.105) which, they argued, conferred on cabinet an independent power of dissolution.[27] The Opposition naturally were equally eager to postpone elections for as long as possible. Assisted by the journalism of OZAKI Yukio[28] (an independent, the doyen of the Lower House, who as early as 1891 had argued that punitive dissolution was unconstitutional), but with very little support from constitutional lawyers[29], the Opposition leaders Katayama (Socialist) and Tomabechi (Democrat) argued that the Constitution empowered cabinet to dissolve the House only in the situation described in a.69, i.e. on the passage of a motion of non-confidence (For Katayama at least, this argument was a *volte face*: while in office he had advocated a dissolution while the coalition still commanded a majority).[30] Briefly their contention was that, since a.4 provides that 'The Emperor shall perform only such acts in matters of state as are provided for in this Constitution and he shall not have powers related to government', a.7(iii) cannot confer a power of dissolution, since dissolution by its very nature is a 'power related to government'. Hence a.7(iii) is to be interpreted as conferring only the power to promulgate dissolutions. Since a basic principle of the Constitution was that the Diet is 'the highest organ of state power' (a.41), representative of, and elected by, 'the people, with whom resides sovereign power' (a.1), any power on the part of cabinet, the servant, to dismiss the legislature, the master, must be expressly conferred. Only a.69 confers such a power - and to a limited degree.

---

27. *Asahi shimbun*, 14 November 1948; *Jiji shimbun*, 14 November 1948.

28. Ozaki was first elected to the Lower House in 1890. His views appeared in substantially the same form in signed articles in the *Daiichi shimbun*, 3 November 1948, *Mainichi shimbun*, 10 November 1948 and *Yomiuri shimbun*, 3 January 1949, in his draft resolution of 11 November 1948 in the House of Representatives (v. *Shuugiin giji sooran, dai 3-4-kai kokkai*) and in his speech in the latter on 16 November 1948 (An English translation of the speech is available in the [English language] *The Official Gazette Extra, House of Representatives, 3rd Session*, no.13, pp.17-26). Ozaki went further than the Opposition and argued that, a.69 notwithstanding, cabinet cannot in any circumstances dissolve the House, since the overriding principle of popular sovereignty must prevail.

His 1891 article arguing that punitive dissolution was unconstitutional appeared under the *nom de plume* Gakudoo in *Kokumin no tomo*, 13 July 1891.

29. Even as late as 1951, whereas numerous articles and textbooks gave cabinet a wide power of dissolution, only a single article by an obscure scholar could be found supporting the restrictive interpretation of a.7 (*Dai 12-kai kokkai : ryooin hooki iinkai kaigiroku*, no.2, 6 November 1951). The latter view, however, prevailed when the subject was discussed at the periodic conference of the Nihon hookakukai (Japan Law Association) in November 1953 (*Jichi kenkyuu*, vol.30, no.4, pp.34-5).

30. *Asahi shimbun*, 13 & 22 August 1948.

On 11 November 1948 Katayama and Tomabechi visited Brig. Gen.Courtney Whitney (Chief, Government Section, SCAP), Col. Charles L. Kades (Deputy Chief) and Dr Justin Williams (Chief, Legislative Division) who supported their interpretation.[31] In private the Americans gave their views in some detail to senior Japanese legal officials:

> Kades. From the time the Constitution was enacted it has been our view that we should give neither the Emperor nor cabinet the power of dissolution. When the draft of the Constitution was being discussed in the room next to that in which we are now sitting, Lt. Esman[32] argued that the power of dissolution should be given to cabinet. However, we said that this was wrong and did not accept it.
>
> Should cabinet arbitrarily try to dissolve, the Diet need pay no attention to it - nay rather, the Emperor, being sensible, would well realise that he did not have such a power, and if the Government tendered such advice he would probably not accept it. Moreover in such a situation he would first call on General MacArthur.
>
> Williams. The provisions of the Constitution relating to this matter are Articles 4, 7, 41 ('The Diet shall be the highest organ of state power ...') and 69. Anyone who studied the Constitution carefully would realise that the power to dissolve the House of Representatives is limited to the circumstances provided in a.69.[33]

Since Kades was the chairman of the SCAP committee that prepared the original draft of the Constitution and since all amendments by the Japanese during the drafting were effected only with his approval, his views are of considerable interest historically. To the present writer, however, his argument is unconvincing on two grounds: (i) In the debates in the

31. Asahi shimbun, 13 November 1948.

32. 1st Lt. Milton J. Esman, who with Mr Cyrus H. Peake, and Mr Jacob I. Miller formed the committee within Government Section, SCAP which prepared the section of the MacArthur Draft relating to the Executive (PRJ, Appendices Volume p.813).

33. This account of discussion between the Americans and FUJISAKI Manri is given by T. Satoo (then a principal law officer) in 'Kaisanken rongi no kaisoo', Jurisuto, no.217 (1 January 1961), pp.14-19.

Diet in the course of the enactment of the Constitution, the Minister-in-charge specifically stated that the power of dissolution was with cabinet as the executive organ and that dissolution was not confined to the situation described in a.69.[34]
(ii) The suggestion that the Emperor may refuse to perform an 'act in matters of state' the performance of which has been advised by cabinet, i.e. that he may withhold consent from a decision of cabinet, is patently at variance with the fundamental principles underlying the Constitution and with the interpretation given by SCAP elsewhere.[35] Nor is it easy to sustain the suggestion that the Emperor has a role, as 'guardian of the Constitution', to restrain cabinet from committing unconstitutional acts: it was in order to fill such roles that the Constitution provided a Supreme Court. The consensus of opinion among Japanese constitutional lawyers is that the Emperor cannot refuse to carry out cabinet's advice.[36]

It is possible that this was a new interpretation on the part of the Americans, adopted opportunistically to meet the particular situation. It is doubtful whether they were at this time particularly enamoured of Yoshida and his party. Furthermore they did not wish the Session to end before the passage of the amendments to the Public Servants Law which they regarded as urgent.

Under SCAP's interpretation of the Constitution, dissolution could take place only when the Opposition parties chose to carry a resolution of non-confidence. The Opposition parties had no intention of obliging. They, moreover, proceeded to use their numerical strength to block the amendments to the Public Servants Law - possibly as a safeguard against SCAP's relaxing its interpretation on dissolution. Finally SCAP broke the deadlock by bringing about a compromise in which the Opposition parties secured a few weeks' respite and some other concessions in return for an undertaking to move a motion of non-confidence at the agreed time.[37] These agreements were honoured and the vote of non-confidence was duly passed on 23 December 1948. At the ensuing election (23 January 1949) Yoshida's party was returned with an absolute majority.

---

34. S. Shimizu, Chikujoo nihon kempoo shingiroku, Yuuhikaku, 1962, vol.3, p.198.

35. E.g. PRJ, p.114.

36. E.g. T. Miyazawa, Nihon koku kempoo, Nihon hyroron shinsha, 1955, p.68.

37. Asahi shimbun, 29 November 1948.

Leaving aside the wording of the Constitution, it is hard to feel great sympathy for Katayama and Tomabechi in the situation under discussion. It is the very situation where, most British writers would agree,[38] it is proper that a dissolution should be available to a minority Government. The Opposition parties had proved that they could not carry on the government and had resigned office. That the Democratic-Liberal minority, were forced to continue in office on the Opposition parties' terms was patently unfair to it and deprived the community of effective government.[39]

The question of dissolution came into prominence with the approach of the Peace Conference. On 29 March 1951 in the House of Representatives MIYAKE Masakazu, on behalf of the Socialist Party, moved that 'the Government promptly tender the advice that the House be dissolved'. The argument on which he laid particular stress was that public opinion should be consulted in advance of the Peace Conference which he argued was a vital issue which would determine the nation's destiny. His speech on this occasion indicates a reversal by the Socialists of their previous attitude towards dissolution. In 1946 their draft Constitution provided dissolution only by referendum.[40] In 1948 they argued that dissolution could take place only in accordance with a.69. Now Miyake argued that the Government of the majority party can dissolve without waiting for a vote of non-confidence.[41]

To someone brought up under the British system, a motion in favour of dissolution is hard to distinguish from a motion of non-confidence in the Government.[42] No Government or Ministerial Member could regard it in any other light. Some

38. It is interesting, however, that Ramsay MacDonald, when about to be commissioned to form a minority Government with the support of a third party in 1924, did not rule out of court the suggestion that in order to prevent too frequent dissolutions the power of dissolution in such circumstances should rest with the House of Commons (J. Ramsay MacDonald, 'What the Three-Party System Involves', The New Leader, 4 January 1924, p.8).

39. The Katayama-Tomabechi interpretation would have limited a minority Government's power to dissolve the Lower House to an extent not dissimilar to that of the power given by the Australian Constitution (Sect.57) to a Government with a minority in the Upper House to dissolve that House. Under Section 57 the Australian Government can dissolve the Upper House only when the latter has not agreed to a bill passed by the Lower House with a period of at least three months intervening. In neither case can the House concerned be dissolve without a specific concerted act or omission by itself (For examples of dissolutions in Australia under Section 57 see H.V. Evatt, The King and his Dominion Governors, Melbourne, Cheshire, 2nd edition 1967, pp.xxii-xxvii, 37-49).

40. Kempoo choosakai jimukyoku, Kenshi soo dai-10, December 1957, p.83.

41. Kampoo googai-dai-10-kai kokkai, shuugiin kaigiroku, no.27, 30 March 1951.

42. At Westminster, the Opposition has on occasion (e.g. 1905 and 1909) chosen for its amendment to the Address-in-Reply a request for a dissolution (C.K. Wang, Dissolution of the British Parliament 1832-1931, New York, Columbia U.P., 1934, p.60). But like any amendment to the Address-in-Reply when the Government has a firm majority, this was mere window-dressing.

years later the following explanation was given of the use of such a motion on this occasion:

> The first[43] occasion on which the Socialist Party moved a dissolution resolution was March 1951. They had wished to move a motion of non-confidence, but there was a lot of the Session still to go and they wanted to keep a motion of non-confidence for a later opportunity.[44]

(Governments have sometimes taken the view that the principle that the same issue cannot be discussed more than once in a Session precludes more than one vote of non-confidence per Session).

The motion was defeated. The Socialists next demanded that there be a dissolution at least before the Diet ratified the Peace Treaty. This, however, was emphatically rejected by the Prime Minister on his return from the Peace Conference (September 1951). Opinion within the Ministerialist ranks was, however, by no means united. In particular, to those party veterans who had been released from the operation of SCAP's purge directive since the last elections, a dissolution was the only means of returning to the Diet. The leader of this group, Hatoyama, pressed strongly for a dissolution.[45] On the other hand, there were influential Ministerialists who in their eagerness to avoid dissolution now cited with approval the precedent accepted by them with such reluctance in 1948.[46]

Report of the Joint Legislative Research Committee

It was in this situation that the Joint Legislative Research Committee of both Houses[47] on 30 October 1951 embarked on a study of the provisions of the Constitution relating to

43. This neglects the unsuccessful dissolution motion moved by the Socialists in company with the Kyoodoo minshutoo and Kokumintoo on 17 December 1946 (before the new Constitution came into effect).

44. Statement by OZAWA Saeki (Liberal-Democrat) in plenary session of House of Representatives, 3 February 1958 (as reported in Mainichi shimbun, 4 February 1958).

45. Yomiuri shimbun, 29 December 1951.

46. See for example the statement of Hirokawa in Asahi shimbun, 1 October 1951.

47. The Joint Legislative Research Committee was a device introduced at the suggestion of SCAP. It was modelled on the Legislative Councils existing in several American States. Its role as described in the Diet Law of 1948 was: '(i) to single out specific problems relating to government and to make recommendations thereon to the Houses; (ii) to make recommendations to the Houses for new legislation or concerning existing laws and cabinet orders; (iii) to investigate and study the laws and regulations pertaining to the Diet and to make recommendations to the Houses for their revision'. This device was later abandoned by the Japanese.

dissolution. Some seven months later, on 17 June 1952, after examining the relevant debates in the Diet, the published views of constitutional lawyers and the evidence of witnesses summoned before it, presented its report, the material part of which was as follows:

> It is proper to interpret the Constitution as permitting dissolution not only in the circumstances provided in a.69 but also in situations where there are sufficient grounds for an objective judgement that it is necessary, from the standpoint of the operation of democratic politics, to seek afresh the general will of the people. We must, however, ensure that dissolution is not performed as a result of the arbitrary decision of cabinet. For example, it is desirable that some such convention be established as that, where the House of Representatives has passed a resolution on dissolution, cabinet shall respect this and give its advice and approval for dissolution underConstitution a.7. Moreover, should there be a suitable opportunity in the future, a democratic system of dissolution should be established by making express provision with respect to these fundamental matters concerning the dissolution system, and constitutional obscurities should be removed.[48]

Obviously a compromise between conflicting points of view, this report is hardly a breakthrough in political theory: the window-dressing in the form of pious aspirations for the future does little more than indicate how hemmed in the Committee was by the essential dilemma of the problem. They had to choose one of two paths and they did so with misgivings. Put more colloquially, their report would seem to amount to something like this: 'The Diet is the "highest organ of state power". Therefore, if we look at it honestly, we can't justify giving cabinet a wide power of dissolution. Nevertheless we must; for otherwise there is the likelihood of gumming up the system - there would be no way out of deadlocks. We wish we could get around this inconsistency, but we can't'.

As has been previously remarked (v. supra p.110) the need specifically to grant the House a power to dissolve itself by

48. Dai-13-kai kokkai : ryooin hooki iinkaigiroku, no.11, 17 June 1952.

resolution seems, to British eyes, redundant. Be this as it may, there have been (and are to-day) numerous European constitutions which provide for dissolution by resolution of the House, independent of any vote of censure on the Executive.[49]

Perhaps the most significant thing about the Report (and about the evidence presented) is how hesitantly and apologetically the case for a wide power of dissolution was put, even by the majority who supported it. The abuse of executive power under the Meiji Constitution, stressed by their opponents, may not have been far from anyone's mind. The justifications advanced in favour of a wide power of dissolution were similar to those advanced in other countries (e.g.: where in a coalition the Government is left in a minority by the defection of its partner; or where the Upper House has rejected a vital Government-sponsored measure approved by the Lower House and the Government wishes to increase its majority in the latter to the two-thirds required to override the Upper House[50]). Another popular argument was in terms of 'checks and balances': dissolution is necessary to prevent the tyranny of the legislature.[51]

The case against a wide power of dissolution was, however, more interesting because, in part at least, it appealed to Japanese history and conditions. It was stated in greatest detail by TAKAHASHI Eikichi, an influential Ministerialist back-bencher, lawyer and provincial newspaper proprietor. The gist of his argument (omitting his textual interpretation of a.7 which is similar to that of Ozaki and Kades) is as follows:[52]

(i) If a power of dissolution wider than a.69 were admitted, there would be no way of confining dissolutions to situations where they were, objectively, justified. Cabinet would dissolve in order to secure or increase a majority - i.e. for

---

49. To-day the Austrian (a.29), Bulgarian (a.30), Yugoslavian (a.70) and East German (a.56) constitutions contain such a provision.

50. See for example the evidence of SEKIGUCHI Yasushi (President of Yokohama Municipal University), Dai-12-kai kokkai : ryooin hooki iinkaigiroku, no.4, 13 November 1951, pp.1-9.

51. See for example the evidence of KANAMORI Tokujiroo (Minister-in-charge of the Constitution Bill during its passage through the Diet), ibid., no.5, 16 November 1951, pp.4 ff.

52. Ibid., no.4, 13 November 1951; no.5, 16 November 1951; no.6, 26 November 1951.

party, political advantage. In Japan the Ministerialists always stand to gain by dissolution.[53] Hence the requirement in the new Constitution that cabinet must resign after the new House is convoked, is not of much significance. Although _to-day_ Cabinet cannot resort to electoral interference to the extent indulged in previously, nevertheless with the present trend towards the centralization of police and other powers the re-emergence of electoral interference is to be feared.
(ii) When an important Government measure is rejected by the Upper House and the Government does not possess the two-thirds majority required to override this veto it should not be able to dissolve: it should abandon the bill, since the latter obviously has little support.
(iii) Where a coalition cabinet splits, the rump cabinet should not have the power to dissolve; for this would mean in practice that the minor partner, fearing dissolution, would support proposals with which it disagreed and which, accordingly, in conscience it should oppose.
(iv) The power of dissolution is unnecessary. It is merely a convention or a product of the history of the countries in which it exists. Japanese local government until quite recently operated satisfactorily without any provision for dissolution.[54] Similarly, government in the U.S.A. proceeds satisfactorily without it. Dissolution is an attribute not of the system of responsible government but of the monarchic system - a system which under the new Constitution no longer exists in Japan.
(v) Under the Meiji Constitution, even though the Emperor dissolved only after hearing the advice of many besides the Prime Minister, the results were nevertheless undesirable. Should a wide power of dissolution now be admitted, it would place greater power in the hands of cabinet, since the other advisory organs have been abolished by the new Constitution.

Among the witnesses Takahashi's position received strong support from Ozaki (v. _supra_ p.107) and ODAKA Tomoo (Professor of Jurisprudence, Tokyo University), particularly on point (i). Ozaki argued that the master, the legislature, could

---

53. This is not completely true, as we have shown in the case of some of the pre-War dissolutions (v. _supra_ p.103).

54. What Takahashi means here is that under the pre-War local government system the _local_ executives had no power of dissolution. The Home Minister, however, had the power to dissolve _any local_ government Council (See for example Prefectural Code, Law 64 of 1899, a.131).

never be dissolved by the servant, cabinet, a.69 notwithstanding. He was influenced by the belief that bribery and intimidation on top of lack of political education and the survival of feudal thought patterns among the people (particularly the newly enfranchised women) produced a more subservient House at each election. Odaka feared that since democracy was not adequately developed in Japan, there was considerable danger of cabinet's abusing a wide power of dissolution. He noted that in Germany it was by dissolving and interfering with the subsequent elections that the Nazis came to power.[55]

These arguments and the Committee's abhorrence of dissolutions performed as a result of the arbitrary decision of cabinet are not surprising in view of the widespread hostility to the authoritarian government of the pre-War period, the low value traditionally accorded in Japanese society to decisions other than those achieved as a result of consensus, and the larger role played by the post-War Japanese Ministerialist back-bencher in policy-making and the legislative process than by his British counterpart. Nevertheless, as might be expected with a problem so difficult of solution, no action regarding the Report was taken by either House or by the Government.

The 'Nukiuchi' ('Sudden Swoop') Dissolution, 28 August 1952

On 28 April 1952 the Peace Treaty came into effect and the Occupation came to an end.

Dissolution was now, of necessity, becoming a practical question. The existing House had been elected on 22 January 1949. A dissolution therefore had to be held before 22 January 1953. Members were accordingly already deserting the House to cultivate their constituencies for the inevitable election. Among the Ministerialists the rift between Hatoyama and Yoshida was steadily becoming deeper. Whereas Yoshida insisted on postponing a dissolution until he had implemented his legislative programme and reconstructed the cabinet, Hatoyama advocated a speedy appeal to the people. Hatoyama's following proved strong enough to thwart Yoshida in his attempts to reconstruct the cabinet. In this impasse, abandoning his original plan of warding off dissolution until November, Yoshida dissolved, without warning, on the second day of

55. Dai-12-kai kokkai : ryooin hooki iinkaigiroku, no.5, 16 November 1951, pp.7-12.

the Session, 28 August 1952.[56] His reasoning presumably was that, since there was no chance of his reconstructing cabinet and going to the country with a ministry that was both favourable to himself and attractive in the eyes of the electorate, the longer the dissolution was delayed the more opportunity it would give to the rising Hatoyama group to woo the electorate. Moreover, the quicker the dissolution the less chance for Hatoyama to accumulate electoral funds.

This dissolution was the subject of litigation which dragged on until 1960 keeping the issues before the public eye and evoking numerous articles in learned journals.

In 1948 one of the leaders of the defeated Ashida coalition who visited GHQ and urged on their willing ears the view that the power of dissolution was confined to the circumstances provided in a.69 was TOMABECHI Gizoo.[57] A leading member of the principal Opposition party, he now once again emerges as a principal figure in the debate on the extent of the power of dissolution.

Tomabechi did not recontest his seat at the election brought about by the 1952 dissolution, but immediately afterwards went to the courts and sought a decision that the dissolution was unconstitutional. Presumably because there was a

---

56. It is appropriate here to note that, admitting that a.7 of the Constitution does empower cabinet to dissolve the House contrary to the latter's wishes, there is one feature of the Constitution which affords a Japanese Government greater freedom in this respect than is the case under the British system: the Queen might well refuse a dissolution until the Government had secured the passage of such legislation (including financial legislation) as was necessary to see the country through the interim until the new Parliament could act. Article 54 of the Japanese Constitution was deliberately designed to allow provisional legislation to be enacted by the Upper House, acting alone, while the House of Representatives stood dissolved. Hence Yoshida on this occasion was able to dissolve even though there was a matter outstanding for which parliamentary approval had to be secured before the forthcoming election. Under Constitution a.79 the appointment of certain justices of the Supreme Court had to be reviewed by referendum at that election. The relevant statute provided that the members of a committee to supervise the referendum should be designated by the Diet. The Diet had not done so. Accordingly Yoshida, on the same day as he dissolved, applied to the President of the House of Councillors to convene an Emergency Session of that House. The House of Councillors duly appointed the Committee and dispersed. To British readers such a system would appear susceptible of abuse. For example, a cabinet at loggerheads with the Lower House could, provided it had a majority in the Upper House, dissolve without waiting for Supply, i.e. without settling grievances as required by the Lower House as the <u>quid pro quo</u> for granting Supply (This was the situation in Japan at the 1953 dissolution - see footnote 75 <u>infra</u>).

57. Tomabechi was first elected in 1946. He was Minister of Transport in the Katayama cabinet in 1947. The same year he became Secretary-General of Ashida's Democratic (Minshutoo) Party. In 1948 he was Minister without Portfolio and Cabinet-Secretary in the Ashida cabinet. Later he became Chairman of the Executive (Soomukaichoo) of the party. He was a delegate at the San Francisco Peace Conference in 1951. He did not stand for re-election to the Lower House after the 1952 dissolution but was in 1953 elected to the Upper House. He died on 29 June 1959 (aged 78), before the Supreme Court had decided his suit.

strong body of opinion in the party that the dissolution was convenient, he placed his resignation with them, but it was not accepted.[58]

Counsel representing Tomabechi was YOSHII Akira who, in addition to relying heavily on an interpretation of Constitution a.4 and a.7 propounded by KOJIMA Kazushi (an associate-professor of Tokyo Municipal University)[59] which is similar to, though more sophisticated than, that of Ozaki (v. <u>supra</u> p. 107) and Kades (v. <u>supra</u> p.108) argued as follows:[60]

(i) The Japanese Constitution does not adopt the British type of relationship between cabinet and legislature. By virtue of a.41 ('The Diet shall be the highest organ of state power ...') and a.70 (whereby cabinet must resign after a general election) cabinet is not the equal but the subordinate of the Diet. It follows that it cannot possess the power of dissolution unless specifically conferred by the Constitution (This again is reminiscent of Ozaki). This restriction of the executive's power of dissolution, he argued, accords with modern concepts and practice - e.g. the power of dissolution is rigorously circumscribed in the French Constitution (1946)[61] and in the Constitution of the Federal Republic of Germany.[62]

(ii) The intention of the American authors of the Japanese Constitution was clearly that cabinet's power of dissolution be confined to the circumstances of a.69.

(iii) Admitting for the sake of argument that the Constitution does give the Emperor the power with the advice and approval of cabinet to dissolve in circumstances other than those provided in a.69, in the present case the essential elements of advice were lacking: although the Emperor's act received the (subsequent) approval of cabinet it was done without the (prior) advice of cabinet. Although at the meeting of cabinet on August 22nd there was agreement that a

---

58. <u>Asahi shimbun</u>, 5 August 1952 (evening edition).

59. K. Kojima: 'Tennoo no kennoo ni tsuite', <u>Hooritsu jihoo</u>, no.269, October 1952, pp.78-84; 'Kaisanken rongi nb tsuite', <u>Koohoo kenkyuu</u>, no.7, 1952, pp.83-93.

60. See the summary of the appellant's case which appears following the Supreme Court's decision in <u>Saikoo saibansho minji hanreishuu</u>, vol.14, 1960, no.7, pp.1219-52.

61. Constitution of France (1946) a.51

62. Constitution of the Federal Republic of Germany, a.68.

speedy dissolution was essential, the formal cabinet resolution to dissolve was not made until the cabinet meeting of August 28th, the day after the Cabinet-Secretary had secured the Emperor's signature to the (undated) dissolution proclamation.[63]

Tomabechi went direct to the Supreme Court seeking a declaration that the dissolution was unconstitutional. The Supreme Court, however, in a unanimous decision, dismissed the suit on the ground that it possessed only appellate jurisdiction and then only 'within the limits necessary for judgement in relation to a concrete legal dispute'.[64] Mano J., however, while concurring in the decision on procedural grounds, indicated in a lengthy supplementary opinion his vigorous agreement with Tomabechi on the merits. Though largely a powerful reiteration of Yoshii's (and Ozaki's) arguments, Mano's opinion is worthy of quotation on two points. He noted that a wide power of dissolution is incompatible with equality of electoral opportunity:

> ... elections under democratic government are based on the premise of equality of opportunity: they operate on the principle that all will compete for votes on a footing of equality and on the basis of fair play. Nevertheless, it is clear that surprise dissolution will give the Ministerial party an unfair advantage over the Opposition party. An election carried out under the conditions of such a handicap would be unfair and would make it impossible for the will of the people to be expressed correctly ....

Some British political scientists would consider Mano's anxieties about the unfair advantage of a surprise dissolution somewhat unreal in this day and age. Some would deny that

63. Evidence of YAMADA Meikichi in the Tokyo District Court, 18 February 1953 [reproduced in A. Yoshii, Kaisankenron (privately published, Tokyo, 1953), pp.91-99]. Also the evidence of YAMADA Meikichi in the Tokyo High Court, 17 July 1954 [Kootoo·benron·choosho (typescript, unpublished)]. To a foreigner it is somewhat surprising that a conservative Japanese Government should subject the Emperor, one of Bagehot's 'dignified parts' of the Constitution, to the indignity of having to sign a proclamation with the date left blank for subsequent insertion by the cabinet. The same thing was done by the 1st Ikeda cabinet at the 1960 dissolution - v. infra footnote 91).

64. Saikoo saibansho minji hanreishuu, vol.7, 1963, no.4, pp.305 ff. This decision including the supplementary opinion of Mano J. is translated in full in J. Maki, Court and Constitution in Japan: Selected Supreme Court Decisions 1948-60, Seattle, Washington U.P., pp.366-83.

such an advantage exists. One of my colleagues, for example, remarked that 'where public opinion can be well informed ... I find it difficult to understand "snap" dissolutions being described as "peremptory and punitive" except where the Government can manipulate the electoral system in its own favour or there are "Khaki" circumstances prevailing'.[65] The fact that, in Britain and some other parts of the Commonwealth, Premiers have of recent years made less effort to achieve surprise[66] goes some way towards supporting this view. Furthermore, in cases

---

65. It can, however, be argued that, irrespective of what other means of information are available, Parliament is both the proper and the best medium for informing the public on the issues to be decided at the election. This point was made in connection with the 1923 dissolution in Britain:

> I still believe that it is of importance that when a great issue is to be decided the fullest information should be in the hands of the people before they are called upon to decide. The importance of discussion in this House is that argument can be met by argument face to face. Speeches on the platform are always one-sided affairs. The importance and the value of this House in our constitutional arrangements is that honourable Members on opposite sides have the opportunity of making statements which can be met in argument and any false statements, arguments, or figures can be tested (Parliamentary Debates, Commons, vol.168, col.45, Mr Pringle, 13 November 1923).

This argument has particular force in Japan to-day where the Committee sessions of the Diet are televised.

Some British writers, however, have gone further than my colleague and have attempted to justify entrusting to the Government the advantage of deciding the timing of elections. Take, for example, the following:

> As part of the normal political process, a part of the normal mechanism for ensuring that governments can sometimes implement policies of change which they believe will be more popular in the long term than in the short, it should normally be the right of a Prime Minister to decide when in any five-year period a general election should be held. A Government in office is inevitably more likely to pile up resentments against itself than an Opposition which is basking in a pleasant lack of responsibility; the right to decide the timing of an election is a legitimate right to redress this imbalance, and to give governments the elbow room in which to govern instead of constantly to electioneer ... (Economist, 20 October 1962, pp.211-12.)

66. The following table indicates the tendency in Britain to give longer notice of elections:

Announcement of Dissolution	Dissolution	Interval between Announcement and Dissolution	Election	Interval between Announcement and Election
13/11/23	16/11/23	3 days	6/12/23	23 days
9/10/24	9/10/24	nil	29/10/24	20 days
24/ 4/29	10/ 5/29	16 days	30/ 5/29	36 days
4/10/31	7/10/31	3 days	27/10/31	23 days
23/10/35	25/10/35	2 days	14/11/35	22 days
23/ 5/45	15/ 6/45	23 days	5/ 7/45	43 days
10/ 1/50	3/ 2/50	24 days	23/ 2/50	44 days
19/ 9/51	5/10/51	16 days	25/10/51	36 days
15/ 4/55	6/ 5/55	21 days	25/ 5/55	41 days
8/ 9/59	18/ 8/59	10 days	8/10/59	30 days
15/ 9/64	25/ 9/64	10 days	15/10/64	30 days

In Victoria (Australia) since the amendment of the Constitution Act in 1961 to permit conjoint elections for both Houses to be held on the same date the Lower House dissolution has on each occasion been timed so that its elections will coincide with those of the Upper House which, since the latter House is not ordinarily subject to dissolution, are virtually 'fixed feasts' occurring triennially. This saves the Treasury about £80,000 at each election. In 1964 for example the Government announced on February 29th that the elections would be held on June 27th and in accordance with this the Lower House was duly dissolved on May 11th.

where there has been little warning, this *per se* has not drawn from the Opposition the howls of yesteryear.[67] Some British writers, however, still consider that surprise can be a considerable advantage to the Government. Take for example, the following comment in the *Observer* (20 September 1964) on the British Leader of the Opposition's position before the 1964 dissolution:

> One politician at this time (April) was as certain as could be that the Tories would have to go for June ... He *knew* it would be June. This was Harold Wilson. Labour's powerful publicity was geared to June, as it was to March. Labour could scarcely afford to be wrong again, for funds were strictly limited. But Wilson, rearing to go, had made a crucial error.

Although the event proved that Wilson's error was not 'crucial', this does not necessarily invalidate the argument. Although the Japanese voter is as well informed as the British thanks to the press, the radio (and to-day television) and the distribution of the manifestos of each candidate to every voter by the Electoral Office at public expense,[68] there are reasonable grounds for thinking that the decision when to commit campaign funds is as important to the Japanese Opposition as to the British. This would at first sight appear to be inconsistent with the provision of the Japanese Electoral Law which, under severe penalties, prohibits electioneering before the writs are issued.[69] It is, however, notorious that this provision has been impossible to enforce effectively. Japanese commentators are agreed that campaign funds are very important indeed in Japanese elections.[70]

---

67. When Mr Gladstone dissolved without warning in 1874 his surprise tactics *per se* were bitterly attacked:

> And why had all that indecent speed been resorted to? He believed it had been purposely taken to give a great pull at the borough elections to the Liberal Members. The Minister well knew that the strength of the Liberal Party lay in the borough constituencies. He knew that possession was nine-tenths of the law. He knew that time and organization, as well as cash, were needed to oust the men in possession. It was to prevent that time and organization from being applied that the election was hurried on (*Hansard's Parliamentary Debates*, vol.218, col.1111, Mr P.B. Smollett, 24 April 1874).

Mr Baldwin's dissolution in 1923, however, was criticized more for the fact that he dissolved in order to seek a mandate on an issue which Parliament had not been given the opportunity to discuss (See *Parliamentary Debates*, Commons, vol.168, col.47, Mr Asquith, 13 November 1923).

68. *Kooshokusenkyohoo* (Law 100 of 1950), a.167.

69. *Ibid.*, a.129.

70. It has been calculated that in the mid-1960s most Liberal-Democratic candidates at election time received about ¥2 million (¥1,000=£sgl) from the Party and at least as much from their faction leader. This is in addition to annual grants of half a million yen from the Party and at least ¥1 million from the faction (H. Fukui, *The Japanese Liberal-Democratic Party and Policy-Making*, Canberra, Australian National University, unpublished Ph.D. thesis, 1967, p.178).

Mano also stressed that a fundamental purpose of the Constitution is to exclude dictatorial government; the power of the executive is strong and is in fact largely wielded by the Prime Minister (by virtue of his power of appointment and dismissal of ministers);[71] a wide power of dissolution would make the Prime Minister even stronger:

> It is as obvious as fire that the excessive powers given a single specific personality, namely, a Prime Minister, can easily be concentrated and as a result can lead readily to dictatorial and tyrannical government. It is well to reflect on this - calmly and dispassionately. Do not our people, who were plunged into the depths of destruction and who received a terrible baptism of fire during World War II, fear and detest the revival of dictatorial or tyrannical government more than anything else? I do not hesitate to declare solemnly that any interpretation of the Constitution ... that will permit the easy revival of dictatorial or tyrannical government and is without any firm foundation in positive law .... is the opinion of a near-sighted group that cannot truly comprehend the basic principles of the establishment of a democratic constitution ...

This, as we have seen, is a recurring theme in Japanese writing on the subject and is not surprising in view of Japan's pre-War history.

Defeated in his initial approach to the Supreme Court, Tomabechi then went to the Tokyo District Court suing for the wages due from the date of dissolution until the date on which his four-year term as a Member would otherwise have ended. The Court on 19 October 1953 found in his favour, holding that: (i) Article 7 conferred on cabinet a power of dissolution not confined to a.69, the pre-eminence of the legislature being sufficiently safeguarded by the requirement that the cabinet resign before the ensuing Session. (ii) In the case in question, although the Emperor's act had the (sub-

71. For the argument that the express power to appoint and dismiss ministers, which the Prime Minister did not enjoy under the Meiji Constitution, has made the Prime Minister too strong, see the evidence of T. Yoshimura before the Commission on the Constitution (Kempoo choosakai, Kempoo choosakai dai-43-kai sookai gijiroku, 1960, pp.7-24).

sequent) approval of cabinet, it was not done with the (prior) advice of cabinet - i.e. it failed because the Emperor's act was not preceded by a formal decision of the cabinet as a whole; if the Emperor were permitted to act without advice subject only to *ex post facto* approval this would give him initiative and personal responsibility inconsistent with the fundamentals of the Constitution.

The State's appeal against this decision was sustained by the Tokyo High Court on 22 September 1954. It held that the general conclusion of cabinet at its meeting on August 22nd that a speedy dissolution was essential constituted 'advice'.

Tomabechi then took the case to the Supreme Court in its appellate jurisdiction. In its decision of 8 June 1960 his appeal was dismissed (Tomabechi had already died of cancer on 29 June 1959 at the age of 78).[72] Of the fourteen judges comprising the Court, ten in a joint opinion did not proceed to the merits, arguing that it was 'beyond the power of the courts to examine acts of the State of a highly political character which directly concern the fundamentals of governing the State'. The remaining four judges, in three separate opinions, argued that:

(i) The Court can and should try such a case.
(ii) Article 7 confers on cabinet a power of dissolution not confined to a.69:

> ... Since ... a dissolution of the House of Representatives is an institution whereby the Government appeals to the people and asks their will, there are circumstances other than the passage of a vote of non-confidence in the cabinet or the rejection of a motion of confidence (e.g. the rejection of a vital Government bill or a budget) where it is equally necessary for the Government to seek the confidence of the people. There are also occasions where, by reason of such circumstances as changes in the size of the Parties, doubts have arisen as to whether the House of Representatives well reflects the wishes of the people whose representative it is. Furthermore new, important developments at home or abroad may make it necessary to seek afresh the wishes of the people. These and other circumstances rendering a dissolution nec-

---

72. *Saikoo saibansho minji hanreishuu*, vol.14, 1960, no.7.

essary exist in large numbers beyond those covered by a.69 ... (Kotani and Okuno JJ).

This does not place cabinet above the Diet since cabinet must resign after the ensuing election.
(iii) The lower court was wrong in attempting to distinguish between 'advice' and 'approval' in a.7: in the present case the requirement of 'advice and approval' is satisfied.

This decision was a forgone conclusion, since the Supreme Court of Japn was unlikely in 1960 to reach a decision that would invalidate every official act performed and every statute enacted since 1952. Brig. Gen. Whitney and his subordinates were undoubtedly sincere in their intention that the Supreme Court should be an effective guardian of the Constitution. They should, however, have realised that it could discharge this role in cases of far-reaching consequence only if they established a system of procedure that enabled such cases to be dealt with as soon as they arose. One of the reasons why the High Court of Australia, for example, has been able to take a positive attitude to constitutional adjudication is that its procedure and the remedies available to it enable it to dispose of such matters urgently by injunction or declaratory judgment. Far from guiding the Japanese in such a direction GHQ insisted that the Japanese Prime Minister be given a power of veto over the issue of injunctions in administrative suits.[73]

Despite this legal victory subsequent Governments have, as we shall see, trodden warily in exercising this power.

The 'Bakayaroo' ('Bloody Fool') Dissolution, 14 March 1953

At the general election of 1 October 1952 produced by the dissolution of 28 August 1952, the Yoshida and Hatoyama factions fought nominally as members of the one party. In reality, however, there were two separate campaign headquarters, fighting each other quite as vigorously as they fought the Opposition. Nevertheless, despite this disunity, they secured between them 240 of the 466 seats in the House (cf. 264 at the previous election). Finally on March 14th a number of Hatoyama's followers supported the Opposition's motion of non-confidence (occasioned by Yoshida's unparliamentary language[74])

73. M. Toyomi in I. Ogawa et al. Gyoosei-jiken-soshoo tokureihoo chikujoo kenkyuu, Yuuhikaku, 1957, p.338.

74. The Prime Minister had retorted 'bakayaroo'! to a Right-Socialist Member who was questioning him (Asahi shimbun, 1 March 1953). The nearest English equivalent is possibly 'You bloody fool!

and formally resigned from the Party. As a result the Government was defeated 229-218. Yoshida dissolved forthwith (14 March 1953).[75]

The Opposition naturally went through the act of deploring this 'repeated' dissolution as on a par with those performed by Itoo and Katsura under the Meiji Constitution. They did not, however, labour the point:[76] they were in no position to form a Government, and they stood to gain by an election.

The election was held on 19 April 1953 with the Yatoyama faction operating as a separate party. The Yoshida Liberals failed to obtain a majority but secured 199 seats. The Opposition parties (Kaishintoo 76, Left Socialists 72, Right Socialists 66, Hatoyama Liberals 35) were unable to work together and Yoshida formed a minority Government drawn solely from his own party.

The 'Ten no Koe' ('Vox populi, vox dei') Dissolution, 24 January 1955

By June 1954 the Hatoyama group had begun conversations with the Kaishintoo to unite forces in a new party to overthrow Yoshida. This new party, the Nihon Minshutoo, was duly formed on November 24th, commanding 121 seats in the House. Parallel defections among the Yoshida Liberals reduced the latter's strength to 185. Finally on December 6th the new party and the two Socialist parties joined forces to introduce a joint motion of non-confidence. Yoshida, as in the past, insisted on a dissolution should the motion of non-confidence be carried. The weight of opinion among inflential members of his party was, however, in favour of resignation and he was forced to give way.[77] The cabinet resigned on December 7th before the motion of non-confidence was put to the vote.

On December 9th both Socialist parties voted with the Nihon Minshutoo in electing Hatoyama Prime Minister and permitted him to form a Nihon Minshutoo cabinet on condition that he would promptly dissolve the House when the Diet reassembled after the New Year recess.

75. As Supply and other legislation necessary to tide him over the election had not been passed, Yoshida thereupon convoked an emergency session of the Upper House which in a three days' session granted two months' Supply.

76. Asahi shimbun, 15 March 1953.

77. Ogata, the Deputy Prime Minister, was rumoured to have threatened that if Yoshida insisted on dissolving, he would not sign the necessary cabinet documents. Since unanimity is required for cabinet decisions, Yoshida would in such circumstances have been able to dissolve only after first dismissing Ogata (Asahi shimbun, 8 December 1954).

The Secretary-General of the new Ministerial party (KISHI Nobusuke, a later Prime Minister) announced that, insofar as they had criticised Yoshida for his undemocratic actions, they definitely would not dissolve 'nukiuchi' (peremptorily, without warning). He pointed out, however, that in the existing circumstances a dissolution in accordance with a.69 would be difficult to effect: if the Government introduced a vote of confidence it would require skilful management to ensure that it did not pass; there would be many Ministerialists, moreover, who could not in conscience vote against it. He therefore proposed that the House of Representatives should pass a resolution in favour of dissolution, in accordance with which cabinet would give 'advice' to the Emperor to dissolve[78] (One of the factors disinclining the Ministerialists from a simple a.7 dissolution may have been the high position in their ranks occupied by Tomabechi whose suit was still pending[79]). The Government sought the cooperation of all parties to this end. Yoshida's Liberals, however, though now in Opposition, insisted that dissolution should be carried out under a.7 and that any accompanying resolution of the House would be unconstitutional (a view not shared by the Government's legal advisers).[80] They felt, no doubt, that the new procedure proposed by the Government would attach even greater opprobrium to Yoshida's 1952 dissolution and might limit their freedom next time they formed a government. Similarly in the Socialist parties, although officially they proposed that the advice tendered by cabinet should be pursuant to a resolution of the House, there were men in high places (notably Kawakami, Chairman of the Executive of the Right Socialists, and Wada, Secretary-General of the Left Socialists) who favoured a simple dissolution under a.7 without an accompanying resolution. Nor was there unanimity among the Ministerialists on this matter.[81] The Government, therefore, abandoned the plan (One factor may have been the fact that in the past most proponents of dissolution by resolution had advocated either a unanimous or two-thirds majority decision, requiring the cooperation of the other parties). The Government then took the un-

78. Yomiuri shimbun, 9 January 1955.

79. This is the explanation given by Professor SATOO Isao (Yomiuri shimbun, 8 January 1955).

80. Nihon keizai shimbun, 8 January 1955.

81. Yokiuri shimbun, 6 & 9 January 1955.

precedented step of placing proposals for the time-table for, and manner of, dissolution, before the Secretary-Generals (and later, the chairmen of the Parliamentary Tactics Committees) of the four principal parties (including the Yoshida Liberals in Opposition) and compromising until agreement was reached. A simple dissolution under a.7 was agreed to, the Socialists reserving their position as to constitutionality, and the Government, at the insistence of the Socialists and Yoshida Liberals, agreeing to extend the time devoted to questions to ministers, which was to precede dissolution.[82] The dissolution took place in accordance with this time-table on 24 January 1955. At the ensuing election (27 February 1955) the Ministerialists were returned as the largest party, but with 59 seats short of a majority. In April conversations began between them and the Liberals with a view to a merger. This was achieved in November, the new party (which commanded 298 seats in the House) being called the Liberal Democrats (Jiyuuminshutoo).

The 'Hanashiai' ('Agreement') Dissolution, 25 April 1958

When the Diet was convoked in December 1957 for its 'regular', 150-day, budget session, a dissolution was predicted either towards the end of the session or, at the latest, during a session in the autumn. The reasoning behind this was as follows. As we have already noted, in Japan dissolution except when the Diet is in session is unprecedented. The term of Members of the House of Representatives would expire in February 1959. If the dissolution were left until the regular session beginning December 1958 this would gravely hamper the preparation and deliberation on the 1959 budget. It was amid such speculation that early in the New Year (1958) SUZUKI Mosaburoo, the Leader of the Socialist Party, when returning a courtesy call by the Prime Minister (Kishi), raised a suggestion made by Professor Miyazawa that the timing of the dissolution should be fixed well in advance by arrangement between the party leaders so that there might be avoided the illegal and expensive (but nevertheless widespread) electioneering which rumours of dissolution always provoked. Kishi after discussing this with the Secretary-General of his party (Kawashima) inclined favourably to some such arrange-

82. Ibid., 18 January 1955, 19 January 1955 (evening edition).

ment provided that there was a parallel agreement between the parties on the passage of government legislation.[83] Similar overtures by Socialists in March were, however, rebuffed by the Prime Minister.

The passage of the Budget on March 31st led to widespread predictions that the dissolution would take place about the middle of April. These were strengthened by the Prime Minister's admission at a press conference on April 2nd that a dissolution within the month was a possibility.

On April 18th the Prime Minister, with the consent of cabinet and the principal officials of his party, approached the Leader of the Socialist Party (Suzuki) and said that now that Japan had a two-party system (established in 1955) he wished to establish a new precedent whereby the timing of an end-of-term dissolution would be decided in consultation with the Opposition party (He distinguished between end-of-term dissolutions such as the present and dissolutions to break a deadlock and go to the country on a particular issue). He proposed April 26th as the date for dissolution and sought Suzuki's cooperation in passing pending legislation with this in view.[84]

Factors disposing the Ministerialists towards 'dissolution by agreement' on this occasion may have included the following: (i) With the 'odour of dissolution' already in the air, Ministerialist Members were neglecting the Diet for their constituencies. It was therefore proving very difficult for the Government to manage the passage of pending legislation. The prevailing mood made a dissolution in the very near future inevitable: only with Socialist cooperation could important legislation be passed before the dissolution. (ii) The Government's 'magnanimity' in abandoning its 'traditional weapon' of unilateral dissolution might be favourably received by the electorate. (iii) Although a dissolution was desirable there was no 'issue' to use as the occasion. (iv) If the session were prolonged the Opposition might embarrass the Government in the face of the electors by raising more scandals like the recent Chiba Bank scandal. (v) If the Socialists withheld

83. Kawashima as quoted in Mainichi shimbun, 18 April 1958. One could argue that a prior announcement of dissolution might increase rather than restrict electioneering. Suzuki, Kishi and Kawashima, however, can be presumed to know what they are talking about when discussing matters of this nature. Possibly since funds are limited and since a prior announcement of the date of dissolution would remove the temptation to gamble on one's prediction and try and steal a march on the others, candidates would concentrate their resources on the final stages of the campaign.

84. Asahi shimbun, 18 April 1958, 19 April 1958 (evening edition), 24 April 1958.

their cooperation in passing legislation and moved a vote of non-confidence, there was not much the Government could do but dissolve. In such circumstances the electorate might be given the unfortunate impression that the Opposition had the initiative.

The Socialists were in a tricky position. They wished to take advantage of precise foreknowledge of the date of dissolution and to wrest what concessions they could in return for providing the cooperation in passing pending legislation which would make an agreed date of dissolution possible. At the same time, by agreeing to the date proposed by the Government, there would not be that degree of confrontation between the parties which an Opposition requires, and they would not be able to claim before the electorate that the dissolution was the outcome of their initiative. Accordingly a very Japanese compromise was reached. The Socialists refused to be associated with fixing the actual date, on the pretext that: 'The Government has the right of dissolution: the date should be determined by the Government'. But provided that some modifications were made to the Government's bill to amend the Criminal Code and Criminal Procedure Code,[85] the Socialists would cooperate in passing the pending Government legislation. They would then, on April 24th, move a motion of non-confidence whereupon the Government would, after making only one speech[86] in reply to the motion, dissolve without putting the motion of non-confidence to the vote (Such a vote would, of course, have been defeated and this would have been unfavourable to the Socialists' image.)

The dissolution duly took place according to this timetable on April 25th, on the advice of cabinet, under Constitution a.7.

The 'Yoyaku' ('Promised') Dissolution, 24 October 1960

The House elected on 22 May 1958 was dissolved on 24 October 1960.

From the beginning of 1960 it became apparent that a strong combination was forming within the Ministerial (Liberal-Democratic) Party to oust Kishi from the leadership. The dis-

85. Asahi shimbun, 19 April 1958.

86. The Socialists rejected a proposal by the Ministerialists that as a quid pro quo for the motion of non-confidence the Prime Minister should be allowed to make a policy statement.

sident factions capitalised on his discomfiture over the Revised Security Treaty issue.

When on 20 May 1960 Kishi used his majority to overcome the obstruction of the Opposition and secure the Lower House's approval of the Treaty, the press and elements among the Ministerialists lent their support to the Opposition's demand that cabinet resign and dissolve the House before completing ratification of the Treaty. Kishi, however, was resolved to see the Treaty through: it was only on June 23rd, the day ratifications were exchanged, that he announced his intention to resign.[87]

Kishi was succeeded by IKEDA Hayato as president of the party on July 14th, and as Prime Minister on July 18th. This 1st Ikeda Cabinet, however, was not a caretaker Government: the new Prime Minister, while admitting that a dissolution within the year was not unlikely, refused to commit himself.[88] Obviously it was in the interest of Ikeda and his party to postpone the dissolution for as long as possible until the Treaty issue was a thing of the past and until an attractive catalogue of electoral promises could be prepared.

On September 2nd, the Cabinet Secretary (a minister) announced that a short Session ending in a dissolution was likely to be convoked as soon as possible after the conclusion of the Inter-parliamentary Union Conference (late September). He added that since it was well known that a dissolution was to take place, it was not proposed to discuss it with the Opposition.[89] On October 8th cabinet determined to convoke the Session on October 17th to last a maximum of five days. The Socialists in reply demanded a longer session so that Ikeda's policies could be more adequately debated. As a compromise, a programme was agreed to in which proceedings would end on October 24th.[90] Both parties adhered to this time-table and the dissolution duly took place on that date.[91]

---

87. Asahi nenkan 1961, p.187.

88. Asahi shimbun, 20 July 1960.

89. Asahi shimbun, 3 September 1960.

90. Asahi shimbun, 14 & 15 October 1960 (evening edition).

91. The manner in which the formalities preceeding this dissolution were conducted resembles in some degree that of the famous Yoshida dissolution of 1952 (v. supra p.119): (i) Cabinet's ultimate decision to dissolve was not taken at a cabinet meeting - the draft resolution was circulated to ministers individually for their signature on the morning of October 23rd; (ii) The Emperor being absent from Tokyo, an official was then despatched to him with the dissolution proclamation which the Emperor signed leaving the date blank so that the Prime Minister, in the words of the Asahi newspaper, could determine the time of the dissolution 'after evaluating the Opposition's demeanour'. Too much, however, should not be made out of the procedural resemblances to the 1952 dissolution. Circulation of papers for signature by ministers is not an uncommon method in Japan for avoiding a special meeting of cabinet on a non-controversial issue. Similarly, with the Emperor several hours distant from Tokyo, it would have been difficult to get his signature expeditiously on the termination of business. In Japan, as we have noticed, the custom is for dissolution to occur during a plenary session of the House: a day's delay to await signature, when Members are so keen to get to their electorates, might be unpopular.

At the ensuing election (20 November 1960) Ikeda's Liberal-Democrats increased their majority, securing 296 of the 467 seats in the House.

The 'Muudo' ('Mood') Dissolution, 23 October 1963

This took place on 23 October 1963 (thirteen months before Members' terms of office would expire). In explaining the date Japanese journalists have given weight to the following factors: (i) If the regular session (commencing in December) were held in an atmosphere of impending dissolution, Members might desert the Diet for their constituencies, and the Government's legislative programme might suffer accordingly. Moreover with electoral promises being bandied about, it would be hard for the Government to keep the size of the budget under control.[92] (ii) With the economic situation deteriorating,[93] it could be argued that, the sooner the election, the better for the Ministerialists. (iii) The Prime Minister's chances of re-election as Party president at the July 1964 Convention would be influenced by his success or otherwise in controlling the House and carrying through his legislative programme in the regular session of the Diet. In the previous year's regular session the Opposition parties had been remarkably successful in using obstructive tactics to prevent the passage of such legislation as they disliked. They could be expected to repeat this performance. Hence the Prime Minister may have felt that it was desirable to face the next regular session with a new House.[94]

On the basis of this reasoning it was frequently argued by the press that the Prime Minister would dissolve before the end of 1963, provided that he could do so without alienating support in the Party and the financial world, and provided that he could devise a suitable occasion for so doing.[95]

92. Nihon keizai shimbun, 4 September 1963.

93. The consumer price spiral was causing increasing discontent among the electorate and the United States Interest Equalisation Tax could be expected to exert a harmful effect on the Japanese economy in theNew Year (Asahi shimbun, 24 August 1963; Nihon keizai shimbun, 4 September 1963, evening edition).

94. Asahi shimbun, 15 September 1963.

95. For my explanation of this dissolution I am endebted to an excellent series of articles 'Kaisan wo yobu mono' appearing in Asahi shimbun, 1-5 October 1965.

The Prime Minister's confidence in his ability to carry the Party with him was no doubt strengthened in mid-July (1963) when, at the periodic reshuffle of cabinet and the principal Party posts, the leaders of the main factions agreed to serve under him. Thus encouraged, on August 8th he deliberately injected into the body politic the virus of election fever: he announced that there was likely to be a dissolution within a year. This, together with activity in the constituencies by the Opposition, caused Ministerialist Members to step up their electoral activities and commit their campaign funds. From then onwards, the sooner the dissolution the better for the sitting back-bencher Member.[96] Though initially reluctant, the principal faction leaders (with the notable exception of Satoo) had come on side by mid-September.[97]

Initially there was considerable opposition to an early dissolution in the business world which as recently as April had been required to pour out considerable funds in support of Ministerialist candidates in the nation-wide municipal elections.[98] As time went on, however, business leaders appeared increasingly to take the view that a speedy dissolution was preferable to the uncertainty engendered by predictions of dissolution.[99]

As we have observed above, the second prerequisite for an early dissolution was that a suitable occasion should present itself. Such Ministerialists, business leaders and newspapers as argued that dissolution should not take place before 1964, or urged the Prime Minister to delay dissolution until the Opposition could be inveigled into providing them with an occasion for dissolution, continually stressed the importance of being able to show the country that they had a

---

96. Tokyo shimbun, 6 September 1963, 2 October 1963.

97. This was interpreted partly as bowing to the inevitable, partly as an indication that they would support Ikeda's candidacy for re-election as president, and partly as an attempt to isolate Satoo who was likely to be the rival candidate.

98. Mainichi shimbun, 29 June 1963.

99. Nihon keizai shimbun, 4 October 1963. The Asahi, in tracing the genesis of the dissolution, lays stress on the strong earnests of its favour expressed by the business community to Ikeda on his departure for his Asian tour at the end of September; the knowledge that the business world was firmly behind him, the Asahi argued, made him confident that he could face an election at any time (Asahi shimbun, 1 October 1963).

'just cause' for dissolution.[100] (This sounds a little quaint to someone used to British politics where nowadays there is no need for a Government to go to much trouble to justify a dissolution to the electorate, provided it does not follow too closely upon the preceding dissolution. As we have already noted, the advantage which the Government has in being able to decide the time hardly worries British theorists, or, indeed, British Oppositions).[101]

In the present case, circumstances which the Ministerialists seem to have felt would be considered a just cause were: (i) the proposal of a motion of non-confidence or a motion for dissolution by the Opposition,[102] (ii) too vigorous an attack on the Government in Opposition questions in reply to Ministers' speeches,[103] (iii) obstructive tactics towards Government legislation.[104]

This anxiety on the part of Ministerialist leaders that there should appear to be a 'just cause' for dissolution may well have stemmed from their feeling that Japanese public opinion regards dissolution as inherently aggressive (and therefore improper) unless in answer to provocation (in which case they feel that it is natural and hence permissible).

In the present case the Opposition seems to have been in two minds as to whether to provide the necessary provocation. As in previous 'end-of-term' dissolutions they appear to have regarded it as desirable to be able to claim that it was they,

---

100. E.g. *Asahi shimbun*, 8 September 1963 (statement by Satoo); *Asahi shimbun*, 14 September 1963 (comment); *Mainichi shimbun*, 16 September 1963 (comment); *Asahi shimbun*, 21 September 1963 (statement by Miki); *Asahi shimbun*, 12 October 1963 (views attributed to Oono, Koono, Fujiyama, Miki and Kawashima). The results of a public opinion poll conducted in Tokyo by the *Tokyo shimbun* from 4-7 October 1963 suggest that at least as regards Tokyo citizens these people were right. Among the people polled, those who claimed to have heard that a dissolution would take place within the year were asked 'In case of dissolution, do you think that it should be brought about by raising a "just cause" - making an important political question the reason?' The answers were as follows: 'A "just cause" is essential', 36.7%; 'The decision should be taken in the light of Diet proceedings and the demeanour of the Opposition', 9.7%' 'A "just cause" is not necessary', 9.3%; 'Dissolution may be carried out at the convenience of the Government and Ministerialist party', 3.8%; 'Dissolution may be carried out by negotiation between the Ministerialist and Opposition parties without a "just cause"', 6.2%; Other answers, 0.8%; 'Don't know' 33.5% (*Tokyo shimbun*, 18 October 1963).

101. V. *supra*, p.119.

102. *Asahi shimbun*, 14 September 1963 (this is the view attributed to Maeo).

103. *Asahi shimbun*, 19 October 1963, 21 October 1963.

104. *Asahi shimbun*, 15 September 1963, 11 October 1963.

not the Government, who had caused the dissolution; that the Government was smarting under their blows to such an extent that the only way in which it could protect itself was to dissolve.[105] Hence even before the adjournment of the 1962-3 regular session in July 1963, we have numerous statements from the Socialists that they would hound the Government into dissolution.[106] When, however, the Government announced in its programme for the 'dissolution' Session the passage of a supplementary budget, the Socialists changed their tune:[107] they were not prepared to run the risk of alienating the electorate by delaying the implemtation of wage rises and disaster relief.[108]

The Government had the initiative: it could introduce the supplementary budget or abandon it as it thought fit. In order that the Government should not have the excuse of provocation to dissolve before entering into budget proceedings, the Leader of the Socialist Party (Kawakami) in his questions in reply to ministers' statements on October 21st, adopted a mild tone.[109] The Ministerialists, however, apparently decided that it would be more to their disadvantage to enter budget proceedings than to dissolve without a 'just cause'. On October 23rd the chairman of the Ministerialist Parliamentary Tactics (kokkai taisaku) Committee rejected a request by the Opposition to commence budget proceedings. He gave as his reason, that the Government was unable to accept the Opposition's assurances of smooth cooperation in such deliberations.[110] The same day, at the end of the agreed period of questions in reply to ministers' statements, the Prime Minister dissolved under a.7 (On October 18th, at the close of Ministers' statements in the Diet, a cabinet meeting had been held at which all the procedures necessary for dissolution were completed).[111]

---

105. The Opposition appears to have been fairly successful in creating this impression. In the Tokyo shimbun public opinion poll referred to in footnote 100 supra those who claimed to have heard that a dissolution would take place within the year were asked 'Why are things moving towards a dissolution within the year?'. The answers were as follows: 'It is convenient for the Prime Minister', 22.7%. 'The Opposition are trying to force a dissolution', 14.2%. 'Because electioneering has already become intense', 7.0%. 'Because it is desirable, by an early dissolution, to bring freshness into the Diet', 25.6%. Other answers, 2.3%. Don't know, 28.2%. Tokyo shimbun, 18 October 1963.

106. Asahi shimbun, 4 October 1963 ('Kaisan wo yobu mono'); Sankei shimbun, 7 July 1963; Tokyo shimbun, 18 July 1963; Mainichi shimbun, 16 September 1963.

107. Asahi shimbun, 28 September 1963, 7, 10 & 19 October 1963.

108. Asahi shimbun, 4 October 1963 ('Kaisan wo yobu mono').

109. Asahi shimbun, 20 October 1963; 21 October 1963 (evening edition).

110. Asahi shimbun, 23 October 1963.

111. Asahi shimbun, 19 October 1963.

The reason why the Ministerialists dissolved before proceeding with the supplementary budget is probably because in committee proceedings attending the passage of financial legislation. the Government is inevitably under Opposition attack - it is subject to more sustained criticism over a wider field and for a longer period than in the Opposition replies to ministers' speeches with which each Session commences.[112] (To dissolve before Opposition replies to ministers' speeches would allienate public opinion as giving the Government the unfair advantage of going to the country having stated its own case and denied speech to the Opposition - the typical pre-War punitive dissolution.)

On this occasion only Nishio, the leader of the breakaway Democratic Socialist Party, challenged the legality of an a.7 dissolution. It is therefore probably safe to regard this once so vigorously debated question as now closed.[113]

That the Prime Minister had misgivings about dissolving without a 'just cause' is apparent from the defensiveness of his remarks on the subject. Take, for example, his remarks at a press conference on the second day of the Session (16 October 1963):

> Q I imagine that the Prime Minister is considering the exercise of the power of dissolution?
>
> A Has not dissolution become implicit in the trend of public opinion and the condition of the Diet? I have under constant consideration whether to exercise the Prime Minister's power of dissolution.
>
> Q Do you think that there is a 'just cause' for dissolution this year?
>
> A Has there ever been in Japan a case where Members have served their full four years? About two years is the average. Three years have already passed. Next year there are the Olympic Games and the IMF General Meeting. Hence there has developed a mood of 'dissolution this year'. Since three years have passed, my feeling is that 'dissolution this year' is the popular will. At this stage I am thinking about after-care for the income-

112. Asahi shimbun, 12 October 1963.

113. Asahi shimbun, 19 October 1963 (evening edition).

doubling plan and wish to consult public opinion. In this connection I do not think that historians at a later date will say that I did not act 'fairly and above board'. After three years have passed, to venture forth and seek the popular will is a possible course.[114]

We have already noted how of recent years Japanese Prime Ministers appear to feel it necessary to say that it is public opinion, not themselves, that is bringing about a dissolution.[115]

It will be observed that the precedent which Mr Kishi sought to establish in 1958 for fixing the date of end-of-term dissolutions by agreement between the leaders of the two parties was not followed. The Deputy Secretary-General of the Ministerialist party stated on September 4th that if there was a dissolution within the year it must be by confrontation between the parties in the Diet and not by agreement.[116] Initially the Socialists proposed what would amount to essentially the same system of consultation and agreement as the 1958 'dissolution by agreement', while denying that this would amount to 'dissolution by agreement'. For example, their Secretary-General (Narita) on October 12th, while emphasizing that they would not agree to discussions between the leaders of the parties on dissolution, continued that there would of course be discussions on the programme of Diet proceedings and that these discussions would probably touch on the time of the dissolution.[117] The following day, however, his Leader (Kawakami) stated less equivocally that, if asked to participate in discussions with the Ministerialists on the timing of the dissolution, he would refuse.[118]

Finally, the Prime Minister on October 16th stated that discussions between the Secretary-Generals on the programme of the Session would be acceptable but that he would not hold discussions on the subject of dissolution, because such would be a bad precedent.[119]

---

114. Asahi shimbun, 16 October 1963 (evening edition).

115. Mr Satoo in 1966 (v. supra pp.96, 97 & 99).

116. Asahi shimbun, 4 September 1963 (evening edition). See also the statement of the Secretary-General (Maeo) the following day, Asahi shimbun, 5 September 1963 (evening edition).

117. Asahi shimbun, 13 October 1963. See also similar remarks by Narita in Asahi shimbun, 7 October 1963 (evening edition).

118. Asahi shimbun, 14 October 1963.

119. Asahi shimbun, 16 October 1963 (evening edition).

Conclusions

The once influential contention that the Constitution permitted dissolution only as an answer to a resolution of non-confidence is now almost dead: cabinet's constitutional right to dissolve under a.7 is generally accepted.

Nevertheless Prime Ministers when dissolving seem to feel constrained to put on record statements in which it is implicit that 'snap dissolutions' would be improper. Moreover, on such occasions, they find it necessary to state that they are not acting arbitrarily, but in accordance with the dictates of public opinion. This seems to have become part of the folklore attending dissolution. Against this background it might now be difficult for Prime Ministers to dissolve 'out of the blue'. They are evidently convinced that influential opinion is hostile to snap dissolutions. This hostility may be explained partly in terms of the following. There is the strong recollection of pre-War examples (which are universally condemned along with pre-War cabinets as totalitarian) and the 1952 dissolution by Yoshida. The new Constitution is regarded as sweeping away arbitrary government and archaic survivals. Moreover, experiments in the working of the new Constitution in its early years led to wide and detailed discussion and analysis of all political institutions and forms (including dissolution), in which these had to be justified against, not tradition, but new, democratic principles including the principle that 'the Diet shall be the highest organ of state power' (a.41) - a principle which even to-day few ministers are prepared overtly to assail. Against this background the consensus emerged that, although without a wide power of dissolution 'responsible government' might not be able to operate smoothly, nevertheless 'we must ... ensure that dissolution is not performed as a result of the arbitrary decision of cabinet' (Report of the Joint Legislative Research Committee v. <u>supra</u> p.112).

The pious hope of the Joint Committee, that Japan might succeed where others had failed and discover a mechanism which gave a wide enough power of dissolution and at the same time an effective safeguard against abuse, was not fulfilled.

In the light of the 1966 dissolution Kishi's attempt to make a precedent out of the 1955 and 1958 dissolutions in which the date was fixed in consultation with the Opposition parties cannot be said to have been entirely unsuccessful. In 1966 in spite of Satoo's refusal to countenance 'dissolution by agreement' his meeting with the Opposition leaders on December 24th seems to have succeeded in achieving this object.

Lastly, once Ministerialist back-benchers 'beat the gun' and begin to spend their limited electioneering funds in earnest, the leaders must bow to this and dissolve before these funds have vanished.

7

LEGACY OF DAVID SISSONS

Keiko Tamura

Ryōtarō Shiba, a bestselling contemporary Japanese author, starts his 1976 short story 'Mokuyōtō no yakai' ('Dinner parties on Thursday Island') with the sentence:[1] 'Thursday Island is far away'.

The story recounts Shiba's visit to Thursday Island to explore the historical presence of Japanese migrant workers on the island before the Pacific War and to meet remaining Japanese residents. He travelled to Thursday Island via Sydney after a close friend in Wakayama introduced him to ex–pearl shell divers and the encounter inspired him to learn about historical migration from Wakayama to the island. Early in the story, Shiba refers to a paper by David Sissons that was published in a Japanese academic journal in 1974.[2] After initially citing his correct full name, Shiba refers to Sissons as 'Professor David', probably assuming that David was his family name. Shiba writes about the personal experiences of those who travelled to Australia to work in the pearl shell industry, but he relies on Sissons' paper to provide the historical background to the migration and analysis of the workers' motives.

Shiba quotes from Sissons' paper and appreciates his insights into the skill of Japanese divers, who were regarded as the best in the pearl shell industry. Sissons argues that they were motivated to excel in the industry by their desire to earn money to send home, rather than the widely accepted theories of racial adaptability and

1 Ryōtarō Shiba (1923–1996) was a Japanese writer of fiction and non-fiction. A number of his historical novels are bestsellers and have been dramatised as films and television programs and have influenced the Japanese public's interpretation of historical incidents. 'Mokuyōtō no yakai' was first published in the journal *Bessatsu Bungei Shunjū* in September 1976 and published as a book with other stories in 1977.

2 David Sissons, '1871–1946 nen no Ōsutoraria no Nihonjin' ['The Japanese in Australia, 1871–1946'], *Ijū Kenkyū*, no. 10, 1974.

ethnic characteristics. Shiba sought an ex-diver's opinion on Sissons' argument and received partial confirmation, including that it was exciting and fun to work under the sea. Shiba praised Sissons' article for its integration of personal stories and success in addressing the essential facts behind the migration to Thursday Island. It is high praise from the famous author.

Shiba's assessment of Sissons' work confirms the rigour of his research and writing. In order to narrate and draw conclusions from historical incidents, Sissons collected individual stories through meticulous research in archives in Japan and Australia. Arthur Stockwin, Sissons' first PhD student, points out that the lengthy closure of the National Diet Library, Tokyo, for rebuilding in the late 1960s led to a fundamental shift in Sissons' research direction.[3] From then on, he carried out extensive research on the history of Australia–Japan relations utilising particularly the Department of Foreign Affair's archive's migration records. I have wondered what, if he had continued his research in diplomatic relations or Japanese politics, he would have done in his academic career. What we know is that researching the stories of ordinary individuals is often more painstakingly difficult than studying archival records of diplomatic relations. While diplomats and politicians are public figures and governments generate official records, pearl divers who migrated from Wakayama to Thursday Island did not generate personal files. Instead, their movements must be traced by checking numerous records in different archives. Sissons started to carry out his groundbreaking work in the 1960s and continued throughout his academic career. That was the time when there were no internet or digital cameras. Databases and catalogues were not available on the web. There were probably no photocopying facilities. He visited each archive and made handwritten notes. He did exactly the same type of work on other areas of research, including Australian war crimes trials, examples of which are published in this volume. With his comprehensive understanding and knowledge of archival classification systems, he had a good idea of where to go and which files to examine, but, nonetheless, collecting information on individual cases required patient and meticulous study.

This was the hallmark of Sissons' research. His work on Australian war crime trials began before the Australian Government released trials records. In this case, as he stated in his 1978 Duntroon lecture reproduced in this volume, he worked with the available Japanese records. An article by Desmond Ball referring to the diplomatic code breaking agency that worked against Japanese diplomatic communication[4] prompted Sissons to begin research on that organisation, for which he had worked as a young translator. He was uncertain if any official documentation of its activities

3 Arthur Stockwin, 'David Sissons, my doctoral supervisor and mentor', in Arthur Stockwin & Keiko Tamura eds, *Bridging Australia and Japan: The writings of David Sissons, historian and political scientist, Volume 1*, Canberra: ANU Press, 2016, p. 20.

4 Desmond J Ball, 'Allied intelligence cooperation involving Australia during World War II', *Australian Outlook*, vol. 31, no. 3, pp. 299–309.

could be obtained; however, following tireless negotiations with the National Archives of Australia (NAA), he managed to access a summary report that was compiled before its closure.[5]

Despite his shyness, Sissons demonstrated a dogged conviction to collect necessary information. This also required commitment and persistence in a research milieu that encouraged devotion to a particular task — a luxury that is not often afforded to researchers today who must identify a certain set of information and data needs even before proposing a research project. Furthermore, today, the period in which research results must be produced is much shorter and tangible outcomes are necessary in order to secure further funding. Sissons was lucky to have a secure, tenured research position at a premier national university during his career.

When existing records did not provide sufficient information, he did not hesitate to get in touch with the informants directly by writing to them. There was no shyness there at all. He wrote extremely polite introductory letters filled with rich background information when approaching an informant for further information. The person who received such a letter would be intrigued enough to respond. Ball, as an editor, insisted on including Sissons' correspondence in *Breaking Japanese Diplomatic Codes* because the letters showed Sissons' methodical approach to collecting information and are an example to all scholars of impeccable academic manners. Sissons was careful to demonstrate his substantial prior research before asking further questions.

However, Sissons' research interests did not fit comfortably in the international relations community in which academic debates and discussions were dominated by a preoccupation with power in politics and diplomacy. His main focus was on Australia–Japan relations illustrated through experiences of ordinary people, who were far away from political power or notable social standing. It must have been rather uncomfortable to announce to his colleagues in the international relations academic community that his research topics were Japanese pearl divers or prostitutes. Throughout the 1970s to 1980s, annual reports of the Research School of Pacific Studies of The Australian National University, with which he was affiliated, recorded his research in a short sentence: 'Mr D. Sissons continued his research on the history of Australian–Japanese relations.' It was probable that some staff members and students did not hold such topics in high regard and expressed some discreet disdain. Sissons was well aware of these views. Yet Ball, who worked in the same department, respected him and his work. Sissons and Ball were a study in contrasts in physique and personality but felt some camaraderie, as is revealed in their correspondence regarding diplomatic code-breaking in Australia.[6]

5 Desmond J Ball & Keiko Tamura (eds), *Breaking Japanese Diplomatic Codes: David Sissons and D Special Section during the Second World War*, Canberra: ANU E Press, 2013, p. 6.

6 Ball & Tamura 2013, annexes 7, 11, 12, 13 and 14.

Sissons' academic research and study was firmly based on individual experiences that examined archival sources. He was also keen to examine how the system functioned. Thus, immigration policy in the case of Japanese migrant workers, or the legal system in the case of war crimes trials, became important aspects of his research. Furthermore, he studied both Australian and Japanese sources.

His pursuit of information was relentless and he did not give up until all the pieces of his particular historical puzzle were assembled.

Sissons' reputation for perfectionism, and his shyness, are regarded as the main deterrents in his limited public speaking activities and published works. And my experience confirms that he was a shy but essentially warm person. His work reveals that he cared about and was interested in the people that he wrote about. He made no moral judgement of the Karayuki-san, Japanese prostitutes who were sent overseas, for example. His interest in lived experience was backed by his commitment to fairness. This was most strongly revealed in his research and writing on war crime investigations and trials. He thoroughly studied each case, regardless of whether the individual was a Japanese war crime suspect or Australian military personnel, and he assessed them within the social and legal framework in which their experience occurred. He sought to grasp all the information in order to arrive at a conclusion.

Bronwen Sissons remembered with affection that her husband found it very difficult to write conclusions. She was usually asked to read his drafts and make comments after which she would compliment him on his writing and content and ask what his conclusion was to be. He often did not manage to give her an answer. I have wondered why he found it so difficult to write conclusions. Over this project's 10 years' duration, I have read and examined his work and come to see that he always remained an objective observer and rarely expressed his own views. With this in mind, I propose an alternative to perfectionism and shyness as the explanation for his limited number of publications. For Sissons, the activity of research and writing was more like weaving original pieces of fabric in which each thread was an individual's story interwoven with historical records. The weaving continued as relevant threads became available and, sometimes, the work was suspended as he went in search of a particular type of thread. Sissons wove his threads thoroughly and meticulously, without a fixed idea of what kind of pattern his cloth would ultimately reveal to his readers.

While compiling a selected bibliography of Sissons' published work for this volume, I realised something of which I was not aware previously. While Sissons did not publish a monograph in his long academic career, his final tally of publications is not small. The archive of his writing is distinctive for the fact that he started to publish early in his career, even before completing his master's thesis. Second, he published regularly in the disciplines of history and political science throughout the 1950s to 1970s, and many of those papers are included in the three posthumous volumes of which this is the final one. Third, from the early 1980s, he was commissioned to write entries on the Japanese in Australia and Australian war crime trials for various encyclopedias and dictionaries. Producing entries for reference works requires intensive research and the writing needs to be concise and the information must be accurate and relevant. Towards the end of his academic career, Sissons produced many such entries while he continued with his research into Australian war crimes trials. His contributions to reference works continue to be cited and are used by many academics as the starting point for extended research projects, despite the decades that have passed since they were first published.

Sissons' woven cloths are assembled here and in the two other posthumous volumes published in 2013 and 2016. Each makes a significant contribution to its relevant field of research, and provides some indication of fruitful opportunities for further investigation.

Personal reflections on David and the project history

In conclusion, I take the opportunity to record my reflections on David Sissons and the history of this project.

I met David in 1997, soon after I started to work for the Australia–Japan Research Project at the Australian War Memorial. This Japanese Government project was part of the Murayama Initiative to commemorate the 50th anniversary of the end of the Pacific War. An international symposium was organised in the early stages of the project to explore the research directions. As one of the guest speakers, David presented his paper on Japanese wartime records, for which he had prepared several handouts.[7] He objected to our proposal to distribute them before he spoke and requested that they instead be distributed during his talk and on his cue. My first impression of him was as controlling and thorough.

It was not until I received a Harold White Fellowship in 2002 to carry out research at the National Library of Australia (NLA) on an expatriate community in Kobe, Japan, that I had the opportunity to get to know David better. My main archival source was the Library's Harold S Williams Collection. Williams (1898–1987) was born in Melbourne, moved to Kobe in his youth and lived there for most of his life as a successful businessman and historian of the Western community in Japan. Williams and David corresponded, and some of their letters were deposited in the collection. I contacted David to find out more about Williams and we met at the NAA for tea.

7 'Sources on Australian investigations into Japanese war crimes in the Pacific', *Journal of the Australian War Memorial*, Issue 30, 1997, www.awm.gov.au/articles/journal/j30/sissons (accessed 12 December 2018).

On that occasion, David confirmed the frugality so well remembered by his students by producing tea bags and biscuits for us to share.[8] He expressed keen interest in my research and provided valuable assistance to my study.

After this encounter, David became more relaxed with me and our friendship started to develop. He occasionally rang me up to ask some questions on computing, a subject on which I was certainly not an expert, but he was always very appreciative of my hesitant advice. We met for coffee a few times and, on one occasion, he even told me some jokes! The last time I saw him was at the NLA after his diagnosis with terminal cancer. He told me of his illness with an exhausted and desperate look. As his health declined, he had come to realise that he did not have enough time to complete his work.

At his funeral in St John's Church, Canberra, in November 2006, one of those gathered remarked on his unpublished manuscripts. Although I was not directly involved in David's research, I thought it was important to make his works available to a wider readership. David's family, particularly his wife, Bronwen, was supportive of the idea. After some false starts, Arthur Stockwin joined the project in 2010. Other professional commitments meant that our progress was slow. In June and November 2011, Arthur travelled twice to Canberra from Oxford to examine and assess suitable manuscripts for publication among the 60 boxes of the Papers of DCS Sissons (MS 3092) at the NLA. During Arthur's second visit, a meeting was arranged with the late Desmond Ball, Professor in the Strategic and Defence Studies Centre at The Australian National University. Arthur taught Des in an undergraduate course at the ANU before he moved to Oxford, and Des and David worked in the same department and respected each other's research. David and Des shared a keen interest in examining Second World War code-breaking organisations. When Des became aware that David had left an unpublished manuscript on D Special Section, the Australian diplomatic code-breaking organisation of that period, he proposed to publish it with an introduction. With the support of Craig Reynolds, chair of the Asian Studies editorial board of ANU Press, Des and I worked together to publish the paper before Des' health deteriorated. The book, *Breaking Japanese Diplomatic Codes: David Sissons and D Special Section during the Second World War*, was published in 2013.

After the first book came out, Arthur and I started to work on the next volume, which covered David's research on Australia–Japan relations. David published little in this field, but each example is stamped with the hallmark of his craftsmanship backed by thorough research. These publications are regarded as essential reading, but over the years since their initial publication, some have become difficult to

8 See Arthur Stockwin & Keiko Tamura eds, *Bridging Australia and Japan, Volume 1*, Canberra: ANU Press, 2016, Chapter 1.

access. We selected several key published and unpublished works with the aim of making them available for readers and researchers with an interest in the relationship between Australia and Japan.

The current volume, *Bridging Australia and Japan: The writings of David Sissons, historian and political scientist, Volume 2*, is the third and last of the project and includes David's writings on the Pacific War, the Australian war crimes trials as well as his early political science writings. We believe Sissons' writings are relevant to contemporary researchers, as proved by Georgina Fitzpatrick's use of Sissons' manuscript in her study on Australian war crimes trials. Just as Georgina managed to discuss the war crimes material with David, I have carried out my own lengthy conversation with David over the years of this project. I am in awe of the vast fields of study that David canvassed throughout his academic career. I am also grateful to have met many unforgettable people as I have worked on David's papers. Most of all are my co-editors, Desmond Ball and Arthur Stockwin, two brilliant academics and good men whom I respect deeply. Over the years and through numerous conversations, Bronwen Sissons told me many stories of David with deep affection. I feel I understand David much more now. I feel David somehow introduced me to them after his death.

DCS SISSONS SELECT BIBLIOGRAPHY[1]

* Reprinted or published in the current volume.

** Reprinted or published in Arthur Stockwin & Keiko Tamura (eds), *Bridging Australia and Japan: The writings of David Sissons, historian and political scientist, Volume 1*, Canberra: ANU Press, 2016.

*** Reprinted or published in Desmond Ball & Keiko Tamura (eds), *Breaking Japanese Diplomatic Codes: David Sissons and D Special Section during the Second World War*, Canberra: ANU E Press, 2013.

**** Published in I Hata et al. (eds), *Sekai sensō hanzai jiten* [Encyclopedia of war crimes in modern history], Tokyo: Bungei Shunjū.

1950 'SCAP's statements on the occupation of Japan', *Australian Outlook*, vol. 4, no. 1.

1952 'The Pacific pact', *Australian Outlook*, vol. 6, no. 1.

1956 'Attitudes to Japan and defence, 1890–1923', Masters thesis, Faculty of Arts, University of Melbourne, hdl.handle.net/11343/38791 (accessed 13 November 2018).

1958 'Ōsutoraria ni okeru kyōshi no kinmu hyōtei' [Teacher evaluations in Australia], Rikizō Uchida (trans.), *Jurisuto*, no. 166.

1959 'The dispute over Japan's police law', *Pacific Affairs*, vol. 32, no. 1.

1960a 'Recent developments in Japan's Socialist movement (1)', *Far Eastern Survey*, vol. 29, no. 3.

1960b 'Recent developments in Japan's Socialist movement (2)', *Far Eastern Survey*, vol. 29, no. 6.

1 Unpublished manuscripts are listed in their year of completion, where known.

1961 'The pacifist clause of the Japanese constitution: Legal and political problems of rearmament', *International Affairs*, vol. 37, no. 1.

1964a 'The Japanese parliament', *Hemisphere*, no. 8, July.

1964b John M Maki, *Court and Constitution in Japan: Selected Supreme Court decisions, 1948–60*, with translations by Ikeda, Masaaki, David CS Sissons, and Kurt Steiner, Seattle: University of Washington Press.

1965 'Human rights under the Japanese constitution', *Papers on Modern Japan*, Research School of Pacific Studies, The Australian National University.*

1968a 'Dissolution of the Japanese lower house', *Papers on Modern Japan*, Research School of Pacific Studies, The Australian National University, Canberra.*

1968b 'Australia and Japan', in JDB Miller (ed.), *India, Japan, Australia: Partners in Asia*, Canberra: Australian National University Press.

1968c 'Australia and Japan, 1961–65', in Gordon Greenwood & Noman Harper (eds), *Australia in World Affairs 1961–65*, Melbourne: FW Cheshire for the Australian Institute of International Affairs.

1971 'History of Australian–Japanese relations', *Australian Heritage*.

1972a 'Early Australian contacts with Japan', *Hemisphere*, vol. 16, no. 4.

1972b 'Immigration in Australian–Japanese relations, 1871–1971', in JAA Stockwin (ed.), *Japan and Australia in the Seventies*, Sydney: Angus and Robertson.**

1972c 'Australian fears of Japan as a defence threat 1895–1971', Senate Standing Committee on Foreign Affairs and Defence — Reference: Japan. *Hansard*, 28 April.

1974a '1871–1946 nen no Ōsutoraria no Nihonjin' [The Japanese in Australia, 1871–1946], *Ijū Kenkyū*, no. 10.

1974b ' Aru imin no ichizoku' [An immigrant family], *Ijū Kenkyū*, no. 10.

1976 'Manchester v. Japan: The imperial background of the Australian trade diversion dispute with Japan, 1936', *Australian Outlook*, vol. 30, no. 3.**

1977a 'Karayuki-san: Japanese prostitutes in Australia, 1887–1916 I', *Historical Studies*, vol. 17, no. 68.**

1977b 'Karayuki-san: Japanese prostitutes in Australia, 1887–1916 II', *Historical Studies*, vol. 17, no. 69.**

1977c 'Japanese in the Northern Territory 1884–1902', *South Australiana*, vol. 16, no. 1.**

1978a 'History of Australian–Japanese relations', in D Pettit & A Hall (eds), *Selected Readings in Australian Foreign Policy*, Melbourne: Sorrett.

1978b 'Australian–Japanese relations: The first phase 1859–1891'.**

1978c 'Japan and the Australian wool industry, 1868–1936'.**

1978d 'Duntroon Lecture, July 1978'.*

1979 'The Japanese in the Australian pearling industry', *Queensland Heritage*, vol. 3, no. 10.**

1980a 'Japan', in WJ Hudson (ed.), *Australia in World Affairs 1971–75*, Sydney: Allen and Unwin.

1980b 'A selector and his family', *Hemisphere*, vol. 25, no. 3.

1980c 'An immigrant family'.**

1981 'Private diplomacy in the 1936 trade dispute with Japan', *Australian Journal of Politics and History*, vol. 27, no. 2.**

1983a 'War crimes', *Australian Encyclopaedia*, 4th edn, Sydney: Grolier.

1983b 'Kitamura, Toranosuke (1866–1930)', *Australian Dictionary of Biography*, National Centre of Biography, Australian National University, adb.anu.edu.au/biography/kitamura-toranosuke-6980/text12129, published first in hardcopy 1983 (accessed 11 December 2018).

1983c 'Kashiwagi, Taira (1868–1954)', *Australian Dictionary of Biography*, National Centre of Biography, Australian National University, adb.anu.edu.au/biography/Kashiwagi-taira-6895/text11955, published first in hardcopy 1983 (accessed 11 December 2018).

1983d 'Komine, Isokichi (1867–1934)', *Australian Dictionary of Biography*, National Centre of Biography, Australian National University, adb.anu.edu.au/biography/komine-isokichi-6997/text121263, published first in hardcopy 1983 (accessed 11 December 2018).

1984 'Kaura horyo shūyūsho no hanran', *Rekishi to Jinbutsu*, no. 165, September.

1984 'Some observations on Australian war crimes trials involving cannibalism/mutilation of the dead'.*

1985 'The trials: were they justice or vengeance?', *Sydney Morning Herald*, 16 August.*

1986a 'The higher direction of a multinational expeditionary force — the JCOSA (Joint Chiefs of Staff in Australia): BCOF (British Commonwealth Occupation Force) experiment, 1954–57', conference paper, Royal Australian Institute of Public Administration 3rd National Conference on Administrative History, Canberra, 17–18 November, National Library of Australia.

1986b 'Murdoch, James (1856–1921)', *Australian Dictionary of Biography*, National Centre of Biography, Australian National University, adb.anu.edu.au/biography/murdoch-james-7690/text13461, published first in hardcopy 1986 (accessed 11 December 2018).

1986c 'Muramats, Jirō (1878–1943)', *Australian Dictionary of Biography*, National Centre of Biography, Australian National University, adb.anu.edu.au/biography/muramats-jiro-7689/text13459, published first in hardcopy 1983 (accessed 11 December 2018).

1987 'James Murdoch 1856–1923', *Transactions of the Asiatic Society of Japan*, 4th series, vol 2.**

1988a 'Japanese', in James Jupp (ed.), *The Australian People: An encyclopaedia of the nation, its people and their origins*, Sydney: Angus and Robertson.

1988b 'Satō, Torajiro (1864–1928)', *Australian Dictionary of Biography*, National Centre of Biography, Australian National University, adb.anu.edu.au/biography/sato-torajiro-8343/text14641, published first in hardcopy 1988 (accessed 11 December 2018).

1990 'Takasuka, Jō (1865–1940)', *Australian Dictionary of Biography*, National Centre of Biography, Australian National University, adb.anu.edu.au/biography/takasuka-jo-8741/text15307, published first in hardcopy 1990 (accessed 11 December 2018).

1993 'Ōsutoraria ni yoru sensō hanzai chōsa to saiban', in T Mitani et al. (eds), *Iwanami Kōza-Kindai Nihon to shokuminchi*, vol. 8, Tokyo: Iwanami Shoten.

1994 'More on Pearl Harbour', *Intelligence and National Security*, vol. 9, no. 2.

1996a 'War crime trials', *The Australian Encyclopedia*, 6th edn, Terrey Hills, NSW: Australian Geographic.

1996b 'Japanese in Australia', *The Australian Encyclopedia*, 6th edn, Terrey Hills, NSW: Australian Geographic.

1997a 'Sources on Australian investigations into Japanese war crimes in the Pacific', *Journal of the Australian War Memorial*, 30, www.awm.gov.au/articles/journal/j30/sissons (accessed 12 December 2018).

1997b 'Japanese intentions towards Australia 1939–42'.*

1997c 'Observations on the trial of Lt Gen Nishimura (Parit Sulong Massacre)'.

1998a 'Selector and his family', in Kinenshi Henshū Iinkai (ed.), *Ōsutoraria no Nihonjin: Isseiki o koeru Nihonjin no sokuseki* [The Japanese in Australia], Sydney: Japan Club of Australia.

1998b 'Australian contacts with Japan in the nineteenth century', *The Japan Foundation Papers*, no. 7.

1999 'Japanese acrobatic troupes touring Australasia 1867–1900', *Australasian Drama Studies*, no. 35.

2000 'Murakami, Yasukichi (1880–1944)', *Australian Dictionary of Biography*, National Centre of Biography, Australian National University, adb.anu.edu.au/biography/murakami-yasukichi-11201/text19967, published first in hardcopy 2000 (accessed 11 December 2018).

2002a 'Honkon-sen ni okeru Eigun horyo no shobun' [Execution of British in Hong Kong (1940)].****

2002b Bisumāku-kai no jūgeki' [After the Battle of Bismarck Sea (1943)].****

2002c '"Akikaze" kanjō no gyakusatsu' [Execution on Destroyer 'Akikaze' (1943)] .****

2002d 'Parawan-tō no Beihei horyo satsugai' [Killing of US POW in Palawan Island (1944)].****

2002e 'Sandakan "shi no kōshin"' [Death march from Sandakan (1945)].****

2002f 'Ōshan-tō no jūmin satsugai' [Massacre of Ocean Islanders (1945)].****

2002g 'Nauru shubihei no 'shi no kōshin' [Death march of Japanese soldiers at Nauru and Ocean Island (1945)].****

2006a 'The Diplomatic Special Intelligence Section: Its origin and history'.***

2006b 'The Australian war crimes trials and investigations (1942–51)'.*

2008 'The voyage of Cyprus mutineers', *The Journal of Pacific History*, 43(2).

2013 *Breaking Japanese Diplomatic Codes: David Sissons and D Special Section during the Second World War*, edited by Desmond Ball & Keiko Tamura, Canberra: ANU E Press.

2016 *Bridging Australia and Japan: The writings of David Sissons, historian and political scientist, Volume 1*, Arthur Stockwin & Keiko Tamura (eds), Canberra: ANU Press.

2016 'The *Lady Rowena* and the *Eamont*: The 19th century'.**

2019 'The fate of the Japanese garrisons at Nauru and Ocean Islands'.*

The Papers of DCS Sissons (MS 3092) are housed at the National Library of Australia in Canberra. The collection consists of 60 boxes and includes published and unpublished manuscripts. The finding aid to the collection is available at nla.gov.au/nla.obj-337994618/findingaid.

www.ingramcontent.com/pod-product-compliance
Lightning Source LLC
Chambersburg PA
CBHW041211100726
47911CB00018B/891

* 9 7 8 1 7 6 0 4 6 3 7 5 5 *